D1602449

Mobile, 1865

Last Stand of the Confederacy

SEAN MICHAEL O'BRIEN

Westport, Connecticut
London

Library of Congress Cataloging-in-Publication Data

O'Brien, Sean Michael, 1944–
  Mobile, 1865 : last stand of the Confederacy / Sean Michael O'Brien.
    p. cm.
  Includes bibliographical references and index.
  ISBN 0–275–97334–4 (alk. paper)
    1. Mobile (Ala.)—History—Civil War, 1861–1865—Campaigns. 2. United
States—History—Civil War, 1861–1865—Campaigns. I. Title.
  F334.M6O27 2001
  973.7′38—dc21   2001016397

British Library Cataloguing in Publication Data is available.

Library of Congress Catalog Card Number: 2001016397
ISBN: 0–275–97334–4

First published in 2001

Praeger Publishers, 88 Post Road West, Westport, CT 06881
An imprint of Greenwood Publishing Group, Inc.
www.praeger.com

Printed in the United States of America

The paper used in this book complies with the
Permanent Paper Standard issued by the National
Information Standards Organization (Z39.48–1984).

10 9 8 7 6 5 4 3 2 1

Contents

An illustration essay follows p. 136.

"I Have Never Seen Such Suffering"

In the blackness of night, the swarm of gray-clad soldiers streamed down the road south of Nashville. Nightfall had saved the army from total disaster. Nightfall and the onset of cold heavy rain. But the Army of Tennessee was shattered, never to fight again, victim of a staggering defeat by a numerically superior Federal army on December 16, 1864. More than 6,000 Rebels were casualties, nearly 4,500 of them prisoners, while Federal losses were a little over 3,000. Nashville was a stunning blow to Confederate morale and the most clear-cut Union tactical victory in the war, a remarkable triumph that should have finished the western Rebel army once and for all.[1]

The Confederate retreat was pure misery. All along the river of mud south of Nashville lay the wreckage of Lieutenant General John Bell Hood's once splendid army: abandoned wagons and baggage, exhausted horses starving and dying by the roadside, debris left by a beaten rabble. Rebel soldiers, many without shoes, without hats, without tents, struggled on in the cold and agony. Now Captain Charles Lumsden's Tuscaloosa battery was "but a name for a command of men without arms." Captain Cuthbert Slocomb's battery, once the pride of New Orleans, was reduced to "forty five bareheaded and half clad men." "Whole regiments," one officer wrote, "are throwing away their guns." Drenched to the bone, Hood's tattered soldiers—"the worst broke down set I ever saw," observed one villager—staggered through Columbia, Tennessee. "Citizens seemed to shirk and hide from us as we approached them," a soldier wrote.[2]

Close on their heels, bluecoated cavalrymen nipped at the Confederates' exhausted rear guard, the infantry brigades of Randall Gibson's Louisianans and James Holtzclaw's Alabamians. "They absolutely gave us no rest at all," Alabama soldier Edgar Jones wrote. "From this time until December 27," another gray-clad recalled, "just one week, the conditions can be summed up in a few words: 'Retreating, fighting all day; retreating, with little rest, all night.' "[3]

The movement south became a nightmare as colder rain and sleet began to fall, turning to snow on the night of December 20 and all the next day. Temperatures plunging into the teens. Frigid blustery wind from the north. Roads and fields encrusted with ice and snow. Supply wagons hopelessly bogged in the mud. Piles of discarded equipment, weapons, dead horses and mules frozen along the roadside. Men with bare feet bleeding in the snow; soldiers hobbling with frostbite. Scarecrows huddling around campfires eating handfuls of parched corn to stay alive. The Rebels' capable cavalry commander, Nathan Bedford Forrest, tried to ease some of the suffering by emptying several wagons and letting many of the barefooted ride.[4]

Mostly the men slogged on in apathetic little groups, abandoning any hint of a military formation. Tempers were short. When a scuffle broke out between an Alabama artillery sergeant and a private, Captain Lumsden, a former instructor at the University of Alabama, pulled the sergeant aside and tried to break the tension. "If a man is insubordinate," he told him, "you have a right to shoot him, but not to strike him with your fist." The sergeant's tired face slowly eased into a smile. Lumsden turned to another wretched soldier, shaking with cold, hobbling on bad feet. "It can't last much longer," Lumsden reassured him.[5]

The Federals seemed less inclined to keep up the chase now. At the head of the Yankee horsemen, Brigadier General James H. Wilson scanned the barren Tennessee countryside, the "worst we had seen," a devastated landscape with appalling roads and pitiful lack of anything that could be used for food. "In all my experience," he wrote, "I have never seen such suffering." Now the Rebels' greatest enemy appeared to be the cold, hunger, and exhaustion.[6]

On a frigid, melancholy Christmas Day, Hood's army reached the Tennessee River, all that separated the graycoats from relative safety. Weary Rebel engineers labored all day and night in a freezing drizzle building a pontoon bridge across the swollen river, and Hood's army began crossing at sunrise. The soldiers were startled to hear heavy firing from downriver. A Union gunboat—an ominous-looking double-turreted monitor—steaming slowly toward them, was under fire from two guns of Captain James C. Cowan's Mississippi battery on the north bank of the river. The graycoats' two Napoleons were no match for the monitor's large Columbiads, and as both sides blazed away, the Rebel gunners received the worst of it, their guns shattered and fifteen men killed or wounded. But on a nearby ridge, a lone Rebel Parrott gun continued to fire, and the Federal gunboat withdrew, allowing the Confederate evacuation to proceed.[7]

Throughout the day of December 26 and the next, Hood's men continued their crossing, the going made agonizingly slow because of the breadth of the river and the swiftness of the current. The rickety bridge swayed as soldiers crossed cautiously in single file. There was still danger from Wilson's Yankee cavalry on their heels, and when sounds of gunfire were heard in the distance, Holtzclaw's Alabama brigade maneuvered to defend the bridge. The Alabamians plunged through a swollen, icy creek, now waist and shoulder deep, the men slipping and struggling up a steep bank on the other side. When they deployed near the river, their clothes were frozen stiff.[8]

Now Francis Cockrell's Missouri brigade, sent westward to construct a Rebel outpost at the mouth of the Duck River only to receive the depressing news of Hood's rout at Nashville, rejoined the retreating army. The Missourians had been badly battered at Franklin, a small hamlet just 18 miles south of Nashville, on November 30, and the brigade numbered only 19 officers and 248 enlisted men. One company had only nine men left. Colonel Peter Flournoy was in command now, with both Cockrell and his second-in-command Colonel Elijah Gates wounded and out of action. "Quite a number of men are barefooted," Lieutenant George Warren recorded in his diary, "and have to be hauled in the wagons." The lieutenant's shoes were only held together with string tied around the soles. A sympathetic farm boy had given Warren an old pair of woolen socks riddled with holes, and he was glad to get them because they were "far better than none."[9]

The sight of the beaten remnant of Hood's dejected army crossing the Tennessee astonished the Missouri men. Warren wrote in his diary, "Nearly all the men I have seen are without arms or accouterments and look very dejected." The Missourians, one of the few Rebel brigades in good order, provided cover for the troops making the crossing. They deployed for battle, but the enemy did not appear. At midnight on December 27 the weary Missourians crossed the bridge. Many soldiers lost their shoes in the knee-deep mud stirred into paste by the hundreds of men, horses, and wagons who had already gone before.[10]

The infantry in the rear guard crossed the river at daybreak. Matthew Ector's ragged Texas brigade, almost constantly in combat since December 15, was last to cross, then the pontoon bridge was dismantled. Once safe on the opposite bank, Hood's army continued its retreat south, hungry and exhausted, many of the soldiers with little clothing and no shoes. "It was a pathetic sight," Edgar Jones wrote, "to see these brave men limping along over the frozen ground with feet tied up in rags or other material, as the best they could do."[11]

On January 3, 1865, the Rebel army straggled into Tupelo, Mississippi, just one third the size it had been before the offensive into Tennessee—an offensive in which it had lost 23,500 men killed, wounded, and captured. No major American army had ever suffered such a devastating defeat.

The Federals elected not to follow their beaten foe across the Tennessee, but some suspected that they might have to fight them once more. The rugged Midwesterners in Major General A. J. Smith's 16th Corps—"Smith's Guerrillas" as they liked to call themselves—would face many of these same gray-clad troops on fields further south. They would fight them again for possession of the Confederacy's last stronghold at Mobile, Alabama, in a battle both bloody and needless—and they would close the Civil War's final chapter. "Some say the war is near over," wrote a weary Union lieutenant, the 21st Missouri's Nehemiah D. Starr, "some say it will never end."[12]

NOTES

1. Mark Mayo Boatner III, *The Civil War Dictionary* (New York: David McKay Co., Inc., 1959), 582; Bruce Catton, *The Centennial History of the Civil War*, vol. 3, *Never Call Retreat* (Garden City: Doubleday & Co., 1965), 414.

2. Larry J. Daniel, *Cannoneers in Gray: The Field Artillery of the Army of Tennessee, 1861–1865* (University: University of Alabama Press, 1984), 180; George Little and James R. Maxwell, *A History of Lumsden's Battery, C.S.A.* (Tuscaloosa: United Daughters of the Confederacy, 1905), 56; Powell A. Casey, *An Outline of the Civil War Campaigns and Engagements of the Washington Artillery of New Orleans* (Baton Rouge, LA: Claitor's Publishing Division, 1986), 85; Phil Gottschalk, *In Deadly Earnest: The History of the First Missouri Brigade, C.S.A.* (Columbia: Missouri River Press, Inc., 1991), 503; Wiley Sword, *Embrace an Angry Wind: The Confederacy's Last Hurrah: Spring Hill, Franklin, and Nashville* (New York: HarperCollins, 1992), 406.

3. Edgar Wiley Jones, *History of the 18th Alabama Infantry Regiment*, compiled by C. David A. Pulcrano (Birmingham, AL: C.D.A. Pulcrano, 1994), 206; James H. McNeilly, "The Retreat from Nashville," *Confederate Veteran* 26 (1918), 306.

4. Sword, *Angry Wind*, 414; Shelby Foote, *The Civil War, a Narrative: Red River to Appomattox* (New York: Random House, 1974), 707–708.

5. Little and Maxwell, *Lumsden's Battery*, 56–58.

6. Sword, *Angry Wind*, 420.

7. Ibid., 421; Daniel, *Cannoneers*, 180; T. G. Dabney, "On Hood's Campaign into Tennessee," *Confederate Veteran* 30 (1922), 409.

8. J. A. Dozier, "Concerning Hood's Tennessee Campaign," *Confederate Veteran* 16 (1908), 192; Jones, *18th Alabama*, 210–211.

9. Gottschalk, *In Deadly Earnest*, 499, 503.

10. Ibid., 504.

11. Sword, *Angry Wind*, 421; J. T. Tunnell, "Ector's Brigade in Battle of Nashville," *Confederate Veteran* 12 (1904), 349; Jones, *18th Alabama*, 213.

12. Leslie Anders, *The Twenty-First Missouri: From Home Guard to Union Regiment* (Westport, CT: Greenwood Press, 1975), 213.

CHAPTER 1

"No Longer an Army"

Major General Dabney H. Maury, commander of Confederate forces at Mobile, was a worried man. Faced with almost certain attack by a massive Federal army, he had only a token force with which to offer opposition.

The situation of the Confederacy at the opening of 1865 was a bleak one. Most of the major cities and seaports in the South—including New Orleans, Pensacola, Savannah, and Atlanta—were already in Federal hands. Union General William T. Sherman had just conducted a devastating march of destruction through central Georgia, severing the eastern Confederacy in two and shattering Southern morale. Only a handful of major cities remained under Rebel control—Richmond, the capital; Charleston, site of the war's start; Wilmington, North Carolina, the last open Confederate port; and Mobile.

Rebel armies in the field were still dangerous, but all were being pressed severely by much larger Union forces. General Robert E. Lee's 60,000-man Army of Northern Virginia, determined to defend Richmond, was under siege by General Ulysses S. Grant's 90,000 Federal soldiers at Petersburg. General Joseph E. Johnston's army of 27,000—with Sherman's 60,000 bluecoats close on its heels—was preparing to make a stand in the Carolinas. Between these two major Rebel armies and the Mississippi, only Lieutenant General Richard Taylor (commanding the Confederate Department of East Louisiana, Mississippi, and Alabama, with headquarters at Meridian, Mississippi) with less than 10,000 scattered troops posed any serious obstacle. Beyond the Mississippi, isolated from the rest of the Confederacy, General Edmund Kirby Smith mustered a command of possibly 40,000 men at best.

Only the most optimistic observers held out any hope at this late date that the Confederacy could pull off a miracle and win a military victory.

Maury's need for military manpower finally received a welcome boost in January 1865 when Taylor, his superior, began transferring units from John Bell Hood's broken army to Mobile. Soon to arrive in the Gulf City were five seasoned brigades—Cockrell's, Sears', Ector's, Gibson's, and Holtzclaw's—as well as some 1,500 artillerymen, about half of the cannoneers in Hood's army. These badly needed veteran troops increased Maury's forces to about 9,000 men.

But how combat-ready were these reinforcements? After the disaster at Nashville, would they fight again? One soldier's observations are worth noting. After three months' absence from the army, Sergeant William Pitt Chambers rejoined Hood's command at Tupelo in January 1865. He was appalled at what he saw: In his old Mississippi regiment, about 150 men left and half of them without shoes. Twenty in his old company left, but none with guns. Not even a stand of colors to be seen in the whole brigade. "All are ragged, dirty and covered with vermin," he wrote, "some not having sufficient clothing to hide their bodies." He found the men in fair spirits considering their wretched circumstances, but they seemed resigned to the fact that the war was lost, "fully convinced that the Confederacy is *gone*."[1]

It was barely two months since Hood had launched his bold offensive into Tennessee. His gray-clad legions—proud veterans of bloody contests from Shiloh to Peachtree Creek—had marched north with red battle flags fluttering and thousands of bayonets glistening in the autumn sun. On November 30, 1864, the little town of Franklin had witnessed the spectacle of the Civil War's last major assault by the embattled Confederacy as Hood's fighting men stormed a line of earthworks hastily thrown up by Major General John M. Schofield's defending Federals. Franklin was a pitiless slaughter—"a living hell," Mississippi soldier R. N. Rea recalled—in which the same bitter lesson of Fredericksburg, Gettysburg, and Kennesaw Mountain was dealt out once again. The grim-faced gray warriors knew this lesson only too well, knew that the day was past when pluck and courage alone could carry fortified earthworks. But courage was not wanting. The gray phalanx hurled itself again and again at the Union works, only to be thrown back over and over. Union officers cited as many as thirteen separate Confederate assaults.[2]

Francis Cockrell's Missouri brigade had been in the very heart of heavy fighting, reaching thirty paces from the enemy works, and "in less than half a minute," one Missouri soldier wrote, "most of them went down." When his horse was felled by enemy fire, Cockrell took an aide's mount and rode on, only to have that horse shot from under him too. Wounded twice in the right arm, once in the left leg, once in the right ankle, Cockrell fell, one of twelve Rebel generals to become casualties that day. Colonel Elijah Gates took command of the brigade; almost instantly he also fell, shot in both arms. In the end, Southern valor was not enough. The Yankee defenders closed ranks, and the gray tide was beaten backward. The earthworks remained firmly in Union hands.[3]

The losses were staggering. Daybreak revealed the horrific carnage of the previous evening's butchery: more than 6,000 Rebels killed, wounded, or missing after five brutal hours of fighting. Five Confederate generals dead, including the capable Irishman Pat Cleburne, regarded as the "Stonewall Jackson of the West." Seven more Rebel generals wounded or captured. Fifty-three field commanders out of action. "Here indeed was a Carnival of Death," Missouri officer George Warren wrote. "There must have been three thousand stiffened corpses lying in this little space, in full view." An Alabama artillery officer estimated that he could have walked half a mile over the bodies of dead Rebel soldiers without touching ground.[4]

Missouri soldier James Bradley wrote, "This has been termed a hard-fought battle, we term it a slaughter." Cockrell's brigade lost nearly two thirds of its men. Only three Confederate brigades suffered higher losses in the whole war. Claudius Sears' Mississippi brigade lost nearly a quarter of its troops. The losses were similar for other Rebel brigades. No other major battle of the Civil War was so costly as Franklin, "combining," historian Shelby Foote observes, "the grisliest features of Pickett's Charge and Spotsylvania's Bloody Angle." Indeed, more Rebel soldiers took part in the assault at Franklin, the Confederacy's last great charge of the war, than in the disastrous Rebel charge at Gettysburg in July 1863.[5]

Despite the appalling losses at Franklin, Hood had urged his troops onward to Nashville. Stunned by the bloodbath of November 30 but with heads still high, the graycoats numbered less than 25,000 now, while their Union opponent had more than twice that number entrenched behind strongly prepared positions in one of the most heavily defended cities in America. No longer strong enough to attack, Hood sought to draw Major General George H. Thomas out into the open and provoke him to assault, hoping to survive the blow and deliver a knockout counterstroke.[6]

On the morning of December 15, Thomas' blue-coated masses poured out of their prepared works in Nashville under thick fog and deployed for battle. After overwhelming several forward redoubts manned by Charles Lumsden's Alabama battery and others, Major General A. J. Smith's bluecoats advanced on the Hillsboro Pike running south from Nashville, where three understrength Rebel divisions crouched behind a stone wall. About 3:00 P.M., the Federal attackers hit the graycoats hard, and after an hour of bloody fighting, the Rebels were fleeing east to take up a new defensive position. Claudius Sears, commanding the Mississippi brigade, was badly wounded.

The Rebel army was not destroyed, and nightfall mercifully brought an end to the fighting for that day. Hood stubbornly refused to withdraw. Federal General John Schofield remarked, "I doubt if any soldiers in the world ever needed so much cumulative evidence to convince them that they were beaten."[7]

The battle resumed the next day. At 3:30 P.M., Federal infantry, spearheaded by the "guerrillas" of A. J. Smith's corps and by Federal cavalry, attacked the new Rebel defensive line at Shy's Hill from two different directions. The graycoats could not hold, and panic quickly set in as veterans tossed down their rifles in a mad scramble to the rear, "like a flock of big birds" taking flight, according to one soldier. A Federal officer wrote, "in those few minutes, an army was changed into a mob." Lieutenant J. A. Chalaron, directing the guns of Cuthbert Slocomb's Louisiana battery on Shy's Hill, wrote, "There was no controlling such a torrent of disorganized troops in their headlong flight." Hood bitterly related, "I beheld for the first and only time a Confederate army abandon the field in confusion." That night would find the proud Rebel commander in tears.[8]

Only on the Confederate right was there any semblance of order remaining, and even here the situation was deteriorating rapidly. Most of James Holtzclaw's Alabama brigade managed to get out, but the bluecoats were close behind. The Rebel army was in total flight all along the line. A Louisiana artillery officer wrote, "I discovered the spectacle of a veritable rout, a mass of fleeing troops without a vestige of organization." The Franklin Pike was clogged with Rebel troops pouring south. There was no rallying these men; finally most of the officers gave up trying.[9]

Gradually a ragged rear guard—Gibson's Louisiana brigade and Holtzclaw's Alabamians—began to form around a lone battery of guns, Lieutenant William J. McKenzie's Eufaula Light Artillery, and only this quick action saved the Rebel army from annihilation. The feeble gray line fired a volley at the Federals, then fell back to a second line in their rear, then repeated the process again. While Rebel cavalrymen—aided by Mathew Ector's Texans, in the last of many scattered engagements fought by the brigade in the last two days—made a desperate holding action against Wilson's pursuing Federal horsemen, Hood withdrew his forces that night, making the narrowest of escapes. And the miserable retreat south of Nashville and across the Tennessee River followed.[10]

In just over two weeks an army had been destroyed. Many Rebel soldiers now felt that the Confederate government and high command had let them down. Alabama soldier Edgar Jones called Hood's actions at Nashville "a foolish thing." To simply wait for Thomas' superior force to attack and destroy them plainly made no sense. Better at least to have attacked first and been beaten.[11]

About the only thing that held many soldiers in the army in January 1865 was a bond that had been forged among them through months of hard fighting and suffering. On the miserable retreat across the Tennessee River, Edgar Jones' good friend, Orderly Sergeant W. E. Ross, suddenly collapsed, overcome with painful stomach cramps. As his mates tried to make him as comfortable as they could, Ross looked up. "I am gone," he said. Jones took out his frustration on the regimental surgeon, who seemed to be too fatigued to care. He whirled on the surgeon and ordered him to do something for Ross quickly, or he would make him pay for it. The doctor fumed and cursed, but seeing that Jones and his comrades meant business, he backed down and quickly administered medicine. Ross recovered, and to the relief of his friends he was able to continue the march south the next morning. Indeed, the Rebel foot soldiers had learned by now that the only ones they could really count on were each other.[12]

Why did these diehard Rebels continue to fight? Most of them neither owned slaves nor grasped the Constitutional issues of secession, but at the start of the war they understood that the North posed a threat to their way of life. Historian Reid Mitchell writes, "Secession probably generated far less enthusiasm among the masses of Southern whites than the war itself did. The prospect of Yankee invasion united the white South." Southerners viewed themselves as the true heirs of the American Revolution, fighting for freedom like the patriots of 1776. Writing in May 1864 to his parents, who had opposed his decision to fight for the South, Texas soldier Francis Asbury Taulman explained, "I was influenced alone by a sense of right and justice. I looked carefully before I leaped, and the result is . . . I have been a Confederate soldier 3 years."[13]

Nourished by decades of sectional friction, many Southerners were inclined to believe the worst of their Northern adversaries. An Alabama soldier wrote to his sister in November 1861, "The men I am trying to kill are not like the men you see everyday—they look just like us but their hearts are mean." Another soldier declared in September 1863, "if we are conquered my opinion is we will be the worst downtrodden people on the face of the earth." On hearing of the mistreatment of his family at home at the hands of the Yankee invaders, a Mississippi soldier wrote, "I intend to fight them as long as I live and after this war stops . . . I intend to kill Every one that crosses my path."[14]

   The reality of wartime hardships and suffering brought despair and bitterness. An Alabama soldier wrote to his wife after the battle of
Murfreesboro in December 1862, "Martha . . . I can inform you that I have
Seen the Monkey Show at last and I dont Waunt to see it no more." And a
Texan wrote home in December 1863, "I am so sick of war that I dont want
to heare it any more till old Abes time is out and then let a man say war to
me and I will choke him." The disaster at Nashville produced a flood of
hopelessness and gloom throughout the South, and most were forced to admit that the war probably was lost.[15]

   Amazingly, soldiers who had given up on the Confederacy itself still felt
loyalty to the army, or at least to their own circle of comrades whom they
had come to know intimately. The soldiers' experiences and hardships had
forged a bond that created a loyalty in itself. The army itself came to em-
body the cause for which they fought, and they were willing to keep fighting as long as the army existed. "I must confess," Missouri officer George
Warren wrote in January 1865, "that I like most of this army am consider-
ably demoralized and would like to get out of it, but I do not wish like them
to give up and go home." Warren went on, "I never was more determined
than at the present to see this matter to the bitter end, fight the Yankees
while my life lasts or our independence is gained."[16]

   In exploring the motivations of the soldiers who fought in the Civil War,
James M. McPherson utilizes the three-category framework of John A.
Lynn in his study of the armies of the French Revolution: initial motivation
(why the soldiers joined), sustaining motivation (why they stayed in the
army), and combat motivation (why they were willing to face danger). In
addition to the secondary influences of patriotism and ideology, it seems
likely that the sustaining motivation of soldiers in the Civil War was "primary group cohesion," first identified by social scientists in studies of British, American, and German soldiers in World War II. The soldier was no
longer fighting for country or cause but for his own band of comrades, who
had become family to him. A World War II veteran summed this up: "Men, I
now knew, do not fight for flag or country, for the Marine Corps or glory or
any other abstraction. They fight for each other."[17]

   "Bonded by the common danger they face in battle," McPherson writes,
"this primary group becomes a true band of brothers whose mutual de-
pendence and mutual support create the cohesion necessary to function as
a fighting unit. The survival of each member of the group depends on the
others doing their jobs; the survival of the group depends on the steadiness
of each individual." To let the group down by showing cowardice or by en-
dangering or abandoning the group could bring contempt or ostracism,
which for the soldier "could be quite literally a fate worse than death; it was

a powerful incentive for fight rather than flight." Reid Mitchell observes, "During the war desertion did not simply mean desertion from some abstract entity called the Confederate States of America; it meant abandoning the men with whom one had fought."[18]

During the last days of World War II, soldiers of the German army stubbornly kept fighting even as the Third Reich disintegrated. Faced with the certainty of defeat, they simply refused to give in. Heavy casualties decimated whole units—the "primary group"—but the soldiers still had German patriotism or Nazi ideology—"ideological cohesion"—to fall back on. When this happened to the South during the Civil War, McPherson observes that "ideals remained as the glue that held the armies together . . . because they believed in what they were fighting for." "Patriotic and ideological convictions were an essential part of the sustaining motivation of Civil War soldiers," McPherson writes, although it is not as easy to assess their influence on combat motivation.[19]

Mitchell observes, "The fact that the soldiers remained loyal to the Confederate cause long after large numbers of their class had abandoned it suggests that the military experience itself was involved in the formation of Confederate loyalties." Hardships forged a permanent bond. Mitchell continues:

[T]he very hardships themselves and the mixture of pride and resentment they produced set soldiers apart from the civilian population. This feeling, combined with the shared dangers of battle and hardships on the march, helped produce the Confederate soldier's *esprit de corps*. . . . The military experience created loyalty in the soldier to those who suffered by his side, whether officers or common soldiers, and a corresponding distance from those civilians who stayed at home.[20]

The loyalty of Confederate soldiers was also a product of their religious conviction. "The hand of God," Mitchell writes, "could be seen in Confederate defeats. . . . But just as divine displeasure could explain military defeat, the possibility of divine favor could lead men to continue the struggle long after it seemed rational." Even as late as February 1865, one Rebel officer wrote his wife that God would make the South victorious. Belief in divine power "encouraged hope in ultimate victory no matter what the odds."[21]

Racial solidarity provided another motivation for Rebel soldiers to keep fighting. When African American troops assaulted the Rebel lines at Nashville, the graycoats seemed to fight with greater intensity, going into a "frenzy" according to one Federal soldier and "slaughtering the poor blacks fearfully." Holtzclaw was barely able to curb his jubilant Alabama troops from jumping the works and going after them as they retreated. For Confederates, capture by black Union soldiers—who might be former slaves—was sheer disgrace.[22]

Ironically, the Federals themselves provided another powerful incentive for Rebel soldiers to fight to the end: their policy of total war toward the South in the last two years of the conflict, with its harsh excesses against civilians. "When they burned or pillaged the Southern countryside," Mitchell writes, "Union soldiers gave Confederates more reason to hate them." In early 1865, as the Confederacy disintegrated, as Hood's army lay beaten, disheartened soldiers by the hundreds were laying down their muskets and walking home. But many others were still willing to fight to the end, no matter what the odds.[23]

On January 13, Hood asked to be relieved of his command. Two days later General P.G.T. Beauregard arrived in Tupelo. He was discouraged at the sight of Hood's wretched troops and wrote, "If not, in the strictest sense of the word a disorganized mob, it was no longer an army." The Army of Tennessee was broken up. Nathan Bedford Forrest continued independent operations in Alabama, and about 5,000 troops joined General Joseph E. Johnston's Confederate army fighting Sherman in the Carolinas. Nearly an equal number headed for Mobile on the Gulf coast, where the last major— and needless—fighting in the war would take place.[24]

Holtzclaw's brigade was ordered to Mobile on January 20. A young soldier in the 36th Alabama described the condition of the brigade on reaching the Gulf City at the end of the month. "We were a sight to behold," he wrote, "black, begrimed with smoke and dust from the boxcars and fires in the cars made out of pine plank." At his own expense, the 36th Alabama's Colonel Thomas H. Herndon provided them with a welcome meal of barbecued meat at a nearby warehouse. The soldier recalled, "At no other time did I enjoy a bath and clean apparel so much." The Alabamians were immediately dispatched across Mobile Bay to Fort Blakely to relieve Alpheus Baker's brigade, which was transferred back to the Army of Tennessee.[25]

Maury was acquainted with Cockrell's Missouri brigade from their service together in the Trans-Mississippi and praised them as "such soldiers as the world has never seen . . . a remnant of battle-scarred, toil-worn veterans." Nathan Bedford Forrest also wanted the Missourians; he recommended that they be furnished with mounts and changed to a cavalry outfit. But Maury had first choice. Around February 1, the Missourians received orders to leave for Mobile. Cockrell and Gates rejoined them along the way, even though Cockrell yet ailed from his wounds—getting about on crutches as best he could—and Gates was missing an arm. Cockrell now was placed in command of Major General Samuel G. French's old division, which included his own, Sears', and Ector's brigades. Gates, with Colonel James McCown as second in command, took charge of the Missouri brigade, which went into camp 5 miles from Mobile on February 3.[26]

At the head of Sears' brigade was Colonel Thomas N. Adaire, who had led his Mississippians to the very crest of the Federal earthworks at Franklin only to fall after being nicked in the head by an enemy musket ball. Trapped in the Yankee works as the Rebels were beaten back, Adaire had lain still until nightfall when he crawled back to his own lines. The Mississippians arrived in Mobile in a pouring rain on February 4. Sergeant William Pitt Chambers wrote in his journal that the soldiers were delighted at being able to obtain some old used army tents, "the first tents we have had since the fall of Vicksburg," he wrote.[27]

The infantry brigades were earmarked for Fort Blakely and Spanish Fort, and a number of the artillery batteries—including Lumsden's, Tarrant's, Garrity's, Slocomb's, Cowan's, and Phillips'—would man the guns there. The rest of the artillerymen—including McKenzie's, which had performed so well during the retreat from Nashville—would be stationed in the defenses around Mobile itself.

Robert E. Lee once said of his soldiers, "There never were such men in an army before. They will go anywhere and do anything if properly led." The reasons for the devotion of Rebel soldiers may be found in emotions that transcended physical hardships, discouragement, and the horrors of battle. They contribute to the character of the Southern soldier, whom historian Bell I. Wiley described as "a soldier of such mettle as to claim a high place among the world's fighting men. It may be doubted that anyone else deserves to outrank him." Confederate soldiers had earned their reputation for courage, loyalty, and perseverance. The question remained, with defeat staring them full in the face, would they fight at Mobile?[28]

NOTES

1. William Pitt Chambers, *Blood and Sacrifice: The Civil War Journal of a Confederate Soldier*, ed. Richard A. Baumgartner (Huntington, WV: Blue Acorn Press, 1994), 197; emphasis in original.

2. R. N. Rea, "A Mississippi Soldier of the Confederacy," *Confederate Veteran* 30 (1922), 288; Michael J. Klinger, "Gallant Charge Repulsed," *America's Civil War* (January 1989), 33.

3. Robert S. Bevier, *History of the Confederate First and Second Missouri Brigades, 1861–1865* (St. Louis, 1879), 252; Phil Gottschalk, *In Deadly Earnest: The History of the First Missouri Brigade, C.S.A.* (Columbia: Missouri River Press, Inc.), 1991), 469.

4. Klinger, "Gallant Charge," 33; Bevier, *Missouri Brigades*, 255; Richard N. Harris, "Historic Sketch of Selden's-Lovelace's Battery," (c. 1907), 5, Selden's-

Lovelace's Battery File, Montgomery: Alabama Department of Archives and History (hereafter cited as ADAH).

5. James Bradley, *Confederate Mail Carrier* (Mexico, MO, 1894), 222; Klinger, "Gallant Charge," 33; Shelby Foote, *The Civil War, a Narrative: Red River to Appomattox* (New York: Random House, 1974), 669; James Lee McDonough and Thomas L. Connelly, *Five Tragic Hours: The Battle of Franklin* (Knoxville: University of Tennessee Press, 1983), 92.

6. Bruce Catton, *The Centennial History of the Civil War*, vol. 3, *Never Call Retreat* (Garden City: Doubleday & Co., 1965), 411.

7. Wiley Sword, *Embrace an Angry Wind: The Confederacy's Last Hurrah: Spring Hill, Franklin, and Nashville* (New York: HarperCollins, 1992), 343; Stanley F. Horn, *The Army of Tennessee* (Norman: University of Oklahoma Press, 1941), 417.

8. Leslie Anders, *The Twenty-First Missouri: From Home Guard to Union Regiment* (Westport, CT: Greenwood Press, 1975), 212; Henry Stone, "Repelling Hood's Invasion of Tennessee," in Robert Underwood Johnson and Clarence Clough Buel, eds., *Battles and Leaders of the Civil War*, vol. 4 (New York: Castle Books, 1956), 464; J. A. Chalaron, "Slocomb's Battery in Tennessee Army," New Orleans *Times-Democrat*, November 22, 1903; John B. Hood, "The Invasion of Tennessee," in Johnson and Buel, eds., *Battles and Leaders*, 437; Gottschalk, *In Deadly Earnest*, 502.

9. Eugenia Persons Smartt, *History of Eufaula, Alabama, 1930* (Eufaula: Author, 1933), 83; Sword, *Angry Wind*, 386.

10. Hood, "Invasion of Tennessee," 437; Smartt, *Eufaula*, 83–84; Joseph Wheeler, "Alabama," in Clement Evans, ed., *Confederate Military History*, vol. 7 (Atlanta, 1899), 419; Larry J. Daniel, *Cannoneers in Gray: The Field Artillery of the Army of Tennessee, 1861–1865* (University: University of Alabama Press, 1984), 179.

11. Edgar Wiley Jones, *History of the 18th Alabama Infantry Regiment*, compiled by C. David A. Pulcrano (Birmingham, AL: C.D.A. Pulcrano, 1994), 196.

12. Ibid., 213.

13. Reid Mitchell, *Civil War Soldiers: Their Expectations and Their Experiences* (New York: Simon and Schuster, 1988), 3; Carl Moneyhon and Bobby Roberts, *Portraits of Conflict: A Photographic History of Texas in the Civil War* (Fayetteville: University of Arkansas Press, 1998), 157.

14. Charles T. Jones, "Five Confederates: The Sons of Bolling Hall in the Civil War," *Alabama Historical Quarterly* 24 (1962), 147; Harry Vollie Barnard, *Tattered Volunteers: The 27th Alabama Infantry Regiment, C.S.A.* (Northport, AL: Hermitage Press, 1965), 68–69; Bell I. Wiley, *The Life of Johnny Reb* (New York: Bobbs-Merill, 1962), 309.

15. Wiley, *Johnny Reb*, 33, 140.

16. Gottschalk, *In Deadly Earnest*, 507.

17. James M. McPherson, *For Cause and Comrades: Why Men Fought in the Civil War* (New York: Oxford University Press, 1997), 12, 85–86, 89.

18. Ibid., 85–86; Mitchell, *Civil War Soldiers*, 172.

19. McPherson, *For Cause and Comrades*, 89; 114.

20. Mitchell, *Civil War Soldiers*, 168, 172.

21. Ibid., 173–174.

22. Ibid., 174–175; Jones, *18th Alabama*, 199; Sword, *Angry Wind*, 362.

23. Mitchell, *Civil War Soldiers*, 175.

24. Sword, *Angry Wind*, 425; Horn, *Army of Tennessee*, 422–423.

25. Milton E. Henderson, *History of Edmond Waller Henderson: His Civil War Service: The Thirty-Sixth Alabama Infantry Regiment in Holtzclaw's Brigade* (N.p., n.d.), in 36th Alabama Infantry Regiment File, ADAH, 26.

26. Bevier, *Missouri Brigades*, 261; Gottschalk, *In Deadly Earnest*, 506.

27. J. C. Rietti, compil., *Military Annals of Mississippi* (Spartanburg: Reprint Co., 1976), 52; Chambers, *Blood and Sacrifice*, 201, 202.

28. Clifford Dowdey, ed., *The Wartime Papers of Robert E. Lee* (New York: Da Capo, 1987), 490; Wiley, *Johnny Reb*, 89.

CHAPTER 2

"The Best Fortified Place in the Confederacy"

By March 1865, Alabama's largest city of Mobile was the last seaport still held by the Confederacy. Although Union control of Mobile Bay since August 1864 had rendered it useless for shipping, the city was still in Rebel hands, an irritant to Yankee aims and pride. Confederate General Joseph E. Johnston called Mobile "the best fortified place in the Confederacy." The city's defenses were formidable. Three stout lines of earthworks, constructed between 1861 and 1864, circled the city to the west. A line of "floating batteries" (some of which were really converted ironclad ships) guarded the city on the Bay side. Across the Bay to the east, Batteries Huger and Tracy protected the water approaches below the Blakely River. Further east, 7 miles away, lay another line of defenses at Spanish Fort and Fort Blakely. Obstructions and naval mines (or torpedoes) lay to the south in Mobile Bay ultimately claiming ten Yankee ships by the end of the war.[1]

The man charged with defending Mobile was 42-year-old Major General Dabney H. Maury, a scrappy little Virginian with an impressive list of credentials. Raised by his uncle, famed oceanographer Matthew Fontaine Maury (called the "Pathfinder of the Seas" for his classic study of the ocean's currents), young Maury received his diploma from the University of Virginia and prepared for a law career but found that it could not hold his interest. He opted for military service instead and graduated from West Point just in time for the outbreak of the Mexican War in 1846. The young officer served with the U.S. Regiment of Mounted Rifles and came out of the conflict with a crippled left arm and a brevet rank of 1st lieutenant. Besides his proven record in combat, Maury accumulated a diverse résumé of military experience in frontier duty in Texas, as an instructor at West Point, as superintendent of the cavalry school at Carlisle Barracks, Pennsylvania, and as assistant adjutant general of the Department of New Mexico.

Commissioned in the Confederate cavalry at the outbreak of the Civil War, Maury served on the staff of Major General Earl Van Dorn in the Trans-Mississippi. He fought at Elkhorn Tavern in Arkansas in March 1862, and Van Dorn praised him as "a zealous patriot and true soldier; cool and calm under all circumstances." Soon he was promoted to brigadier general, and in Mississippi he led a division at Iuka in September 1862 and at Corinth in October. Promoted to major general, Maury commanded troops in defense of Snyder's Bluff on the Yazoo River above Vicksburg, and his experience in directing heavy artillery against enemy gunboats—in addition to his combat experience at Elkhorn Tavern, Iuka, and Corinth—made him a shoe-in for the command post of Mobile in May 1863. He did not seek the appointment; he would have preferred a divisional command in Virginia. Still he welcomed the Mobile assignment over an unsatisfying stint as head of the Confederate Department of East Tennessee at Knoxville, a post that claimed a high turnover of Rebel commanders frustrated with the mountain area and its lack of support for the Confederacy.[2]

Some of Maury's soldiers bristled at his fondness for rigid discipline, but he soon earned their respect and affection. He was popular with the troops at Mobile who called him "Little Dab" and "Old Puss in Boots." Louisiana artilleryman Philip D. Stephenson wrote that Maury was " 'every inch a soldier,' but there were not many inches of him," since the little general stood no more than 5 feet 4 inches. Maury proved to be a good choice for command at Mobile and showed himself to be energetic, capable, and popular with the civilians of the town as well as the soldiers.[3]

Mobile's impressive fortifications were the result of three years of hard work by four capable Confederate engineer officers. Brigadier General Danville Leadbetter, a 52-year-old career engineer from Maine, designed or built most of the forts along upper Mobile Bay, including Fort Blakely, Spanish Fort, and Batteries Huger and Tracy. Leadbetter graduated third in the West Point class of 1836, and for four years during the 1850s he was stationed in Mobile constructing forts. The Mobile Bay defenses were part of a chain of coastal forts designed by army engineers for use in the event of invasion by a foreign power. Leadbetter received able assistance during the first two years of the war from Colonel Samuel H. Lockett and Captain Charles T. Liernur. From the fall of 1863 on, direct responsibility for finishing the Mobile defenses fell to German-born Lieutenant Colonel Viktor Von Sheliha. A veteran of the Prussian Army, Von Sheliha at times could be caustic and ill-tempered; he often complained of a "chronic disease of the liver."

But he was a highly competent chief engineer, a keen observer of military and social affairs, with an impressive command of the English language.[4]

The entire Mobile defenses were so widespread that it took several days in February 1864 for Maury, Von Sheliha, and Colonel Jeremy F. Gilmer, chief of the Confederate Corps of Engineers, to tour the entire works. Gilmer was pleased and wrote, "If a little more time be allowed us, it will be a hopeless task for the Yankees to undertake the capture of Mobile by way of the Harbor." He cautiously added, "The land defences are not so complete as I would wish."[5]

Von Sheliha proved to be a hardworking and attentive officer, but the choleric Prussian lost patience with the burdensome problems that faced him. What discouraged him most was the lack of manpower available for constructing earthworks, digging rifle pits, and emplacing the big guns. Slave labor seemed to be the most practical way to go, but owners were loath to release their slaves for this type of work. In frustration Von Sheliha even requested (unsuccessfully) to be reassigned in June 1864 and wrote, "My earnest appeals for laborers have met with no success whatever. . . . [F]or the last three months especially work here has been dragging along pitifully slowly for want of hands."[6]

Mobile became a major target of Union forces because of its strategic and economic importance. After the fall of New Orleans in April 1862, Mobile emerged as the South's major seaport on the Gulf and a favorite destination of blockade runners. Also, the capture of Mobile took on political importance in the summer of 1864 because of the approaching U.S. presidential election. Faced with considerable opposition from war-weary Democrats, Lincoln needed a military victory to bolster public support for his policies. Federal operations against Mobile Bay had been planned for some time but had been delayed, because available Union forces were diverted to the Red River campaign in western Louisiana from March through May 1864. Union Admiral David G. Farragut had to wait until land and naval movements could be effectively coordinated before his planned thrust against the Bay forts could get under way.

The naval battle of Mobile Bay, on August 5, 1864, gave Farragut control of the gateway to Mobile. Farragut, with four ironclad monitors and fourteen wooden warships, encountered Confederate Commodore Franklin Buchanan's sole ironclad ram (the formidable C.S.S. *Tennessee*) and a few wooden gunboats. The Rebel squadron was soundly defeated, and Buchanan was wounded and taken prisoner.

The Federals also began land operations against the coastal forts at the entrance to Mobile Bay 30 miles south of the city. Fort Morgan, a massive masonry fort built in 1834, lay on a narrow peninsula of land on the eastern side of Mobile Bay. Fort Gaines, also an older brick fort, sat on Dauphin Island on the western side of the Bay. Six miles northwest of Fort Gaines, the Confederates had constructed Fort Powell, an incomplete earthwork battery on Tower Island at the mouth of Grant's Pass.

On August 3, 1864, Major General Gordon Granger landed 1,500 Union troops on the western end of Dauphin Island and moved against Fort Gaines, garrisoned by the 21st Alabama Infantry Regiment under Colonel Charles D. Anderson. Shelled by Federal monitors by sea and Granger's troops by land, Fort Gaines surrendered on August 8, 1864. Maury was extremely critical of Anderson for giving up the garrison so soon, and Mobile's nationalistic newspapers quickly labeled the surrender a disgrace to Confederate arms.

Similar controversy surrounded the evacuation of Fort Powell, commanded by Lieutenant Colonel James M. Williams of the 21st Alabama. A U.S. flotilla anchored in Grant's Pass began shelling Fort Powell on August 4. Williams ordered the little fort blown up and the garrison withdrawn to Mobile. Williams later wrote, "I decided promptly that it would be better to save my command and destroy the fort than to allow both to fall into the hands of the enemy." But Maury disagreed. "Colonel Williams should have fought his guns," he wrote. Maury relieved Williams of command, but later the officer was cleared of all charges.[7]

Fort Morgan, the largest of the Alabama coastal forts, withstood an eighteen-day siege. A five-sided brick structure with eighty-six guns, Fort Morgan was commanded by Brigadier General Richard L. ("Ramrod") Page, a 56-year-old former naval officer, and was garrisoned by 600 troops of the 1st Alabama Artillery Battalion and the 21st Alabama Infantry. Farragut's naval vessels and Granger's land forces hammered Fort Morgan for days. On the night of August 22, 1864, the Union shelling set off a fire inside the fort. A Rebel officer wrote, "Six or eight shells could be counted in the air at once and every shot appeared to take effect. . . . The interior of the fort had become a mass of smoking ruins." All but two of the big fort's guns were disabled. The fires inside the fortress threatened to spread to the powder magazine, and much of the fort's gunpowder had to be sacrificed. Page surrendered the fort on August 23.[8]

When the coastal forts fell, Von Sheliha took it as a negative reflection on his competence as an engineer. He contended that his engineers were not to blame for the loss of the forts, for they had "ever worked faithfully and judiciously." He offered his resignation and made plans to return to Europe with his wife, but Maury refused to accept it. The Prussian then decided to stay on in Mobile. In 1868 Von Sheliha would publish a treatise on the lessons learned in coastal defense during the war. The main lesson, clear to other observers as well, was that the old masonry fortresses like Fort Morgan that dotted the eastern coast of the United States were obsolete because of advances in rifled artillery. When the coastal forts were designed, they were intended to withstand the firepower of 8-inch Columbiads, the biggest guns in use at the start of the war. But the first year of the war alone witnessed development of larger and more powerful guns by both sides, with greater range and more destructive capabilities.[9]

The capture of Forts Morgan and Gaines gave the Federals control of Mobile Bay, and plans could now proceed for land operations against the city of Mobile itself. U.S. troops probably could have taken the Rebel stronghold in August 1864, because at the time there were few Confederate troops available to Maury for defense. But Major General Edward R. S. Canby, who had been placed in charge of the Federal offensive, was cautious and was unaware of the true state of Mobile's defenses. With winter approaching, he preferred to wait for a more suitable time to launch an attack. Large numbers of blue-coated troops were based at Pensacola and at Fort Gaines, and reinforcements continued to augment the Federal force as 1865 approached.[10]

The fall of the coastal forts did not cause hysteria in Mobile. Most citizens regarded the extensive fortifications at the upper end of the Bay as adequate protection against the invaders. An editorial in the Mobile *Daily Advertiser* of August 11, 1864, reminded readers that the enemy "has to encounter the inner line of defences. When he does that he is no nearer to taking Mobile than Grant is to taking Petersburg. . . . In other words this city is a long ways from 'going up.'" A local resident, 67-year-old Richard Spencer, wrote his son-in-law on August 26, 1864:

> Our upper fortifications and the obstructions in the river are our main defence. In these, as I understand, our Military men place the utmost confidence. . . . The citizens do not appear to be alarmed. All is quiet as usual. Some families are leaving for the up country but not in a panic. Most of the women and children even are determined to remain and risk the dangers of a bombardment.[11]

The effect of the war on Mobile's civilian population was minimal in the first three years of the conflict. Mobilians went about their business as usual and kept up their social life as though no war was going on. They held frequent dances, balls, parties, concerts in the park, and parades. The Gulf City replaced New Orleans as the lively center of social and cultural activity. One wartime resident recalled, "Mobile was called the Paris of the Confederacy . . . and gay indeed it was."[12]

Confederate military personnel found duty in Mobile to be an enviable one. Entertainment, food, and drink were plentiful, and there was a cheerful atmosphere. A Missouri soldier recalled, "a man could come nearer getting the worth of Confederate money there, than any other place in the department." A favorite delicacy was oysters, harvested from Bon Secour Bay. Several Kentucky soldiers stationed in Mobile were caught by their brigade commander, Colonel Robert P. Trabue, entering the Battle House Hotel, although they were supposed to be confined to camp. They lamely explained to Trabue that they were looking for stragglers. "You are looking for straggling oysters," the colonel replied. "I know what you are up to." The city's pleasant environment was conducive to romance. Several officers and enlisted men married Mobile women; preachers performed as many as ten weddings in one day.[13]

The Union victory at Mobile Bay provided a needed boost to Lincoln's campaign for reelection as president of the United States. The election in November 1864 drew interest among Mobile townspeople largely because of speculation on the policies of the candidates toward a defeated South. Although Democrat George B. McClellan was the peace candidate, many Mobilians seemed to prefer Lincoln as the lesser of two evils, reasoning that military occupation of the South was inevitable and that a civilian president would be less harsh than a former Union general. Many were attracted by Lincoln's lenient "ten percent plan" of reconstruction, which pledged readmission to the Union without penalty for any Southern state in which just ten percent of the voting population took a loyalty oath to the United States.[14]

Federal naval control of the Bay also brought an end to Mobile's long-held reputation as a haven for blockade running. Before August 1864, Yankee gunboats patrolled outside the Bay, but swift Rebel vessels—aided by the guns of Fort Morgan—usually could outrun them, carrying Southern cotton to be exchanged for European arms and supplies. Some of the Rebel captains sailed for patriotic reasons, some purely for profit. Earlier in the war, a number of the blockade runners, like William "Black Bill" Wilson, made their homes at Pilot Town (or Navy Cove), 5 miles east of Fort Morgan on the Bay side of the peninsula. Lieutenant Robert Tarleton, an Alabama artillery officer at Fort Morgan, described Pilot Town as "simply a long straggling row of dilapidated one-story houses, paintless and shapeless, built immediately on the shore." Wilson, a Dubliner, was captured at Fort Morgan and sent to prison in New York. Reportedly he turned down an offer of $50,000 and safe passage for his family in return for piloting Federal ships into Mobile Bay.[15]

Even before the Union naval victory in August 1864, it was not easy to get in and out of Mobile Bay, but once in the Gulf the blockade runners could reach Havana, Cuba, in three days barring unforeseen problems. Early in 1862, the schooner *Cuba* sailed from Mobile with 127 bales of cotton and weighed anchor at Pilot Town, where the crew waited two or three days for favorable winds. Then on a dark and stormy night, without lights, the *Cuba* evaded two Union gunboats and sailed out into the Gulf bound for Havana. Even in daylight resourceful runners could break the blockade. Disguised as a British ship, the Rebel cruiser C.S.S. *Florida* was able to throw Union patrol boats off guard long enough to slip into Mobile Bay in September 1862. The *Florida* slipped back out three months later under cover of darkness and subsequently managed to capture or destroy millions of dollars in Federal shipping on the high seas.[16]

Not all blockade running escapades ended successfully. In June 1864, the Yankees captured the *Donegal*, a steamer carrying 400 barrels of gunpowder and rifles bound for the Rebel army. On the night of July 1, the *Ivanhoe*, an English steamer on her first trip carrying supplies to Mobile, ran aground about a mile east of Fort Morgan. After August 1864, the blockade runners' days were over.[17]

Federal control of the Bay aggravated the problem of wartime shortages in Mobile. One item in short supply was salt. The Confederates had a salt works near the mouth of the Fish River on Bon Secour Bay. Once a month they sent schooners carrying 60-pound sacks of the commodity to Mobile. Mobilians paid about $40.00 per sack. Federals destroyed the salt works in September 1864.[18]

Even before August 1864, many items were becoming scarce, and prices were high. In September 1863, molasses sold for $7.00 a gallon, sugar for $1.50 to $2.00 a pound, bacon for $4.00 a pound, butter for $5.00 a pound, flour for $90.00 a barrel. Military bureaucracy sometimes interfered with the free market distribution of goods. A problem arose when Lieutenant General John C. Pemberton, Confederate commander at Vicksburg, insisted that Mobile obtain its supplies from Alabama rather than Mississippi. To circumvent this restriction, one entrepreneur purchased a supply of bacon in Mississippi and smuggled it into the Gulf City in a 6-foot pine coffin labeled "John Shoat, 32nd Alabama Regiment, Mobile, Ala."[19]

The most visible example of public unrest in Mobile was the "bread riot" of September 4, 1863. Grabbing up brooms, hatchets, hammers, or whatever else was handy, several hundred poor women of the city assembled on Spring Hill Road to protest the shortage of food. Banners proclaimed, "Bread or Peace" and "Bread or Blood." What began as a peaceful march down Dauphin Street into the downtown business area soon got out of hand. The women broke ranks and began to loot stores and parcel out clothes and food items amongst themselves. Curious crowds gathered to gawk, and thousands of onlookers, many of them in sympathy with the women, egged them on. When Maury dispatched troops to arrest the rioters, the soldiers refused to confront the "Amazonian phalanx," as one spectator called the women. Finally the city's mayor, Robert H. Slough, met the crowd head on and promised to make food available if they would go home. The women agreed to disperse. Later that day Slough issued an appeal to the citizens of Mobile for contributions to buy food and clothing for needy families in the city. He set up a Special Relief Committee to oversee the distribution, and the committee followed through in the next few months, easing some of the distress caused by food shortages.[20]

For some local farmers things were not all that bad. Richard Spencer wrote in June 1864, "It is true provisions are scarce and high, but everything else is equally so. My sales more than meet my expenses. I have never in my life made so much money (if we may call it money) as within the past two years, and everybody else who will work and raise anything for market, is doing as well or better than I." Cabbages were selling for $.75 to $1.00 a head, "a good size onion" $.50 to $1.00, Irish potatoes $2.00 a quart, milk $2.00 a gallon, butter $5.00 a pound, eggs $2.50 a dozen, "good size chickens" $6.00 or $7.00 each, sweet potatoes $20.00 a pound, common fire wood $25.00 to $30.00 a cord. "The greatest drawbacks we have," Spencer wrote, "is the rogues. The deserters and worthless soldiers and vagabonds about the country, kill the hogs and cattle, so that we have hard work to raise our meat. And meat is so enormously high we cannot buy it."[21]

With the Federals in control of the Bay, items like coffee and some meats and vegetables were in short supply, and especially oysters, which now became very expensive and out of the reach of most townspeople. The Rebel army impressed river steamers in January 1865 to carry supplies intended for the military, and this halted transportation of many civilian goods.[22]

When war broke out in April 1861, Mobilians had responded patriotically, and several military companies quickly appeared. But as the war dragged on, enthusiastic volunteers were harder to find. When the Confederacy implemented conscription in April 1862, townspeople resisted. Many were upset in July 1864 when Confederate authorities conscripted the city's firemen. "Wonder what next the military will organize," one disgruntled local wrote, "perhaps the Bank of Mobile."[23]

The war also had a significant impact on the city's African American population. The Mobile area boasted nearly 1,200 free blacks in 1860, about as many as in the entire rest of the state. Many were descendants of free blacks who had lived in the area when Spain controlled the region and were called "Creoles," a term commonly used in Mobile to refer to people of mixed race, or mulattos. They undoubtedly participated in the military defense of the city. One individual, seeking to form a company of Creoles, described them in April 1862: "They are mostly property-holders, owning slaves, and a peaceable, orderly class, and capable of doing good service." Mobile's Congressman Edmund S. Dargan approved the idea, confirming that "I know the character of the population he proposes to enlist, and think they will render as efficient aid as any class we have." Although the Confederate War Department declined to accept their offer of service, Alabama's state legislature in November 1862 approved the recruitment of Creole companies into the state militia, with the condition that the officers must be white. The "Creole Guards," a company formed in December 1862, served as guards for government warehouses in Mobile.[24]

In November 1863, Maury appealed to Confederate authorities to approve the enlisting of Creoles. He wrote that the Creoles were "admirably qualified" for duty as artillerymen and that "they were very anxious to enter Confederate service." Confederate Secretary of War James A. Seddon responded, "Our position with the North and before the world will not allow the employment as armed soldiers of Negroes." But he added, "If these creoles can be naturally and properly discriminated from Negroes, the authority may be considered as conferred." Maury authorized enlistment of Creoles and free blacks in October 1864. A "Native Guards" company was on duty in the spring of 1865, with Mobile's Assistant Chief of Police as commander and Creoles holding the other officer positions.[25]

Slaves furnished most of the labor for constructing the elaborate system of forts and earthworks surrounding Mobile. One fourth of the city's population in 1860 was slave, most of them working in the town's cotton presses. Maury and Von Sheliha at first appealed to local slave owners to supply workers voluntarily, but at times the Rebels resorted to impressing them. Runaway slaves became more numerous as the war dragged on, and many fled to Federal lines rather than be impressed into the Confederate labor force.[26]

The use of captured black soldiers was another thorny issue. After Nathan Bedford Forrest had 800 to 900 black Federal soldiers (captured at Fort Pillow, Tennessee, in April 1864 and at Athens, Alabama, in September 1864) sent to Mobile, Maury assigned them to work on the city's defenses. Gordon Granger protested to Maury but was unable to win their release, even after he threatened to impress captive Rebel soldiers in the same way. Maury informed Granger that the Confederacy regarded the blacks as property of their owners and not as prisoners of war, but he pledged that they would not be mistreated. A few of the black prisoners who managed to escape reported that this was not so, that abuse did occur. The issue remained unresolved at the beginning of 1865.[27]

In the fall of 1864, Maury prepared for the expected Federal land offensive against Mobile. He sought more troops from Alabama Governor Thomas H. Watts, who recommended that he reduce the city to "a heap of ashes" before leaving it to the enemy. But Maury had virtually exhausted the small supply of Alabama state troops available to him; they were already on duty in Mobile. Although Hood had sent him Baker's Alabama infantry brigade of 700 soldiers at the end of August, Maury still needed more men. Baker's brigade, stationed at Spanish Fort, was the only veteran infantry brigade he had. Sickness was a problem in Maury's army in the fall of 1864; many men were down with fever and chills. At Battery McIntosh, on the Bay shore outside the city, an officer recorded in his diary, "Thirty six men out of three companies are all we have for duty today." In one of the Rebel brigades only 100 out of 900 men were found fit for duty. Maury had less than 3,000 men at the end of October. Things would look brighter with the reassignment of troops from Hood's army to Mobile in January 1865.[28]

Von Sheliha worked to complete the city's defenses. He faced enormous obstacles: defense works covering over 20 miles of land and water, a scarcity of workers, with only one steamer and eight teams to supply them. The Prussian's engineers concentrated on Fort Sidney Johnston (Redoubt "N") south of the city and kept 500 slaves working day and night to finish it. An observer wrote, "They are in such numbers that they look like ants on the side of an ant hill." The work was hampered by cold weather and heavy rains in November.[29]

Across the Bay to the east, the engineers had nearly finished the Spanish Fort defenses, with four redoubts completed by the end of September; and the gun embrasures were finished by the end of the year. The workers dug more than 250 yards of rifle pits and cleared trees for 300 yards in front, beginning to construct an abatis to protect the works from an enemy assault. Further north, the work crews erected a battery at Blakely and began felling trees in front of the proposed line of rifle pits. More obstructions were placed in the Apalachee and Blakely rivers, including heavy rafts to stop Federal ships from sailing upstream and getting behind the Rebel forts.[30]

Work on Fort Blakely was delayed because the Rebels had to send fifty laborers north in November to repair the Mobile and Great Northern Railroad, recently raided by Federal cavalry. Workers continued to clear land and to load barges with earth bound for Batteries Huger and Tracy. They concentrated on earthworks in December, and by end of the year they had four redoubts ready along with 50 yards of rifle pits.[31]

By the end of the year, Rebel engineers had finished their work on Battery Tracy and Battery Huger, which received more attention because it lay closer to the Yankee fleet. A new magazine, fortified by the addition of 8 feet of dirt and a mounted gun, was built, and workers improved and thickened the south parapet. Von Sheliha's men spent the last few weeks of 1864 repairing damage caused by the bad weather of the previous two months. But poor health continued to plague Von Sheliha as the year came to an end. He asked for and was granted a six-month leave to return to Germany for rest.[32]

With Mobile Bay in Federal hands, the vital Mobile and Ohio Railroad across Mississippi became the principal means of transport for supplies to Mobile, especially for war materials like arms, gunpowder, and iron. The Alabama and Florida Railroad running from Montgomery to the little town of Pollard 60 miles northeast of Mobile was extended to the Tensas River, with goods either shipped by barge from there to Mobile or hauled overland. Federal cavalry raids continually disrupted the flow of supplies on the railroads. In December 1864, Brigadier General Benjamin H. Grierson led 3,500 blue-coated horsemen on a raid across northern Mississippi. The Yankee troopers tore up 100 miles of track and destroyed nine locomotives and many supplies. The raid did considerable damage but did not seriously disrupt supply to Mobile.[33]

In mid-December, the Federals launched a surprise raid on Pollard. From Pensacola, about 800 black troops headed overland, their objective the rail line at Pollard. On December 16, they reached the little town, where they burned several buildings and tore up the railroad tracks after scattering the Rebel cavalry under Brigadier General James H. Clanton. Withdrawing to Pensacola, the raiders were intercepted about 6 miles south of Pollard by Rebel infantry and cavalry under Brigadier General St. John Liddell, commander at Blakely. The Rebels pursued the Federals for about 30 miles, skirmishing all along the way, then finally gave up the chase. The Federals suffered 81 casualties. The Confederates had the railroad at Pollard repaired by Christmas.[34]

As Confederate Mobile's last winter wore on, Rebel hopes of winning the war appeared more and more illusory. Many residents, called "Croakers" by the city's die-hard Rebels, simply hoped for an end to the fighting. Their main concern now was for salvaging what they could of the city's businesses so that the economy could revive after the war was over. Most affected by this defeatist attitude were the city's working-class people.[35]

Friction between townspeople and soldiers intensified as well. Some of the local citizens accused soldiers of stealing vegetables from private gardens. One wrote the Mobile *Register* in January 1865 that "the market gardeners are in despair. They say it is useless to attempt to raise vegetables for the Mobile market, for the soldiers will allow nothing green to sprout without pouncing on it." Another contended, "scarcely a day passes without our hearing of some chicken coop, pig pen or larder being robbed." They also complained about drunk and unruly soldiers carousing in the city's bars. Governor Watts in February 1865 issued an order closing the barrooms in Mobile, but barkeepers and soldiers generally ignored the law. An Alabama artillery officer, Captain Stouten Hubert Dent, wrote his wife in February 1865 that there was plenty of whiskey available in Mobile in spite of the Governor's order. "The only difference now," the Mobile *Register* editorialized, "is between 3 to 5 dollars a drink and thirty dollars a quart." Maury finally cracked down on the town's bars, shutting them down on April 1, as attack by the Federals loomed close.[36]

Soldiers resented the closing of the bars and felt they were unfairly singled out. One of them wrote,

> Nothing to drink. I can't get a drop.
> For the Governor has closed every rum shop.
> It rains every day; don't you think he ought to
> give us whiskey to mix with the water.[37]

Shortages now hit Mobile's residents hard. Veterans of Hood's army who had arrived in Mobile were curious to see what their Confederate money would buy. Sergeant James R. Maxwell of Lumsden's Alabama Battery wrote:

> Fish and oysters were plentiful, as well as eggs and vegetables. But for coffee we had to take whatever substitute was available. Usually sweet potatoes, okra or sage. For sweetening either long sweetening [molasses] or short sweetening [a moist clammy dark brown sugar]. For cream, if wanted, a beaten egg answered, but most of us preferred the 'coffee' 'barefooted and baldheaded,' i. e. without cream or sugar, or 'straight.' Some little new corn whiskey, white as water, could be had also 'sub rosa.' Occasionally, at a social call at some private residence, home-made wine from grapes or blackberry might be set before the caller, but real coffee or tea, or white sugar was hardly to be had, for love or money.[38]

Long lines formed to buy goods, and fights frequently broke out as civilians, mostly women, pushed and shoved to get scarce items like cornmeal, wheat, flour, sugar, and coffee. One woman, Mary Conley, was fined $25 in the Mobile mayor's court for disorderly conduct and was said to be "good with her fists as well as her tongue, and made free use of both." Reports of petty thefts and burglaries also became common, with soldiers and slaves getting much of the blame.[39]

What made things worse was the inflated prices charged by some merchants and outrageous prices charged by speculators who simply exploited the poor. Lieutenant Colonel James M. Williams of the 21st Alabama Infantry may have had such men in mind when he wrote in October 1864, "the day is not far distant when a man will be ashamed to hold up his head and say that he did not 'serve in the wars'—Money will not shield him from the contempt that is the portion of a coward." Some businesses were more civic-minded and advertised that they would sell "to families only," or "only to the town's poor." Some patriotic individuals organized a "supply association" to buy and grind corn for sale to the poor at cost.[40]

At first, cotton had been thought to be the South's trump card. Richard Spencer wrote in December 1860: "Our cotton alone can save us. Europe and the North can't do without our great staple, and may remain at peace with us." But as the war unfolded, Southerners discovered to their dismay that Europe could do without their cotton, and foreign military intervention was not to be.[41]

Now some cotton merchants were hoarding their crop in hopes of making a big profit when the war ended. They were angered when Maury threatened to seize the crop, as well as resin and turpentine, and burn it rather than let it fall into Federal hands. James M. Williams wrote in March 1865 that Confederate authorities conducting intense searches of homes in Mobile were uncovering cotton hidden in unusual places, including a single bale masquerading as a bed. When Union forces occupied the city, there were 20,000 bales of cotton yet undestroyed.[42]

Mobile's political and social institutions continued to function nearly as normal. Mayor R. H. Slough and the town council continued to run the city government and courts. The city still had a police force. City schools, including the Barton Academy and Catholic College at Spring Hill, continued to operate, as well as a Confederate military academy. Citizens enjoyed theatrical productions of *Macbeth* and *Richard III* and comedies as well. They also held charitable benefits, with proceeds going to soldiers' widows, orphans, sick and wounded soldiers, and the town's poor. Confederate nurse Kate Cummings wrote on February 20, "Mobile never was as gay as it is at the present; not a night passes but some large ball or party is given. Same old excuse: that they are for the benefit of the soldiers; and indeed the soldiers seem to enjoy them." Churches continued to conduct services. Even in the final months of the war, many Mobile women busied themselves in local soldiers' aid societies sending food and medical supplies to the troops stationed in the area. Meanwhile refugees were flocking into Mobile by the hundreds, fleeing turmoil and the loss of their homes elsewhere in Alabama.[43]

The desperate plight of the Confederacy late in 1864 prompted the Congress at Richmond to confront the controversial issue of slave emancipation. As early as August 1863, the Alabama legislature had passed resolutions requesting that Congress consider enlisting slaves into the army to alleviate the Confederacy's manpower problem. Mobile's Congressman Edmund S. Dargan came out publicly for freeing the slaves if such a course of action offered the only chance of European recognition of the Confederacy. Von Sheliha proposed the creation of an engineer laborer corps, in which freed slaves could be enlisted. This would provide the engineers at Mobile with enough manpower to finish the defensive works around the city so that they would "stand any siege." Von Sheliha felt that this would be more efficient and economical than the old slave impressment and would release white soldiers for more critical combat assignments, but his superiors declined to act on his proposals.[44]

Robert E. Lee also endorsed the recruiting of black troops. Although at first opposed, Jefferson Davis gradually—and in the end, too late—came around to the idea of enlisting black soldiers. Yet even desperation could not overcome the fears of many white Southerners for whom the dreaded slave uprising seemed a very real prospect. Richard Spencer wrote in December 1860: "If war is commenced, the whole of the slave states will probably join us, but with eight millions of white population and four of slaves, we shall be a feeble power; and if they instigate the negroes to insurrection our difficulties and dangers will be greatly increased."[45]

On February 13, 1865, Mobile citizens held a public meeting at Temperance Hall to discuss the slave emancipation issue. Several prominent town businessmen, including newspaper editor John Forsyth, endorsed the Davis proposals. The result was a resolution asking the Confederate Congress to authorize the arming of 100,000 blacks for the defense of the South.[46]

There were also efforts to gauge the attitude of the Rebel soldiers assigned to duty in Mobile. On February 17, the men of Sears' Mississippi brigade held a meeting to air their feelings about continuing the war and about the question before Congress of freeing and arming the slaves. Most soldiers were sick of the war, but what choice did they have but to see it out to the bitter end? Pitt Chambers wrote in his journal, "These resolutions are to be *for show*, I suppose. The time for *big talk* has passed. Disguise the fact as we may, the *real sentiment* of this brigade and this division is for peace on almost any terms." That morning Chambers had confessed to having the "blues." It seemed evident that the North would accept nothing other than the South's unconditional surrender, and so the war would go on. "It seems a useless waste of life," he lamented. "We have no armies to fight our victorious foes."[47]

Colonel William S. Barry, who had just rejoined the brigade after recovering from a wound in October 1864, told the soldiers, "There is hope in fighting, in submission none." The soldiers voted a resolution to continue the fight. The question of arming the slaves also was discussed, but the men were unable to reach any agreement on the issue. Chambers wrote that he was "opposed to it on higher ground than expediency—*it is not right.*"[48]

The following day a division meeting was held to discuss the same questions. The soldiers heard speeches from Cockrell, Barry, and Colonel David Coleman of Ector's brigade, as well as political dignitaries from the city. This time in a vote of support for the Confederate leadership the men approved a resolution endorsing the freeing and arming of the slaves. Chambers did not attend the meeting. "I do not know what is best," he admitted, "I am simply resolved to do my whole duty as nearly as I can." Congress passed the slave emancipation bill into law, and it went into effect on March 13, 1865, too late to have an effect on the war's outcome.[49]

The early days of March brought more rain, cold wind, and gloom to Mobile. Soldiers attended prayer services each night and sometimes during the day. There were a number of baptisms, including several in Ector's brigade performed by Captain Jacob Ziegler, a Baptist preacher now in command of the 10th Texas Cavalry. Rumors of imminent action persisted, with the swelling Union army at Pensacola poised to launch a major offensive. Rebel soldiers observed an increased movement of Federal vessels in the Bay. All furloughs were canceled. Chambers wrote, "On every side we are losing ground. I very much doubt whether the *morale* of this army or of the citizens of the land is equal to the emergency that confronts us. All of us are weary of this ceaseless turmoil and bloodshed—we long so much for peace."[50]

After a stormy, windy night, the weather turned "spring-like" on March 8. Although they had carried unloaded Austrian rifles since their arrival at Mobile—"all the picketing we have done here, though in sight of the enemy, has been done with 'empty guns,'" Chambers had written—Sears' brigade finally received ammunition. March 11 was observed as a "fast day," with routine activities suspended. Chambers noted that it was a cold day with frost in the morning and a prayer meeting in Sears' brigade at 10:00 A.M.[51]

Maury sent out circulars to civilians and soldiers detailing what to do when the enemy attacked. He encouraged noncombatants to leave the city (and later wrote that they created a problem by declining to do so). He spoke confidently of success and assured the public that with an ample supply of food and plenty of ammunition, the city's defenses could with-stand a long siege. By now the pipes in the city's waterworks had been torn out to be melted down into lead for bullets.[52]

Mobile resident Laura Roberts Pillans wrote on March 12:

> The weather clear & cold. twenty one vessels in the bay; five of them monitors. . . . It is supposed that our trial is approaching. I believe our people will meet the attack with calmness & resolution & will sustain the spirit & resolution of the soldiers sent here for defense.[53]

It rained all day March 23. On March 24, Cockrell's division was ordered to Fort Blakely. Sears' brigade left on the steamer *Magnolia* at 8:00 P.M. and arrived at the fort around midnight. Holtzclaw's brigade was already there, and Gibson's brigade was deploying for action near Spanish Fort.

Among the soldiers, opinions varied on the Rebels' chances of success. Eufaula attorney Stouten Hubert Dent, 31-year-old grandson of a Revolutionary War soldier, had been wounded at Shiloh, Atlanta, and Nashville. His men were veterans commended many times for their faithfulness; at Shiloh one of their commanders had said, "With such batteries there could be no failure." Nashville had been a disaster for them, and now they were manning heavy guns on the outskirts of Mobile near the Bay. Although they had been promised to be sent back to the field soon, Dent felt that the scarcity of horses made this highly unlikely. He expressed pessimism about the city's ability to repel the invader and wrote his wife on February 10, "There seems to be a good deal of discipline here on paper and very little elsewhere. I do not wonder at the success of the Yankees in taking our cities if the defenses of all others were like those about Mobile."[54]

Robert Tarleton was irrepressibly optimistic. A graduate of Princeton, the 26-year-old artillery lieutenant had been captured with the Fort Morgan garrison in August 1864. After one unsuccessful escape attempt, he broke through the roof of his prison in New Orleans and made his way through the Louisiana swamps to marry his sweetheart, Sallie B. Lightfoot of Pass Christian, Mississippi. Tarleton then returned to Mobile to fight to the end. He wrote Sallie on April 2, 1865, "Our city is not at all changed in appearance—the band plays in the square as usual and to judge from the display on such festive occasions, You would never suppose it is in a state of siege." And the young officer assured his bride that the city's defenses would hold:

> You often hear the expression, "Spanish Fort is the key to Mobile." No such thing! It is only an outpost. So unless the enemy has some very

strong card hidden away somewhere which he is keeping back to play at the decisive moment, I think we are going to win this little game. So I don't want you to be one of those who say, "Of course the enemy will take the place—they always do."[55]

NOTES

1. Christopher C. Andrews, *History of the Campaign of Mobile* (New York, 1867), 10.

2. Arthur W. Bergeron, Jr., "Dabney Herndon Maury," in William C. Davis, ed., *The Confederate General* (Harrisburg, PA: National Historical Society, 1991), vol. 4, 165; Arthur W. Bergeron, Jr., *Confederate Mobile* (Jackson: University Press of Mississippi, 1991), 29.

3. Bergeron, *Confederate Mobile*, 29; Philip D. Stephenson, "Defence of Spanish Fort," *Southern Historical Society Papers* 39 (1914), 119.

4. Chester G. Hearn, *Mobile Bay and the Mobile Campaign: The Last Great Battles of the Civil War* (Jefferson, NC: McFarland and Company, Inc., Publishers, 1993), 47; Ezra J. Warner, *Generals in Gray: Lives of the Confederate Commanders* (Baton Rouge: Louisiana State University Press, 1959), 176–177; Milton F. Perry, *Infernal Machines: The Story of Confederate Submarine and Mine Warfare* (Baton Rouge: Louisiana State University Press, 1965), 183–184.

5. James L. Nichols, "Confederate Engineers and the Defense of Mobile," *Alabama Review* 12 (1959), 185.

6. Ibid., 188.

7. John Kent Folmar, ed., *From That Terrible Field: Civil War Letters of James M. Williams, Twenty-First Alabama Infantry Volunteers* (University: University of Alabama Press, 1981), 136.

8. Doris Rich, *Fort Morgan and the Battle of Mobile Bay* (Foley, AL: Underwood Printing Co., 1986), 57.

9. Nichols, "Confederate Engineers," 190–191, 193–194.

10. Hearn, *Mobile Campaign*, 136.

11. "The Situation at Mobile," Mobile *Daily Advertiser*, August 11, 1864; Charlie Holcombe Pitcher, "Spencer-Holcombe Letters Written in the 1860s," *Louisiana Genealogical Register* (March 1972), 46.

12. Bergeron, *Confederate Mobile*, 92.

13. Ibid., 93.

14. Joe A. Mobley, "The Siege of Mobile, August, 1864–April, 1865," *Alabama Historical Quarterly* 38 (1976), 269.

15. Rich, *Fort Morgan*, 17; William N. Still, Jr., "The Civil War Letters of Robert Tarleton," *Alabama Historical Quarterly* 32 (1970), 58.

16. Bergeron, *Confederate Mobile*, 115; Rich, *Fort Morgan*, 15–16, 19.

17. Rich, *Fort Morgan*, 21.

18. Ibid., 15; Hearn, *Mobile Campaign*, 139.

19. Pitcher, "Spencer-Holcombe Letters," 45; Bergeron, *Confederate Mobile*, 100.

20. Bergeron, *Confederate Mobile*, 101–102.

21. Pitcher, "Spencer-Holcombe Letters," 45–46.

22. Bergeron, *Confederate Mobile*, 102–103.

23. Mobley, "Siege of Mobile," 260.

24. Bergeron, *Confederate Mobile*, 104–106; Richard Rollins, *Black Southerners in Gray* (Murfreesboro: Southern Heritage Press, 1994), 25–26.

25. Ibid.

26. Bergeron, *Confederate Mobile*, 104, 109.

27. Ibid., 114.

28. Ibid., 158, 160–161.

29. Hearn, *Mobile Campaign*, 141; Bergeron, *Confederate Mobile*, 159.

30. Bergeron, *Confederate Mobile*, 160.

31. Ibid., 164.

32. Ibid., 163; Perry, *Infernal Machines*, 184.

33. Hearn, *Mobile Campaign*, 141–143.

34. Bergeron, *Confederate Mobile*, 165.

35. Mobley, "Siege of Mobile," 251.

36. Ibid., 252–253; S. H. Dent to his wife, February 10, 1865, Stouten Hubert Dent Papers: Confederate Letters. RG #86, Auburn University Archives.

37. Mobley, "Siege of Mobile," 254.

38. George Little and James R. Maxwell, *A History of Lumsden's Battery,* C.S.A. (Tuscaloosa: United Daughters of the Confederacy, 1905), 64.

39. Mobley, "Siege of Mobile," 255, 257.

40. Ibid., 257–258; Folmar, *Terrible Field*, 146.

41. Pitcher, "Spencer-Holcombe Letters," 44.

42. Mobley, "Siege of Mobile," 259–260; Folmar, *Terrible Field*, 155.

43. Mobley, "Siege of Mobile," 266–268; Sidney Adair Smith and C. Carter Smith, Jr., eds., *Mobile: 1861–1865 Notes and a Bibliography* (Chicago: Wyvern Press, 1994), 39.

44. Bergeron, *Confederate Mobile*, 114.

45. Ibid., 109; Pitcher, "Spencer-Holcombe Letters," 44.

46. Bergeron, *Confederate Mobile*, 109.

47. William Pitt Chambers, *Blood and Sacrifice: The Civil War Journal of a Confederate Soldier*, ed. Richard A. Baumgartner (Huntington, WV: Blue Acorn Press), 202–203; emphasis in original.

48. Ibid., 203; emphasis in original.

49. Ibid., 204.

50. Ibid., 204–206; emphasis in original.

51. Ibid., 206.

52. Mobley, "Siege of Mobile," 267; Bergeron, *Confederate Mobile*, 171–172.

53. Smith and Smith, *Mobile: 1861–1865*, 44.

54. Mattie Thomas Thompson, *History of Barbour County, Alabama* (Eufaula: N.p., 1939), 390–391; Wheeler, "Alabama," in Clement Evans, ed., *Confederate Military History*, vol. 7 (Atlanta, 1899), 337; Dent to his wife, February 10, 1865, Dent Papers.

55. Still, "Tarleton Letters," 78–79.

CHAPTER 3

"Every Thing Wet and Not Enough to Eat"

The architect of the Federal offensive against Mobile was Major General Edward Richard Sprigg Canby, a 47-year-old career officer whose chief claim to fame lay in thwarting the Confederacy's attempt to occupy New Mexico. A native Kentuckian, Canby's record at West Point was not particularly outstanding; "Sprigg," as he was nicknamed, graduated next to last in his class in 1839. As a young officer he fought Seminoles in Florida; commanded troops in the removal of Creeks, Cherokees, and Choctaws to Arkansas; and served as chief of staff of a brigade in the Mexican War. Canby saw substantial frontier duty in the 1850s, and the outbreak of the Civil War found him stationed at Fort Defiance in the New Mexico Territory. In May 1861 he was made colonel of the newly authorized 19th U.S. Infantry Regiment and placed in command of the Department of New Mexico.[1]

In February 1862, the Confederates launched an offensive into New Mexico as 3,500 Texas troops led by Brigadier General Henry Hopkins Sibley streamed northward along the Rio Grande from Fort Bliss. Canby assembled as many Federal troops to oppose them. The Rebels won the first round. Sibley stung Canby at Valverde forcing him to retreat, then went on to capture Albuquerque and Santa Fe. But Canby, reinforced by 900 troops rushed south from Colorado, turned the tables on the Rebels and smashed them at Glorietta Pass. Sibley's ragtag army withdrew to Texas.

Although minor in comparison with events in the East, the Union victory was significant. Had they secured New Mexico, the Confederates intended to invade California, and a Confederate California with its valuable gold deposits and harbors free from Yankee blockaders could have caused much damage to the Union. Canby made brigadier general in May 1862, and the next year and a half brought him staff duty back east. He earned a reputation for being a methodical, hard working officer, and by May 1864 he was a major general placed in charge of Federal forces recently beaten by the Rebels in the calamitous Red River campaign. He coordinated Federal troops with Farragut's naval forces in the capture of Fort Morgan and Fort Gaines in August 1864.

In November 1864 while conducting operations in an area where Rebel guerrillas were active, Canby received an embarrassing but potentially dangerous wound from a sniper who fired on him from a Louisiana river-bank. At first the general was not expected to live. Canby had been struck in the left buttock, and the musket ball had passed out of his body through the thigh just below the groin. He was in a lot of pain but was lucky because the bullet did no damage to nerves or blood vessels. Still Canby did not recover for a couple of months. Even after returning to duty, he continued to get about with the aid of a walking stick as late as March 1865.[2]

As the last year of the war opened, Union army commander Ulysses S. Grant envisioned a master strategy to smite the exhausted Confederacy with a final death blow. With his own Army of the Potomac poised before Robert E. Lee's besieged army in Petersburg, Virginia, Grant wanted Canby and George H. Thomas to launch major offensives in coordination with William T. Sherman's march into the Carolinas. Neither Canby in New Orleans nor Thomas in Nashville had gotten under way. Grant expected Thomas to unleash two powerful Federal cavalry operations: Major General George Stoneman into western North Carolina and Major General James H. Wilson into north Alabama. Canby was to move up from the Gulf and join Wilson for operations against Selma, a major Rebel industrial center, and Montgomery. Grant considered Canby a major linchpin in his plan, and to help him carry out his part of the mission, he transferred Major General A. J. Smith's corps—18,000 infantrymen fresh from their victory at Nashville—to Canby in January 1865.

It was obvious to Grant that the anticipated Federal troop movements could not be coordinated unless Canby got under way, but "Sprigg" seemed to be dragging his feet. It was already too late to support Sherman's movements in the Carolinas. Late in February 1865, Canby received a message from Army Chief of Staff Henry ("Old Brains") Halleck urging him to begin the campaign: "I hope your expedition will be off before this reaches you, for Genl Grant is very impatient at delays & too ponderous preparations. He says that nearly all our generals are too late in starting & carry too much with them."[3]

Canby cited recent heavy rains and impassable roads for the delay, with only seven days of decent weather in the forty days prior to March 7. But Grant was "extremely anxious to see the enemy entirely broken up in the West" while still "an easy job." He insisted that if the Rebels were pressed hard enough, desertion would thin their ranks, and he stressed the importance of destroying their crops, railroads, and manufacturing facilities. "It is also important," Grant wrote, "to get all the negro men we can before the enemy put them in their ranks." But still Canby moved at a snail's pace, complaining of the bad weather, and when he requested a construction corps to repair 70 miles of railroad track between Pensacola and Pollard, it was the last straw for a thoroughly exasperated Grant. "You need not send an article of railroad material or a man to Canby," he wrote to Quartermaster General Montgomery C. Meigs on March 9. "We have no time for building railroads there now." "Take Mobile and hold it," he ordered Canby, "and push your forces to Montgomery and Selma." On March 13 the disgusted Grant wired Halleck, "I have seen but little from Canby to show that he intends to do or have anything done."[4]

In a caustic communication with Secretary of War Edwin Stanton on March 14, Grant wrote, "I am very much dissatisfied with General Canby. He has been slow beyond excuse. . . . On the 1st of March he is in New Orleans, and does not say a word about leaving there." His patience clearly at an end, Grant requested that Major General Philip Sheridan be sent from Virginia to replace Canby. Grant also disagreed with Canby's choice of Gordon Granger for command of one of his two corps, the 13th. Grant did not like Granger and wanted his old West Point classmate Frederick Steele to be given the command.[5]

Major General Gordon Granger, a 42-year-old New Yorker, was a graduate of the 1845 class of West Point, which boasted fourteen general officers during the Civil War. He served in the Mexican War and on the western frontier, and he rose rapidly in rank after the start of the Civil War. Granger's timely actions at Chickamauga in September 1863 helped save the Union army from disaster when—against orders—he rushed his Reserve Corps into the battle at just the right moment. When his troops gave out of ammunition, Granger ordered, "Fix bayonets and go for them." The Reserve Corps suffered 44 percent casualties in less than two hours at Chickamauga. Because he had commanded the Federal land forces during Farragut's August 1864 campaign in Mobile Bay, Granger was familiar with the area around Mobile, with the terrain, and with the character of the war here, and Canby considered him an able commander despite Grant's disapproval. J. S. Fullerton, Granger's chief of staff at Chickamauga, described him as "rough in manner, but he had a tender heart. He was inclined to insubordination, especially when he knew his superior to be wrong. Otherwise he was a splendid soldier."[6]

In New Orleans Canby was meticulously planning his offensive, which would finally get under way before the boiling-mad general-in-chief could carry out his threat to replace him. By March 1865 Canby had about 45,000 troops in the area, compared with Maury's 9,000. As he opened operations against Mobile's defenses, Canby decided to concentrate on the Rebel forts to the east of the Bay rather than the triple line of defenses to the west. The Federal advance would be made in two columns. The main one under Canby—32,000 soldiers of the 13th Corps led by Granger and the 16th Corps under A. J. Smith—would leave from Fort Morgan and Fort Gaines. The other column under Frederick Steele—13,000 troops from Pensacola—would move north in a feint toward Montgomery to divert Maury's cavalry away, then would turn south to join Canby for operations against Spanish Fort and Blakely. Canby planned to use the Fish River, which emptied into Mobile Bay just 20 miles south of Spanish Fort, as a supply route. Federal ships could transport men, guns, and material across Mobile Bay from Dauphin Island, travel several miles upriver, and deposit them. Federal troops could move up the Fish River toward Spanish Fort, and gunboats moving along the eastern shore of the Bay could provide support.

Because Mobile was no longer of use to the Rebels as a seaport, Grant regarded Selma and Montgomery as more significant military objectives, and it made more sense to him for Canby to bypass the Gulf City and advance into central Alabama for the proposed linkup with Wilson, but only if Mobile proved too formidable an obstacle. If Mobile fell quickly, he could still make the rendezvous. What Grant did not want was a protracted operation that would tie Canby's forces down against Mobile. But the ever-cautious Canby had no intention of leaving Fort Blakely and Spanish Fort in his rear; he must first neutralize these Rebel strongholds before moving inland. And Grant had specifically ordered him to take Mobile. By March 18, Wilson's 10,000 horsemen were under way on their sweep into central Alabama. When Canby's troops settled in for prolonged siege operations around Spanish Fort and Fort Blakely, it became obvious to Grant that he would not be able to link up with Wilson as planned. But at least Canby had been prodded into finally doing something.

As the time approached for the Federal offensive to begin, Granger's division commanders in the 13th Corps were getting their troops ready for the coming movement across the Bay. Brigadier General James C. Veatch, a 45-year-old lawyer and Indiana state legislator, was a veteran of Shiloh, Corinth, and the Atlanta campaign. He commanded the 1st Division, which disembarked at Navy Cove. Brigadier General William P. Benton, a

36-year-old former district attorney and judge of common pleas court in Wayne County, Indiana, was a combat veteran of the Mexican War and was said to be the first man in the county to sign up after Lincoln called for 75,000 volunteers. A popular officer, he had fought at Port Gibson, Jackson, and Vicksburg. He led the 3rd Division marching east from Fort Morgan. Brigadier General Christopher C. Andrews with two brigades in his 2nd Division had been sent to augment Steele's forces at Pensacola, leaving with Granger the one brigade of Colonel Henry Bertram, a German immigrant and veteran of the Mexican War.[7]

The 29th Iowa Infantry in Benton's division was a product of Lincoln's second call for volunteers (300,000 men for three years' service in July 1862). It had not been a particularly good time for young men to go off to war, with crops needing harvesting, but the threat of conscription caused many to sign up. Ultimately 76,000 men, more than half the Iowa population of military age, served in the Union army. Thomas Hart Benton, Jr., raised the 29th Iowa and became the regiment's first colonel. The new recruits went into training at Camp Dodge in Council Bluffs and were officially mustered on December 1, 1862. Most were farmers from the western frontier of the state, having migrated to Iowa from the East, and a number of them had immigrated from Europe. The 29th Iowa saw service in the Trans-Mississippi Department, mostly in Arkansas where the regiment quickly became familiar with frontier warfare. C. C. Andrews called the 29th Iowa "a regiment of splendid material and discipline to match."[8]

Typical of the young Iowa soldiers was Charles O. Musser, 20 years old when he enlisted in the 29th Iowa. A local farm boy from Council Bluffs, Musser stood 5 feet 6 inches tall, with gray eyes and brown hair. His parents, who had come from Ohio in search of better land in Iowa, were not overjoyed when Charles signed up; they could have used the extra hands around the farm. Charles wrote in July 1863, "I done wrong in enlisting, but i thought it was my duty to Serve my country above all things." Charles may have shared the feelings of another Iowa soldier, John P. Moulton of the 34th Iowa, who wrote that his desire was to "fight for my country so long as I can shoulder my musket" for the principles of "free Speach, free press and free Governments in General." And, like many Northern youths, he may have been attracted by the lure of adventure, the desire to avoid the stigma of conscription, and by the promise of a bounty. Charles did well in the army and by June 1864 was wearing sergeant's stripes. Charles' brother William chose the Confederacy, joining the 8th Missouri Infantry in September 1862; he spent much of the war in a Federal prison camp and remained at odds with his family after the war.[9]

Throughout the war Charles kept up a detailed correspondence with his family and friends, commenting on his experiences as a soldier, on the South and its people. He was weary of it by January 1865 when he wrote that the war couldn't go on past the end of the year, and added, "I want to *see* it end before I go home." He felt that his accounts of the war might be worth looking back over some day and asked his family to save his letters so that he could read through them when he returned home.[10]

Charles' regiment departed Council Bluffs in December 1862. First stop was Saint Joseph, Missouri ("considerable of a town . . . three times as large as the bluffs"), then Saint Louis, and then down the Mississippi River to Helena, Arkansas, where Charles got his first taste of combat in July 1863. He also learned that there was a more deadly enemy to face. Illness in the form of measles, diarrhea, and malaria swept through the Federal camps, and soldiers soon called the low lying river town "Hell-in-Arkansas." Iowa had the highest percentage of deaths by disease of any Union state—12.5 percent—and the 29th Iowa was especially hard hit. So many Union soldiers lay in graves nearby that Musser wrote his father from Helena that he hoped when he finally left there that the Mississippi River would "cover it so deep that no lead can Sound the bottom." He also wrote that he wished he could be home to help with the farm chores, but he wanted to wait until his soldiering was finished.[11]

Like the 29th Iowa, Lieutenant Colonel Edmund B. Gray's 28th Wisconsin Infantry in Benton's division had been raised in August 1862 following Lincoln's call for 300,000 more volunteers. The regiment was formed in the dairy farmland of Waukesha County west of Milwaukee, and recruitment meetings were held at schools and communities throughout the area. The captains of the companies included the school superintendent, clerk of the circuit court, and district attorney. Oconomowoc's postmaster, Thomas N. Stevens, was captain of Company C.[12]

In March 1865, Stevens was a few weeks short of his 30th birthday. Born in New York, he had struck out on his own at the age of 17 and had made his way to southern Wisconsin. Stevens married Caroline E. Silsbee of Columbus, Wisconsin, in 1857. He wrote many letters to "Carrie" during the war, expressing concern for his family and their well-being. A staunch Republican, Stevens enlisted in the 28th Wisconsin out of patriotism. A very religious and moral man, he cared deeply about his soldiers, and he wanted no rank above captain, although he could have received promotions. The men of his company respected him. Stevens was a restless man. He planned to settle somewhere with his family after the war, and he even considered moving to the South.[13]

The 28th Wisconsin sailed from New Orleans to Fort Morgan in February 1865. Stevens wrote Carrie that their voyage across the Gulf was a rough one accompanied by a heavy rainstorm, their ship thrown about in the sea leaving nearly everyone seasick. "I stood it till about half past ten," he wrote, "when I had to make for the ship's side and toss my breakfast to the fishes." At Fort Morgan the Wisconsin boys got their first taste of South Alabama life. "Nothing here but sand & weeds," Stevens wrote.[14]

From Fort Morgan the 28th Wisconsin moved to Navy Cove, where a heavy all-night rain on March 7 left the men soaked, although Stevens wrote, "I'm used to that—it don't hurt me a bit." Stevens commented on the military buildup in the area and speculated that the army would soon move on Selma or Montgomery, because "Mobile would be worth little to the rebs" once these other key cities fell. The mood of the soldiers was optimistic, having just received news of the February 22 capture of Wilmington, North Carolina, and rumors promised the end of the war any day. "I hope it may," Stevens wrote, "but hardly think it will. . . . [I]t does seem that the rebels must soon be overcome—*conquered*. When that is done the war is ended—*and not till then*."[15]

As they prepared to move overland from Fort Morgan toward the Fish River, the men of Benton's division received their marching orders. They must each carry four days' rations and fifty rounds of ammunition, plus an ax and entrenching tool for each dozen men. Soldiers could bring only one extra shirt, change of underwear, pair of socks, pair of shoes, woolen blanket, and shelter half. "Just think of *that* load," Musser wrote. There would be swamps to wade through, wagons and guns to be pulled by hand out of the mud, and anywhere from 5 to 20 miles of hard marching to do each day. Then at night, earthworks to throw up, rifle pits to dig, and up before daybreak with the same work to do all over again.[16]

On March 17, 1865, the grand Federal offensive against Mobile's defenses—so long anticipated by Grant, by Canby, and by common soldiers like Charles Musser and Thomas Stevens—finally got under way. Smith's 16th Corps had a relatively easy passage by transports from Fort Gaines across the Bay and 6 miles up the Fish River, disembarking at Dannelly's Mills. But Granger's 13th Corps, marching overland from Fort Morgan and Navy Cove eastward along the peninsula and then northward through the woods toward Spanish Fort, had a much harder time of it. Swampy terrain, bad roads, and heavy rain made for slow progress. No serious resistance was encountered, although the bluecoats spotted Rebel scouts several times.

The first leg of the march from Fort Morgan and Navy Cove took the Federal column through swamps and sand banks. "Scrubby Pine and Live Oak," Musser wrote, "roads getting worse and worse fast." Stevens called it a "barren, miserable desert." Things only got worse as the column reached Bayou Portage, turned and pushed north toward the Fish River.[17]

Colonel Henry Bertram's brigade led the way. In the vanguard was Colonel John McNulta's 94th Illinois Infantry. About one fourth of Canby's troops hailed from the Prairie State. Most were farm boys like those in the 94th Illinois, recruited in August 1862 in the central Illinois corn belt of McLean County. The recruits who left their plows to don the Union blue were responding to Lincoln's second call for volunteers. By the fall of 1862, the 94th Illinois was on duty in Missouri, and on December 7 the volunteers took part in the battle of Prairie Grove, a Federal victory that secured northern Arkansas for the Union. More campaigning in Arkansas and Missouri followed, then in June 1863 the 94th Illinois was sent across the Mississippi to participate in the Federal siege of Vicksburg. After the Rebel garrison surrendered, the 94th was on duty at Port Hudson and at New Orleans. In the fall of 1863, the 94th Illinois set out for the Rio Grande as part of a U.S. move to counter the recent French military intervention in Mexico. The Illinoisans crossed the river to Matamoros and escorted the U.S. consul back to Brownsville, where the regiment was stationed for nine months. In August 1864, the 94th Illinois was among the Federal troops besieging Fort Morgan and had been stationed in the area ever since.[18]

The rainy weather slowed the 94th Illinois' advance. On March 18, 31-year-old William M. Macy wrote in his diary, "Roads very good in forenoon and in the afternoon very bad swampy and muddy." On the march north Macy commented on the scarcity of dwellings. He recorded on March 19, "stopped at one house and carried their rails to build a Bridge across a swampy place. Marched 8 miles and camped in the pinery."[19]

The next two days brought eighteen hours of heavy rain, and wagons and artillery quickly sank in the mire. A drencher flooded the country on March 20. When the downpour finally let up about 1:00 P.M., Musser and his companions all pitched in to help pull guns and wagons out of the waist-deep mud. As soon as they could get them on good ground, they would harness the horses to them. Musser mused, "one may judge how the roads is when 8 large Horses cant move a 12 Pounder Napoleon gun." At the end of the day, tired and muddy soldiers, with no dry change of clothing, built camp fires from pine branches and huddled around the smoky fires until they looked "more like contrabands than white men."[20]

It rained again all day on March 21 making for a miserable time for the men who had to drag cannon and wagons out of the mud by hand. Exhausted soldiers labored to convert the miry trails into "corduroy roads," cutting trees and laying the trunks across the road to provide some traction for wagons and cannon. "Mud & water from ankle to waist deep," Thomas

Stevens wrote. "Every one wet." Granger reported that the roads were "of the worst possible description—the heavy rains of the 20th and 21st converting the country into a boggy swamp." In the 94th Illinois at the head of the column, William Macy summed it up: "every thing wet and not enough to eat."[21]

The next day there was more backbreaking work, more corduroy roads to build. For Musser, this was "the worst country I ever saw for an Army to march through." The ground appeared firm enough, but after several wagons or caissons pulled through, they would sink axle deep. Musser recalled, "Then it's 'halt,' 'front,' 'Stack Arms, Boys and help those teams out of the mud.' " "Then we pull the donkeys," a soldier in the 35th Wisconsin Infantry wrote, "mud up to our knees, but those long-ears weren't dumb. When things didn't move, they layed down."[22]

Although the going was slow and rough, there was encouragement along the way. The men seemed to bear the ordeal without complaint. Musser recorded, "they all seem in the best of spirits and care not what comes." At one point, Brigadier General Benton himself shed his coat and toiled along with his soldiers pushing a wagon out of the mire. An elderly black woman cheered on soldiers of the 33rd Iowa as they struggled through the swamp. "Glory, Hallelujah! The Lord's done heard us. There's eight hundred of us praying for you at Mobile!"[23]

On March 22, Bertram's vanguard reached Dannelly's Mills on the Fish River, where the 16th Corps had already arrived. It had taken five days to travel some 40 miles. Exhausted from their long march overland through the swamps, Benton's division finally arrived around 3:00 P.M. on March 23, its bands blasting "Oh, ain't you glad you're out of the wilderness." Veatch's division arrived on the following day. Stevens quipped, "This point is called Danly's Mills. I 'don't see' the Mill."[24]

Canby waited until most of his troops—about 30,000 men—were up, then the column pushed on toward Spanish Fort, again with Bertram's brigade in the lead. It was the 13th Corps that first made contact with the enemy—members of Gibson's Louisiana brigade—at daybreak on March 27. Gibson had planned a surprise attack to throw the Yanks off guard, and 400 gray-clad infantrymen poured out of their earthworks. The Rebels discharged a volley that quickly scattered the Federal pickets and gamely charged into a gap between two Union regiments, both of which fell back. Then the blue-coated masses formed their own line of battle, and when they realized the true size of the force in front of them. the Rebels wisely fell back to Spanish Fort.[25]

The next day from dawn until dark the Yankees were busy with axes, shovels, and guns. Canby's troops had the enemy garrison under siege, but—as the Federals had learned the hard way—the Rebels were far from predictable. March 30 was marked less by firing than by the tedious work of digging trenches. But at 1:00 A.M., gunfire suddenly erupted as Gibson's Louisiana troops again poured over their works and launched a surprise attack on the 94th Illinois on the extreme left of the Federal siege line. The graycoats got within 50 yards of the Yankee works, but the 19th Iowa was rushed up and the Federals beat back the attack. The Rebels withdrew to the fort leaving nine of their men dead and three Federals wounded.[26]

Canby made his headquarters 2 miles from Spanish Fort on the main road. As siege operations extended at Spanish Fort, Musser wrote on March 31, "Boys all well and full of fight, just as soon fight as not." On the same day a sleepy, worn out Thomas Stevens wrote, "We are now 'in the field,' sure."[27]

NOTES

1. Ezra Warner, *Generals in Blue: Lives of the Union Commanders* (Baton Rouge: Louisiana State University Press, 1964), 67–68.

2. Max L. Heyman, Jr., *Prudent Soldier: A Biography of Major General E.R.S. Canby, 1817–1873* (Glendale, CA: Arthur H. Clarke Co., 1959), 219–224, 227.

3. Shelby Foote, *The Civil War, a Narrative: Red River to Appomattox* (New York: Random House, 1994), 848–849; Bruce Catton, *The Centennial History of the Civil War*, vol. 3, *Never Call Retreat* (Garden City: Doubleday & Co., 1965), 433.

4. Heyman, *Prudent Soldier*, 224–225.

5. Ibid., 226.

6. Warner, *Generals in Blue*, 181; J. S. Fullerton, "Reenforcing Thomas at Chickamauga," in Robert Underwood Johnson and Clarence Clough Buel, eds., *Battles and Leaders of the Civil War*, vol. 3 (New York: Castle Books, 1956), p. 667.

7. Warner, *Generals in Blue*, 30–31, 525–526; Mark Mayo Boatner III, *The Civil War Dictionary* (New York: David McKay Co., Inc., 1959), 62.

8. Barry Popchock, ed., *Soldier Boy: The Civil War Letters of Charles O. Musser* (Iowa City: University of Iowa Press, 1995), 1; Christopher C. Andrews, *History of the Campaign of Mobile* (New York, 1867), 65.

9. Popchock, *Soldier Boy*, 4, 7–8; Bell I. Wiley, *The Life of Billy Yank* (Baton Rouge: Louisiana State University Press, 1978), 40.

10. Popchock, *Soldier Boy*, 8–10.

11. Ibid., 11, 21, 58–59.

12. George M. Blackburn, ed., *"Dear Carrie . . .": The Civil War Letters of Thomas N. Stevens* (Mount Pleasant, MI: Clarke Historical Library, Central Michigan University, 1984), xiv–xv.

13. Ibid., xii–xiii.

14. Ibid., 299–300.

15. Ibid., 301–302; emphasis in original.

16. Popchock, *Soldier Boy*, 195; emphasis in original.

17. Ibid.; Blackburn, *"Dear Carrie . . . ,"* 303.

18. Jasper Gilmore, Diary, Mobile Public Library, Living History and Genealogy Division, Mobile, AL.

19. Ibid.; William M. Macy, "Civil War Diary of William M. Macy," *Indiana Magazine of History* 30 (1934), 191–192.

20. Popchock, *Soldier Boy*, 196.

21. Blackburn, *"Dear Carrie . . . ,"* 304; *War of the Rebellion: A Compilation of the Official Records of the Union and Confederate Armies* (Washington, DC: Government Printing Office, 1880–1901), Series I, Vol. 49, Part I, 141; Macy, "Civil War Diary," 192.

22. Popchock, *Soldier Boy*, 196; Chester G. Hearn, *Mobile Bay and the Mobile Campaign—The Last Great Battles of the Civil War* (Jefferson, NC: McFarland and Company, Inc., Publishers, 1993), 155.

23. Ibid.; James Huffstadt, "The Last Great Assault: Campaigning for Mobile," *Civil War Times Illustrated* (March 1982), 10.

24. Popchock, *Soldier Boy*, 196; Hearn, *Mobile Campaign*, 155; Blackburn, *"Dear Carrie . . . ,"* 304.

25. Hearn, *Mobile Campaign*, 161; Andrews, *Campaign of Mobile*, 49–50; Popchock, *Soldier Boy*, 198.

26. Andrews, *Campaign of Mobile*, 79.

27. Popchock, *Soldier Boy*, 199; Andrews, *Campaign of Mobile*, 59; Blackburn, *"Dear Carrie . . . ,"* 305.

CHAPTER 4

"Mutilated and Sacrificed"

Major General Dabney H. Maury had known that a Federal offensive was looming, but where would the main thrust come? On the western side of the Bay? On the eastern side? The primary attack might come from Dauphin Island, or from Fort Morgan, or from Pensacola. When he received the unwelcome news that his scouts had spotted large numbers of Federal troops landing near the mouth of the Fish River, Maury dispatched his veteran infantry brigades from the city to Brigadier General St. John R. Liddell at Blakely. He planned to make a stand south of Spanish Fort and challenge the enemy. If the advancing Federal force was not too large, there was a chance that he might be able to take the Yanks by surprise and sting them with a quick reverse before the better part of their army arrived.

On March 26, 1865, Gibson's Louisiana brigade under Colonel Francis L. Campbell dug in on the hilly north bank of D'Olive's Creek a few miles south of Spanish Fort. Cockrell's division was about 4 miles northeast at Alexis Spring. Rebel scouts reported two separate Union columns coming up the roads from the south toward each position. Liddell was confident that either Gibson or Cockrell could meet the advancing Federal troops and defeat them piecemeal. Reports from Colonel Philip B. Spence's 16th Confederate Cavalry indicated that the invaders were part of Gordon Granger's 13th Corps. Liddell felt that muddy roads would delay the bluecoats in front of Cockrell and that the main attack would come at D'Olive's Creek. The Rebs drew their battle line—Cockrell on the left, Gibson on the right, Spence's cavalry in between, Holtzclaw's brigade in reserve—and waited for the Yankees to arrive.

But the bluecoats did not attack at D'Olive's Creek. Instead they side-stepped to the north and east, swinging around the Rebels' thin left flank toward Blakely. Liddell was being outflanked. And to his dismay the Federal force was much larger than he had hoped. The bluecoats advancing in front of Cockrell were troops of A. J. Smith's 16th Corps, "Smith's Guerrillas." The Rebels faced two enemy corps, an entire Yankee army of some 30,000 men. Liddell pulled all his troops back and withdrew toward Blakely with Cockrell's division, the bulk of the Rebel force. Gibson fell back to Spanish Fort with his Louisiana brigade, Alabama reserves, and artillery and took command of the post there.[1]

Gibson hoped to delay the Federals long enough for his men to prepare for a siege. That evening he instructed them to set numerous campfires in front of Spanish Fort to deceive the advancing Yankees into thinking that he had a larger force. And when Federal pickets approached the Rebel works at daybreak on March 27, the Louisianans gave them a warm reception before falling back. Gibson had seriously considered launching a major attack, but when his officers reported that the enemy was too strong, he thought better of it. "I concluded not to attack," he informed Liddell.[2]

Thirty-two-year-old Brigadier General Randall Lee Gibson was a son of Louisiana's planter aristocracy. Raised on his father's plantation, Live Oaks, in southern Louisiana's Terrebonne Parish, and educated by a private tutor, Gibson graduated from Yale in 1853 and from the University of Louisiana's law school in 1855. He continued his studies in Europe and spent six months as an attaché to the U.S. embassy in Madrid before returning to Louisiana and settling into the comfortable life of a planter in Lafourche Parish. Gibson's military career showed promise from the very start of the war. He received a position as aide-de-camp to Louisiana Governor Thomas O. Moore, served briefly as an officer in the 1st Louisiana Heavy Artillery, and in September 1861 became colonel of the 13th Louisiana Infantry Regiment, recruited in the southern part of the state.[3]

The dashing young colonel first gained the attention and praise of his superiors on the battlefield at Shiloh in April 1862. Already in temporary command of a brigade, Gibson led his troops in four unsuccessful assaults on the Federal stronghold called the "Hornet's Nest," which witnessed the bloodiest fighting ever seen in North America up to that time. The 4th Louisiana Infantry Regiment suffered 209 casualties in the engagement. At Perryville, Kentucky, in October 1862, Gibson received accolades "for skill and valor" from his brigade commander, Louisiana attorney Daniel W. Adams, who had lost an eye at Shiloh. At Murfreesboro in December 1862, Gibson replaced Adams, who had been wounded again, and commanded his brigade

for the rest of the engagement; Major General John C. Breckinridge complimented Gibson for showing "marked courage and skill."[4]

Not all of Gibson's superiors agreed. After Shiloh, Major General
Braxton Bragg criticized Gibson for failing to take the "Hornet's Nest" and
in a letter to his wife termed the young Louisianan "an arrant coward."
When word of Bragg's criticisms got back to him, Gibson requested that the
army convene a court of inquiry to investigate the charges, but the War Department declined to pursue the matter. Gibson and Bragg remained on un-
friendly terms afterward.[5]

The Louisiana brigade suffered heavy losses at Chickamauga in September 1863, over 40 percent casualties in several regiments. Adams was
wounded again and was captured, and Gibson took over the brigade. He finally received his promotion to brigadier general in February 1864. The
Louisiana brigade was busy throughout the Atlanta campaign, taking
heavy casualties on July 28 at Ezra Church and on August 31 at Jonesboro,
where Gibson grabbed up a regimental flag and personally led his men forward against enemy earthworks. Major General Henry D. Clayton, his division commander, praised him for bravery and for inspiring his men. He
continued to lead the Louisiana brigade through Hood's Tennessee offensive and in the rear guard action in the retreat from Nashville.[6]

On March 27, 1865, Gibson prepared to defend Spanish Fort with 1,810
troops. The Rebels expected an attack, and they occupied a strong position.
The Confederate defenses formed a line of works a mile and a half long,
"shaped a good deal like a horseshoe pressed open," Gibson noted. For 300
yards in front of the lines, trees had been cleared and obstructions placed
for the oncoming Federals. A tangled abatis stretched about 15 feet deep
along the whole front, and in front of the breastworks ran a ditch 8 feet wide
and 5 feet deep. Rebel sharpshooters manned rifle pits scattered in front of
the six batteries or redoubts that crowned the crest of red bluffs running
along the line. Both the northern and southern flanks lay open and unforti-
fied, ending in the Bay Minette swamp on the north and in the marshy
mouth of D'Olive's Creek on the south. "It was apparent," Gibson observed,
"that an immense work with the spade, pick, and ax was before us, and that
some decisive measure must be adopted to prevent the large army already
upon our front from coming upon us vigorously or by an onset."[7]

Gibson's Louisiana Brigade, which had seen such hazardous duty as the
rear guard during Hood's retreat from Nashville, provided infantry support on the right of the Rebel line at Spanish Fort. Gibson's soldiers were
from all parts of their state, from the piney woods of western Louisiana to
the swampy Cajun delta lands in the south. Many officers and enlisted men
came from the city and surrounding parishes of New Orleans, where one

fourth of the state's people lived. The most populous and most cosmopolitan city in the South, New Orleans thrived on trade with the Midwest, although the state's economy was also dependent on cotton and slavery. The Crescent City had been in Federal hands since April 1862.

About a fifth of the Pelican State's population was foreign born. French was commonly spoken in many Louisiana military units, and the French influence was evident in names and uniforms. Members of the Orleans Guards Battalion of New Orleans began the war in their French Army style red kepis and dark blue frock coats and pants. Confederate troops serving with the Louisianans dubbed them "red caps." In Gibson's old command, the 13th Louisiana Infantry, six companies wore French Army-inspired blue Zouave jackets trimmed with gilt lace, baggy red Zouave pants, and the red fez. The similarity to Union blue caused much confusion early in the war, especially at Shiloh, and most units soon switched to Confederate gray.[8]

With Gibson in command at Spanish Fort, his senior colonel, 28-year-old Francis Lee Campbell, assumed control of the Louisiana brigade and commanded the Confederate right flank. Raised on his father's farm in Concordia Parish, Campbell was the youngest of fourteen children by his father's first marriage. He was a civil engineer and surveyor.[9]

Ranking second to Campbell in the Louisiana brigade was Lieutenant Colonel Robert Hume Lindsay, a 31-year-old Scottish pharmacist, the fifth child in a family of twelve children. In 1851, he immigrated to America and settled in Shreveport, Louisiana, where he branched into cotton in 1857. At the beginning of the war, he helped organize a local volunteer company, the "Caddo Fencibles," which joined the 16th Louisiana Infantry. Lindsay was elected captain of the company in November 1861, was promoted to major in 1862, and finally made lieutenant colonel of the regiment. A capable officer liked by his men and noted for his bravery and unruffled demeanor, he played a conspicuous role in the rear guard action after Nashville.[10]

Lindsay told of using a ruse to learn the disposition of enemy troops just south of Nashville before the battle in December 1864. Waving a white handkerchief, the unarmed Lindsay approached the railroad bridge across Brown's Creek and waited for a like signal from the opposite side. A Federal officer and two cavalrymen met him on the bridge and asked him what he wanted. Lindsay replied, "a ball of shoe thread to make a pair of boots," and offered to pay for it in tobacco. The Federal said, "That is a queer thing for a flag of truce," and doubted his superiors would agree to it. "Well," Lindsay told him, "let me know to-morrow morning." The two officers shook hands, and as he turned to go, Lindsay casually asked the two Federal enlisted men what regiment they belonged to. "Second Kentucky," they replied. "Ah, boys," Lindsay told them, "you should be on my side."

The soldiers grinned, and Lindsay returned to his side of the bridge, with the information he had wanted. The identity of the Federal unit in front of him would enable him to ascertain their brigade and division as well. The Yankees did not fall for the trick twice, though. The following morning, one of Lindsay's officers, Captain Samuel Haden, approached the bridge with the same deception in mind. This time the Federals were wary. "I saw them point their rifles at him and force him to enter their lines," Lindsay wrote, "and thus I lost one of my most gallant and skillful captains." Lindsay did not see Haden again until eighteen years later, when Haden (by then a Baptist minister) came to Shreveport for the dedication of a church.[11]

Perhaps illustrative of the officers in Gibson's brigade was Captain Lewis Fortin of the 30th Louisiana Infantry. He was originally a member of the Orleans Guards Battalion of New Orleans, later incorporated into the 30th Louisiana and garbed in Confederate gray. During the Atlanta campaign, the 30th Louisiana took some hard knocks. By August 1864, Fortin was one of only a few officers left and was dejected over the heavy losses and needless suffering. "I have seen you fall," he told his men, "mutilated and sacrificed in an unnecessary attack." Fortin died just two days later, the victim of a Yankee sharpshooter.[12]

By November 1864, Gibson's brigade was only a shade of what it once had been. In one regiment, the 1st Louisiana Regulars, just thirty-nine men were present. The Nashville campaign claimed a substantial toll. In Mobile in February 1865, the skeleton regiments of Gibson's brigade underwent drastic consolidation: The 1st, 16th, and 20th Louisiana Infantry Regiments were combined into one regiment under Lieutenant Colonel Robert H. Lindsay. The 4th Battalion and 25th Louisiana Regiment Infantry were merged into one under Colonel Francis C. Zacharie. The 4th, 13th, 19th, and 30th Louisiana Infantry Regiments were all consolidated under Major Camp Flournoy. And the Louisiana Battalion Sharpshooters was led by Colonel Francis L. Campbell. Gibson's brigade was down to about 500 men when it dug in at Spanish Fort.[13]

By the afternoon of March 27, the approaching Federals were testing the Spanish Fort defenses. When the Yankees were within half a mile of the fort, Gibson unleashed the firepower of his formidable arsenal—six heavy guns, fourteen field pieces, and twelve Coehorn mortars—which quickly silenced the cheering and yelling blue-coated troops. "No Sabbath-school was ever more quiet," a Yankee newspaperman reported. But with their overwhelming numbers the Federal troops began to encircle the Rebel fort, and by nightfall the investment of Spanish Fort was a reality. Gibson settled down for a siege. He had lost five soldiers killed and forty-four wounded. "The boys are worn down already," he reported.[14]

It soon became apparent that the Union gunboats in the Blakely River could not get close enough to Spanish Fort to do much damage, and the Federals were not prepared to risk a frontal attack by land. During the next couple of days both sides busied themselves with strengthening their positions and settling in for a lengthy siege. To demonstrate that the Rebels were still a force to be reckoned with, Gibson sent plucky Lieutenant Colonel Lindsay with 550 men on a midnight sortie on March 29, and in a pouring rain the Rebels surprised a group of 400 Federal soldiers. Remarkably, most of the Yankees were unarmed, because they were working on a battery, but they put up a stubborn fight and in hand-to-hand combat kept the Rebels at bay. Lindsay withdrew to the fort with several prisoners and some captured arms, but the raid cost him seven men killed and fourteen wounded.[15]

When Maury visited Spanish Fort on March 28, he could see that Gibson needed more men, but he had few to spare. It was a matter of placing his hard-pressed troops where they could do the most good. To bolster Gibson's besieged garrison, he ordered one of Holtzclaw's Alabama regiments to come down from Blakely, along with a detachment of Rebel sharpshooters toting the deadly accurate Whitworth rifles so feared by the Yankees. Maury was at the fort again on March 30, and because casualties continued to mount, he agreed to send more troops from Blakely to strengthen the beleaguered garrison. By March 31, Gibson received welcome reinforcements from Liddell: Ector's and Holtzclaw's brigades. Ector's Texans would defend the left flank at Spanish Fort, Holtzclaw's Alabamians the center. Holtzclaw would command the Rebel left wing. In return, Gibson sent Liddell the Alabama reserves under Brigadier General Bryan Thomas.[16]

The soldiers of Matthew D. Ector's Texas brigade, which had seen much hard service since coming east of the Mississippi, were a rugged lot, used to frontier life, and acquainted with adversity. Cotton and vast available land had brought these men and their families to the plains of eastern Texas. Many of them hailed from up near the Red River, from the Sabine River valley, and from northeast Texas towns like Tyler, Paris, and Sulphur Springs. Although most of them had enlisted to fight as cavalry, the scarcity of mounts had long since reduced them to the status of common foot soldiers.

The guiding spirit behind the Texas brigade was Brigadier General Matthew Duncan Ector, 42 years old, a veteran of the Mexican War and a former attorney and state legislator. Born in Georgia, Ector served as an enlisted man in a regiment of Georgia volunteers in the war of 1846–1848. While stationed in Texas, the young soldier liked what he saw. He settled in the little East Texas town of Henderson in 1849 and opened his law office there. Ector served in the Texas state legislature from 1855 to 1861, when the start of the war prompted him to enlist as a private in the Rebel army. He quickly advanced to officer grade. Commended for gallantry at Wilson's Creek in August 1861 and at Elkhorn Tavern (Pea Ridge) in March 1862, Ector soon attracted the eye of his superiors. In May 1862 he was elected colonel of the 14th Texas Cavalry Regiment.[17]

Ector led his regiment in the Confederate invasion of Kentucky in August 1862. His brigade commander wrote that at Richmond, Kentucky, on August 30, Ector "particularly distinguished himself, being in front of the battle and cheering on his men." He was made brigadier general the following month. Ector's brigade carried out a dawn surprise attack at Murfreesboro on December 31, 1862, and again he received praise for his "cool and dauntless courage, as well as skill." Brigade losses were heavy at Murfreesboro, as high as 34 percent in the 10th Texas Cavalry. The brigade suffered 63 percent casualties at Chickamauga in September 1863.[18]

Through the Georgia campaign of 1864, Ector was tireless and energetic, had only one staff officer to aid him, but managed to lead the brigade with efficiency. The Texas brigade took part in the desperate fighting around Atlanta. On July 27, Ector was hit by a piece of enemy shell while he was directing artillery fire from the Rebel earthworks. He was badly wounded above the left knee, and his leg was amputated. It appeared that his fighting days were over, and he made his way back across the Federal-held Mississippi to Texas to recover.[19]

With Ector out of action, 26-year-old Colonel William H. Young, who had been wounded four times during the war, took command of the brigade. But in October 1864, Young was wounded yet again, this time nearly losing his left foot. He was captured and spent the rest of the war in a Federal prison. Command now went to 41-year-old Colonel David Coleman, a graduate of the U.S. Naval Academy at Annapolis, more recently a member of the North Carolina legislature. It was Coleman who led the brigade during Hood's Tennessee offensive. And it was to Coleman's troops, withdrawing to Shy's Hill after the first day's disaster at Nashville, that Hood himself rode up, imploring his fellow Texans not to lose heart: "Texans," he told them, "I want you to hold this hill regardless of what transpires around you." The men replied, "We'll do it, General," and when darkness fell, they still held the hill. After Nashville the brigade was drastically reduced by deaths and sickness. Colonel J. A. Andrews took over command at Spanish Fort, and there is evidence to indicate that Ector himself managed to rejoin his brigade there in April 1865.[20]

A typical junior officer in the Texas brigade was Captain James A. Howze from Ector's old command, the 14th Texas Cavalry. Howze joined a cavalry company in Rusk County in the fall of 1861 and eventually became its captain. Steady under fire, yet calming and encouraging to his men, he helped keep the Texans focused. The night after Chickamauga he returned to the scene of slaughter to bury three of his men who had fallen in one spot on the field of battle. Near Atlanta, while the 14th Texas was doing rear guard duty for Hood's retreating army, Howze coolly and quickly snapped up an enemy artillery shell that had landed amongst his terrified men, with fuse still smoking, and hurled it over the earthwork before it exploded.[21]

Ector's Texas brigade spent most of the war fighting as dismounted cavalry. In the summer of 1863, while taking part in an unsuccessful attempt to relieve the besieged Rebel garrison at Vicksburg, the footsore men of the 14th Texas, upset at not being remounted despite promises to the contrary, staged a mutiny. Shouting "Hell or horses," they stacked their weapons and refused to fight. "Now, boys," Howze told them, "don't do that. I do not want a man of my company to lay down his gun. If the government does not see fit to give us our horses, let's serve our country in any capacity they want us to." All the companies in the regiment except Howze's continued the mutiny until compelled by force to pick up their muskets and obey orders. Two weeks later the entire regiment was in action again, and Ector let them redeem themselves by forcing back Union troops and reclaiming their picket line. Howze's company came to be known as the "Star Company" of Ector's brigade.[22]

The rank and file of Ector's brigade was drawn from soldiers like 25-year-old John E. Logsdon, 9th Texas Infantry, who enlisted in William H. Young's original company, was wounded in the right arm at Murfreesboro and in the right wrist at Nashville. Logsdon was nearly down with illness during the Atlanta campaign, but when comrades urged him to report for sick call, he declined. "I told them no, not as long as I could walk," he wrote later. "I would rather risk my chances on the firing line than in any army hospital." Orderly Sergeant C. M. Gingles, 22 years old, 10th Texas Cavalry, was wounded at Murfreesboro, at New Hope Church, and at Nashville; 19-year-old Robert C. Graves, an orderly sergeant in the 32nd Texas Cavalry, lost his right arm at Chickamauga. Most soldiers sought little recognition for their sacrifices. Francis A. Taulman, a 23-year-old private in the 32nd Texas Cavalry, explained, many years later, "I merely 'went with the crowd,' never halting short of the firing line and faithfully 'shucked my part of the corn.' While many of my comrades fell around me I was mercifully spared. . . . I marvel that so many of us were permitted to survive the ordeal."[23]

Added to Ector's brigade during the 1864 Georgia campaign were two regiments of infantry recruited in the mountains of western North Carolina. The 29th and 39th North Carolina Infantry Regiments were organized in the little town of Asheville in the late summer of 1861. Many of these men had never even seen a slave, much less owned one. Support for secession was weak in the mountains, and most of the tough highlanders would have been content to be left alone in their isolated coves and cabins in the Blue Ridge and Smokies. The mountain boys already had seen action in East Tennessee. The 29th North Carolina suffered 22 percent casualties at Murfreesboro and 110 casualties at Chickamauga. During the Atlanta campaign, men of the 39th North Carolina got sick on bad whiskey. "It was a pathetic sight," an officer reported, "to see at least five hundred men vomiting at the same time, and none able to assist his comrades." The 39th North Carolina was the last command to cross the Tennessee River during Hood's retreat from Nashville.[24]

So great was the problem of desertion in the Confederate army that commanders had questioned the wisdom of assigning Alabamians to the Mobile area, for fear the temptation to run away would be too great. But when James T. Holtzclaw's fine Alabama infantry brigade and several Alabama artillery batteries were earmarked for Mobile, no one raised any serious objection. Three of the regiments in the brigade (the 32nd, 36th, and 38th Alabama Infantry) had been organized in Mobile and had been stationed there (as was the 18th Alabama Infantry) at times prior to their assignment to Holtzclaw's brigade near the end of 1863. Several of the original companies had even been recruited in the Mobile area, although the majority of the brigade's soldiers came from other parts of the state. Most were poor farmers from the western counties, north central hill country, southern wire grass, or the south central black belt.

Montgomery attorney James T. Holtzclaw grew up in eastern Alabama's Chambers County and was educated at the Presbyterian high school in Lafayette. In 1853 he obtained an appointment to West Point, but he declined it because his older brother had just died and he felt that his absence would put too great a financial strain on the family. Later Holtzclaw took up residence in the state capital, practiced law, and became an officer in the prestigious Montgomery True Blues, the oldest military company in the state. Holtzclaw received a post as major in the 18th Alabama Infantry in August 1861 and made lieutenant colonel by the end of the year. In action at Shiloh in April 1862, he was standing next to the regimental colors and drew the attention of a Yankee rifleman who sent a musket ball through his right lung. Holtzclaw was not expected to live, but he was back with his command in ninety days. At Chickamauga in September 1863 he was injured when his horse ran against a tree and he was thrown off. The 18th Alabama lost two thirds of its men in the engagement. During the Atlanta campaign in July 1864 Holtzclaw was promoted to brigadier general; and he spent his

31st birthday leading his brigade in the rear guard action for Hood's army falling back from Nashville.[25]

At 28 years of age, Colonel Bush Jones was the senior colonel of the brigade. A graduate of the University of Alabama and an attorney in Uniontown, Jones married Carrie Evans, sister of writer Augusta Evans Wilson. He enlisted as a private but quickly gained officer status, and eventually he became colonel of the 58th Alabama Infantry, which captured four pieces of artillery on the first day at Chickamauga, losing 148 killed and wounded out of 254 men. A few weeks later Jones' regiment was consolidated with the 32nd Alabama. Jones commanded the Alabama brigade at times during the Atlanta campaign, during the retreat from Nashville, and at Spanish Fort. Major Harry Thornton, a former San Francisco lawyer who was wounded at Chickamauga and Atlanta, took over command of the regiment at these times.[26]

The 36th Alabama's Colonel Thomas H. Herndon, a graduate of the University of Alabama and Harvard, was another outstanding brigade officer. A distinguished looking Mobilian, with brown eyes and hair and a full beard and mustache, Herndon was a 36-year-old attorney and state legislator who had been wounded at Chickamauga and Atlanta. Commended by Bush Jones for "dashing and conspicuous gallantry" and up for promotion to colonel in July 1864, he remarked, "The truth is, I would never do for a colonel of a regiment. I cannot divest myself of sympathy for the men, nor look upon them as mere machines to be worked by me." But his officers and men thought differently.[27]

Greenville attorney Eddie Crenshaw, a graduate of the University of Alabama and the University of Virginia law school, was just 19 when he enlisted in the Rebel army, but before he reached his 21st birthday he was already the senior captain in Bush Jones' 9th Alabama Infantry Battalion, soon to become the 58th Alabama. Crenshaw was wounded at Chickamauga. In May 1864 he left the 58th Alabama to enter the Confederate States Marine Corps and served as an officer on the C.S.S. *Tallahassee*, a Rebel privateer that captured some forty Yankee ships during the war.[28]

Crenshaw wrote in his diary about the 58th Alabama in July 1863:

We were as well officered a little regiment as there was in the army, nearly all of the officers being young men, and thirsting for glory and distinction. Col. Bush Jones was a tall and exceedingly fine looking officer, cool and fearless in battle, and a good disciplinarian. Lt. Col. Inzer was a tall and spare built man a good officer—brave as a lion but excitable in battle. Major Thornton was a small but very handsome and graceful man, and would have done credit to the days of Coeur De Lion and Bayard.[29]

Almost as soon as they arrived in Mobile, the Alabama brigade was sent across the Bay to Liddell, but this didn't stop some of the soldiers from making the best of their situation. When their transport steamed out for Blakely, many of the men were suitably intoxicated and were still drinking on board. One of the soldiers had met his father in Mobile, and the old man accompanied him on the steamer, planning on spending some time with him at Blakely. During their carousing, the son fell overboard. He was never seen again. When the boat docked at Blakely landing, two more soldiers took a misstep on some loose boards and fell through a hole in the wharf. Other soldiers pulled the soaked inebriates—who had sobered up quickly—out of the water. The heartbroken father spent several fruitless days around the Bay in an unsuccessful attempt to recover his son's body.[30]

The Alabamians spent February and most of March 1865 near Blakely working on the completion of the fort's earthworks, fishing, and debating among themselves on the prospects of peace. In the 18th Alabama, Corporal Edgar Jones argued, "Let's fight it out." The soldiers were able to go into Mobile on passes and enjoy some of the pleasures of the Gulf City. As in Gibson's and Ector's commands, Holtzclaw's brigade was much reduced in strength, and in some regiments only junior officers were left to command. There was little doubt among the veterans that the hardest fighting they had ever faced probably lay ahead.[31]

Gibson had resolve and battle-hardened troops on his side, but so did the enemy. And there was no doubt as to which side had overwhelming superiority in numbers and in guns. Gibson would depend on his guns and the strength of the Rebel works to keep the Yankees at bay. "You must dig, dig, dig," he warned his soldiers. "Nothing can save us here but the spade."[32]

NOTES

1. Arthur W. Bergeron, Jr., *Confederate Mobile* (Jackson: University Press of Mississippi, 1991), 175; Chester G. Hearn, *Mobile Bay and the Mobile Campaign: The Last Great Battles of the Civil War* (Jefferson, NC: McFarland and Company, Inc., Publishers, 1993), 156–157.

2. Hearn, *Mobile Campaign*, 161; Christopher C. Andrews, *History of the Campaign of Mobile* (New York: 1867), 49–50; *War of the Rebellion: A Compilation of the Official Records of the Union and Confederate Armies* (hereafter cited as *OR*) (Washington, DC: Government Printing Office, 1880–1901), Series I, Vol. 49, Part II, 1164.

3. Arthur W. Bergeron, Jr., "Randall Lee Gibson," in William C. Davis, ed., *The Confederate General*, vol. 1 (Harrisburg, PA: National Historical Society, 1991), 185.

4. Ibid.; Ezra J. Warner, *Generals in Gray: Lives of the Confederate Commanders* (Baton Rouge: Louisiana State University Press, 1959), 1; Joseph H. Crute, Jr., *Units of the Confederate States Army* (Midlothian, VA: Derwent Books, 1987), 143.

5. Bergeron, "Gibson," 185.

6. Ibid.

7. *OR*, Series I, Vol. 49, Part I, 314–315.

8. Frederick P. Todd, *American Military Equipage, 1851–1872*, vol. 2, *State Forces* (New York: Chatham Square Press, Inc., 1983), 835, 843, 849, 856.

9. *Biographical and Historical Memoirs of Louisiana*, vol. 1 (Baton Rouge: Claitor's Publishing Div., 1975), 336.

10. Colonel R. H. Lindsay, Obituary, *Confederate Veteran* 18 (1910), 581.

11. R. H. Lindsay, "Trick to Learn Position of the Enemy," *Confederate Veteran* 8 (1900), 75.

12. Carl Moneyhon and Bobby Roberts, *Portraits of Conflict: A Photographic History of Louisiana in the Civil War* (Fayetteville: University of Arkansas Press, 1990), 106.

13. Crute, *Units*, 139–156; Hearn, *Mobile Campaign*, 218; John Dimitry, "Louisiana," in Clement Evans, ed., *Confederate Military History*, vol. 10 (Atlanta, 1899), 158.

14. Vincent Cortright, "Last-Ditch Defenders at Mobile," *America's Civil War* (January 1997), 60; *OR*, Series I, Vol. 49, Part II, 1163, 1164.

15. Hearn, *Mobile Campaign*, 168–169; Andrews, *Campaign of Mobile*, 65–66.

16. Bergeron, *Confederate Mobile*, 176–177.

17. Lawrence L. Hewitt, "Matthew Duncan Ector," in William C. Davis, ed., *The Confederate General*, vol. 1 (Harrisburg, PA: National Historical Society, 1991), 94.

18. Ibid., 95; Crute, *Units*, 329; R. Todhunter, "Ector's Texas Brigade," *Confederate Veteran* 7 (1899), 312.

19. Hewitt, "Ector," 95; Mamie Yeary, compil., *Reminiscences of the Boys in Gray, 1861–1865* (Dayton, OH: Morningside House, 1986), 316.

20. Warner, *Generals in Gray*, 348–349; F. A. Sondley, *A History of Buncombe County, North Carolina* (Spartanburg: Reprint Co., 1977), 768; Shelby Foote, *The Civil War, a Narrative: Red River to Appomattox* (New York: Random House, 1974), 695; *OR*, Series I, Vol. 49, Part I, 318; Andrews, *Campaign of Mobile*, 90; Hewitt, "Ector," 95.

21. W. Bailey, "The Star Company of Ector's Texas Brigade," *Confederate Veteran* 22 (1914), 404–405.

22. Ibid., 404.

23. Yeary, *Reminiscences*, 268, 277, 445–446, 740.

24. Crute, *Units*, 228; Richard B. McCaslin, *Portraits of Conflict: A Photographic History of North Carolina in the Civil War* (Fayetteville: University of Arkansas Press, 1997), 201, 202.

25. Joseph Wheeler, "Alabama," in Clement Evans, ed., *Confederate Military History*, vol. 7 (Atlanta, 1899), 417–419.

26. W. Stuart Harris, *Perry County Heritage*, vol. 2 (N.p., 1991), 22; Wheeler, "Alabama," 221–222.

27. Thomas M. Owen, *History of Alabama and Dictionary of Alabama Biography*, vol. 3 (Spartanburg, SC: Reprint Co., 1978), 803; Col. Thomas C. Herndon Obituary, *Confederate Veteran* 8 (1900), 542.

28. Owen, *History of Alabama*, 423.

29. Edward Crenshaw, "Diary of Captain Edward Crenshaw of the Confederate States Army," *Alabama Historical Quarterly* 1 (1930), 443–444.

30. Edgar Wiley Jones, *History of the 18th Alabama Infantry Regiment*, compiled by C. David A. Pulcrano (Birmingham, AL: C.D.A. Pulcrano, 1994), 216.

31. Ibid., 217.

32. *OR*, Series I, Vol. 49, Part I, 314; Part II, 1180.

CHAPTER 5

"The Worst Roads
I Ever Saw"

Major General Frederick Steele's Federal column was winding its way from the northwest toward Blakely after a difficult hundred-mile march overland from Pensacola. A 46-year-old New Yorker, Steele had been a distinguished officer during the Mexican War and had served on the western frontier prior to the outbreak of the Civil War. He became colonel of the 8th Iowa Volunteers in September 1861, was promoted to brigadier general in January 1862 and to major general in March 1863. Steele commanded a division at Vicksburg, and he took part in the unsuccessful Red River campaign.[1]

Even as Canby's blue-coated troops unloaded their equipment at Dannelly's Mills, Sprigg had selected Pensacola as a secondary Federal supply base. Pensacola had been the focus of early wartime activity in 1861 as Confederate forces marshaled for an assault against Federal-held Fort Pickens off shore on Santa Rosa Island. Dominating the excellent harbor of Pensacola Bay, Fort Pickens for a short while was the only major Southern coastal fort held by the Union. The expected Rebel assault on Fort Pickens never materialized. As a growing fleet of Union warships gathered in the Gulf and as reinforcements continued to enlarge the Federal garrison, the Confederates backed off, and soon their troops were sent to more critical scenes of combat in western Tennessee. The Rebels evacuated Pensacola in May 1862. Steele's forces assembled at Fort Barrancas, a former Rebel post outside of the town. C. C. Andrews' division from the 13th Corps arrived at the beginning of February 1865 and was joined by Canby's brother-in-law, 36-year-old Brigadier General John P. Hawkins, at the head of a division of

U.S. Colored Troops, and by Brigadier General Thomas J. Lucas with his cavalry division in early March.

Brigadier General Christopher Columbus Andrews was a 35-year-old New Englander whose passion for new places and new experiences led him to Kansas in 1854 and to Minnesota in 1857. An attorney at 21 years of age, Andrews became an accomplished writer and a state legislator on the Minnesota frontier. When the war erupted, he enlisted as a private but soon was elected captain in the 3rd Minnesota Infantry. Andrews was captured at Murfreesboro in July 1862 but was exchanged in October. A distinguished looking dark-bearded officer, he rose rapidly in rank, first to lieutenant colonel, then colonel in 1863, and finally to brigadier general in January 1864.[2]

Andrews' troops—mostly farm boys from Illinois, Indiana, Iowa, and Ohio—settled in for a stay at Fort Barrancas. They pitched their camp in the form of a small town "laid out with five streets to a regiment, with tents for two companies on a street, the companies facing." Soldiers created artificial groves from cut evergreen trees along the streets and carved cannons, mottoes, and other decorative designs in the sand. Andrews wrote, "These soldiers were some of the best young men of the West. . . . The plates on their accoutrements were kept brightly polished, and their muskets and accoutrements always neat." Andrews' two brigade commanders were Colonel William T. Spicely and Colonel Frederick W. Moore, an Ohio officer with experience in the Red River campaign.[3]

The 83rd Ohio Infantry, Moore's old command, had been formed in August 1862 following Lincoln's second call for volunteers. Rushed across the Ohio River into Kentucky to meet Confederate General Braxton Bragg's invasion of that state in September, learning to drill and march as they went, the volunteers missed seeing action as the Rebels withdrew, but soon the 83rd was sent to Arkansas where they took part in the capture of Fort Hindman (or Arkansas Post) on January 11, 1863. Next came campaigning in Louisiana and the siege and July 4 capture of Vicksburg, Mississippi, where Ohio soldier Isaac Jackson wrote, "The Rebels are entirely penned up. The worse fix they was ever in." Jackson observed "the most glorious Fourth I ever spent" when the Rebel garrison surrendered. But more hard campaigning lay ahead, and the 83rd Ohio served in Louisiana in the Teche Bayou expedition in the fall of 1863 and in the Red River campaign in the spring of 1864.[4]

Twenty-two-year-old Isaac Jackson, the son of a pottery maker, was born in Harrison, Ohio, west of Cincinnati. In apprenticeship as a tinsmith, Isaac joined the 83rd Ohio in August 1862. Like many Yankee recruits, he left for the war burdened down with equipment he would never use: white shirts, "store bought" shoes, and a "water purifier." (Jackson described it as a rubber tube about 6 or 8 inches long with a "small sand-stone" attached to the end, through which water was drawn into the mouth.) Assigned as a skirmisher, Jackson saw his first action in the capture of Fort Hindman. Although he thanked "good fortune, hard fighting and some tall running" for coming out safe in the Teche Bayou expedition, he was impressed by Louisiana and even considered moving there after the war. He especially liked New Orleans and Baton Rouge ("the nicest place I ever saw"). Late in 1863 Isaac transferred to the 17th Ohio Battery. He enjoyed serving in the artillery and hoped to stay on, but he was sent back to the 83rd Ohio in June 1864.[5]

Jackson was a religious, basically shy young man who became a good soldier, adjusting well to military life. The army agreed with him so much that he put on thirty pounds during his first eighteen months of service. He found the idea of slavery repugnant, and he felt it his duty as a Christian to help save the Union. All through the war he maintained a positive spirit in light-hearted correspondence in which he commented to his family on all the minutiae of soldier life: the hardships, the welcome letters from home, national politics (the pro-Lincoln Jackson hated Ohio's pro-Southern Copperheads), Southern food, and Southern girls. Isaac wrote his sister from New Orleans in June 1864, "Well, Sallie, I was to church yesterday. I heard a pretty good sermon.... And what is more I seen some pretty girls there, too ... but I seen them and that was all.... If I could only get to speak to them I would be a little better satisfied."[6]

Jackson described the 83rd Ohio's rocky voyage from New Orleans to Fort Barrancas in which most of the men were kept busy "heaving away." At Fort Barrancas there was "nothing to be seen here but 'sand' & Pine trees. Every thing sand. Go to eat a piece of bread you will find sand. Or take a piece of meat, you will be sure to find sand. Comb your hair you will find sand. In short, sand seems to form part of everything here." He had no idea why he and his comrades had been sent to Barrancas but wrote that he had discovered one advantage: "There is no mud—no matter how much it rains." Isaac spent his off-duty time on the beach collecting seashells, which he mailed home.[7]

Isaac liked most of his officers in the army, and he was favorably impressed by his new division commander, C. C. Andrews, who drilled the men morning and afternoon at Barrancas. Isaac wrote his brother Ethan on February 17 that Andrews told them they were "going on some hard campaigning and that we were agoing to have some very hard fighting and that he could rely on us to do it."[8]

Also in the 83rd Ohio was Corporal Frank McGregor, a 26-year-old Scottish immigrant who had come to the United States at age 13 with his parents, three brothers, and four sisters in 1851. The McGregor family had a farm in Glendale, Ohio, north of Cincinnati. Frank became a staunch Republican and enlisted in the 83rd Ohio in 1862 to fight for the Union. He wrote regularly to his sweetheart Susan Brown, a 20-year-old teacher from Lockland, a few miles south of Glendale.[9]

More philosophical than his easy-going fellow soldier Isaac Jackson, Frank McGregor often addressed the deeper anguish of men at war: the horrors of death and the longing for home and loved ones. He described the interior of the captured Rebel post at Fort Hindman in January 1863, a "dreadful sight" with its "shockingly mangled human beings." McGregor was also sad that he had lost Susie's two photographs and two letters during the battle, but the letters were retrieved by a comrade later. Already Frank was sick of the war. Marveling at how much his attitude had changed in his short period of service, he wrote Susie on January 30, 1863, "The whole army wishes only for one thing, and that is *Peace*, Peace almost at any price." His sentiments were echoed by fellow Union soldier John N. Moulton of the 34th Iowa Infantry (in the same brigade with the 83rd Ohio in the Mobile campaign) who despite his earlier enthusiasm for the war wrote his sister from near Vicksburg in March 1863, "I am lonesome and down hearted in Spite of my Self. I am tired of Blood Shed and have Saw enough of it."[10]

Frank McGregor contracted malaria during the cold rainy winter of 1863. He nearly died and was in a coma for almost a week. From April to October 1863 he spent time recovering in the hospital. But the experience brought him closer to God, and when he had regained his strength, Frank served as a male nurse in the hospital. The duty brought him time to think and to reflect and to long for Susie and home. He wrote Susie that of seven or eight soldiers from the 83rd Ohio who entered the hospital with him only one besides himself was still alive. A friend who had been wounded had lost an arm. "Poor fellow," Frank wrote, "I feel for him, he can never paint a picture again." Soon Frank became anxious to rejoin his regiment. He wrote Susie in June 1863 that he was confident God would bring him home safely and reunite them, knowing that he and his fellow soldiers had "done our duty in assisting to crush this unholy rebellion that has for its main pillar the keeping of fellow man in bondage."[11]

Frank returned to duty in the spring of 1864 in time for the Red River campaign in Louisiana. On April 8 he took part in the engagement at Sabine Cross Roads (or Mosses Lane) where the Federals were taken by surprise and routed. "Under terrible fire," he wrote Susie, "all confusion. . . . It's a terrible thing, but such is war, who is to blame?"[12]

In December 1864, Frank spent Christmas in Natchez, Mississippi, where he lent a hand decorating a church for Southern ladies. He wrote, "I have said often that of all the places in the south, this I like the best." But he was not to stay there, because the 83rd Ohio shipped out for New Orleans and from there to Fort Barrancas. Frank speculated on the next move. He expected some hard marching because the soldiers had been advised to pack an extra pair of shoes.[13]

Steele's column got under way from Pensacola on March 20, 1865. Their objective was the south Alabama railroad town of Pollard, although the movement was really designed as a feint toward Montgomery. Canby expected that Steele could actually move on to Montgomery if the Mobile defenses fell quickly. If not, Steele was to turn west from Pollard and join Canby with the main army on the eastern shore of Mobile Bay. Carrying ten days' rations, Steele's 12,000 troops and 270 wagons encountered very slow going because of the bad roads and rainy weather, the same conditions that delayed Granger's soldiers in their movement overland from Navy Cove. Sometimes the column could travel no more than a few miles a day. There were heavy rains the night of March 20, and the troops spent the next day building corduroy roads. "We have to drag the wagons through by ropes nearly all the way," Isaac Jackson wrote, "they are the worst roads I ever saw."[14]

The Federals had little to fear from the two small brigades of Rebel horsemen sent to delay the Union advance. Once the Confederate cavalry had been a menace and a terror to the Yankees, but by the fourth year of the conflict dwindling sources of manpower and horses had sapped much of the life out of the South's cavalry arm, whereas three years of combat experience plus a vast superiority in numbers and equipment had made the North's horse soldiers a formidable arm of service. The senior cavalry officer assigned to the defense of Mobile was 38-year-old James H. Clanton, a graduate of the University of Alabama and a veteran of the Mexican War. A brigadier general since November 1863, Clanton had made a reputation for himself as a hard-hitting cavalry leader, and Braxton Bragg called him "gallant to rashness." Clanton's command had been cut up in a skirmish with Federal Major General Lovell H. Rousseau's raiders at Ten Islands on the Coosa River in July 1864, and all his staff officers had been either killed or wounded in the engagement.[15]

It was the job of Brigadier General Thomas J. Lucas' cavalry division to ride ahead of Steele's column and brush Confederate resistance aside. A watchmaker's son from the Ohio River town of Lawrenceburg, Indiana, the

36-year-old Lucas had served as an officer during the Mexican War and had been wounded three times at Vicksburg. Lucas moved forward with one cavalry brigade and a battery of artillery to protect Steele's column. Meanwhile Lieutenant Colonel Andrew B. Spurling, who hailed from the little coastal town of Orland, Maine, was leading his cavalry brigade on a wide sweep to the east and north to cut Rebel rail and communications between Mobile and Montgomery and to deceive the Confederates into believing that a major Federal raid on the state capital was in progress. Spurling's troopers first occupied Milton, Florida, and then struck out northward to Andalusia, Alabama, where they destroyed Confederate property on March 23.[16]

Spurling's brigade included his old regiment, the 2nd Maine Cavalry, farther from home than any other command in the Mobile campaign. Formed late in 1863, the 2nd Maine had seen action in the Red River campaign and in the Federal incursion against Pollard in December 1864. Also riding with Spurling was the battle-hardened 2nd Illinois Cavalry, which began their service after just four weeks of training with crude wooden swords and in December 1862 put up a stubborn resistance (losing nine men killed and thirty-nine wounded) against a surprise Rebel attack on the Federal supply base at Holly Springs, Mississippi. Later the cavalrymen showed spirit and ingenuity when, in a joint operation with the 69th Indiana Infantry, they leapt from their horses and paddled small boats across the bayou to capture Richmond, Louisiana, in March 1863. In May 1863, in what their division commander called "one of the most brilliant cavalry engagements of the war," the 2nd Illinois drew sabers and made a vigorous charge against Rebel infantry near Vicksburg, pushing the enemy back 5 miles, taking 30 prisoners, and killing or wounding 12.[17]

The bluecoats circled west to Evergreen, Alabama, where Spurling surprised a Rebel officer and two scouts a few miles from town. Hidden behind a fence, Spurling waited until the three men had walked past, then sprang to his feet with revolver drawn and demanded that they surrender. Startled, the Rebels whirled around and called on him to identify himself. "I am a live Yankee," Spurling replied. The graycoats lifted their rifles to fire, but the Federal officer was faster. The Rebel officer and one of his scouts fell wounded, the other raised his hands. The wounded officer turned out to be the son of Alabama Governor Thomas H. Watts. On March 24, Spurling's men cut the telegraph lines north of Evergreen severing communications between Mobile and Montgomery, tore up railroad tracks on the Alabama and Florida Railroad, and derailed and destroyed two locomotives, one of which was carrying troops bound for Mobile. The Federals then rode south toward Pollard where they were to join Steele.[18]

As Steele's slow moving column plodded north through the Florida swamps, Lieutenant Colonel Washington T. Lary's 6th Alabama Cavalry kept the bluecoats under observation. The Rebel troopers used all their wits to delay the enemy advance. They burned bridges in the path of the Yankees, ambushed Federal detachments, and hit isolated enemy wagons. Soon the rest of Clanton's cavalry joined Lary in harassing the enemy column. Although they could not stop Steele, they did delay him. Federal engineers had to repair a bridge over Pine Barren Creek that the Rebels had destroyed on March 23. With considerable effort, Yankee engineers built a 300-foot bridge across the Escambia River, and the column prepared to cross. The blue horsemen had no problem, but Steele's supply wagons and artillery became bogged in the mud almost immediately on reaching the opposite side of the river. At this point, Steele decided to send Lucas' remaining cavalry brigade forward to occupy the bridge across Big Escambia River and neutralize the Rebel threat.[19]

On March 25, Rebel and Yankee horsemen fought a running series of skirmishes along the streams feeding the Escambia. Colonel Charles P. Ball's 8th Alabama Cavalry, which had seen combat in Georgia and against Rousseau's raiders the previous summer, succeeded in burning part of the bridge over Mitchell Creek and then dug in on the opposite bank to receive the enemy advance while Clanton's brigade remained in reserve. Lucas moved to flank Ball from two directions. Colonel Algernon S. Badger and his 1st (Union) Louisiana Cavalry rode downstream, dismounted and crossed on foot, and launched an attack on Ball's left. Colonel Morgan H. Chrysler with the 2nd New York Veteran Cavalry was to move upstream, cross, and attack the Rebel right, but the New Yorkers were unable to ford the creek. Badger and the Unionist Louisianans charged into the Rebel left flank and drove the graycoats back. Lucas ordered the bridge repaired and pushed forward.[20]

Ball contested the Yankee advance again at Cotton Creek, where the Rebels had erected a log barricade across the road. Sixteen-year-old Rebel cavalryman Robert Posey recalled his first and only action under fire there:

Our pickets soon returned and reported that they were coming and we were ordered to get ready. I had an Enfield rifle which was captured from the enemy, and when they came rushing up on the other side of the little river we commenced firing. I shot at least twenty times and others did as well, but owing to the smoke we could not tell what damage we did. We learned afterward that several were killed. Some one set fire to the bridge just as the Federals came up, which saved us from being captured. . . . We made a "good run instead of a bad stand," as they had about 1500 troops.[21]

The Rebels drew another line in the sand at Canoe Creek and again were pushed back, fighting all the way. Ball withdrew to William's Station, but about a mile north of Bluff Springs, Florida, at Pringle's Creek, Clanton's senior colonel, Lary, decided to make a stand. Lary's troopers alighted from their horses and erected a barricade of fence rails north of the creek as the bluecoat cavalry zeroed in on them. Ball failed to support Lary because he apparently expected him to follow suit and fall back. Lucas' horsemen reached the creek, and Lary's troopers opened fire. But the Federal cavalry was too strong, and the Rebels were driven back again. At this point Clanton arrived from Pollard, ordered Lary to "dress up on the colors" and prepare to move back in order. Lary replied that there was no time, he was being flanked. Badger ordered the 1st Louisiana forward with a yell, and the Rebels were overrun. The Federals captured over 100 Confederate soldiers and seventeen of their officers (Lary included), losing two killed and eight wounded. Private Thomas Riley of the 1st Louisiana captured a Rebel battle flag for which he was later awarded the Congressional Medal of Honor. Many of the Rebels fled into the swamps, others headed for the Big Escambia bridge. They did not know that recent floods had swept away a span of the bridge, and most of them plunged into the rain-swollen river to drown.[22]

Refusing to surrender, Clanton shot and wounded a Yankee officer then attempted to make a run for it but was struck in the back by a Federal musket ball, which passed through his intestines. The Rebel general fell from his horse and was captured. At first he was not expected to live; he instructed his chief of staff who also had been taken prisoner to make out his will. But Clanton survived and was left with other wounded prisoners under a surgeon's care at a nearby house while the Federal cavalry moved on. The Federals ordered him to turn himself in at Pensacola when he was able to travel. Back in Steele's column the Federal foot soldiers were relieved to hear of Clanton's defeat and capture. "A pretty good day's work," Isaac Jackson wrote.[23]

By March 26, Andrews' division finally reached Pollard on the rail line to Montgomery. Confederate forces had abandoned the post, and the bluecoats proceeded to destroy the railroad tracks as well as supplies bound for the defenses of Mobile. By now Steele had heard from Canby and was ordered to turn west and join the main army besieging Blakely. But the Rebel troops had left Pollard with no food supplies, and Steele's 12,000 soldiers were running low on rations after their long march from Pensacola. Even the return of Spurling's cavalry with 120 Rebel prisoners in tow failed to bring needed food. An all-day rain set in on March 27, and the next two days were spent in building corduroy roads. Isaac Jackson—hungry and impatient to get to the column's destination so that they could get something to eat—

recorded on March 31, "We see nothing but the pine forest with an occasional cabin, very seldom with any one living in them."[24]

By scavenging surrounding communities, Steele's cavalry managed to bring in enough beef and corn to feed the troops, and by April 1 the column was in camp in front of Fort Blakely. Frank McGregor wrote Susie on April 3, "Our prisoners told us when we came to Blakeley that we would find a warm reception from their old comrades. So far they have predicted truly." Indeed, the veteran Federal soldiers in the western theater had developed a deep respect and even admiration for their stubborn adversaries. "The Rebles," an Illinois soldier wrote in early 1863 not long after the Fort Hindman engagement, "are a motly looking crew but they fight like Devills"; and he even admitted, "I hope I did not hit any person [even] if they are Rebles."[25]

NOTES

1. Ezra J. Warner, *Generals in Blue: Lives of the Union Commanders* (Baton Rouge: Louisiana State University Press, 1964), 474–475.

2. Ibid., 8–9.

3. Christopher C. Andrews, *History of the Campaign of Mobile* (New York, 1867), 24; Mark Mayo Boatner III, *The Civil War Dictionary* (New York: David McKay Co., Inc., 1959), 563.

4. Joseph Orville Jackson, ed., *"Some of the Boys . . .": The Civil War Letters of Isaac Jackson, 1862–1865* (Carbondale: Southern Illinois University Press, 1960), ix–x.

5. Ibid., vii–xi.

6. Ibid., xi–xv.

7. Ibid., 232–233, 235.

8. Ibid., 234–235.

9. Carl E. Hatch, ed., *Dearest Susie: A Civil War Infantryman's Letters to His Sweetheart* (Jericho, NY: Exposition Press, Inc., 1971), Introduction.

10. Ibid., 26, 38; Bell I. Wiley, *The Life of Billy Yank* (Baton Rouge: Louisiana State University Press, 1978), 280.

11. Hatch, *Dearest Susie*, 52–53.

12. Ibid., 68.

13. Ibid., 98, 105.

14. Jackson, *"Some of the Boys . . . ,"* 240.

15. Arthur W. Bergeron, Jr., "James Holt Clanton," in William C. Davis, ed., *The Confederate General*, vol. 1 (Harrisburg, PA: National Historical Society, 1991), 189–190.

16. Warner, *Generals in Blue*, 285–286; Andrews, *Campaign of Mobile*, 112–113.

17. William E. S. Whitman and Charles H. True, *Maine in the War for the Union: A History of the Part Borne by Maine Troops in the Suppression of the American Rebellion* (Lewiston, ME, 1865), 563–569; Stephen Z. Starr, *The Union Cavalry in the Civil War*, vol. 3, *The War in the West, 1861–1865* (Baton Rouge: Louisiana State University Press, 1985), 18–19, 182–183; Colonel Thomas L. Snead, "The Conquest of Ar-

kansas," in Robert Underwood Johnson and Clarence Clough Buel, eds., *Battles and Leaders of the Civil War*, vol. 3 (New York: Castle Books, 1956), 451.

18. Andrews, *Campaign of Mobile*, 113.

19. Ibid., 103–106.

20. Ibid., 107–108.

21. Mamie Yeary, compil., *Reminiscences of the Boys in Gray, 1861–1865* (Dayton, OH: Morningside House, 1986), 619.

22. Andrews, *Campaign of Mobile*, 108–110; *War of the Rebellion: A Compilation of the Official Records of the Union and Confederate Armies* (hereafter cited as *OR*) (Washington, DC: Government Printing Office, 1880–1901), Series I, Vol. 49, Part I, 302–303, 308–309.

23. Bergeron, "Clanton," 191; Jackson, *"Some of the Boys . . . ,"* 241.

24. Jackson, *"Some of the Boys . . . ,"* 242.

25. *OR*, Series I, Vol. 49, Part I, 203–204, 280–281; Hatch, *Dearest Susie*, 107; Wiley, *Billy Yank*, 351.

CHAPTER 6

"It Looked Like Refined Cruelty"

At Fort Blakely, General Liddell had learned that—in addition to Canby's Union army besieging Spanish Fort to his south—yet another Yankee column from Pensacola under Steele was swinging down on him from the north. He had placed a screen of pickets east of the fort to scour the landscape for approaching bluecoats. William Pitt Chambers' regiment, the 46th Mississippi Infantry—about 100 soldiers under Captain J. B. Hart—was 4 miles up the Stockton Road above Blakely posted behind a pile of fence rails thrown up as a barricade. Around noon on April 1, 1865, they spotted enemy horsemen from Andrew Spurling's advance Federal cavalry trotting down the road toward them.

The Rebels let loose a volley that "emptied several saddles," according to Chambers, and the bluecoats whirled about and headed to the rear. A mounted courier from Francis Cockrell rode up with a message directing Captain Hart to fall back to the fort. But Hart, overconfident after the easy repulse of the Federal horsemen, replied that he could hold the enemy and sent the courier galloping away. Soon the Mississippians discovered to their alarm that Yankee troops were flanking them through the woods to their left.[1]

Troopers of the 2nd Maine Cavalry advanced on foot on both sides of the road, while the 2nd Illinois Cavalry with drawn sabers followed on horseback. The Maine boys quickly sent the graycoats flying with a blistering volley from their repeating rifles. Badly outnumbered, the Rebels fell back firing and reloading as they went, keeping up a running fight for about a mile until they were cut off by Federal cavalry who had moved around

them through the open pine woods. Swinging their sabers, the mounted Illinois troops charged, and the graycoats were overwhelmed. The little Mississippi regiment disintegrated on the spot. Hart managed to get away on
horseback, and Lieutenant R. N. Rea, wounded in the right hand and left
leg, was bundled into the saddle by several of his men and sent flying toward Blakely. "It was the first time I had ridden horseback during the entire
war," Rea wrote. The Mississippians lost three officers and seventy-one enlisted men and their colors. Chambers and three of his comrades dove into
a thicket and managed to escape into the woods.[2]

The Federals chased the fleeing Rebels back to their outer lines at Fort
Blakely where soldiers of Cockrell's Missouri brigade were posted in a
nearby ravine. Their skirmishers were taken by surprise at first as the Yankee horsemen nearly galloped over them, but they fell back to warn the
main body of troops who stood and peppered the bluecoats with musket
fire. The Federal advance ran into more trouble when Rebel batteries in the
fort also opened fire, and the Yankee horsemen turned back, unable to out-
flank and overwhelm the Missourians as they had done the 46th Mississippi. Lieutenant George Warren wrote, "it must have been a downfall to
their pride to know that they had been whipped and routed by less than an
[sic] hundred ragged Missouri infantry."[3]

Fort Blakely was defended by a pitifully understrength garrison of 2,700
troops. The earthen fortress, built in the shape of a crescent, enclosed the
small town of Blakely on the east bank of the Tensas River. The Rebel lines
ran for about three miles, with nine earthen forts or redoubts strung out
along the line. As at Spanish Fort, the outnumbered Confederates expected
an attack and intended to give the Yanks a warm reception. More than forty
pieces of artillery dotted the lines. In front of the earthworks were ditches
four to five feet deep. Abatis made of felled trees covered the ground for 300
yards out, with a liberal seeding of land mines made with twelve-pound
shells, and Rebel rifle pits were scattered behind.

To the rear of the Confederate lines that buzzed like a busy ant hill, the
little town of Blakely was only a shadow of what once had been a thriving
community. Founded by Josiah Blakely in 1814, Blakely was a natural port
for entrance to the Alabama River and experienced a short growth boom
that witnessed the launching of Alabama's first steamboat, the *Tensas*, in
1819. By the mid-1820s Blakely already boasted several hotels and stores,
warehouses, churches, and docks, and many began to see it as a potential ri-
val to the larger city of Mobile just 10 miles across the Bay. But by the late
1820s a yellow fever epidemic and overspeculation in land by greedy in-
vestors had burst the bubble.

The county seat of Baldwin County, Blakely once had a population of 3,000 people, but so many had deserted it for greater opportunities in Mobile that barely 100 now remained. The river landing was flanked by several big moss-covered oaks, and from there the ground gradually rose for about a mile to the Confederate earthworks. An old two-story white brick courthouse, which served as Liddell's headquarters, stood amid leafy oaks 200 yards from the landing with several old wooden buildings nearby. Pitt Chambers called it "a pretty village . . . surrounded by pine woods." Low swamps, covered with hardwood trees and dense vines and weeds, lay on each side of the little town. Two well-traveled roads spread out from the landing at Blakely, one running northeast to Stockton, the other running southeast toward Pensacola.[4]

On the Confederate left at Fort Blakely, troops of Claudius Sears' Mississippi brigade manned Redoubts 1 and 2. Less than 800 of these combat-hardened veterans from the Magnolia State remained to fight at Blakely.

Sears' Mississippi brigade had served with Cockrell's Missourians and Ector's Texans through the long Atlanta campaign, and there was a close bond between them. The second Southern state to secede, Mississippi led the United States in cotton production in the 1850s, yielding more than 22 percent of the nation's crop. The state's economy was inseparably tied to cotton and slavery. Yet most of the Mississippi brigade's soldiers were not slaveowners, but small farmers from the rural central Mississippi prairie and from small towns like West Point, Corinth, and Columbus. They had enlisted with green enthusiasm, and the names they gave to some of their volunteer companies spoke to their youthful truculence: Attala Yellow Jackets, Sons of the South, Invincible Warriors, Zollicoffer Avengers, Yankee Hunters, Edwards Tigers, Newton Hornets, Yazoo Pickets, Jeff Davis Rebels. The 46th Mississippi's R. N. Rea recalled, "I still thought I could whip ten Yankees, even though there did come a time when I was convinced of the fallibility of this conviction."[5]

The old man of the brigade, 47-year-old Massachusetts native Claudius W. Sears was a West Point graduate who had left the U.S. Army in 1842 to become a mathematics instructor at St. Thomas' Hall in the north Mississippi town of Holly Springs. When the war broke out, Sears became colonel of the 46th Mississippi. Captured at Vicksburg, paroled and returned to command, Sears was promoted to brigadier general in March 1864. At Nashville, a Federal shell tore off his right leg and killed "Billy," his favorite roan horse who had been with him through the whole war. Through blinding pain, Sears managed to mumble, "Poor Billy," as tears streamed down his face. Removed from the field and taken prisoner a few days later, he remained a captive for the rest of the war.[6]

At Blakely, 43-year-old Colonel William S. Barry took command of Sears' brigade. Barry had played a leading role in Mississippi's decision to secede from the Union. Barry's father, a veteran of the War of 1812, had settled with his wife in Columbus, where he operated the Eagle Hotel and Tavern. Young Barry appeared to have a promising career ahead of him; after graduating from Yale in 1845, he took up the practice of law in his hometown. Although a gifted speaker, he found the legal profession boring. Politics was more to his liking, and friends encouraged him to seek office in the state legislature in 1849. Barry was elected and soon gained attention as a powerful and persuasive orator.[7]

Barry became an influential member of the Mississippi legislature, as well as a capable soldier. Although a political enemy, Unionist Presbyterian minister James A. Lyon of Columbus, characterized him as "an accomplished and perfectly unscrupulous demagogue," he quickly built an impressive political following. Barry was president of the state's secession convention and closed the meeting with an appeal to Mississippians to stand firm. "What lies before us," he said, "will test the heroism, the higher, the nobler qualities of our race, inherited from revolutionary sires." Barry became colonel of the 35th Mississippi Infantry, formed in the spring of 1862, and led his troops at Corinth and at Vicksburg. During the Atlanta campaign in 1864, he often commanded Sears' brigade while the ex-professor was ailing. A shoulder injury at Allatoona, Georgia, on October 5 put Barry out of action during the Tennessee offensive, but he rejoined the brigade at Mobile in February 1865.[8]

The Mississippi brigade's enlisted men and junior officers were drawn from men of hardened caliber. William Denson Evans, from the little south Mississippi community of Stringer, formed a volunteer military company with some of his friends at the local schoolhouse in December 1861. The following spring they joined the 7th Mississippi Infantry Battalion, which suffered serious casualties at Corinth in October 1862. Evans lost his left eye while charging a Federal battery but managed to help carry his badly wounded commander, Lieutenant Colonel James S. Terral, off the field and sit with him until he died. "He was shot all to peaces," Evans related, "boath leges were broke[,] boath arms was broke[,] and 4 or five bullits were shot in his boddy." "We done what he told us to do," Evans wrote, "and spiked the big guns." Evans later was wounded at Champion's Hill, captured at Vicksburg, exchanged, wounded again in the Atlanta campaign, promoted to first lieutenant, and wounded at Franklin.[9]

James M. Brownlee of the 35th Mississippi Infantry also fought at Corinth, where he was wounded and captured. After being exchanged, he returned to his regiment. On May 22, 1863, the 35th Mississippi held off three

Federal attacks at Vicksburg. Brownlee was captured at Vicksburg, was paroled, rejoined his regiment, and later was promoted to second lieutenant.[10]

The grueling siege at Vicksburg held especially painful memories for soldiers of Sears' brigade. R. N. Rea wrote in 1922, "I remember to this day the pangs of hunger, and I remember also how good my ration of mule meat was to me." He described the Rebel garrison's surrender on July 4, 1863: "There was placed a small white flag on the breastworks of our entire line, and the army in perfect order passed over the parapets and stacked their arms in silence." Rea told of inducing a Federal soldier to try some mule meat. "It was fun to see him gag," he wrote, "but we made him swallow his dainty morsel."[11]

Eighteen-year-old Henry Lacy joined the Rebel army in January 1864 and served as a private in the 36th Mississippi Infantry. Lacy was wounded at Kennesaw Mountain five months later. At New Hope Church near Atlanta, Lacy and his comrades crouched behind a log while munching on their rations. Out of the blue, one of his companions remarked, "I am going to kill a Yankee as soon as I eat this bread." After taking the last bite, he raised his weapon and rested it on the log, waiting for his chance. Directly he lifted his head above the barricade and fired, and at the same moment an enemy musket ball plowed into his forehead, "scattering his brains in every direction." The soldier lived for two more hours and never spoke again.[12]

With the fall of Atlanta, many of the Mississippians began to despair of ever gaining their independence. Confidence in the Confederate leadership had been shaken. R. N. Rea told of seeing fellow Mississippian President Jefferson Davis when he reviewed Hood's army after the fall of Atlanta. "I was surprised," he wrote. "Time had made a great change in his appearance. I now saw a man whose face was very sad, his countenance old, and his body thin and weak."[13]

Typical of the soldiers of Sears' brigade was 25-year-old Sergeant William Pitt Chambers, whose family of yeoman farmers had moved to southern Mississippi's Covington County in the 1830s. As a child, Pitt Chambers was an avid reader and a serious student; as an adult he became a teacher. When war loomed, Chambers joined a volunteer company called the Harvey Desperadoes, but when it was disbanded, he cast his lot with another outfit, the Covington Rebels, in March 1862. The recruits, mainly older family men, brought their own arms, mostly shotguns, from home; they received no muskets from the state until August, six months later. By the end of the year the Covington Rebels became Company B of the 46th Mississippi Infantry.[14]

Chambers kept a daily journal that expanded to a remarkable several hundred pages by the war's end. Much of it he nearly lost when he left it in a friend's home in 1864; Federal raiders looted the home. The journal, dirty and wadded up, was found later in an abandoned Yankee camp and miraculously made its way back to Chambers. A deeply religious man, Pitt Chambers' faith helped sustain him through difficult days, as he dutifully recorded the events of suffering and the deaths of good friends. He wondered if it all was worth it, writing in 1864 that the deaths of so many could never justify "nominal freedom . . . to some four or five millions of an inferior race, that will probably be invested with the right of suffrage without intelligence to use it."[15]

Wounded at Allatoona in October 1864, Chambers was out of action during the devastating events at Franklin and Nashville. He rejoined his regiment in January 1865 near Tupelo, where he found Sears' brigade drastically reduced in numbers.[16]

Redoubts 3 and 4, near the center of the Rebel lines, were held by Francis Cockrell's Missouri brigade, now reduced to 400 soldiers. The Missourians occupied the strongest and best fortified part of the lines at Blakely. Colonel Elijah Gates held command, with Cockrell moved up to division head and assistant commander of the fort.

To the veteran soldiers in Cockrell's Missouri brigade, the war had become a way of life. As a border slave state where much antislavery feeling also existed, Missouri had been involved in civil war fully five years before the rest of the nation. Although St. Louis was a great hub of commerce for river traffic on the Missouri and the Mississippi, and Kansas City served as a jumping off point for trails west, the rest of the state was frontier farming country, thinly settled. The Kansas troubles of the 1850s brought the slavery issue to the boiling point. Border raids along Missouri's western frontier pitted pro-slavery "Border Ruffians" against antislavery "Kansas Jayhawkers."

In May 1861 Unionist forces led by Brigadier General Nathaniel Lyon descended on Camp Jackson near St. Louis and broke up the pro-Southern Missouri volunteer militia. The capture of Camp Jackson triggered civil war within the state. The pro-Southern Missouri legislature and Governor Claiborne Jackson at Jefferson City reacted by forming the Missouri State Guard, a small army of about 3,600 poorly armed, rural militiamen under white-haired Major General Sterling Price. In the summer of 1861 Lyon and the Unionists struck hard, scattering the State Guard and driving it into the hills of southwestern Missouri where it continued a largely futile resistance against the better supplied Union army. A new pro-Union state government was formed in Jefferson City. On August 10, 1861, Lyon attacked Price at Wilson's Creek. Southern forces won the day, and Lyon was killed, but the Rebels never regained control of the state. The Confederacy lost Missouri, although one of the thirteen stars on her flag symbolically represented the border state.

The State Guard was unable to continue the military struggle in Missouri without outside support, which the Confederate government at Richmond seemed disinclined to provide. Finally the State Guard was broken up in December 1861. Veterans of the frontier fighting force went into the Confederate army as two infantry brigades, one of which came to be Cockrell's. Some former State Guardsmen joined guerrilla bands, including William Clarke Quantrill's notorious gang that played havoc on the western frontier.

The Missouri Confederate brigade became a kind of "foreign legion," fighting a war in exile. An armed force of Missourians that never fought a major battle in their own state but for four long bloody years saw combat on both sides of the Mississippi from Arkansas to Georgia, their courage and determination were unequaled. Yet they were never to return to their native state to liberate it from the blue-coated occupation army.[17]

The majority of soldiers in the Missouri brigade were not slaveowners. Most were rugged yeoman farmers who fought primarily in defense of the Jeffersonian concept of democracy. The federal government in Washington was to them an alien authority that no longer represented their interests and that threatened their independent way of life. They viewed themselves as latter day American patriots standing up to a tyrannical power, as their forefathers had stood for their rights against Britain in the Revolutionary War. Private Isaac Vincent Smith wrote that the Missourians "thought that their civil rights were being taken away from them." Secession and the Confederacy represented the best chance of preserving those rights. Missouri Confederates feared that the federal government under Lincoln would take away the small farmer's property, reducing him to slavery. Private Absalom Roby Dyson wrote, "I cannot think of going back until I can go as a free-man . . . as a white man and not as a slave." One Missouri brigade soldier put it more plainly: "When the Yankees came in our part of the country, we got after them."[18]

The Missouri brigade's excellent combat record forged an esprit de corps that was exceptional even among the most veteran Confederate troops. Its frontier makeup made class distinctions far less apparent, and the self-sufficient Missourians were some of the most independent-minded soldiers in the Confederate army, quite a distinction in an army of Rebels who prided themselves on their stubborn individuality.[19]

Most members of the Missouri brigade were of English or Scotch-Irish blood, but St. Louis contained a sizable Irish population. The rough environment of the St. Louis docks furnished the 5th Missouri Infantry with a colorful group of Irish immigrants—many of whom were already veterans of the State Guard—who filled the ranks of Company F, the "Fighting Irish Company." An officer once called them "the best soldiers on duty and the worst off, the best fighters and the most troublesome men in the army." Often utilized as skirmishers advancing boldly in front of the brigade, the Irish saw continuous action, and over 70 percent of them were wiped out at Corinth in October 1862. Captain Patrick Canniff, a 23-year-old St. Louis saddle maker recently emigrated from Ireland, led the "Fighting Irish Company." Bold, thoughtful to the needs of his men, the popular young officer with the flowing auburn hair died with a bullet through his head at Franklin.[20]

Missouri historian Phillip Thomas Tucker credits the Missouri brigade's first-class service record to the tough frontier character of its members, prior military service in the State Guard, and outstanding leadership. Most of the Missouri soldiers were young, hailing from the Mississippi and Missouri River valleys, recruited as one of them put it, "of the youths of the first families of Central and Northern Missouri." Farmers, hunters, outdoorsmen, they knew how to shoot and ride and were familiar with the ways of the woods and fields. They were rough and self-reliant, "a damned hard set," a member of the State Guard called them. Many had seen service on the frontier before the war and had fought Indians, border raiders, and outlaws. Service in the Missouri State Guard had acquainted them with military discipline, a discipline sustained throughout the war in the face of frustrating setbacks and hardships. Their esprit de corps endured to the bitter end. The Missouri brigade benefited enormously from a distinguished officer corps that included graduates of West Point, Virginia Military Institute, and Kentucky Military Institute.[21]

Forty-year-old Brigadier General Francis Marion Cockrell had become the preeminent leader of the 1st Missouri Brigade. Born on the state's western plateau in the little town of Warrensburg some 50 miles southeast of Kansas City, Cockrell graduated from Chapel Hill College in 1853 and returned briefly as an instructor of Greek and Latin before opening a law practice in his hometown. In 1859 his wife died in childbirth, and Cockrell was left with two young sons to raise. Although not a secessionist, Cockrell felt obliged after Camp Jackson to take a stand, and he enlisted in the State Guard on June 20, 1861. The men of his company elected him captain the next day. Cockrell fought at Wilson's Creek, and by January 1862 he was an officer in the newly formed 2nd Missouri Infantry. In May 1862 he was elected lieutenant colonel of the regiment, and in June he replaced Colonel John Q. Burbridge as commander of the 2nd Missouri when the latter stepped down due to illness.[22]

Cockrell had a touch of a rough-hewn Stonewall Jackson about him, the Bible and Hardee's *Tactics* his constant companions. Grave and earnest, reserved, his philosophy was a fusion of Southern nationalism and Presbyterian religious zeal. The "praying captain," as he once was called, refrained from drinking or swearing. He had no formal military training, was "green as a gourd in military affairs." But he was a natural leader, practical, sharp, and aggressive. "While the other fellows were fussing and fuming about the ranks and grades," one of his soldiers explained, "Cockrell was fighting, and between battles was lying flat on his belly in his tent studying Hardee's tactics." In combat Cockrell "told us to come on, not go on."[23]

Cockrell quickly earned the respect and loyalty of his troops. He was a strict disciplinarian; one soldier wrote, "when he wasn't fightin, [Cockrell] used to turn loose and drill us till the tongues hung outen our mouth." But he showed no favoritism and was at home with the most humble private soldier as well as the most aristocratic senior officer. He had a charisma that energized and motivated the Missourians and inspired confidence. A commanding presence at 6 feet 1 inch and 215 pounds, the blue-eyed Cockrell, with his long brown hair and beard and his bright smile, was, according to one soldier, "one of the finest looking officers in the army. . . . [M]en would have followed him anywhere." Cockrell's political colleague Champ Clark wrote that he tirelessly tended to his men's needs in sickness, when wounded, when discouraged. The secret of his control over his soldiers lay simply in "his personal courage and his unfailing kindness. . . . He was the father of his soldiers."[24]

Colonel Elijah P. Gates, the 34-year-old commander of the 1st Missouri Cavalry, had left Kentucky to search for gold in California's Sierra Nevada mountains in 1852. He came out empty-handed and moved to Missouri with his wife, settling as a yeoman farmer in frontier Buchanan County in the Platte River valley north of Kansas City. Like Cockrell, he had no formal military training, but he was a natural leader and proved himself to be a master of rough-and-tumble cavalry tactics, excelling in ambushes and raids. Thick-set, broad-shouldered, Gates had a fiery temper, and Sterling Price said he "had no superior for bravery." So far in the war, the obstinate Gates had been taken prisoner three times (and had escaped twice) and had ridden at the head of his horsemen in too many reckless charges to count. Only Cockrell was more highly regarded by the Missouri soldiers than Gates, who now commanded the brigade.[25]

Gates' second in command was Colonel James C. McCown of the 5th Missouri Infantry. A 47-year-old Virginian raised by Irish parents, McCown was a well-to-do landowner and pro-secession politician in Cockrell's home community of Warrensburg. In March 1861 Cockrell had defended

McCown from a bloodthirsty mob after McCown's son had killed a prominent Unionist in an altercation. McCown led the 5th Missouri from the beginning of the war to the end. While he was away, Federal militia burned
his home in March 1862, leaving his wife and children without shelter in
the winter cold.[26]

Younger officers—those who were still alive—now were taking on
greater responsibility too, and all bore scars of their four years of service.
Lieutenant Colonel Stephen Cooper, a 26-year-old farmer before the war,
had been considered quite a catch for any young lady until his left arm was
shot away at Corinth in October 1862. Captain Joseph H. Neal was a
24-year-old cavalry officer who had demonstrated excellent leadership
qualities under Gates. Part of his jaw was blown away at New Hope
Church in May 1864, and he carried a tiny box containing his "menagerie,"
teeth and bone fragments from the hideous facial wound. Captain Charles
L. Edmondson, a former merchant from St. Louis, had proven to be an outstanding infantry officer, distinguished at Shiloh in April 1862 and
wounded in August 1864. Former St. Louis firefighter Joseph Boyce, an officer in the 1st Missouri Infantry, was wounded eleven times during the
war. He came to be the unofficial historian for the Missouri brigade.[27]

The Missourians had proven themselves in many tight scrapes from
Elkhorn Tavern to Franklin. In February 1862, they were in the rear guard of
Sterling Price's army, retreating across the state line into the rugged Boston
Mountains of northwestern Arkansas. Fighting bitter cold and driving
snow, their clothes wet and freezing, the tired and hungry Missourians
turned and formed an ambush for their Federal pursuers. Gates' cavalrymen—many of them former partisans in the border war—already were
skilled in the hit-and-run tactics of dismounted cavalry that were still
largely unfamiliar to both sides in the Civil War but that they had learned
well in years of border warfare with the Kansas Jayhawkers. A private in
the 2nd Missouri Infantry wrote that he and his comrades were "rather silent, very mad, and somewhat moody . . . and fight was much preferred to
being dogged any farther." It was also in the Boston Mountains that the
Missourians became acquainted with Colonel Dabney H. Maury, who
served as their interim commander.[28]

In March 1862 at Elkhorn Tavern the Confederates suffered a decisive re-
versal, although the Missouri brigade fought with distinction. Missouri
was left firmly in Union hands. The Missouri brigade was dispatched east
of the Mississippi River and went into camp near Tupelo, Mississippi, in the
summer of 1862. Oppressive heat made drilling all the more the difficult,
but the men kept at it. For recreation, the Missourians amused themselves

with card playing, drinking, writing home, and chicken fights. Lieutenant George Warren noted a great demand for "pugalistic fowls."[29]

Next came heavy fighting at Corinth in October 1862. Cockrell's favorite war horse, "Old Yellow," was shot from under him as a Yankee cannon ball tore through the mount's body, yet immediately the colonel was on his feet brandishing his sword and leading his men in a charge against Battery Powell, the strong enemy earthwork. He barely escaped death again when an enemy bullet grazed his throat. Although the Missouri brigade captured Battery Powell with its reserve of enemy artillery, Corinth proved to be another costly Confederate defeat.[30]

Their first major battles in Mississippi cost the Missouri brigade dearly, for scarcely a third of its soldiers remained alive. But the Missourians were praised by their commanders. General Joseph E. Johnston remarked that he had "never [seen] better discipline, or men march more regularly." And a newspaperman wrote, "These veteran soldiers never falter in battle. They are never whipped!" The ragged soldiers of the Missouri brigade now received new uniforms for the first time, gray caps and pants and gray jackets with light blue trim on the collars and cuffs. They were the first uniforms the Missourians had been issued, and they were proud of them. By May 1863 the brigade received new arms as well, Enfield rifles to replace their old Springfields.[31]

The Missouri brigade was by no means a perfect command. Examples of ill discipline existed, as in any military organization, Northern or Southern, and there were murderers, drunkards, and scoundrels in its ranks. One officer wrote, "when far away from all the wholesome restraints of social life, soldiers are sad dogs." In January 1863 one company in the 5th Missouri refused to fall out for dress parade, in protest against an order requiring them to have signed passes to leave camp. When guards were sent to arrest them, the mutineers seized their muskets and refused to be taken. Soldiers from other companies joined them, and the incident threatened to engulf the whole brigade until more moderate heads prevailed and the mutineers finally agreed to settle down.[32]

Many brigade members also despaired of ever seeing their home state again, as the unit fought on far-flung battlefields. "Being as we are used to seceding," one cynical Missouri soldier wrote, "I'd secede the second time, take this brigade, go over into Missouri, and I'd be durned if I didn't fight anything that came to me, Yankee or secesh." But overall, the loyalty and courage of the Missouri brigade remained unquestioned.[33]

The long siege of Vicksburg in the summer of 1863 was a trying test for the Missouri brigade. For seven grueling weeks, the city was shelled night and day by General Ulysses S. Grant's blue-coated army. Civilians took refuge in caves dug into the bluffs along the Mississippi River. As food and supplies gradually gave out, townspeople and soldiers turned to eating mules. "If you did not know it," one Missouri soldier said, "you could hardly tell the difference, when cooked, between it and beef."[34]

The position of the beleaguered Vicksburg garrison grew increasingly desperate, as hope of reinforcement evaporated. But Cockrell said his men were "desirous of holding out and fighting as long as there was a cartridge or a ration or mule or horse, and when the garrison capitulated they felt, and were, distressed, but in no wise whipped, conquered, or destroyed." On July 4, Vicksburg surrendered, bringing the Mississippi under Union control and splitting the Confederacy in two. The Missourians were prisoners of war and were completely cut off from their native state. By the end of the summer the prisoners were exchanged. Cockrell, just promoted to brigadier general, immediately organized a new Missouri brigade and led it throughout the campaign in Georgia the following year.[35]

During the campaign for Atlanta, Cockrell's brigade formed a close association with Sears' Mississippians and Ector's Texans, sharing many hard fought engagements with the soldiers of these units. The Missourians played a critical role in beating back Union attackers at Kennesaw Mountain in June 1864. During the fighting around Atlanta, Cockrell lost several fingers. The Missourians were in the rear guard during the Confederate evacuation of Atlanta, which Lieutenant Joseph Boyce described as "the dark side of war." The looting and burning they witnessed "really appalled us," he wrote."[36]

Finally came the bloodbath at Franklin and the disastrous retreat from Tennessee. In January 1865 the brigade was a skeleton of what it once had been. The Missourians had come full circuit back to Tupelo after two years of hardship and struggle. Lieutenant Colonel Robert S. Bevier of the 5th Missouri Infantry wrote, "They had been purified and refined in the crucible and the alembic, and all that was left was of the virgin gold."[37]

As he witnessed the veterans of Hood's army deserting by the hundreds, Lieutenant George Warren expressed some of the feelings of the Missourians when he wrote home to his brother from camp near Tupelo on January 15, 1865, "It is truly distressing to see the demoralized state of affairs in this department." Warren was especially concerned about his family. The Missourians had not received any mail from home since mid-November.[38]

News from home meant a lot to these exiled Missouri soldiers so far away from their families. Earlier in the war, one soldier had written to his wife that only the joy of the South's winning independence could bring him greater satisfaction than to receive "a small scrape of a pen from you." And earlier in the war, they strove to maintain contact with their loved ones in

Federal-occupied Missouri. Absalom C. Grimes, a former steamboat pilot and good friend of Samuel (Mark Twain) Clemens, used his familiarity with the Mississippi to brave the Federal gunboat blockade on the river and slip back into Missouri. He became a regular mail runner for the Missouri brigade and brought back letters from home. Many of the soldiers' wives in Missouri helped create a regular underground mail service and kept up a correspondence at considerable personal risk.[39]

As Warren continued his long letter to his brother, with fingers so numb he could hardly write, he spoke of the bitterness the Missouri soldiers felt at their treatment by the Confederacy, which seemed so often to take the Missouri brigade for granted. Warren wrote, "the boys have taken up the idea that Missourians are outsiders that will do very well to do the rough fighting." But he was cheered by the welcome arrival of mail from home, and his letter began to take a more optimistic tone. He was lucky to have survived the ordeal of the Nashville campaign. He had heard plenty of complaining from both officers and enlisted men, but now everyone seemed to be pulling together again.[40]

The loss of so many good officers in the carnage at Franklin—nineteen killed, thirty-one wounded, and thirteen captured—meant that the small consolidated regiments of the brigade would be led by junior officers. The 1st and 4th Missouri Infantry was commanded by Captain Charles L. Edmondson. Lieutenant Colonel Stephen Cooper commanded the 2nd and 6th Missouri. The 3rd and 5th Missouri Infantry was led by Captain Benjamin E. Guthrie. And the 1st and 3rd Missouri Cavalry (consolidated and dismounted) was commanded by Captain Joseph H. Neal. Cockrell's entire division of 162 officers and 1,530 men was scarcely larger than a regiment and a half at normal strength.[41]

The sadly depleted state of the brigade was in the hearts and minds of the weary Missouri veterans as they sat on the earthworks and around their campfires at Fort Blakely. Captain Joseph Boyce wrote, "All wore a saddened, softened look." No more talk of battles and heroism, but thoughts turned to their fellow soldiers and friends dead at Franklin. And of the survivors, just how many of them had been wounded some time during the war? The general consensus was that there was not one of them in the brigade who did not bear at least one injury from the conflict, and some had even been wounded six times. The Missouri regiments had lost so many men, Boyce reflected, "that it looked like refined cruelty to ask men to fight again."[42]

Most of the Rebel infantry stationed at Blakely were the teenage soldiers and reluctant draftees of Brigadier General Bryan Morel Thomas' Alabama reserves. Supporting Redoubts 5 through 9, the center and right of the Confederate line, they held the weakest sector of the Rebel defenses. Largely untested in combat, the Alabama reserves were not expected to do much. "Our brigade could hold its lines," remarked a Missouri officer, "but we also knew that the old men and boys to our right, who had never been under fire, would get excited when the assault came, and shoot the tops of the trees off, and the Yanks would bulge right in on them."[43]

Bryan Morel Thomas, a 28-year-old Georgian, had graduated from West Point in 1858, a rather undistinguished 22nd out of 27 in his class. As an infantry lieutenant he was stationed in New York and on the western frontier. He tendered his resignation at the outbreak of the Civil War and entered Confederate service. By the time he was assigned to Maury's command at Mobile, Thomas had acquired considerable experience as a staff officer in charge of ordnance and artillery, had commendations for "intelligence and efficiency" as well as an endorsement from Braxton Bragg, and had recruited a small cavalry brigade that never quite got up to strength. With an additional recommendation from Maury, Thomas was promoted to brigadier general in August 1864. Gibson reported Thomas' brigade at 950 soldiers at Spanish Fort. Included were two reserve regiments, the 62nd and 63rd Alabama Infantry, with James M. Williams' 21st Alabama Infantry attached. (When Thomas' two reserve regiments were sent north to Blakely, the 21st Alabama stayed at Spanish Fort and was attached to Holtzclaw's brigade.)[44]

Little was expected of them, but many of the teenage soldiers of the 62nd Alabama Infantry had in fact already seen combat. The previous July they had received their baptism of fire at Chehaw Station, on the railroad line between Montgomery and Auburn. Major General Lovell Rousseau with two brigades of Federal cavalry swept down from the north to disrupt railroad communications between Atlanta and Montgomery. Rushed out to meet the raiders on July 18, 1864, was Lockhart's Battalion of state troops (at no more than 600 teenage boys), plus a company of fifty-four University of Alabama cadets on furlough in Montgomery and a company of conscripts, the only Rebel forces available, under the command of Bryan M. Thomas, then a major.

In the skirmish with the Federal cavalry, Lockhart's Battalion lost forty-eight killed and wounded, the cadets two, and the conscripts fifteen. The boy soldiers turned back Rousseau's raiders and received the compliments of Governor Thomas H. Watts for their performance. At 16 years of age, David Marshall Scott was the youngest soldier in Lockhart's Battalion. When he was 12 years old, a militiaman had paid him 25 cents to fill in for him on "muster day," and the excited little boy had used his "service pay" earned for a few hours' work on a hot summer day to buy ginger cakes and pop. Scott described his first experience under fire, writing that Thomas tricked the Federals into thinking that they faced a much larger Rebel force than really was there:

> Major Thomas had the conductor and engineer of the train, that was fired on, while we were on the train go back to Franklin Station, below Chehaw, and about every hour would come up to Chehaw Station blowing the whistle with a vengeance. Major Thomas had all the boys set up a yell when the whistle was blown, and Rousseau thought we were getting reinforcements all the time, when the fact was that we had no reinforcements whatever, nearer than Mobile, 225 miles distance.[45]

Using Lockhart's Battalion as a nucleus of soldiers who at least had "seen the elephant," the Rebels organized a new regiment at Mobile later that month: the 62nd Alabama Infantry (or 1st Alabama Reserve Regiment) with Daniel E. Huger, a 28-year-old cotton merchant from Mobile, as colonel. More underage recruits were added like 17-year-old Asa M. Piper, a blacksmith's son from Columbiana. David Scott became an orderly sergeant in Company F. Also serving as an orderly sergeant was 17-year-old Thomas Seay, a future governor of Alabama. Scott wrote that with the exception of the officers every soldier in the "Boy Regiment" was under the age for being drafted; all were volunteers. He recalled that the young men were given their choice of either remaining in state service or entering the Confederate army and that the entire regiment stepped forward to join up.[46]

In Mobile the regiment prepared to help garrison the city's defenses. Asa Piper recalled that his company exchanged their short Mississippi rifles for Enfields, which he considered superior weapons. Four companies of the 62nd Alabama were stationed at Fort Gaines and were captured with the rest of the garrison in August 1864. After a harsh confinement at New Orleans and Ship Island off the Gulf coast, they were exchanged in January 1865. On March 15 the regiment was ordered to Spanish Fort, and Piper's company performed picket duty near the Fish River. "On the 26th of March," Piper wrote, "we were driven into the ditches about 8 A.M. and the Battle of Spanish Fort opened with good and heavy cannonading from both sides."[47]

About twenty cadets from the University of Alabama became officers in the 62nd and 63rd Alabama. C. C. Oliver, one of the cadets, accompanied the cadet corps to Sibley's Mills near Blakely where the two new regiments were being organized in July 1864. One cadet was assigned to each company as a drillmaster, and later many of these same cadets were elected as officers in the regiments. Oliver became a 2nd lieutenant in Company I, 63rd Alabama.[48]

The 63rd Alabama Infantry (2nd Alabama Reserves) under Colonel Junius A. Law of Macon County was the other regiment in Thomas' brigade. Many of the officers already had experience, but most of the men, with the exception of Companies A and B, were conscripts. Zach T. Smith, in Captain William B. Fulton's company from Randolph County, wrote that the 1st and 2nd Reserves were "two fine well drilled regs of soldier Boys." Smith expressed apprehensions when his command was driven into Spanish Fort. "So there we were," he wrote, "surrounded by the Yanks on one side and water on the other."[49]

The boy soldiers generally received good marks for their service at Spanish Fort, although Louisiana artilleryman Phil Stephenson felt that their youthful pride exposed them to unnecessary risks. "In vain did we tell them," he recalled, "when going to the skirmish line to shelter themselves as much as possible. They thought it was 'not soldierly,' and they stood up and were shot down like sheep." At Fort Blakely their courage would be tested indeed.[50]

As at Spanish Fort, the earthworks at Blakely bristled with heavy guns in need of experienced handlers. Liddell was glad to have several companies of the 1st Mississippi Light Artillery Regiment, which arrived on April 1. Company K, Captain George F. Abbay's battery, manned the guns of Redoubt 4 near the Missouri brigade. Abbay's battery was raised in Claiborne and Jefferson Counties in May 1862 and left Port Gibson to join the 1st Mississippi Light Artillery at Jackson. The battery was captured at the fall of the Rebel garrison at Port Hudson, Louisiana, in July 1863. Enlisted men went to a Federal prison camp at Enterprise, Mississippi, officers to Johnson's Island, Ohio. Later the prisoners were exchanged and were stationed at Mobile. Company G, Captain James C. Cowan's battery from Vicksburg, had fought in the Atlanta campaign, been battered at Franklin—which 21-year-old Corporal Louis Spencer Flatau called "the bloodiest battle that was ever fought in this world, where guns were used that burned powder"—and dueled with a Federal gunboat during the retreat across the Tennessee River.[51]

Two more veteran companies served with the Alabama reserves at Blakely. Captain William C. Winston's Tennessee Battery was stationed at Redoubt 5 near the 63rd Alabama Infantry, and Lieutenant J. L. Moses' South Carolina Battery manned the guns at Redoubt 9, near the 62nd Alabama.

Captain Edward C. Tarrant's Alabama Battery manned eight heavy guns on the Rebel left at Redoubt 1 with the Mississippi brigade. The former school superintendent of Tuscaloosa County, Tarrant became an officer in Lumsden's battery in November 1861, along with his son Edward William Tarrant, a former University of Alabama cadet who had already seen action with the 5th Alabama Infantry. Tarrant resigned in June 1863 to raise his own command, an artillery company with new recruits mainly from the western part of the state, and E. W. Tarrant transferred to his father's battery as an officer. At Nashville, the battery suffered near annihilation, with one of its sections overrun and so many men and horses killed in the remaining section that no one was left to pull the guns off.[52]

Probably no one was more aware of Fort Blakely's vulnerability than its commander, Brigadier General St. John Richardson Liddell. At 5 feet 9 inches with gray eyes and dark hair, the tough 49-year-old officer was just what Maury had needed to take charge of the Rebel outposts on the eastern side of the Bay in September 1864. Like Gibson, he hailed from the Pelican State, with a home in Catahoula Parish, and he boasted a wide range of military experience.

The grandson of an Irish immigrant and Revolutionary War soldier, John Liddell was born on his father's plantation near the southwest Mississippi town of Woodville. As a young man he seemed to lack focus in his life. He fretted away his freshman year at the University of Virginia and through his father's political connections wrangled an appointment to West Point in the summer of 1833. While at the Academy, he chummed with future Confederate officers like Braxton Bragg who would become valuable allies. But he was unhappy at West Point too and by December was wanting to return home. Liddell was dismissed in February 1834 for "deficiency in studies." Rumor held that the young hothead was asked to resign after a duel in which he wounded a fellow cadet, and records at the Academy charged him with "conduct highly subversive of good order and discipline."[53]

In an attempt to get his restless son to settle down, Liddell's father bought him a plantation in Catahoula Parish, Louisiana. Finally John found success as a cotton planter and worked hard at making his business productive. He married socially prominent Mary Metcalfe Roper, whom he had met in Natchez, in 1841. The couple raised ten children as well as an orphaned niece. But Liddell could not shake a bent toward violence that dogged him all his life. Liddell was a blunt man, sometimes brazen and biased. The same obstinacy with which he defended slavery and the Southern way of life made him a tenacious adversary if provoked. An ongoing feud with neighboring planter Charles Jones apparently began when a woman acquaintance of Liddell shot and wounded Jones. When two of Jones' friends turned up dead later, Liddell was arrested and charged with the murders, but a jury found him not guilty in 1854.[54]

When the Civil War broke out, Liddell utilized his family connections and his friendship with Rebel generals P.G.T. Beauregard, Braxton Bragg, and William J. Hardee, to secure a position in the new army. With no real military credentials, he persuaded Hardee to take him on his staff as a volunteer aide and served without pay until May 1862. His first command, a small brigade at Corinth, earned him approval and promotion to brigadier general in June 1862. Liddell led an Arkansas brigade at Perryville in October 1862 and received high praise from Pat Cleburne at Murfreesboro, where his brigade suffered 589 casualties but saved Cleburne's left flank from being turned by the Federals. In September 1863 he commanded a small division at Chickamauga, where half of his force was wiped out in two days of hard fighting. Liddell had hammered out a name for himself as a hard-hitting, reliable officer.[55]

Liddell left the Army of Tennessee and transferred to Louisiana where he served under Major General Richard Taylor in the Red River campaign in the spring of 1864. But animosity with Taylor, who was equally as blunt as Liddell, turned the experience sour. Liddell later wrote, "It seems that Taylor's senselessness kept the whole department stirred up." He accused Taylor of issuing "indiscriminate orders to drive out of the lines whole families of women and children, who happened to have had some members that had deserted to the enemy." Reassignment to Mobile in September 1864 was a welcome change for the no-nonsense Liddell, who got along well with Maury only to have Taylor, "to my disgust," become Maury's superior.[56]

Like many of his officers and soldiers, Liddell had reservations about being stationed at Blakely, and he yearned for happier times in the Army of Tennessee. He wrote his wife Mary in February 1865, "I wish for more active service rather than being confined to fortifications." Liddell ran into a former colleague, Brigadier General George Maney, one day in Mobile. "Why did you leave us?" Maney asked him. "What did you quit the Army of Tennessee for?" Liddell recalled of the meeting, "I only stammered out some excuse that there were enough general officers without me, but that I now regretted not having taken up Hardee's offer as chief of staff." Liddell was unaware that Generals Simon B. Buckner and Edmund Kirby Smith had both petitioned the War Department to promote Liddell and assign him to a division command in the Trans-Mississippi; Maury had vetoed the proposal.[57]

One night during the siege of Fort Blakely, Liddell welcomed a friend from Mobile who had brought another visitor with him. While the three men sat and talked around the general's table, a musket ball suddenly plopped down on the table from out of the darkness. The stranger was startled. Liddell wrote later, "I explained to him that the sharpshooters in the rifle pits were firing all night long and balls frequently fell near, glancing from trees sometimes, and that shells exploded sometimes near." The visitors were not reassured at all and abruptly terminated their social call. "You are bound to go up," Liddell's friend told him, as he turned to leave. "I feel sorry for you. Good-bye. I hope you live through all this."[58]

NOTES

1. William Pitt Chambers, *Blood and Sacrifice: The Civil War Journal of a Confederate Soldier*, ed. Richard A. Baumgartner (Huntington, WV: Blue Acorn Press, 1994), 210.

2. Chester G. Hearn, *Mobile Bay and the Mobile Campaign: The Last Great Battles of the Civil War* (Jefferson, NC: McFarland and Company, Inc., Publishers, 1993), 179–180; Chambers, *Blood and Sacrifice*, 210–211; R. N. Rea, "A Mississippi Soldier of the Confederacy," *Confederate Veteran* 30 (1922), 289.

3. Phil Gottschalk, *In Deadly Earnest: The History of the First Missouri Brigade, C.S.A.* (Columbia: Missouri River Press, 1991), 514; Robert S. Bevier, *History of the Confederate First and Second Missouri Brigades, 1861–1865* (St. Louis, 1879), 262.

4. Christopher C. Andrews, *History of the Campaign of Mobile* (New York, 1867), 121–122; Chambers, *Blood and Sacrifice*, 209.

5. Carl Moneyhon and Bobby Roberts, *Portraits of Conflict: A Photographic History of Mississippi in the Civil War* (Fayetteville: University of Arkansas Press, 1993), 19; W. J. Tancig, *Confederate Military Land Units, 1861–1865* (New York: Thomas Yoseloff, 1967), 54, 60, 61; Rea, "A Mississippi Soldier," 264.

6. Ezra J. Warner, *Generals in Gray: Lives of the Confederate Commanders* (Baton Rouge: Louisiana State University Press, 1959), 271–272; R. N. Rea, "Gen. G. W. Sears: A Pathetic Incident," *Confederate Veteran* 11 (1903), 327.

7. Lee T. Wyatt III, "William S. Barry, Advocate of Secession, 1821–1868," *Journal of Mississippi History* 39 (1977), 339–341.

8. Ibid., 350, 354; Moneyhon and Roberts, *Mississippi*, 32; Charles E. Hooker, "Mississippi," in Clement Evans, ed., *Confederate Military History*, vol. 12 (Atlanta, 1899), 214.

9. Moneyhon and Roberts, *Mississippi*, 168, 357.

10. Ibid., 255, 353.

11. Rea, "A Mississippi Soldier," 264.

12. Mamie Yeary, compiler, *Reminiscences of the Boys in Gray, 1861–1865* (Dayton, OH: Morningside House, 1986), 414.

13. Rea, "A Mississippi Soldier," 287.

14. Chambers, *Blood and Sacrifice*, 2–3.

15. Ibid., 1, 4.

16. Hearn, *Mobile Campaign*, 219.

17. Phillip Thomas Tucker, *The South's Finest: The First Missouri Confederate Brigade from Pea Ridge to Vicksburg* (Shippensburg, PA: White Mane, 1993), xix.

18. Ibid., xxi–xxii, xxiv.

19. Ibid., xix, 5.

20. Ibid., xxii, 56–57, 69; Gottschalk, *In Deadly Earnest*, 79.

21. Tucker, *South's Finest*, xix–xx, xxii–xxiii; Gottschalk, *In Deadly Earnest*, 77.

22. Anne Bailey, "Francis Marion Cockrell," in William C. Davis, ed., *The Confederate General*, vol. 1 (Harrisburg, PA: National Historical Society, 1991), 7; Tucker, *South's Finest*, 53.

23. Tucker, *South's Finest*, 52; Gottschalk, *In Deadly Earnest*, 523.

24. Tucker, *South's Finest*, 53; Gottschalk, *In Deadly Earnest*, 326.

25. Tucker, *South's Finest*, 5, 15; Phillip Thomas Tucker, "The First Missouri Confederate Brigade's Last Stand at Fort Blakeley on Mobile Bay," *Alabama Review* 42 (October 1989), 271–272.

26. Tucker, *South's Finest*, 56.

27. Tucker, "Last Stand," 272–274; Gottschalk, *In Deadly Earnest*, 77.

28. Tucker, *South's Finest*, 15.

29. Ibid., 53.

30. Ibid., 73.

31. Ibid., 98, 99, 103.

32. Ibid., xxiii, 103.

33. Ibid., 99.

34. Bruce Catton, *The Centennial History of the Civil War*, vol. 3, *Never Call Retreat* (Garden City: Doubleday & Co., 1965), 204.

35. Bailey, "Cockrell," 7.

36. Ibid.; Gottschalk, *In Deadly Earnest*, 398.

37. Bevier, *Missouri Brigades*, 261.

38. Gottschalk, *In Deadly Earnest*, 507.

39. Tucker, *South's Finest*, 54.

40. Gottschalk, *In Deadly Earnest*, 507–508.

41. Ibid., 490, 506–508; Hearn, *Mobile Campaign*, 219.

42. Gottschalk, *In Deadly Earnest*, 512–513.

43. Tucker, "Last Stand," 276.

44. Benjamin E. Snellgrove, "Bryan Morel Thomas," in William C. Davis, ed., *The Confederate General*, vol. 6 (Harrisburg, PA: National Historical Society, 1991), 42–43; *War of the Rebellion: A Compilation of the Official Records of the Union and Confederate Armies* (Washington, DC: Government Printing Office, 1880–1901), Series I, Vol. 49, Part I, 314.

45. David Marshall Scott, "The Evolution of the Alabama National Guard," Jefferson County National Guard Association, *The History of the Alabama National Guard of Jefferson County* (Birmingham, 1909); David Marshall Scott, letter to Thomas M. Owen, July 1, 1910, 62nd Alabama Infantry Regiment File, Alabama Department of Archives and History (hereafted cited as ADAH); Samuel Will John, "Alabama Corps of Cadets, 1860–1865," *Confederate Veteran* 25 (1917), 12–14.

46. Ibid.

47. Asa M. Piper, "Some Recollections of an Old Soldier," 62nd Alabama Infantry Regiment File, ADAH.

48. C. C. Oliver, letter to Thomas M. Owen, February 22, 1911, 63rd Alabama Infantry Regiment File, ADAH.

49. Zach T. Smith, letter to T. M. Owen, October 15–November 3, 1910, 63rd Alabama Infantry Regiment File, ADAH.

50. Philip D. Stephenson, "Defence of Spanish Fort," *Southern Historical Society Papers* 39 (1914), 122.

51. Dunbar Rowland, *Military History of Mississippi, 1803–1898* (Spartanburg, SC: Reprint Co., 1978), 465–466; Yeary, *Reminiscences*, 227.

52. Levin Vinson Rosser, "Tarrant Family–Columbia Institute," *Alabama Historical Society Collections*, vol. 2 (1897–1898), Tarrant's Battery File, ADAH; Rev. Edward William Tarrant obituary, *Confederate Veteran* 30 (1922), 108; Willis

Brewer, *Alabama: Her History, Resources, War Record, and Public Men from 1540 to 1872* (Montgomery, 1872), 704.

53. Nathaniel C. Hughes, ed., *Liddell's Record* (Dayton, OH: Morningside House, Inc., 1985), 11–13.

54. Ibid., 8–10, 14–15.

55. Terry L. Jones, "St. John Richardson Liddell," in William C. Davis, ed., *The Confederate General*, vol. 4 (Harrisburg, PA: National Historical Society, 1991), 74–75.

56. Hughes, *Liddell's Record*, 186.

57. Ibid., 193.

58. Ibid., 194–195.

CHAPTER 7

"Burning with an Impulse to Do Honor"

After the December 1864 Federal strike on the rail line at Pollard, the raiding column—about 800 troops of Colonel George D. Robinson's 97th U.S. Colored Infantry—headed south toward their base at Pensacola. But Liddell's cavalry from Blakely caught up with them about 6 miles south of Pollard and gave chase, skirmishing on the run for about 30 miles. As they would do again in March 1865, the Rebels burned bridges across the creeks emptying into the Escambia to delay the Federals, and Liddell nipped at the enemy's heels, striking him at each burned bridge. Liddell wrote, "The Negroes fought well, obstinately, and pressed us back steadily." He acknowledged that none of the black soldiers surrendered or was captured. At nightfall on December 17, Liddell struck the enemy column at Pine Barren Creek, where the Rebels killed or wounded eighty of the bluecoats, and ten wagons fell into their hands. The remainder of the Yanks escaped only because the Rebels' mounts were simply too exhausted to go on.[1]

Liddell's comments on the fighting ability of the black soldiers amounted to high praise indeed coming from a Confederate general and a slaveholder. Liddell expressed his opinion on the slave emancipation issue later that same month. He wrote to Louisiana's senator Edward Sparrow that he was convinced the war was lost unless the South could either secure foreign military support or free the slaves and enlist black troops. "We ought to have done this for effect," he commented later, "at the time of Mr. Lincoln's Emancipation Proclamation." General Robert E. Lee was in agreement with Liddell on the slave emancipation issue and was anxious to

have black soldiers, insisting "he could make soldiers out of any human being that had arms and legs."[2]

But even if Confederate officers like Liddell, Lee, and Pat Cleburne accepted the combat potential of blacks, the Rebel rank and file still regarded
them with contempt. A soldier in Colonel Charles P. Ball's 8th Alabama
Cavalry gave a graphic account of the encounter at Pine Barren Creek
where he alleged that a Rebel trooper scalped one of the dead black soldiers. The soldier adorned his hat with the scalp and wore it for several
days explaining that he had scalped the dead man because the blacks had
killed his uncle in the engagement.[3]

Ten percent of Canby's army in the Mobile campaign—and nearly a
fourth of the Federal force in front of Fort Blakely—was African American.
C. C. Andrews described the soldiers in Brigadier General John P.
Hawkins' division as "burning with an impulse to do honor to their race."
They would play a critical role in the final battle for Mobile. Though the motives of many whites in joining the Union army are unclear, it is easier to understand the willingness of African Americans to put on the blue. Most
blacks enlisted in the Union army to do their part in a war to end slavery.
They clearly saw military service as a way to prove their patriotism and to
show white Americans that they were worthy of citizenship. "Once let the
black man get upon his person the brass letters, U. S.," abolitionist and former slave Frederick Douglass once stressed, "let him get an eagle on his
button, and a musket on his shoulder and bullets in his pocket, and there is
no power on earth which can deny that he has earned the right to citizenship in the United States."[4]

Blacks may have been willing to fight for the Union, but their white comrades in arms generally were less than enthusiastic about serving with
them. Many shared the feelings of an Ohio soldier who wrote, "I dont think
enough of the Niggar to go and fight for them. I would rather fight them."
Most white soldiers—especially Irish immigrants and those from border
states—brought strong antiblack prejudices into the army with them. Contact with blacks in the army sometimes softened but more often intensified
these prejudices. Many white soldiers felt that the black man was the cause
of the war and blamed him for the hardships they had to endure. Many
viewed black soldiers as a threat to white superiority. Others were convinced that blacks were just not soldier material. Some whites even threatened to desert rather than serve in the army with blacks. White Federals in
New Orleans waylaid black soldiers on the street, stripped their uniforms
off them, and sent them naked back to their commands.[5]

Although many whites never accepted blacks in the Union army, most
came to tolerate them once the government began to actively recruit them

in 1863. Many Yanks welcomed the notion that a black soldier could take a Rebel bullet meant for a white man. White soldiers also liked the idea of being freed for combat duty, while blacks performed tedious fatigue and garrison chores. Many white enlisted men took advantage of the opportunity of receiving commissions in black regiments. Gradually in the last two and a half years of the war, most whites came to accept black soldiers because they became more accustomed to seeing them in uniform.[6]

Only grudgingly did the 29th Iowa's Charles O. Musser accept Lincoln's Emancipation Proclamation. "I never did like the darky," Musser admitted, conceding that he would have to make the best of an unwanted situation. Gradually Musser's attitude changed, and he came to embrace the idea of black soldiers in the Union army. Writing his father from Helena, Arkansas, in June 1863, he granted that most of the white soldiers now favored the enlistment of blacks. Musser thought blacks would fight even more fiercely because they knew that they would be reduced to slavery if captured by the Rebels, and he wrote, "[I] say arm every nigger of them and let them fight."[7]

In the 83rd Ohio Frank McGregor and his comrades reacted to emancipation in a similar way. McGregor wrote in January 1863 that the white troops felt "it has come down to be a nigger war, fighting for the Blacks, etc." But two months later he revised his opinion, concluding that if it took black troops to quell the rebellion, then so be it. McGregor acknowledged that black soldiers had performed well in combat, and although at first opposed to the recruitment of black troops—and still uneasy with putting blacks on the same level as the white volunteers—he now agreed that it was a wise decision. He added, "I think the using of the slave to shoot down his master will go rather against the Butternuts."[8]

Marching in Hawkins' black division in March 1865 were men of the 73rd Regiment United States Colored Troops, which—in an ironic twist of fate—had its origin in a Louisiana Confederate command. New Orleans boasted a large population of free African Americans who demonstrated their loyalty to the Confederacy by forming their own regiment, the Louisiana Native Guards, in May 1861. When Federal forces under Major General Benjamin Butler occupied the Crescent City in April 1862, the Native Guards remained in the city and were assimilated by the Union Army. The 1st Regiment Louisiana Native Guards became the first black command to be admitted into the U.S. Army on September 27, 1862. Four more black regiments, recruited mostly from former slaves, were formed by March 1863. Meanwhile Major General Nathaniel Banks had replaced Butler as commander in New Orleans. In May 1863 he created the Corps d'Afrique, under Brigadier General Daniel Ullmann, to recruit more former slaves, and the Louisiana Native Guards became part of that organization.

The commander of the 1st Louisiana Native Guards was Major Chauncey Bassett, an officer in the 11th Michigan Infantry, but the regiment's high-spirited young line officers were all African Americans. The captains included men like Alcide Lewis (a mason), H. Louis Rey (a clerk), and Andre Cailloux (a cigar maker)—all former officers in the Confederate regiment. Cailloux—proudly styling himself "the blackest man in New Orleans"—also boasted a Paris education, an impressive standing as a horseman and boxer, and widespread admiration in the black and white communities of the city. Sixteen-year-old 2nd Lieutenant John H. Crowder may have been the youngest officer in the Federal army. Crowder's heart filled with pride when he wrote these lines to his mother: "If Abraham Lincoln knew that a colored Lad of my age could command a company, what would he say."[9]

The Louisiana Native Guards were given the chance to prove themselves on May 27, 1863, in a bloody assault on the strongly entrenched Rebel garrison at Port Hudson, Louisiana. On the right of the Federal army the 1st and 3rd Louisiana Native Guards braved half a mile of marshy timber-laden ground under heavy fire to hurl themselves against the enemy works at least three times, and one witness said the blacks made six separate assaults. They sustained nearly 200 casualties, among the dead the young lieutenant, John Crowder. Cailloux, bellowing orders in both English and French, his left arm smashed, urged his men forward and managed to reach within 50 yards of the Confederate works before he was struck and killed by an enemy shell. Color Sergeant Anselmas Planciancois—who earlier had vowed to "bring back the colors with honor or report to God the reason why"—was shot down at the head of the troops, and the regimental flag was immediately snatched up by two corporals, one of whom fell wounded. When an officer noticed a wounded soldier hobbling from the direction of the hospital toward the battle, he inquired where he was headed. "I been shot bad in de leg, Captain," the soldier explained, "and dey want me to go to de hospital, but I guess I can gib 'em some more yet." The Federals failed to take the fort, and the Rebels refused to allow them to remove the bodies of the black soldiers. Cailloux's body was not recovered until after Port Hudson finally surrendered, six weeks later on July 9. Both blacks and whites were present at his impressive funeral in New Orleans.[10]

Port Hudson showed conclusively that African Americans would fight and forced many white officers to rethink their attitudes toward black soldiers. Ullmann wrote to Secretary of War Stanton that the black troops without question "behaved with dauntless courage." The *New York Times* praised these inexperienced troops who behaved like veterans under fire. They had charged heavily defended enemy works, and "The men, white or black, who will not flinch from that will flinch from nothing." Even Banks had to admit that their determination in the face of the enemy "leaves upon my mind no doubt of their ultimate success."[11]

Just eleven days later on June 7, 1863, four untrained and poorly armed black regiments with two white companies from the 23rd Iowa Infantry— about 1,000 men in all—fought a heroic action defending the Federal post at Milliken's Bend, Louisiana, against a determined assault by 1,500 Confederate Texas troops under Brigadier General Henry E. McCulloch. The inexperienced black soldiers were not able to reload fast enough and were overwhelmed; but they used the bayonet and resisted stubbornly. As savage hand-to-hand fighting raged on the levee, the Iowa soldiers fell back. "The white or true Yankee portion ran like whipped curs," McCulloch recorded; but the blacks fought on with "considerable obstinacy." The bluecoats held the fort, although 35 percent of the black troops were killed or wounded. The 1st Mississippi Infantry (African Descent)—later to become the 51st Regiment, U.S.C.T., in the Mobile campaign—fought on the left of the Federal line. "Many of the severely wounded," wrote their commander, "voluntarily returned to the ranks after washing their wounds." One soldier with a jaw so badly shattered that he could not speak refused to abandon his post until ordered by the commander; the soldier died after the battle. Former New York journalist Charles A. Dana reported to Secretary of War Stanton that the black soldiers' courage at Milliken's Bend had led many white officers to change their thinking about the use of black troops. "Prominent officers, who used in private to sneer at the idea," he wrote, "are now heartily in favor of it."[12]

One white Yankee soldier who changed his mind about African Americans was the 83rd Ohio's Frank McGregor recuperating in the hospital at Milliken's Bend and praising the blacks for their stand there in "one of the bloodiest short engagements of the war." McGregor wrote that the black soldiers "never flinched but made a desperate resistance. . . . [T]he ground strewed with dead bodies showed there had been hot work." Witnesses accused the Rebels of massacring wounded blacks and of executing two of their white officers during the battle. McGregor claimed to have seen one black soldier with six bayonet wounds in his body after he had already been struck down by a rifle shot.[13]

After a fearless but unsuccessful assault by the black 54th Massachusetts Infantry at Fort Wagner, South Carolina, on July 18, 1863, whites in the North could no longer ignore the combat performance of African American troops. The sacrifice of this Northern regiment of blacks in the bloody assault and the death of its commander, 25-year-old Bostonian Colonel Rob-

ert Gould Shaw, opened the door to enthusiastic Federal recruitment of
black soldiers.

Their grudging admission that blacks would fight did not mean that
whites considered them equal. Prejudice against black troops persisted,
and racist attitudes worked against the black soldier. If black troops proved
themselves well disciplined, some whites attributed it to slavelike subser-
vience. If they fought the Rebels with untamed fury, then it was because
they were savages anyway—fitting to fight the Rebels, because both were
less than civilized, but that hardly qualified them to be accepted as good citizens, much less the equal of whites.[14]

One of the earliest examples of discrimination against African American
troops was a purge of black officers. Despite the clear evidence to the contrary—his own Inspector General's Office in September 1863 reported that
black officers of the 1st Louisiana Native Guards "exhibited as much
promptness and intelligence and knowledge of their duties, as a majority of
the white officers of other regiments"—Nathaniel Banks disapproved of
blacks in command positions. Constant harassment soon made it impossible for black officers to function. Captain Joseph Follin of the 1st Louisiana
Native Guards resigned in disgust in February 1864 writing, "Daily events
demonstrate that prejudices are so strong against Colored Officers, that no
matter what would be their patriotism and their anxiety to fight for the flag
of their native Land, they cannot do it with honor to themselves." Gradually all the other black officers in the regiment turned in their resignations
but one, Captain Louis A. Snaer, whose skin was reportedly "as white as
that of any officer in the regiment" and who stubbornly held on to his position to the end of the war.[15]

Even more irritating to the soldiers in the 1st Louisiana Native Guards
was the army's refusal to allow them to emblazon their battle flag with the
name "Port Hudson." A member of the regiment bitterly complained that
the only inscription carried by the flag was "the blood stain of the noble sergeant who bore it in this fierce assault."[16]

When the black officers left, their places were taken by whites, some of
whom were capable leaders, but others who were incompetents foisted off
by white commanders eager to get rid of their own dead wood. Daniel
Ullmann complained that higher commanders who contended that blacks
were incapable of being good soldiers created a self-fulfilling prophecy "by
appointing ignoramuses and boors" as officers over them," men so igno-
rant that they cannot write three consecutive sentences without violating
orthography and syntax."[17]

Black soldiers often resented white officers and found subordination to
whites an unpleasant reminder of slavery; but although it was often easier

to get a commission in a black regiment, white soldiers sometimes were equally reluctant to serve with blacks. Whites frequently could not overcome their personal biases and pressure from peers and families. Sergeant James K. Newton of the 14th Wisconsin Infantry had an opportunity in 1863 to advance to lieutenant by accepting a commission in a black regiment. Even though the increase in pay was a sore temptation for Newton, who sent whatever money he could home to his parents, he decided to decline the offer because his mother "took a decided stand" against it.[18]

On the other hand, there were white officers who seemed genuinely happy to serve in black commands and who did their duty with efficiency and dedication. Henry Crydenwise, a New Yorker, served for two years as an enlisted man before receiving a commission in December 1863 in the 1st Louisiana Native Guards. In a letter to his parents, he expressed his attitude toward black soldiers. "I dont know what your feelings or prejudices may be in regard to colored troops," he wrote. "I am well aware that many are strongly prejudiced against colored soldiers and that with some I should loose caste by becoming an officer in a colored regiment. [B]ut I cannot think that the petty prejudices or even the frowns of others should deter us from persuing what we conceive to be a line of duty." He went on to say that most of the officers of the black regiments were moral men who must pass a strict exam before being offered a position.[19]

Captain Crydenwise became an enthusiastic and energetic officer. He never belittled his black recruits, and he worked hard to make his company a model of good conduct. Crydenwise's company earned two commendations for displaying the most soldierly appearance in the 73rd U.S.C.T. (In April 1864 African American Union regiments were all renumbered under the designation "United States Colored Troops." The 1st Louisiana Native Guards became the 73rd Regiment, U.S.C.T.)

Others were critical of the officer exams for the black regiments. Although he scored well himself, Daniel Densmore, an officer in the 68th U.S.C.T. (formerly the 4th Missouri Colored Regiment), questioned the criteria used in the officer selection process. "The object of the examining board seems to be to ascertain whether the applicant is a live man," he wrote to his brother in February 1864. Densmore felt there was too much emphasis on mere outward appearance and shiny boots.[20]

Fortunately, some senior white officers took an enlightened approach to commanding black soldiers. Daniel Ullmann felt that whites tended to make the mistake of looking at black troops "as a unit, as a whole, as being all alike—the inferior specimens are selected as examples of all." He believed good leadership provided the key. "I have seen colored regiments," he wrote,"—weak, disorganized, inefficient—which stripped of their miserable officers, and placed in the hands of men who both knew their duty and discharged it, were raised speedily to a high degree of discipline and effectiveness."[21]

When Brigadier General George L. Andrews, a distinguished West Point graduate and veteran of combat in Virginia, took command of the post of Port Hudson in July 1863, he applied common sense and fairness to make the Corps d'Afrique one of the finest units in the Federal army. Immediately he issued orders to protect the black soldiers from abuse. The black soldier, he ordered, "is entitled to respect and consideration, and to the protection and support of his military superiors, particularly when performing any duty which has been imposed on him." For those who violated his prohibition against mistreatment of black troops, Andrews promised punishment "with unrelenting severity." He also pushed for high standards in the officer ranks. The 1st Louisiana Native Guards' Lieutenant Colonel Samuel M. Quincy—a Bostonian, graduate of Harvard, where his grandfather was president, and former officer in the 2nd Massachusetts Infantry—wrote, "General Andrews is making excellent troops of the negroes by insisting on the strictest discipline among the officers & showing no mercy to the worthless or incompetent until he gets rid of them." Andrews set up and personally oversaw a school of instruction for the white officers.[22]

Andrews also stressed education for the black enlisted men and established schools for each regiment. Crydenwise contended that the Federal government "while it makes use of the negro in crushing out this rebellion also seeks to elevate and enlighten him that he may be prepared for the future which shall open before him." He found it to be "a great field for Christian & philanthropic labor. a field where great good may be accomplished." Quincy was amused to see black soldiers so anxious to learn, "grown men . . . making great staggering letters on their slates with great muscular exertion." When he noticed a soldier lagging behind a column of troops and was about to chide the man for his conduct, he held back because the man was studying his spelling book and trying to march at the same time.[23]

Brigadier General John P. Hawkins, a West Point graduate and veteran of service on the northwestern frontier before the Civil War, had commanded his black division since February 1864. A solid believer in firm discipline but not humiliation, he outlawed the practice of bonding—tying up soldiers—as a form of punishment because it was too great a reminder of slavery. Besides encouraging more humane treatment for black soldiers, Hawkins advised the assignment of more junior officers to help provide the needed training. And he also lent his voice to the campaign for equal pay for black soldiers.[24]

Discrimination in pay was a universal complaint among African American troops. Federal army privates normally received $13 per month, but black soldiers were paid only $10 per month, with $3 deducted out of this for uniform expenses. Officers were paid the same as in white commands. Some of the white officers protested, and commanders of the black units lobbied for a redress, but not until June 1864 did Congress finally act to provide equal pay for all soldiers. The question of back pay was still up in the air. Only black soldiers who had been free on April 19, 1861, could qualify for back pay. In March 1865, when Hawkins' black division was marching on Blakely, Congress finally passed legislation guaranteeing equal pay for all black soldiers.[25]

Despite the best efforts of commanders like Ullmann, George Andrews, and Hawkins, cases of abuse toward black soldiers still occurred. Some of the black enlisted men in the 73rd U.S.C.T., assigned in April 1864 to Colonel William H. Dickey's brigade during the Red River campaign, charged that Dickey publicly cursed them and called them "dam Smart Nigers." Dickey denied these charges. In December 1864 the 73rd was sent with the 92nd U.S.C.T. on an expedition against Confederate raiders in Louisiana. Because the 92nd had broken ranks to loot property on a previous expedition, white officers were stricter this time, cursing and beating the black troops. Samuel L. Gardner, chaplain in the 73rd, registered a strong complaint with Ullmann pointing out that white troops would never submit to such treatment. Gardner wrote, "The discipline of the service ought to present to them a contrast to the irresponsible cruelties of slavedriving, instead of a too faithful reproduction of them."[26]

Verbal and physical abuse of black soldiers was commonplace. The 124th Illinois' Corporal Charles Henry Snedeker recorded in his diary on February 20, 1865, at Vicksburg that a Federal staff officer "broke a Negroe's skull with his sabre." He added, "The wound is considered dangerous. It was a brutal and cowardly act."[27]

The actions of one white officer touched off a mutiny in the 4th Regiment Corps d'Afrique (later the 76th Regiment U.S.C.T.) in December 1863. Lieutenant Colonel Augustus W. Benedict had earned the hatred of his soldiers for numerous acts of physical abuse, including hitting soldiers with his fist, striking them with his sword, and spreading molasses on the face, hands, and feet of a soldier staked spread eagle on the ground—a punishment that lasted for two days. After Benedict flogged two drummer boys at Fort Jackson near New Orleans—and the regiment's commander, Colonel Charles Drew, witnessed the act but made no move to stop it—the regiment erupted in mutiny. Once order was restored, an investigation was launched resulting in Benedict's dismissal from the army. He was replaced by Major William E. Nye, who had been conveniently unavailable for duty during the Fort Jackson mutiny. Eight of the mutineers received prison sentences.[28]

The new commandant of Fort Jackson, Brigadier General William Dwight, probed further into charges of brutality in the regiment. The investigation led to the arrest of six white officers charged with sexual assault on black women who served as laundresses for the regiment. And in February 1864, Dwight charged Colonel Drew with "kicking a private who is slow, striking and kicking a first Sgt. who is out of quarters without permission; striking with a stick a Sergt. who is from sickness unable to drill, and using all sorts of threats of violence towards a Private who does not face properly in saluting." The six officers who had forced their way into the black laundresses' quarters were dismissed from the army. But Drew managed to wriggle free and was in fact bumped up in the chain of command. As the black troops advanced on Blakely, Drew commanded the 3rd Brigade in Hawkins' division, a brigade that included his old regiment, the 76th U.S.C.T.[29]

Adding to the anger of African American troops over ill treatment by racist officers was their keen disappointment in not getting a chance to fight, despite the good combat performance of black soldiers at Port Hudson, Milliken's Bend, Fort Wagner, and other actions. Many Federal commanders, like Nathaniel Banks, simply saw black soldiers as laborers, doing the work that white troops disliked doing. So the lot of most black soldiers was to dig latrines and trenches and to perform guard duty. Ullmann charged that "many high officials outside of Washington have no other intention than that these men shall be used as diggers and drudges." Samuel Quincy complained that the troops "are mostly employed in the dirty work of the army & not given a chance to fight." Continued complaints led Secretary of War Stanton to direct army commanders in June 1864 to have white troops do the same amount of fatigue duty as blacks, but misuse of black troops persisted. Morale was especially low during the summer of 1864 when sickness from diarrhea, fever, and dysentery swept through the camps of the U.S.C.T. In black regiments the death rate from sickness was twice that of white units, and there never were enough doctors to provide medical care.[30]

Major Daniel Densmore in the 68th Regiment U.S.C.T. became so disgusted that he considered transferring to another department. He complained that his soldiers were kept on fatigue duty most of the time to perform work considered too dirty for the white soldiers. In a letter to his brother in December 1864 he wrote bitterly, "We have been discussing the propriety of going back to the former nomenclature, as being much more in Keeping with our business, to wit: Col. to be 'Ole Massa,' and the remainder of us to be 'bosses.' "[31]

Conscientious officers in the black regiments experienced their share of despair over what seemed to be overwhelming obstacles of discrimination and prejudice. "Nobody really desires our success," Samuel Quincy wrote in April 1864, "and it is uphill work." In July he wrote from Port Hudson that army authorities "are opposed to our success and will not treat either officers or men as on equality with other troops." It was frustrating to see his troops who had drilled and worked so hard to be good soldiers treated with apathy and indifference by the high command. When the 73rd held a dress parade in honor of Independence Day, Quincy was struck by the bitter irony of it all. "A review looks funny without any spectators," he wrote, "drums beating colors flying—everybody galloping around in full uniform apparently for the edification of two contrabands & a mule."[32]

Black enlisted men coped with the hardships of discrimination, ill treatment, and burdensome service by laboring harder to be good soldiers. Discipline helped weld the black recruits together and give them cohesion. They quickly caught on to the elements of drill and soldier life and became reliable troops. Major General N.J.T. Dana chose the 68th Regiment U.S.C.T. as the best drilled regiment in his department. And even as they worked hard, the black soldiers also played hard. Music and recreation helped alleviate the boredom of garrison duty. At Christmas 1863, Quincy wrote that his soldiers chased greased pigs, held wheelbarrow races, and scaled greased poles.[33]

The Confederacy's policy toward black Union soldiers was a harsh one. Any black soldiers taken prisoners by the Rebels could expect to be returned to slavery. White officers of black regiments who were captured were to be executed. Such treatment actually helped create a bond between the white officers and their black enlisted men. The commander of the 82nd Regiment U.S.C.T. put it to his troops this way: "They have left their homes and come among you, knowing that they are liable of being hung by the rebel govt should they be taken prisoner and why? Because they instruct you to be soldiers. Because they teach you how to fight for liberty they would wish you to enjoy."[34]

African American troops faced real danger from the Confederates. In February 1864, Rebel guerrillas surprised a foraging party of twenty soldiers from the 51st Regiment U.S.C.T. led by a lieutenant. After the Yankees surrendered, the Rebs killed and mutilated the prisoners, shot the lieutenant in the face, and left him for dead.[35]

The most notorious example of Rebel mistreatment of black prisoners was the April 12, 1864, assault by Nathan Bedford Forrest's troops on Fort Pillow, a Federal garrison on the Mississippi River in Tennessee. The Rebels overwhelmed the 557 defenders, half of whom were black, and captured the fort. What happened next still generates controversy, but most scholars agree that atrocities took place at Fort Pillow and that some black soldiers were massacred. When the guns finally fell silent, 231 Federal soldiers were dead, 100 were wounded, and the rest were prisoners. Northerners accused the Rebels of shooting men after they had surrendered, with burying black soldiers alive, and with setting tents of the wounded on fire. The Confederates denied these charges and insisted that only black soldiers who refused to surrender were killed. After the Fort Pillow incident, many black troops refused to give quarter to Rebels, and nearly a year later, black soldiers marching on Blakely clung to their grim vow to "Remember Fort Pillow."[36]

The long march from Pensacola to Pollard to Blakely starting on March 20, 1865, "was a severe one on the men," Hawkins reported, "being attended with constant labor, making corduroy roads to get the wagons through the almost impassable swamps." Lieutenant Colonel Henry C. Merriam of the 73rd U.S.C.T. wrote, "Our wagons actually dropped to their axles while standing in the park and our animals were floundering in mire at the picket lines unable to move until rolled and dragged out by the men." Chaplain C. W. Buckley of the 47th Regiment U.S.C.T. commented on the good conduct of the black troops on the march. He wrote, "when hunger or pillage were the only parts of the alternative, hunger was preferred to disobedience of orders." He added, "During the whole march I have not heard a word of reproach cast upon a colored soldier."[37]

On April 1, the black division moved up to support the Federal cavalry driving in Rebel skirmishers in front of Fort Blakely. Spurling's cavalry brigade had routed the 46th Mississippi Infantry earlier in the afternoon, and the black regiments pitched camp east of Fort Blakely on the right of the Federal line. They spent the night tired and hungry, with their muskets handy, but in the morning, cheers greeted supply wagons sent from Spanish Fort, and corn—"two ears and a 'nubbin' "—was distributed to each soldier.[38]

Spearheaded by a detachment of pickets from the 68th Regiment U.S.C.T. led by Lieutenant Albert H. Taisey, Colonel Charles W. Drew's black brigade (48th, 68th, and 76th U.S.C.T.) moved out on the Stockton Road in front of Fort Blakely at daybreak. Taisey's party saw no sign of the Rebels and even began to hope that the enemy might have evacuated during the night. But a sudden hail of bullets from the woods ahead showed them that the Rebels were expecting them. Drew moved up with the brigade and halted within half a mile of the Confederate works. "Not a man lagged," C. C. Andrews wrote, "but with eager strides to the front, they kept the horses of the mounted officers on the trot." About a mile and a quarter from the fort, the soldiers encountered heavy resistance from Rebel skirmishers in a deep and densely wooded ravine. Colonel J. Blackburn Jones of the 68th U.S.C.T. formed a heavy skirmish line—six companies from each of the three brigades (soon to be increased by nine more companies)—and moved forward. The Confederates stubbornly contested every inch of ground, and it took three hours to push them back 800 yards to their rifle pits outside the fort. Jones, who had two horses shot from under him, halted his line within 120 yards of the rifle pits. There were forty casualties in the black division, including Lieutenant Edward E. Talbot of the 68th killed and Colonel Frederick M. Crandall of the 48th wounded by a Rebel shell. To the left of Drew's brigade, Brigadier General William A. Pile, a Methodist minister and former chaplain, moved his brigade (73rd, 82nd, and 86th U.S.C.T.) to within 900 yards of the fort. Colonel Hiram Scofield's brigade (47th, 50th, and 51st U.S.C.T.) came up next as a reserve.[39]

By April 3, the Federals completed their investment of Blakely, as two more divisions—Garrard's of Smith's corps and Veatch's of Granger's—arrived from Spanish Fort. Garrard's division planted itself on the Union left facing Thomas' Alabama brigade, and Veatch's troops occupied the ground to their right. Andrews' two brigades were in the center opposite Cockrell's Missouri brigade and the strongest part of the Rebel line, Redoubts 3 and 4. Hawkins' black division held the right of the Federal line facing Sears' Mississippians.

Would Blakely become a Fort Pillow in reverse? A Connecticut artilleryman wrote, "Our colored boys fight well, better than the white troops. I pity the poor Johnnies if they ever get a chance at them." The Confederates had no doubts about what to expect. On April 1, Liddell sent word to Thomas that "the force of the enemy now in our front is composed principally of negroes, and will not spare any of our men should they gain possession of our works. In view of the above, he directs that you station your men in the rifle-pits, and impress upon their minds the importance of holding their position to the last, and with the determination never to surrender."[40]

NOTES

1. Nathaniel C. Hughes, ed., *Liddell's Record* (Dayton, OH: Morningside House, Inc., 1985), 191–192.

2. Ibid., 192.

3. W. H. O'Bannon, Letter to T. M. Owen, June 1910, Alabama Department of Archives and History, 8th Alabama Cavalry Regiment File, 3–4.

4. Christopher C. Andrews, *History of the Campaign of Mobile* (New York, 1867), 200; James I. Robertson, Jr., "Negro Soldiers in the Civil War," *The Negro in the Civil War* (Philadelphia: Eastern Acorn Press, 1988), 33.

5. Bell I. Wiley, *The Life of Billy Yank* (Baton Rouge: Louisiana State University Press, 1978), 109, 112,120–121.

6. Ibid., 120–121.

7. Barry Popchock, ed., *Soldier Boy: The Civil War Letters of Charles O. Musser* (Iowa City: University of Iowa Press, 1995), 8, 58.

8. Carl E. Hatch, ed., *Dearest Susie: A Civil War Infantryman's Letters to His Sweetheart* (Jericho, NY: Exposition Press, Inc., 1971), 37–38.

9. Mary F. Berry, "Negro Troops in Blue and Gray: The Louisiana Native Guards, 1861–1863," in Donald G. Nieman, ed., *The Day of the Jubilee: The Civil War Experience of Black Southerners* (New York: Garland Publishing, Inc., 1994), 25–26, 32–33; Joseph T. Glatthaar, *Forged in Battle: The Civil War Alliance of Black Soldiers and White Officers* (New York: Macmillan, Inc., 1990), 124–125.

10. Glatthaar, *Forged in Battle*, 126–129.

11. Ibid., 129–130.

12. Ibid., 131–135.

13. Hatch, *Dearest Susie*, 53–54; Glatthaar, *Forged in Battle*, 133.

14. Reid Mitchell, *Civil War Soldiers: Their Expectations and Their Experiences* (New York: Simon and Schuster, 1988), 196–197.

15. James G. Hollandsworth, Jr., *The Louisiana Native Guards: The Black Military Experience during the Civil War* (Baton Rouge: Louisiana State University Press, 1995), 78; Henry C. Merriam, "The Capture of Mobile," in *War Papers (Read Before the Commandery of the State of Maine. Military Order of the Loyal Legion of the United States)*, vol. 3 (Wilmington, NC: Broadfoot Publishing Co., 1992), 247.

16. Noah Andre Trudeau, *Like Men of War: Black Troops in the Civil War, 1862–1865* (Boston: Little, Brown & Co., 1998), 397.

17. Hollandsworth, *Louisiana Native Guards*, 79.

18. Glatthaar, *Forged in Battle*, 113; Stephen E. Ambrose, ed., *A Wisconsin Boy in Dixie: The Selected Letters of James K. Newton* (Madison: University of Wisconsin Press, 1961), xvi.

19. Wiley, *Billy Yank*, 122.

20. Glatthaar, *Forged in Battle*, 51–52.

21. Dudley Taylor Cornish, *The Sable Arm: Negro Troops in the Union Army, 1861–1865* (New York: Longmans, Green, & Co., 1956), 262–263.

22. Hollandsworth, *Louisiana Native Guards*, 85.

23. Wiley, *Billy Yank*, 122; Hollandsworth, *Louisiana Native Guards*, 86–87.

24. John T. Hubbell and James W. Geary, eds., *Biographical Dictionary of the Union: Northern Leaders of the Civil War* (Westport, CT: Greenwood Press, 1995), 244.

25. Hollandsworth, *Louisiana Native Guards*, 88.

26. Glatthaar, *Forged in Battle*, 197; Hollandsworth, *Louisiana Native Guards*, 100.

27. Mildred Britton, ed., *The Civil War Diary of Charles Henry Snedeker*, 1966, Auburn University Archives, RG 844.

28. Fred Harvey Harrington, "The Fort Jackson Mutiny," in Donald G. Nieman, *Day of the Jubilee: The Civil War Experience of Black Southerners* (New York: Garland Publishing, Inc., 1994), 164–169.

29. Ibid., 169–175.

30. Hollandsworth, *Louisiana Native Guards*, 97–98.

31. Glatthaar, *Forged in Battle*, 184.

32. Hollandsworth, *Louisiana Native Guards*, 90, 99, 116.

33. Glatthaar, *Forged in Battle*, 120; Hollandsworth, *Louisiana Native Guards*, 88–89.

34. Glatthaar, *Forged in Battle*, 204.

35. Ibid., 157.

36. Mark Mayo Boatner III, *Civil War Dictionary* (New York: David McKay Co., Inc., 1959), 296; Mitchell, *Civil War Soldiers*, 193; Glatthaar, *Forged in Battle*, 156–157.

37. *War of the Rebellion: A Compilation of the Official Records of the Union and Confederate Armies* (Washington DC: Government Printing Office, 1880–1901) (hereafter cited as *OR*), Series I, Vol. 49, Part I, 287; Trudeau, *Like Men of War*, 399.

38. Andrews, *Campaign of Mobile*, 123.

39. Ibid., 123–125.

40. Noah Andre Trudeau, *Out of the Storm: The End of the Civil War, April–June 1865* (Boston: Little, Brown & Co., 1994), 167; *OR*, Series I, Vol. 49, Part II, 1188.

CHAPTER 8

"All That Men Could Do"

At the start of the siege at Spanish Fort, the Rebel garrison was able to hold its own while its outnumbered defenders labored around the clock to strengthen their works. Gibson relied on the fort's big guns to keep the Federals at a distance. He wrote, "For the first ten days my artillery, aided by well-trained sharpshooters, was able to cope with that of the enemy, sometimes silencing his guns, and often broke up his working parties in handsome style." After nearly four years of combat with the Confederates, Yankee soldiers had learned to have a healthy respect for Rebel cannoneers.[1]

The artillery was still a somewhat specialized branch of service in the Civil War. A good cannoneer needed some basic technical skills as well as the stamina and endurance of the common foot soldier. Artillery required more training than other branches of the military. In the western Confederacy, most recruits were drawn to the infantry (because it was the most common type of company formed in home towns) or the cavalry (because it was viewed as the more dashing arm of service). Most of the older volunteer militia artillery companies were found in the eastern Confederacy in Virginia, South Carolina, or Georgia. There were few experienced artillery officers. As the war lengthened, the Confederacy encountered far more problems than the Union in equipping its artillerymen with guns, horses, and caissons.[2]

But those drawn to the artillery helped create a veteran fighting arm. Most volunteers were young, curious, eager to learn, hailing from towns or cities like New Orleans, Mobile, and Tuscaloosa. Youthful enthusiasm made up for the lack of training and experience. Recruits soon learned their places in a standard six-man gun crew. Cannoneer Number 1 sponged out the cannon's bore and vent to prevent sparks from setting off a fire. Number 2 deposited a round (a projectile and powder charge measured into a cloth cartridge bag) into the muzzle of the gun. Number 1 used a rammer to push the round into the bore. Number 3 inserted a small wire called a pick into the vent hole on the top rear of the barrel which punctured the cartridge bag. Number 4 placed a friction primer into the vent; this allowed a flame to be carried down the vent to the gunpowder. The supervising gunner, usually a sergeant, sighted and adjusted for elevation. Pulling the lanyard attached to the friction primer set off the powder charge, and the gun fired. Numbers 5 and 6 brought ammunition from a limber chest. An experienced crew could load and fire two rounds a minute.[3]

The Confederate artillery employed several types of guns. Caliber eight to thirteen-inch Columbiads, mounted in coastal forts, were the biggest. Parrott guns were also heavy rifled guns that fired ten-, twenty-, and thirty-pound shells. Twelve-pounder smoothbore Napoleons were the most common Rebel guns, used in field batteries as well as in forts. Mortars, or "Coehorns," were squat, small pieces designed to fire shells over enemy earthworks; lightest of the guns at 300 pounds, they were equipped with handles so that they could be hand-carried by four men. Projectiles also varied. Solid shot or cannon balls generally were used at long range for tearing down enemy works. For use against personnel at short range (100 to 200 yards) there was canister (hundreds of small iron balls discharged like a shotgun blast from a metal cylinder into the ranks of advancing infantry), grapeshot (deadly clusters of two-inch iron balls), or exploding charges timed with a percussion fuse to detonate in air or on contact.[4]

The guns in Spanish Fort's strongest and best defended positions were manned by soldiers of the 22nd Louisiana Consolidated Infantry (also called the 22nd Louisiana Heavy Artillery). Old Spanish Fort (Redoubt 1), built by the Spanish in 1780, sat on a high bluff by the Bay and inside the "open horseshoe" of the Rebel works. The earthwork bastion was armed with six heavy guns—eight-inch Columbiads and thirty-pounder Parrots—which faced the Bay from atop a thirty-foot-thick parapet to lend support to Batteries Huger and Tracy about a mile upstream. Some 107 men, three companies of the 22nd Louisiana, were stationed there.[5]

The 22nd Louisiana came about from the consolidation of eight battered Louisiana infantry commands in January 1864. Most men in the new regiment were from the old 22nd Louisiana Infantry, which had served as heavy artillery at Vicksburg and at Snyder's Bluff, and the other members soon adapted to artillery service as well. Given the Confederacy's shortage in manpower, it was not uncommon for some infantry units to perform duty as artillery. The 22nd Consolidated reported to Maury in February 1864 and was assigned to man the guns in several forts around Mobile. The Louisianans were on their way to reinforce Fort Gaines in August 1864, but before their transport could land them, the fort fell, sparing them confinement in a Union prisoner of war camp. Colonel Isaac W. Patton, a former U.S. Army artillery officer with experience in the Mexican War, commanded the 22nd Louisiana Consolidated. Gibson eventually placed Patton in overall command of his artillery at Spanish Fort.[6]

The 22nd Louisiana also garrisoned Battery Huger, the small earthwork on an island in the fork formed by the Apalachee and Blakely Rivers. Major Washington Marks commanded two companies of Louisianans there, along with Captain L. A. Collier's Mississippi battery, bringing his strength up to about 200 men to handle the little fort's eleven guns. Battery Tracy lay 1,000 yards from Huger on the west bank of the Apalachee River. Major Marks also commanded Battery Tracy (although Huger was where he made his headquarters) where two more companies of the 22nd Louisiana (120 men) under Captain Ambrose A. Plattsmier manned five guns.[7]

More Louisianans garrisoned Fort McDermott (Redoubt 2, called Fort Alexis by the Federals), which anchored the southern end of the Rebel works about 400 yards from Old Spanish Fort. A somewhat smaller bastion but decisively commanding the high ground, Fort McDermott boasted a six-inch Brooke rifle, two twenty-four-pounder howitzers, six six-pounder smoothbores, and six Coehorn mortars. Stationed there was Captain Samuel Barnes' company of the 22nd Louisiana. Also on duty during the siege were Captain Thomas L. Massenburg's Georgia battery, Captain J. C. Thrall's Arkansas battery, and Captain T. J. Perry's Florida battery (the Marion Artillery).[8]

The elite 5th Company of New Orleans' Washington Artillery, veterans of hard-fought campaigns from Shiloh to Nashville, manned Redoubt 3 in the center of the Rebel lines, with ninety men and six guns. The men of Slocomb's Battery, as the company was called, named their redoubt "Battery Blair" in honor of one of their own, Lieutenant Thomas M. Blair, killed at Chickamauga. But the Federals called the Rebel bastion "Red Fort" for the red earth thrown out in front of the earthwork by the graycoat soldiers.

Slocomb's Battery represented one of the oldest and most distinguished units present at Spanish Fort. Formed in 1838, the Washington Artillery had a long history of service. With the onset of war, recruits flocked to its banner, and expansion swelled the unit to battalion size by May 1861. Its four companies promptly marched off to serve in Virginia, but Lieutenant W. Irving Hodgson and twenty men who remained in New Orleans organized a fifth company in March 1862. The New Orleans business community, city council, and the Louisiana legislature all chipped in to buy arms, equipment, and distinctive uniforms. The new recruits, with Hodgson as their captain, marched off smartly in their red kepis, dark blue shell jackets with red piping, and blue jeans pants. The company's membership reflected New Orleans' urban background. Included were five attorneys, two doctors, an architect, ten merchants, forty-seven clerks, eight artisans, eleven students, three riverboat pilots, thirty-one laborers, and three planters. Philip D. Stephenson, who joined the company in March 1864, wrote that the majority of the members were French or of French ancestry.[9]

Although they continued to designate themselves as "Headquarters, 5th Company, Battalion Washington Artillery," fate dictated that the enthusiastic cannoneers would never join the rest of their battalion serving in Virginia. Instead, they were to forge their own splendid combat record in places like Shiloh, Murfreesboro, and Chickamauga. Early in the war the company was known as the "White Horse Battery" because of the large numbers of white or gray horses pulling its caissons. A Confederate soldier described the high-spirited artillerymen shortly before their first battle at Shiloh in April 1862: "Their uniforms were fresh. They sang, joked and laughed aloud as they cooked their meals at the campfire."[10]

Shiloh was an eye-opening shock to people in both the North and the South, with over 23,000 casualties in two days of the worst killing ever seen in North America. In some of the heaviest fighting the New Orleans battery fired 723 rounds before it ran out of ammunition and was nearly overrun. Seven gunners were killed, along with most of the horses. Among the twenty men wounded was 30-year-old Lieutenant Cuthbert H. Slocomb, who had joined the company with six months of service under his belt with the battalion in Virginia.[11]

The battery reorganized, and two months later the popular Slocomb replaced Hodgson who resigned due to illness. Confederate artillery batteries took the names of their commanders, and now the unit was referred to as Slocomb's Battery. Slocomb earned a reputation as a gifted officer in the Army of Tennessee. He was wounded again during the Atlanta campaign in August 1864 and was out of action for several weeks. By the time the battery reached Mobile, he was back and in command of a battalion.

Charismatic, energetic Lieutenant J. Adolph Chalaron led the company during Hood's Tennessee campaign and at Spanish Fort. A life-long resident of the Crescent City, Chalaron was 28 years old, older than most of the men in the battery. Cited several times for bravery, Chalaron turned down promotions so that he could stay with the company.

The New Orleans battery never lost its youthful exuberance. During action at Jackson, Mississippi, in July 1863, the company was stationed along the railroad tracks south of the city, and the men took advantage of breaks in the fighting to sing and pound out tunes on a piano found in an abandoned house nearby. At the keyboard, Sergeant Andy G. Swain, a former Mississippi riverboat skipper, entertained the troops who stopped singing when firing started again. As soon as the guns were silent, the singing commenced once more.[12]

But months of exhausting fighting capped off by the bloodbath at Franklin in November 1864 was more than many in the battery could stand. Chalaron wrote, "Demoralization was openly expressed by many" over the "useless slaughter and blundering sacrifice of the flower of the Army of Tennessee." Meanwhile the battery was assigned to Major General William Bate's division for operations around Murfreesboro, and the cannoneers found themselves in deep trouble in an action at Overall Creek on December 4.[13]

Chalaron's battery at Overall Creek had been shelling an enemy blockhouse, and skirmishing had gone on for most of the afternoon when the Federals launched a strong attack on the Rebels at dusk. The Louisianans' infantry support suddenly melted away. The little battery stood alone with enemy cavalry bearing down on them in large numbers. While Lieutenant Abram I. Leverich's section of guns opened fire with canister, Chalaron and Lieutenant C. G. Johnson struggled to limber up his section to move to the rear. But there was no time; a cloud of dust was already approaching. Chalaron turned to Johnson, "Leverich has failed to check them!" he warned. "They're on us! Have you a weapon?" "Not a penknife," Johnson answered. The two officers braced for the shock of impact, and Chalaron threw up his arm expecting a blow from a Yankee saber. About thirty or forty riderless horses stampeded past the guns. Chalaron suddenly realized that Leverich's canister had done its work, but without infantry support the battery still was in peril. Leverich's section retired, while Johnson's opened up with shrapnel on the enemy troopers. Using the common field artillery tactic of withdrawing one section at a time, with one section firing while the other retired, Chalaron pulled the battery out of harm's way, and nightfall brought the cannoneers out of jeopardy. A greatly relieved Bate grabbed Chalaron's hand and blurted, "You have saved my division." "I know I have," the cocky Chalaron shot back. But the action had cost the battery one man killed and three wounded.[14]

Two weeks later came the disaster at Nashville and the brutal retreat from Tennessee in the freezing rain and snow. In February 1865 the cannoneers learned that they were being sent to Mobile, where they would be armed with muskets and assigned to man heavy guns in the city's forts. The Louisianans arrived in Mobile by rail on open flat cars in the freezing rain.

They were not happy with their new assignment and would have preferred being sent to the field again. On March 4 Slocomb, Chalaron, and the officers and men of the company requested transfer to Joseph E. Johnston's army in North Carolina so they could return to duty as light artillery. The war was over before Johnston could reply to their appeal.[15]

Their disappointment at being used as heavy artillery did not stop the Louisianans from enjoying themselves in the Gulf City. Some of them had just been paid, and they were anxious to spend their Confederate money for coffee at a dollar a cup or boots for $100 a pair. Soon word came down that the battery was to be sent to Spanish Fort, and the cannoneers crossed the Bay and started digging in at the Red Fort.[16]

Some of the veterans were apprehensive. "We felt ourselves to be in a trap as soon as we took in the situation," Phil Stephenson reflected. With its back to the Blakely River, Spanish Fort seemed all too vulnerable. Stephenson feared shelling from the rear by Yankee naval vessels, and he visualized Federal ships steaming into the river and cutting the fort off. A few days later he eyed an escape route, "a chain of little, low, marshy islands, hardly above the water," lying not far off the shore. "If the place be taken by assault," he wrote, "we might make for one of these and by swimming from one to the other, finally get to Blakely."[17]

Inside Redoubt 3 the Louisianans became well acquainted with the guns they would use during the coming siege. The artillerymen gave nicknames to the four heavy guns: "Lady Slocomb" (for Slocomb's wife), "Cora Slocomb" (for their daughter), "Lady Vaught" (for the wife of 1st Lieutenant W.C.D. Vaught, out of action after losing his hearing from a concussion), and "Gen. Gibson." The two Coehorn mortars were called "Louise" and "Therese" for two good-looking women who sold apples and peanuts at the Battle House Hotel. The favorite was "Lady Slocomb," an eight-inch Columbiad. "Ah, my lads!" one of the Rebels gloated, "Look out now for the Lady Slocomb; when she speaks the Yanks must hush up and hide." And her fire proved deadly indeed. On March 31 a shell from the "Lady Slocomb" struck a limber of the 14th Indiana Light Artillery and killed one Federal soldier in the explosion. The Rebel gunners also named the Federal guns, calling them "Anna Maria," "Sarah Jane," and "Elizabeth Ann."[18]

To the left of Slocomb's battery, Redoubts 4 and 5 were manned by Tennesseans—Captain J. W. Phillips' Battery, which had served in the same battalion with Slocomb's at Nashville. At Chickamauga in September 1863, Confederate Major General John C. Breckinridge called it an "excellent battery," and it was heavily engaged throughout the Atlanta campaign in 1864. Like Slocomb's Battery, the Tennesseans had lost their guns at Nashville, and in February 1865 they were sent to Mobile. John A. Thomas, a Kentuckian who served with the unit, wrote that they were drilled for about a month as heavy artillery and "fattened up for the next 'killing.' "[19]

During the siege at Spanish Fort, Phillips' Tennesseans were reinforced by James Garrity's Alabama battery of about seventy men. Garrity's Battery was the pre-war Alabama State Artillery Company from Mobile. Formed in 1836, the unit rivaled the better known Washington Artillery of New Orleans, and there seems to have been a close association between the two. The Mobile company may have imitated the blue uniforms of the Washington Artillery, which visited the Gulf City in 1860. The Mobile cannoneers departed for the war in May 1861 dressed in their "handsome service uniform of indigo blue, trimmed with red, and brown gaiters." In a letter to his brother, Lieutenant Philip Bond in July 1861 referred to the war as a "severe test of patriotism." Bond, who led the battery in the summer of 1864, was killed near Atlanta. [20]

Like the 5th Company of the Washington Artillery, the Mobilians received their baptism of fire at Shiloh—"one of the hardest fights that has ever taken place on this Continent," Lieutenant Bond wrote. They lost seven men killed and wounded and were highly commended by their brigade commander. Rough campaigning followed. The battery was especially hard hit at Murfreesboro, where it suffered twenty-seven casualties in December 1862. Although wounded at Murfreesboro, James Garrity took command of the battery in January 1863. There was more fighting at Chickamauga, at Chattanooga, and in Georgia, and Garrity's battery was among the wreckage of Hood's army after Nashville in December 1864. At Mobile, Garrity was promoted to battalion level, and Lieutenant Henry T. Carrell commanded the battery at Spanish Fort.[21]

On the left of the Rebel line was Redoubt 6, manned by Charles L. Lumsden's Alabama battery, with four six-pounders and three Coehorn mortars. Sergeant James Maxwell wrote that the guns "seemed like pop guns in comparison with the 12 pounder Napoleons, that we had handled so long." After their position was overrun at Nashville, Lieutenant General Alexander P. Stewart had told Lumsden, "You and your men did all that men could do," and a Federal artillery captain admitted to one of the Rebel prisoners that Lumsden's battery "gave him hell." The veteran gunners had built a commendable reputation for themselves on battlefields from Perryville to Atlanta.[22]

Lumsden, a Virginia Military Institute graduate, was a former commandant of cadets at the University of Alabama. Major Felix I. Robertson, his battalion commander at Chattanooga, described him as "a man below medium height, but unusually alert and preposessing in appearance, well fitted by education and temperament to be a successful commander of a battery of field artillery." Half the men in his company were college gradu-ates or students from the Tuscaloosa area. His four original lieutenants in-cluded Dr. George W. Vaughn (later a regimental surgeon) and his brother-in-law Ebenezer H. Hargrove, county sheriff Henry H. Cribbs, and county school superintendent Edward Tarrant (later to command his own battery). Sergeants Andrew Coleman Hargrove, a 27-year-old Tuscaloosa lawyer and Alabama alumnus, and John A. Caldwell both would be lieutenants at Spanish Fort. Dr. George Little, a college professor, was orderly sergeant, and his younger brother John, a college administrator, was a scout.[23]

When the war broke out, George Little was a 23-year-old chemistry pro-fessor at Mississippi's Oakland College. Since turning 19, he had spent much time in Europe and had not followed the political issues over slavery during the 1850s. He had ignored all the rhetoric about a coming civil war. "I did not take it seriously," he wrote, "as I could not believe that the people of the United States were so foolish as to go to war." But when war became apparent, he resolved to sign up with the Confederate army at the end of the school term in June 1861. "The question of slavery may have had much weight with the men higher up," he explained, "but it did not enter into the minds of the rank and file of the soldiers of the Confederate army; with us it was purely a question of our right to manage our own affairs without inter-ference from other states." Little and his roommate, mathematics professor W. L. Baird, pulled an atlas from the shelf and looked up the population of the North and South, and "found that in white population they outnum-bered us five to one. I asked Baird what he was going to do and he said that he was going to stay right there; I told him that I was going into the army." Little would serve with Lumsden's battery until September 1863 when he was promoted to lieutenant and assigned to staff duty.[24]

The Tuscaloosa battery's first service was at Fort Gaines on Dauphin Is-land, where from the fall of 1861 to the spring of 1862 the recruits learned the art of soldiering and handling the big guns. Hands unaccustomed to hard physical labor became blistered and callused from wielding crowbars and shovels, and faces were burned from working in the "semi-tropical sun." The dull routine of camp life replaced the lively convivial calendar of Tuscaloosa society. Little wrote, "Released from restraints of home, church and public sentiment, it did not take long for many to learn to be quite ex-pert gamblers." Camp sicknesses like measles and mumps claimed some victims. On the other hand, parents and friends came down by steamboat from Tuscaloosa to visit, bringing articles from home. "Nothing was too good for the boys at the front," Little explained, "and fish and oysters were abundant in season." The men thought they had it rough, but Little wrote, "The time soon came when they could look back to their first year's experience of soldier life as luxurious, in comparison to rags and semi-starvation that afterwards fell to their lot for months at a time."[25]

Meanwhile the young soldiers yearned to be sent into action. They missed out on Shiloh in April 1862 because Captain Charles P. Gage's Mobile battery was sent north instead (political pull, Lumsden's boys asserted). But in mid-April, Gage's company came limping back to Mobile after taking a battering at Shiloh, and they remained in the Gulf City for the rest of the war. Lumsden's battery inherited Gage's guns and equipment and was at last sent into the field.

Late April and early May 1862 found Lumsden's battery in northern Mississippi with the Confederate army falling back after Shiloh. Cold rain and bad roads made for rough service, and poor drinking water and lack of sanitation led to sickness. In Lumsden's battery, 60 men out of 170 were down with pneumonia, measles, typhoid fever, or diarrhea. "At one time," Little recalled, "there were so many sick men in our company that we had barely enough left to ride the horses and none to work the guns." Five unlucky cannoneers died. On May 9, the battery saw its first action at the little community of Farmington 5 miles from Corinth, an artillery duel with a Federal battery that cost Lumsden no casualties but earned the Tuscaloosans compliments from their brigade commander for their "fine shooting." Lumsden's battery went on to become a dependable unit with service at Perryville, Murfreesboro, and Chickamauga.[26]

James R. Maxwell, who became a fine N.C.O. with Lumsden's battery, was just 16 years old when he entered the University of Alabama in January 1861. His planter father, fearing a Southern defeat and dreading the prospect of a Yankee-incited slave uprising, resolved to take the family to England for safety, but James refused to join them and stayed in Tuscaloosa. Young Maxwell was burning to enlist in the Confederate army, but university president Landon Garland would hear none of it. Instead, he allowed the cadet to serve as a drillmaster for Confederate recruits, and in April 1862 Maxwell was assigned to the 34th Alabama Infantry Regiment. Maxwell accompanied the regiment into Kentucky where he was captured and sent to a prison camp in the North. During his confinement, diarrhea nearly killed him, and he was down to ninety pounds when he was exchanged. But as soon as he recovered, he returned to duty. Not yet 19, he joined Lumsden's gun crews—as Number 6 cannoneer, preparing fuses—and was in combat at Missionary Ridge on November 25, 1863. Before long he was promoted to corporal, then to sergeant.[27]

From his father's plantation Maxwell brought good-natured Jim Bobbett as his servant. Lumsden's company had about a dozen black servants, some attending officers, others private soldiers. Most of them served as cooks. Maxwell wrote, "they were liked by all, and were glad to assist any and all soldiers for small rewards and even for personal thanks." The servants proved to be very skillful foragers and earned cash performing odd jobs around the camp. They "usually had money in their pockets, when their masters had none," according to Maxwell. A "handy fellow all round," Jim rarely had less than $100 in his money belt, and his skill as a handyman, barber, and clothes cleaner—as well as his charming ways with the women he met from time to time—served him well. Jim and his cronies kept Lumsden's men supplied with scarce food items; and although they had numerous chances to escape to Federal lines, Maxwell asserted, "none attached to our company ever deserted."[28]

Nashville was a disaster for the Rebel artillery, and after the first day's action a weary Lumsden counted his losses: all four guns abandoned, twenty-two men captured, and six good men killed, including 17-year-old Hilen L. Rosser, youngest of three brothers in the battery, with the top of his head shot off. As the captain ran his hands over his face, something clung to his beard, and brushing it out he turned to Maxwell. "Maxwell," he said grimly, shaking his head, "that is Rosser's brains I'm picking out." When the remnants of Hood's army were reassigned, the Tuscaloosans were sent to Mobile. "We were soon well drilled in the handling of siege artillery," Maxwell recalled, "and also had some practice with small Coehorn mortars, firing at targets out in the marsh." The duty was not too rigorous after their experiences in Tennessee, and the men were able to spend their spare time dining or carousing in the city.[29]

The battery assembled for Maury's review of his troops on Government Street in Mobile. Several of Lumsden's men were still without coats and pants, and Lumsden told them that they did not have to appear, but if they did it might shame the commander into doing something. When Maury spotted several men "down to shirts and drawers" standing conspicuously in the front rank of the Tuscaloosa company, he turned to Lumsden. "Captain," he said, "what does that mean, those men in ranks, in that condition?" "They have no clothing, Sir," Lumsden innocently replied, "but what they have on, and I have exhausted all means to obtain it, by requisition after requisition." "Can't you think of some way, Captain?" Maury asked. "If you will allow me to detail a man to go to Tuscaloosa," Lumsden suggested, "I do not doubt we can get all the clothes needed, in some way." Maury okayed the proposal, and Maxwell was to go up to Tuscaloosa to handle the business. But the company was ordered to Spanish Fort before he had the chance to leave.[30]

Like the 22nd Louisiana Consolidated, one other command at Spanish Fort was long used to doing double duty as infantry and artillery—a local outfit, Lieutenant Colonel James M. Williams' 21st Alabama Infantry occupying the center of the earthworks near Redoubt 4. In this badly depleted little regiment, Rebel spirits were high, despite recent losses on all fronts of the war.

The 21st Alabama was formed in Mobile in October 1861, and many men from the town's working class joined. The regiment was intended to be a carbon copy of the 3rd Alabama Infantry, the first Alabama command to be sent into the war in Virginia and that included several of the old volunteer militia companies from Mobile. Many of the younger brothers and relatives who didn't make it into the 3rd Alabama enlisted in the 21st Alabama and formed companies with the same names as those in the old 3rd. Most of the young recruits shared the patriotic sentiments of James M. Williams, who wrote in December 1861, "my country calls me—and my own self respect forces me to make the sacrifice."[31]

The recruits went into training at Hall's Mill south of Mobile and then to their first duty post at Fort Gaines. Yearning for action, the new regiment first came under fire at Shiloh in April 1862. The 21st Alabama suffered 200 casualties out of 650 men and had six color bearers shot down, and Williams wrote, "it will take me months to describe what I saw on that terrible field." Returning to Mobile, the regiment spent the rest of the war garrisoning forts around Mobile Bay and filling in as heavy artillery.[32]

Six companies of the 21st Alabama were stationed at Fort Gaines, two at Fort Morgan, and two at Fort Powell when the Rebel forts fell in August 1864. The two companies under Lieutenant Colonel Williams at Fort Powell escaped, were stationed in Mobile and for a short period during December 1864 at Batteries Huger and Tracy, "each of which," Williams wrote, "is about as much of a Fort as Powell." In January 1865 the Alabamians were back in Mobile where they were joined by many of the men taken at Fort Gaines and recently swapped out in a prisoner exchange. Then on March 10 the little regiment was ordered to Spanish Fort, becoming part of Bryan M. Thomas' brigade of Alabama reserves. When Holtzclaw's Alabama brigade arrived from Blakely on March 31, the 21st Alabama was transferred to that command.[33]

The 21st Alabama's commander, James M. Williams, was something of an anomaly himself. The 27-year-old officer was born in Ohio, the son of a watchmaker and silversmith who moved his family to the plains of Iowa in 1856. When things failed to pan out well there, James was sent to Augusta, Georgia, to work as a clerk for a friend of his father's. James, then 21 years old, was captivated by Southern culture and society. He joined a baseball club and a choral group, learned to dance, and even joined the Clinch Rifles, a prominent local volunteer militia company, but most importantly he fell in love with a 17-year-old local girl, Eliza Jane Rennison. By December 1860 he had married "Lizzy" and moved to Mobile, where he had landed a better paying job as a bookkeeper for the firm of a local silver engraver.

The transplanted Yankee soon was caught up in the political issues dividing the North and South. Thoroughly won over to the Southern way of life, Williams became a vocal advocate for Southern independence and joined the 21st Alabama Infantry in October 1861. He served as 1st Sergeant of Company A, the Washington Light Infantry (#2), but in December 1861 he resigned his position in protest over what he considered the ineptness and apathy of the company's officers. As a private soldier, he liked having few responsibilities, and he became a favorite among the regiment's enlisted men who waited for the opportunity to elect him to officer status. The chance for advancement came when the regiment was ordered north to western Tennessee in March 1862. Williams was elected lieutenant and led his company at Shiloh where he was commended for gallantry. In May 1862 he was elected captain, was advanced to major the following October, and made lieutenant colonel in June 1863.

Throughout the war Williams wrote frequently to his wife, displaying humor and insight and filling the margins of his letters with whimsical sketches and cartoons illustrating the life of the soldier. He was devoted to Lizzy and to their son George who was born in May 1863. Like many Southern women, Lizzy provided moral encouragement and support to her husband in spite of the separation caused by the war and the despair brought by defeats. Williams wrote about Lizzy to his father in August 1862, "She is indeed my good angel."[34]

Williams also was a die-hard Rebel who never gave up hope of a Southern victory in spite of setbacks on all fronts. He wrote to his father from Fort Morgan in August 1862, "My whole soul is in the sucess of our struggle for independence; which *sooner or later we will win*—If I should not survive the war to see you again be assured that I feel that my life has been devoted to a good cause." And to Lizzy from Fort Morgan in July 1863, he wrote that news of the fall of Vicksburg had not left him depressed, because "brave hearts and strong arms are left to our Country, and will save it yet."[35]

After his evacuation of Fort Powell on August 6, 1864, Williams came under fire from Maury for not putting up a fight. He was relieved of command while the army conducted an inquiry into the matter. Although a military tribunal exonerated Williams in September 1864, Maury was dissatisfied with the decision and refused to return him to command. (Williams remained the 21st Alabama's senior officer, because the regiment's commander, Colonel Charles D. Anderson, was a prisoner of war; after the prisoner exchange in January 1865 Maury placed Anderson under arrest for his part in the surrender of Fort Gaines.) The lengthy process of trying to clear his name through the indifferent military bureaucracy was a strain on Williams. He lashed out at Maury, whom he referred to as the "old granny" and the "Lord of Panic." In frustration he wrote Lizzy from Mobile in October 1864, "I am coming to have a perfect contempt for the corrupt and imbecile administration of our military department here."[36]

Williams finally was reinstated in December 1864. He assumed command of Batteries Huger and Tracy, and he wrote Lizzy on December 20 that he anticipated a feast of bacon and corn bread for Christmas dinner. Williams and the 21st Alabama were ordered back to Mobile in January 1865. He wrote Lizzy on January 11 that he felt they would be stationed in the city as heavy artillery. "I hope so," he added, "for I like the big guns." But the regiment's destination proved to be Spanish Fort.[37]

Not particularly overjoyed at being assigned to Spanish Fort, Williams wrote Lizzy on March 19, "I don't think that my future crown of laurels is growing on the hills of this fort." The day before, the brigade had witnessed a military execution of which Williams was in charge; and on March 31, Privates Thomas Elam and Elijah Winn, both local men who had deserted from the 21st Alabama in September 1863, were shot by a firing squad. Williams' letters during this period remarked on the rainy weather, his recent bout with diarrhea, and continuous rumors of a Federal attack soon.[38]

Williams welcomed the impending enemy attack. He wrote to Lizzy on March 22 that Spanish Fort was rife with rumors of action, but the men were used to such scuttlebutt and were not excited. Half of his soldiers were busy at work in the trenches, and the rest, "like so many school boys," were shooting marbles outside his tent. "If the Yankees don't come this time I will be vexed," he wrote, "for I want to see them in front of my boys once more."[39]

As the Federal columns closed in on Spanish Fort, Williams soon had his wish. On March 27, he and the 21st Alabama Regiment—225 men strong— were hidden in the bushes on the north side of Bay Minette Creek waiting in ambush for the approaching blue-coated troops. The Alabamians opened fire on the startled 81st Illinois Infantry advancing some 400 yards away taking them by surprise and nearly claiming as a victim none other than Major General A. J. Smith who barely escaped with his life. The Yankees quickly rallied, returned fire, and Williams and the 21st Alabama melted away into the swamp.[40]

NOTES

1. *War of the Rebellion: A Compilation of the Official Records of the Union and Confederate Armies* (Washington, DC: Government Printing Office, 1880–1901), Series I, Vol. 49, Part I, 315.

2. Larry J. Daniel, *Cannoneers in Gray: The Field Artillery of the Army of Tennessee, 1861–1865* (University: University of Alabama Press, 1984), 7.

3. Ibid., 8–9, 12–13.

4. Bell I. Wiley, *The Life of Johnny Reb* (New York: Bobbs-Merrill, 1962), 300–303.

5. Chester G. Hearn, *Mobile Bay and the Mobile Campaign: The Last Great Battles of the Civil War* (Jefferson, NC: McFarland and Company, Inc., Publishers, 1993), 159; Arthur W. Bergeron, Jr., "The Twenty-Second Louisiana Consolidated Infantry in the Defense of Mobile, 1864–1865," *Alabama Historical Quarterly* 38 (1976), 208–209.

6. Bergeron, "Twenty-Second," 204–207.

7. Ibid., 208.

8. Ibid., 209; Daniel, *Cannoneers*, 9.

9. Daniel, *Cannoneers*, 8–9; Frederick P. Todd, *American Military Equipage, 1851–1872*, vol. 2, *State Forces* (New York: Chatham Square Press, Inc., 1983), 850; Nathaniel C. Hughes, Jr., ed., *The Civil War Memoirs of Philip Daingerfield Stephenson, D.D.* (Conway, AR: UCA Press, 1995), 163.

10. Powell A. Casey, *An Outline of the Civil War Campaigns and Engagements of the Washington Artillery of New Orleans* (Baton Rouge, LA: Claitor's Publishing Division, 1986), v, 53.

11. Ibid., 55.

12. Ibid., 63.

13. J. A. Chalaron, "Hood's Campaign at Murfreesboro," *Confederate Veteran* 11 (1903), 439.

14. Ibid., 440; Hughes, *Stephenson*, 299.

15. Casey, *Washington Artillery*, 85–86.

16. Hughes, *Stephenson*, 357–358.

17. Philip D. Stephenson, "Defence of Spanish Fort," *Southern Historical Society Papers* 39 (1914), 120.

18. Casey, *Washington Artillery*, 87; J. A. Chalaron, "The Slocomb's History," *Mobile Register*, January 3, 1896; Christopher C. Andrews, *History of the Campaign of Mobile* (New York, 1867), 238.

19. Civil War Centennial Commission, *Tennesseans in the Civil War: A Military History of Confederate and Union Units with Available Rosters of Personnel*, (Nashville, 1964), 143–144; John A. Thomas, "Mebane's Battery," *Confederate Veteran* 5 (1897), 167.

20. James G. Terry, compil., "Record of the Alabama State Artillery Company," *Alabama Historical Quarterly* 20 (1958), 303, 312.

21. Ibid., 313; Joseph Wheeler, "Alabama," in Clement Evans, ed., *Confederate Military History*, vol. 7 (Atlanta, 1899), 313.

22. George Little and James R. Maxwell, *A History of Lumsden's Battery C.S.A.* (Tuscaloosa: United Daughters of the Confederacy, 1905), 66; James R. Maxwell, "Lumsden's Battery in the Battle of Nashville," Lumsden's Battery File, Montgomery, Alabama Department of Archives and History, 103, 105.

23. Felix I. Robertson, "Service of Dr. James Thomas Searcy," *Confederate Veteran* 28 (1920), 251; Little and Maxwell, *Lumsden's Battery*, 3–4, 56.

24. George Little, *Memoirs of George Little* (Tuscaloosa, AL: Tuscaloosa Chamber of Commerce, 1929), 40–41.

25. Little and Maxwell, *Lumsden's Battery*, 5–7.

26. Ibid., 8–9; Little, *Memoirs*, 43.

27. G. Ward Hubbs, *Tuscaloosa: Portrait of an Alabama County* (Northridge, CA: Windsor Publications, Inc., 1987), 42.

28. Little and Maxwell, *Lumsden's Battery*, 19, 60–61.

29. Ibid., Insert 56–57, 63.

30. Ibid., 65.

31. John Kent Folmar, ed., *From That Terrible Field: Civil War Letters of James M. Williams, Twenty-First Alabama Infantry Volunteers* (University: University of Alabama Press, 1981), 8, 161.

32. Ibid., 53; Willis Brewer, *Alabama: Her History, Resources, War Record, and Public Men from 1540 to 1872* (Montgomery, 1872), 623.

33. Folmar, *Terrible Field*, 150.

34. Ibid., 101.

35. Ibid., 102, 115.

36. Ibid., 147, 149, 157.

37. Ibid., 151, 152.

38. Ibid., 157, 179.

39. Ibid., 158.

40. Andrews, *Campaign of Mobile*, 51.

CHAPTER 9

"Smith's Guerrillas"

As A. J. Smith's 16th Corps moved against Spanish Fort on March 27, 1865, the scrappy general was not in the best of moods. He had already had a close call when his column was ambushed at Bay Minette Bridge by James M. Williams' 21st Alabama Infantry. Riding with his leading regiment, the 81st Illinois, Smith had nearly been hit when the Rebels unleashed an unexpected volley from the shelter of the brush. Several men in the 81st Illinois had been wounded before the Yanks returned fire and the Rebels fell back.

About a mile from Spanish Fort, Smith ordered his divisions to deploy for battle, hoping to keep his movements secret from the Rebels. But as "Old Baldy" rode past the 49th Missouri Infantry, the soldiers began cheering him, and because the noise was loud enough to be heard in the Rebel fort, Smith sternly chided the troops for giving their position away. His fears were realized, for almost instantly a Rebel shell came sailing from the fort and dropped near the 49th Missouri. Startled, the men broke formation and backed away. "Stand up to it!" Smith yelled. "You had no business cheering."[1]

The awe with which "Smith's Guerrillas" regarded their chief helps explain why soldiers would risk enemy fire just to cheer him. Major General Andrew Jackson Smith, now a month short of his 50th birthday, had devoted over half of his life to the U.S. Army, mostly in the hard school of combat on the western frontier. Named after Andrew Jackson, his father's commanding officer in the War of 1812, Smith was an 1838 graduate of West Point, and he had been stationed at scattered army posts throughout the West until the outbreak of the Civil War. The balding, white-bearded veteran was made brigadier general in March 1862, and he had led his troops in hard fights from Arkansas Post to Vicksburg to the Red River to Nashville. Smith dubbed his soldiers the "lost tribes of Israel," and indeed their service had carried them to many a faraway place. Old Baldy was the only Federal commander to have defeated the feared Nathan Bedford Forrest in a clash at Tupelo, Mississippi, in July 1864. Smith "fights all the time," William T. Sherman once said. "He rides along with a word for any soldier that passes by," wrote Lieutenant Sidney Robinson of the 117th Illinois, "and when a gun fires he perks up his ears and before you can hardly think, he is there." Robinson added, "He has one fault; he gets pretty tight sometimes on the battlefield."[2]

Smith's soldiers received their nickname from Major General Nathaniel Banks during the Red River campaign, a poorly conceived and badly executed Federal operation aimed at the occupation of Shreveport, Louisiana—and control of potential millions of dollars in Rebel cotton—in the spring of 1864. With the cooperation of Admiral David Porter's Federal gunboats, Banks' 30,000 troops were to rendezvous with 15,000 troops under Frederick Steele and 10,000 more under A. J. Smith at Alexandria, Louisiana, before pushing upriver toward the Rebel garrison at Shreveport. Smith's corps reached Alexandria first, and when Banks saw them—an ill-equipped lot in worn clothing, with no tents, in need of wagons—he was flabbergasted. "What, in the name of Heaven," Banks blurted, "did Sherman send me these ragged guerrillas for?" But Banks soon had cause to respect these tough Midwesterners. After Richard Taylor smashed the Federal advance at Sabine Crossroads on April 8, 1864, Smith's Guerrillas saved Banks' army the next day by defeating Taylor at Pleasant Hill. Banks took advantage of the Rebel setback to withdraw his army, and the Federals hastily evacuated Alexandria on May 14. Porter, whose gunboats were nearly marooned due to the falling water level of the Red River, acknowledged Smith's Guerrillas as "the happiest looking soldiers ever seen under arms" and remarked that they were "the only part of the army that was not demoralized."[3]

Smith's Guerrillas were not anxious to continue serving under Banks, though. With the campaign finally at an end, Sergeant James K. Newton of the 14th Wisconsin wrote, "we are out of Banks' Dep't. I hope we may never go near it again." And Corporal Charles Henry Snedeker, a soldier in the 124th Illinois, wrote of the return of the Red River troops on May 24, 1864, "They look rough as though they had seen hard service. . . . They give Banks an awful name. Not one had a good word to speak for him. but all speak in praise of Gen. Smith."[4]

Smith and his Guerrillas furthered their reputation as a hard-fighting command by successfully beating back a Confederate attempt to invade

Missouri in October 1864. A month later the "lost tribes of Israel" traveled from Kansas City to Nashville where they helped to destroy Hood's army. When George H. Thomas observed Smith's corps advancing at Nashville, breaking ranks in their eagerness to move forward, he turned to Smith. "General," he said, "I notice your men are not keeping good formation." Old Baldy replied, "I only notice they are fighting like hell."[5]

Smith's capable division commanders were also an asset to the 16th Corps. Brawny and outspoken John McArthur, a 38-year-old Scottish immigrant blacksmith-turned-foundry owner, had an excellent combat record from the beginning of his service as captain of the Chicago Highland Guards to his promotion to brigadier general in March 1862. It was McArthur's division that had carried the Rebel earthworks on Shy's Hill at Nashville, where McArthur—annoyed that his men had not been ordered in sooner to deliver the coup de grace to Hood's army—urged his troops forward with orders "to fix bayonets, not to fire a shot and neither to halt nor cheer until they had gained the enemy's works." His three brigade commanders were equally seasoned veterans: Colonel William L. McMillen, a 35-year-old Ohioan who had served as a surgeon with the Russian Army in the Crimean War; Colonel Lucius F. Hubbard; and 39-year-old Colonel William R. Marshall.[6]

Kenner Garrard, a 37-year-old Kentuckian, studied at Harvard for a year before going on to West Point where he graduated 8th in his class in 1851. Like A. J. Smith, he had served as a cavalry officer out west, and by August 1862 he was colonel of the 146th New York Infantry. Although distinguished at Fredericksburg, Chancellorsville, and Gettysburg, and promoted to brigadier general in July 1863, Garrard raised the ire of William T. Sherman while leading Federal cavalry in the Atlanta campaign. Accusing Garrard of retreating "if he can see a horseman in the distance with a spyglass," Sherman replaced him with the aggressive Judson Kilpatrick. But Garrard went on to receive a brevet major general's promotion as Smith's 2nd Division commander at Nashville. Garrard's brigade commanders in March 1865 included Colonel John I. Rinaker, Colonel Charles L. Harris, and Brigadier General James I. Gilbert who had only recently been promoted. The 41-year-old Gilbert—a former lumberman, Indian trader, real estate salesman, and store owner—had no combat experience before the spring of 1864 when his regiment, the 27th Iowa Infantry, joined Smith's command for the Red River campaign. He was in charge of a brigade by December 1864 and earned praise for his service at Nashville.[7]

Eugene A. Carr, 35 years old, was another veteran Indian fighter. He had entered West Point at age 16 and graduated 19th in his class in 1850. The young cavalry officer was seriously wounded in a skirmish with Indians in

Texas in 1854. He was wounded three times at Pea Ridge in March 1862, had to be bandaged while sitting on his horse because he refused to leave the field, and received the Congressional Medal of Honor. Carr led a division at Vicksburg and was not with Smith at Nashville but took over his 3rd Division prior to the Mobile campaign. His brigade commanders were Colonels Jonathan B. Moore, Lyman W. Ward, and James L. Geddes.[8]

More than a fourth of Smith's corps sprang from the agricultural heartland of Illinois, which sent a quarter of a million boys to war for the Union. With Chicago becoming an important industrial center, and railroads rapidly crisscrossing the state, Illinois' population had doubled in the past decade. Though there was significant pro-Southern feeling and Copperhead activity in the southern part of the state, most of the Prairie State's people supported the Union. While not all Illinois soldiers claimed to be abolitionists or even idealists, most of them enlisted out of patriotic motives and resolved to see the conflict through for the good of the nation. The state's regiments, often formed from companies raised in the same hometowns and communities, gave them a sense of pride and comradeship.[9]

The 33rd Illinois Infantry, called the "Teacher's Regiment" or "Normal Regiment," was recruited in August 1861 on the campus of the Illinois State Normal School near Bloomington. Most of the volunteers were young, most of them teachers and college students. One company in the 33rd Illinois contained no less than thirteen college graduates, all of them enlisted as privates. The regiment was the pet project of the school's founder, Charles Edward Hovey, who became the unit's first colonel. Hovey was promoted to brigadier general and was distinguished in the action at Fort Hindman in January 1863, only to be wounded and retire from the army.[10]

Like their zealous counterparts in the Confederacy, most of the Illinois boys marched off to war with little military experience, although many of their officers had served in the Black Hawk War of 1832 or the Mexican War of 1846–1848. As in the Southern regiments, commissioned and noncommissioned officers were elected by the men of each company. Although enthusiasm was high, training was inadequately brief, and decent weapons were lacking. Recruits in the 33rd Illinois complained that their poor-quality Austrian muskets had an unsettling habit of discharging when placed at parade rest. Volunteers in the 47th Illinois (a unit that would serve with the 33rd Illinois in McArthur's division at Spanish Fort) drilled with hickory sticks in place of rifles. Now both regiments were equipped with Enfields or Springfields.[11]

The 33rd Illinois saw its first combat on the Missouri border. One weary soldier in the 33rd wrote home in May 1862 that he was nearly "gin out" by all the hard marching, but still his spirits were high. "Who would not be a soldier!" he wrote. But Rebel bushwhackers and toilsome marches were not the only problems the Illinois boys faced. Sickness devastated the army camps. "Our men lay sick by the hundreds," an Illinois officer wrote in October 1861. They began to see the face of the enemy at close range, as in the case of the naive young private in the 33rd who stopped to fill his canteen from a stream and looked up to find himself surrounded by enemy guerrillas. "Please, gentlemen," he implored them, "don't shoot, I'm not well."[12]

The "Normal Regiment" had come a long way since those early days. They had seen campaigning in Louisiana, had visited New Orleans, and had traveled to Brownsville on the Rio Grande. They joined Smith's corps too late to participate in the fighting at Nashville. Colonel Charles E. Lippencott, a hardy young doctor who had been to California in the 1850s and had returned to teach at the Normal School, now led the regiment, assigned to McArthur's division.

Also in McArthur's division was the 8th Wisconsin Infantry, the "Eagle Regiment," led by 35-year-old Lieutenant Colonel William B. Britton, a furniture manufacturer from Janesville who had been wounded at Nashville. Companies from all over the Badger State—like the Janesville Fire Zouaves, the Eau Claire Badgers, the Rough and Ready Guards from Fitchburg, and the Sheboygan County Independents—formed the 8th Wisconsin in September 1861. Farmers, including sizable numbers of Norwegian and German immigrants, filled the enlisted ranks, but there also were mechanics, carpenters, laborers, lumbermen, and blacksmiths. The 8th Wisconsin was most famous for its mascot "Old Abe," a 3-year-old bald eagle adopted as an orphaned eaglet by a frontier couple in northwestern Wisconsin and donated to the regiment in 1861. A living symbol of the Union, Old Abe boosted the soldiers' morale through thirty-seven battles and skirmishes. He was no longer with the 8th Wisconsin in the Mobile campaign. The men of the Eagle Regiment had voted to "retire" Old Abe in September 1864, and the old veteran spent his remaining years on public display at the State Capitol in Madison until his death in 1881.[13]

Kenner Garrard's division, moved up to the Fort Blakely front on April 3, contained some rugged commands, and none had seen more hard fighting than the 21st Missouri Infantry. Missourians made up about 15 percent of the 16th Corps. Formed in February 1862 from two of Nathaniel Lyon's Union Home Guard regiments, the 21st Missouri was first commanded by Colonel David Moore, the son of Irish immigrants and a veteran of the Mexican War. The Missourians had already been through some scrappy campaigning in their home state before being sent east of the Mississippi, much as their Rebel counterparts in Cockrell's Missouri brigade. Some of the young officers and enlisted men who would remain with the regiment to the end included Sergeant Nehemiah D. (Nick) Starr, a Quaker who had taught school before the war; Lieutenant Henry McGonigle, an Irish Catholic from Pennsylvania; Captain Charles Yust, a German immigrant who spoke only broken English but was a tough and wily veteran of the Prussian army; and Quartermaster Sergeant Charles W. Tracy, a young engineer from Canton. William H. Matlick was just 16 when he joined the regiment; Michael Cashman at 15 lied about his age to get in. All of them had seen arduous service since the regiment was formed.[14]

The 21st Missouri was the first Federal command to be engaged at Shiloh in April 1862. When the Missouri boys ran headlong into the Confederate surprise attack, Moore recalled, "it appeared like a volcano at full blast . . . the air was filled with lead and iron." As the Rebel assault intensified, the 21st Missouri participated in the heavy fighting in the Hornet's Nest, where they helped hold off the Confederate attack until finally overwhelmed. Many of the Missourians were killed or captured, and Moore was wounded in the leg; but the next day the balance of the regiment participated in the Federal counterattack that turned the battle into a Union victory. The 21st Missouri lost eighteen killed, forty-six wounded, and fifty-eight missing.[15]

Fighting at Iuka and Corinth followed, then garrison duty at Memphis, and part of the regiment took part in the Red River campaign. The 21st Missouri joined Smith's 16th Corps in June 1864 and reveled in his victory over Forrest at Tupelo, where—after unleashing a point-blank volley into the charging Rebels—the Missourians counterattacked "with a yell like that of demons" and pushed the enemy from the field. In December 1864 came the shattering victory over Hood at Nashville, where the Missourians stormed Shy's Hill amidst "the heaviest musketry and cannonading I ever heard," according to one soldier.[16]

In January 1865, the 21st Missouri was in camp at Eastport, Mississippi. The rigors of the Nashville campaign with its cold and snow had left many in the regiment sick, and rations were low. During the month new recruits came in, and several veterans were lost to disease or death. Nick Starr, one of the original sergeants in the regiment who was recovering from near pneumonia, was promoted to 1st lieutenant. Colonel David Moore was promoted to brigadier general. Colonel Charles W. Tracy, who had originally been quartermaster sergeant in the regiment, took over command of the 21st Missouri in February 1865. There were 210 soldiers out of 350 in April 1865 who had been with the regiment from the beginning.[17]

Many of the Missourians were weary of the war now. Lieutenant Charles C. Morrey, a 34-year-old former 1st sergeant soon to be detached from the regiment for service with the Ambulance Corps, wrote early in March that he was "tired and would like to come home; but I take things as patiently as possible for there is no use to fret. The better a man is satisfied, the less trouble he will have, and I try to think of home as little as possible." Starr wrote his fiancée, "I do want to come home more particularly on your account than anything else."[18]

Garrard's division also contained the 117th Illinois Infantry, known as the "McKendree Regiment" because of its association with McKendree College in the town of Lebanon 20 miles east of St. Louis. Colonel Risdon M. Moore, a 38-year-old St. Clair County native and McKendree graduate, had tutored students in Latin and Greek and taught mathematics and astronomy. A popular instructor, Moore stood nearly 6 feet tall, with blue eyes, brown hair, and a ruddy complexion. He was a staunch Republican and had actually met Lincoln twice. Moore's father had fought in the Black Hawk War of 1832 and was now an officer in the 32nd Illinois Infantry. Two grandfathers had fought in the Revolutionary War, and his brother was an officer in the 40th Illinois.[19]

Thirty-year-old Lieutenant Colonel Jonathan ("Bigfoot") Merriam was a towering figure at 6 feet 2½ inches, 240 pounds, with dark eyes and hair. He was just 12 years old when his father died leaving him and his brother with the responsibility of looking after their mother and running the family farm in Tazewell County. Merriam taught in a rural school for a while and later married one of his former students. Merriam was a student at McKendree but did not finish due to health problems. The tragic death of his wife in 1861 left him with a daughter to raise, and he left her with his mother while he enlisted in the 117th Illinois in September 1862. "Bigfoot" later married Lucy White, the regimental chaplain's daughter, in November 1864.[20]

The 117th was filled with men like Captain Henry Clay Fike, the 31-year-old quartermaster officer from Mascoutah, a McKendree graduate and a veteran teacher and high school principal. Twenty-three-year-old Lieutenant Benjamin R. Hieronymus loved to tell how during an action at Meridian, Mississippi, in February 1864, General William T. Sherman personally ordered him to advance with the regiment's colors. His younger brother Thomas was in the same company. Hieronymus kept a diary, as did Corporal Richard H. Saunders, a farmer from Marine, who turned 21 on March 26, 1865. Corporal Adolphus Phillip Wolf, from Edwardsville in Madison County, was 23 years old; after serving four months in the 19th Pennsylvania Infantry, he enlisted in the 117th Illinois and became color bearer for Company F. His brother Otto, who was 15 when he enlisted in the 117th, was a drummer boy.[21]

Formed in November 1862, the McKendree Regiment was primed to be sent down the Mississippi to take part in Federal operations against

Vicksburg. But Sherman dismissed their Belgian rifles as "worthless"; and because better weapons were unavailable, the regiment remained at Memphis during the Vicksburg campaign. The 117th Illinois finally received Springfield muskets but saw little action until January 1864 when the regiment was assigned to Smith's corps. The McKendree boys took part in the Meridian action in February 1864, the Red River campaign in the spring, the engagement at Tupelo in July, and the decisive Union victory at Nashville in December.[22]

"I never was so near give out in my life," Adolph Wolf wrote of his experience at Nashville. "We had to charge nearly two miles on a run with a heavy load on our backs and the mud was shoemouth deep." Wolf told of missing his chance to capture a Rebel flag from one of the beaten defenders of Shy's Hill. "I was the first to see him," Wolf wrote, "but was so near tired out that I told one of the boys standing by (Wilbur Moore) to get him and he did so." The Rebel captive turned out to be a color bearer who surrendered his flag to Moore. "Now, may I not box my own ears?" an exasperated Wolf wrote. "I think I would be justified in doing so. Instead of having a sixty-day furlough, I am here living on half-rations. It is too bad but serves me right."[23]

Soldiers in E. A. Carr's division also had seen some heavy combat. The 44th Missouri, in Jonathan B. Moore's brigade, suffered the highest casualties in the Union army at Franklin: thirty-four killed, thirty-seven wounded, and ninety-two missing. In the same engagement, Lieutenant Colonel Joseph Stockton's 72nd Illinois lost ten men killed, sixty-six wounded, and seventy-five missing, and every field officer sustained wounds.[24]

Also in Moore's brigade was the 33rd Wisconsin, where 37-year-old Jerome Burbank served as an army surgeon. Jerome helped raise eight siblings after the death of his father, but by 1847 he was off to embark on a medical career. An 1851 graduate of the medical college in Keokuk, Iowa, Burbank established his practice in southern Wisconsin in the little town of Avon, where he married Jerusha Kinney, daughter of a justice of the peace, in 1853. The couple had four children before the war. Jerome was a loyal Republican and took a commission in the 22nd Wisconsin Infantry in 1862. A dedicated physician and devoted family man, he wrote often to Jerusha, his "Absent Companion," always concerned about the well-being of his wife and children. When chronic dysentery forced him to leave in September 1863, every officer and private in the regiment signed a certificate of appreciation for his service. By July 1864, he was back in uniform as surgeon in the 33rd Wisconsin.[25]

In Lyman W. Ward's brigade in Carr's division, 22-year-old James K. Newton was a sergeant in the 14th Wisconsin Infantry, which had seen action in the Red River campaign and at Nashville. James grew up on his parents' farm in DePere, Wisconsin, not far from Green Bay, with three boys and five girls in the family. The 6-foot-tall, 180-pound young man was teaching in a small one-room county school when he signed up for military duty in October 1861. James' older brother Edward had already enlisted, and James felt honor-bound to help defend the Union. A Republican and an admirer of Lincoln, James never became an abolitionist, but like many young Northerners, he was a patriotic and resolute soldier. His introduction to army life was "one of the greatest times I ever went through," and he was proud of his company, the "best drilled, best behaved, and best looking" in the regiment. James' first action was at Shiloh in April 1862. "All I need say about the 14th," he wrote, "is that they *didn't run*."[26]

Newton was captured during the Confederate attack on Corinth in October 1862, but in December he was exchanged and made his way back to the 14th Wisconsin. His letters to his parents were full of perception and humor. Although he had no sympathy for the Confederate leaders, he felt no hatred toward Southerners in general. "I can't pity the rebels themselves," he wrote from Vicksburg, "but it does seem too bad for the women and children in the city." On July 4, 1863, the 14th Wisconsin entered Vicksburg proudly at the head of their brigade. The young Wisconsin soldier prayed for a conclusion of the conflict and wrote, "If the settlement of this war was left to the Enlisted men of both sides we would soon go home."[27]

In another company in the 14th Wisconsin, 18-year-old Elisha Stockwell had just been promoted to corporal on March 1, 1865. Elisha grew up in Alma in the dairy and cattle country of Jackson County in the western part of the state. In February 1862, he signed up with the 14th Wisconsin at the age of 15. In his baptism of fire at Shiloh, on April 7, 1862, he was wounded twice, the only time he was hurt during the war. By March 1865, he was a seasoned veteran and a newly married man of one year (he had wed Katherine Hurley of Milwaukee while home on furlough), so he felt well qualified to advise his brother Frank about joining the army. He wrote his mother on March 31, "if he knows when he is well off he had better stay to home. . . . I think he will do more good to home raising murphys and sowbelly."[28]

Not all Federal soldiers were volunteers, and conscription played a major role in filling the ranks of Union regiments. About fifteen conscripts were assigned to Elisha Stockwell's company before the Mobile campaign began. One Irish draftee in particular, Stockwell wrote, seemed to enjoy rankling the volunteers with his defense of the Rebels' right to be left alone. He said that if he found himself in combat with them, he would fire high so as not to hit them. This angered many of the soldiers who wanted to know why he didn't join up with the Rebs if he felt that way about them. The fellow would just laugh at them. Stockwell went on to say that the man became a good soldier and was one of the first to apply for his pension on returning home. "I think he talked for the sake of an argument," Stockwell concluded.[29]

Carr's 3rd Brigade had been added to the 16th Corps since Nashville and included the 81st Illinois (veteran of the Red River and Nashville campaigns) plus the 108th and 124th Illinois and the 8th Iowa. The brigade commander, 37-year-old Scottish-born Colonel James L. Geddes, was a former officer in both the British Army in India—where he served in the elite Royal Horse Guards—and the Canadian Army. A farmer and teacher in Iowa, he began the Civil War as lieutenant colonel of the 8th Iowa in September 1861. Wounded and captured at Shiloh, Geddes was exchanged and saw combat at Vicksburg before joining Smith's Guerrillas in January 1865.[30]

Lieutenant Colonel William B. Bell, a former blacksmith, now led Geddes' old command, the 8th Iowa Infantry, "distinguished for discipline and gallantry," according to C. C. Andrews. Formed in September 1861 in the Mississippi River town of Davenport, the regiment's eager young soldiers headed downriver by steamer toward St. Louis, burning for battle although they had no arms or uniforms. They picked up their weapons in Keokuk, but they were not pleased with the Belgian muskets that the Iowans called "pumpkin slingers." Some of the barrels on the weapons were crooked, and soldiers joked that they could shoot around hills. At St. Louis they received uniforms and equipment and also their first taste of the infamous hardtack, which nearly caused a mutiny. Just two weeks of training, and then the Iowans were off for several weeks of fruitless campaigning in Missouri. By the time they went into winter quarters in Sedalia, many were dying from disease.[31]

On April 6, 1862, the 8th Iowa was conspicuous in defending the Hornet's Nest at Shiloh from a determined Rebel assault led by none other than Randall L. Gibson. The graycoats finally took the battery the Iowans had been ordered to protect, but the 8th Iowa launched a vigorous counterattack and recaptured the guns. But as the afternoon wore on, the Union position became hopeless. "We were completely surrounded and whipped," one Iowa officer wrote, "but did not know it." The 8th Iowa was captured around sundown. Beaten but still proud, Colonel Geddes reported, "I claim the honor for my regiment of being the last to leave the advanced line of our army on the battle-field of Shiloh on Sunday, April 6." The regiment lost 30 men killed, 72 wounded (several of them shot down when they refused to surrender their muskets and began bashing them against trees), and 379 missing or captured, many of them not released until October 1862. The 8th

Iowa was reorganized in January 1863, participated in the siege of Vicksburg, and guarded the railroad in Mississippi for the rest of the year. The regiment was stationed at Memphis early in 1864 and remained there until January 1865 when they joined the 16th Corps.[32]

The 124th Illinois Infantry (the "Excelsior Regiment") was raised in August 1862, took part in engagements at Port Gibson and Champion's Hill in 1863 and in the siege of Vicksburg. Charles Henry Snedeker, a 28-year-old enlisted man in Company H, wrote in his diary on the surrender of Vicksburg, "The most quiet fourth of July that I ever knew." A modest, religious man, Snedeker received corporal's stripes in January 1864, obtained a welcome thirty-day furlough home in June, and returned to the 124th still stationed at Vicksburg. On Christmas Eve, news came of the defeat of Hood's army at Nashville. "A Gill of Whiskey is issued to each man to keep Christmas with," Snedeker recorded. Soon the regiment was added to the 16th Corps.[33]

Smith's corps had the most extensive and the most recent hard combat experience of any of the troops in Canby's army, and spirits were high after their victory over Hood at Nashville. After Grant assigned the 18,000 soldiers to Canby in January 1865, a flotilla of forty-three river steamers and seven barges was dispatched to carry them—along with 5,000 of James Wilson's cavalrymen with their horses and equipment—down the Tennessee, Ohio, and Mississippi Rivers to New Orleans. Elisha Stockwell recalled, "we concluded we were going to have a boat ride, where to, we had no idea and cared less. It would beat marching anyway." Even Smith was unsure of the corps' destination. When he wired for instructions, he received a cryptic reply from Henry Halleck. "Continue on your exodus as the Wandering Tribe of Israel," the chief of staff advised. "On reaching the land of Canby you will have a number and name."[34]

Smith landed his entire force at Vicksburg only to learn the following day that only Wilson's cavalry was to remain there. Smith's infantry had to drag all their equipment back on the steamers and continue their "wandering" down the Mississippi to New Orleans. They arrived there on February 21 and went into camp on the site of Andrew Jackson's encampment prior to the Battle of New Orleans in 1815. Smith's Guerrillas had two weeks to enjoy in the Crescent City. On March 1, Charles Henry Snedeker took in the sights, enjoying the statues of Jackson and Henry Clay and the marketplace with its fresh vegetables and fruit. "Nearly every man in the Regt. visited the City today," he wrote.[35]

"One would hardly think that they knew anything about cold weather down here," James Newton observed in a letter to his parents, noting that he had seen rain every day except one since arriving in New Orleans. Newton speculated that the destination of Smith's corps was Mobile and doubted that the Rebels could hold out much longer. "I begin to think that they'll get scared & capitulate," he predicted, "as soon as we *start for 'em.*" A few days later Newton received a letter from his mother and jokingly responded, "I had begun to think that you had forgotten all about 'poor me' now that I had got so far down in this heathenish country." James told her to expect an overcoat and blanket that he had just mailed home and went on to explain that he would not need them because the weather was turning warm. "I advise you to hang them out doors & maybe scald them," he added, "for there's no telling how many tenants they have."[36]

Relations with the New Orleans townspeople were generally good, but Elisha Stockwell described one heated encounter involving an irate "French Creole" woman who rushed out of her house to confront several soldiers near her garden. Sleeves rolled up and ready for business, cursing like a man, she lit into the Yanks calling them "nigger thieves." They laughingly assured her they were not interested in her vegetables, but she continued berating them and "told them to come up there two at a time and she would lick the whole bunch." Stockwell headed back to camp having witnessed enough of the scene.[37]

As their stay in New Orleans drew to a close, Smith's Guerrillas found themselves seaborne once again, heading on transports for Dauphin Island (where Canby's army was assembling) and ailing from the seasickness that had afflicted the 13th Corps on its passage. In the 6th Minnesota Infantry, 40-year-old Corporal Andrew Thompson wrote in his diary on March 7, "soon as We got in to the salt Watter about all got Sea sick and then we had a Time of it all day Vomiting." A tall, fair-haired Irish immigrant, Thompson had received a federal land grant for a farm in Greenwood Township, Minnesota, in 1860. He had became a U.S. citizen and enlisted in the 6th Minnesota in August 1862.[38]

Whereas the officers occupied the cabins of the transports in relative comfort, the enlisted soldiers were packed together on decks and in holds "like so many cattle or hogs," according to Charles Henry Snedeker. Only by lying on top of one another could Snedeker and his comrades lie down, and at one point during the voyage someone accidentally spilled a pail of water under them. A soldier in the 119th Illinois wrote, "This riding on the seas is disturbing to a well regulated stomach, but we heaved with the sea, and finally landed."[39]

Elisha Stockwell also described the trip to Dauphin Island and his first experience on salt water beyond the sight of land. The day was still, Stockwell wrote, "but the white-caps were rolling, and it looked plenty rough enough to suit most of us, especially with that old tub of a boat." Stockwell could see the sea gulls following overhead and porpoises trailing alongside the craft, a sign of a coming storm according to some of the old hands on board. Stockwell and his mates were relieved when they finally reached Dauphin Island, which appeared "embarrassingly small."[40]

While they were camped on Dauphin Island, Smith's Guerrillas enjoyed a brand new experience for many of them. A delighted Private Byron Cloyd Bryner of the 47th Illinois Infantry wrote, "the oyster beds furnished a new and hitherto unknown addition to the army rations." "Traditional army food was wholly neglected," Colonel Lucius F. Hubbard commented. Stockwell and his mates waded out into the Bay to catch oysters and groped with their bare feet under the water until they could feel them. They were "the first raw oyesters that I ever ate," he wrote, and "went down as though they were greased. what a Soldier cant eat no one else nead to try to." But some had more than their fill of the delicacy. Surgeon Jerome Burbank wrote his wife on March 21, "I have eaten oysters boiled, oysters stewed and oysters raw until I do not care any more about oysters than I would a nice chicken well cooked."[41]

Until orders came to begin the long-awaited campaign, the Yankee soldiers had little to do but pass the time on Dauphin Island. They amused themselves with games of marbles, cards, and wrestling. Jerome Burbank was impressed with the site for his field hospital on the beach with its sugary white sand. He wrote Jerusha on March 15, "I think this is the healthiest location that we have occupied since I have been with the regt."[42]

All was not entirely pleasant for everyone. On March 18, a brigade of Federal troops landed at Cedar Point north of Dauphin Island. The movement was a feint aimed at diverting Maury's attention to the western side of Mobile Bay, while Canby massed his troops for an offensive on the eastern shore. (After brief skirmishing with Confederate troops from Mobile, the Federals withdrew on March 22 and headed for the eastern shore.) On picket duty at Cedar Point, Private Edward Q. Nye of the 33rd Illinois wrote in his diary, "The mosquitoes are out in force. I never saw anything like it. They sting like bees." He added that they "seem bound to have their fill of Yankee blood, which luxury they have not been able to procure until lately."[43]

Nye and his comrades would see much more of the "infernal mosquitoes," as the 16th Corps crossed Mobile Bay by transports and landed at Dannelly's Mills, the rendezvous point for Canby's army on the Fish River. Nye commented on the heavily wooded Alabama terrain and on the brownish water of the Fish River, not very wide but just broad enough for a vessel to turn around in. "Our company is on pickett," he wrote on March 23. "I seen several Rebs 500–600 yards off. We soon made them travel."[44]

Snedeker took note of the religious activity in camp. About twenty Illinois soldiers were baptized in the river with a sizable crowd in attendance. Andrew Thompson was doing picket duty on March 24 and recorded that all was quiet at sundown as he rested on a log.[45]

By March 25, the 16th Corps was in motion again, marching north toward Spanish Fort where, Nye predicted, "we will be apt to have a hard fight." Snedeker recorded, "I did not see a house nor any kind of a building during the march." The rolling terrain, Jerome Burbank observed, was covered with "pitch pine, not a tree of any other timber to be seen during the day." He wrote that the sandy soil, muddy from recent rains, would not support the wagons, which sank down to their axles. The troops were foraging, and Nye wrote on March 26, "we have supplied ourselves with all the chickens, sweet potatoes, fresh pork, corn meal and molasses that we need for supper and breakfast."[46]

On March 27, the Federals closed in on the defenders of Spanish Fort. Snedeker wrote in his diary of the skirmish between the 81st Illinois and James M. Williams' Rebel infantry. Federal sharpshooters were now within 800 yards of the Confederate bastion. "They shell us terrifically," Nye wrote, "cutting the pine trees all around us. We have got them pretty well hemmed in."[47]

Smith's aggressive division commanders expected to attack Spanish Fort on March 27. As the 16th Corps deployed for battle, Carr sent Geddes' brigade ahead, and the 8th Iowa plus the 108th and 124th Illinois pushed the Rebel skirmishers back to their rifle pits. After noon the rain began, and impatient soldiers waited, wet and anxious, for the orders to go forward. The Rebels were on the run, Carr thought. Now was the time for a general advance, and the works might be taken without a costly siege. Smith agreed. He requested Canby's consent to attack. But only two divisions, Carr's and McArthur's, were in place, and the deliberate Canby questioned the wisdom of an assault. He asked McArthur what he thought of the situation. "My division will go in there if ordered," the Scot replied, "but if the rebels stay by their guns it will cost the lives of half my men." Canby shook his head. "It won't pay," he decided.[48]

Smith's corps lost ninety-one men killed and wounded on March 27. Casualties included Lieutenant W. E. Smith of the 124th Illinois, along with his color sergeant, and Captain W. M. Bullock of the 108th Illinois. Spanish Fort appeared to be a powerful stronghold, Stockwell recalled, "it would be hard to take by storm." Snedeker wrote, "Soon after dark we began building Breastworks and were at it nearly all night."[49]

Jerome Burbank set up his temporary field hospital behind a hill out of the line of fire. Division casualties were heavy that day, and two of the wounded had arms amputated, no legs yet. Sitting under a tree and using his amputating case as a writing table, he wrote Jerusha on March 29 that he had observed some of the big Rebel shells pass overhead, "but they were all shot high so they did not affect us, only to make us skulk as they passed." Burbank assessed the strength of the Rebel fort and the task that lay before them: "I antisipate that they have strong works and men enough to hold us at bey a few days at least, and if they can reinforce at pleasure they will hold us a long time."[50]

NOTES

1. Christopher C. Andrews, *History of the Campaign of Mobile* (New York, 1867), 51–52.

2. Ezra J. Warner, *Generals in Blue: Lives of the Union Commanders* (Baton Rouge: Louisiana State University Press, 1964), 454; Leslie Anders, *The Twenty-First Missouri: From Home Guard to Union Regiment* (Westport, CT: Greenwood Press, 1975), 209; Edwin G. Gerling, *The One Hundred Seventeenth Illinois Infantry Volunteers (The McKendree Regiment), 1862–1865* (Highland, IL: Author, 1992), 8–9.

3. Gerling, *One Hundred Seventeenth Illinois*, 17; Bruce Catton, *The Centennial History of the Civil War*, vol. 3, *Never Call Retreat* (Garden City: Doubleday & Co., 1965), 339.

4. Stephen E. Ambrose, ed., *A Wisconsin Boy in Dixie: The Selected Letters of James K. Newton* (Madison: University of Wisconsin Press, 1961), xiv; Mildred Britton, ed., *The Civil War Diary of Charles Henry Snedeker*, 1966, Auburn University Archives, RG844 (hereafter cited as *Snedeker Diary*).

5. Byron Cloyd Bryner, *Bugle Echoes: The Story of Illinois 47th Infantry* (Springfield, IL, 1905), 150.

6. Warner, *Generals in Blue*, 288–289; Mark Mayo Boatner III, *The Civil War Dictionary* (New York: David McKay Co., Inc., 1959), 514, 537; Henry Stone, "Repelling Hood's Invasion of Tennessee," in Robert Underwood Johnson and Clarence Clough Buel, eds., *Battles and Leaders of the Civil War*, vol. 4 (New York: Castle Books, 1956), 463, 464.

7. Warner, *Generals in Blue*, 167–168, 174–175, 622 n. 141.

8. Ibid., 70–71; Chester G. Hearn, *Mobile Bay and the Mobile Campaign: The Last Great Battles of the Civil War* (Jefferson, NC: McFarland and Company, Inc., Publishers, 1993), 162.

9. Victor Hicken, *Illinois in the Civil War* (Urbana: University of Illinois Press, 1966), vii–ix.

10. Ibid., 8; Warner, *Generals in Blue*, 236;

11. Hicken, *Illinois*, 8–9, 14.

12. Ibid., 16–18.

13. Richard H. Zeitlin, *Old Abe the War Eagle* (Madison: State Historical Society of Wisconsin, 1986), 1, 3–4, 65, 91.

14. Anders, *Twenty-First Missouri*, 49–52.

15. William B. Allmon, "The 21st Missouri," *America's Civil War* (September 1996), 12, 16.

16. Ibid., 82; Anders, *Twenty-First Missouri*, 212.

17. Anders, *Twenty-First Missouri*, 229.

18. Ibid., 223–224.

19. Gerling, *One Hundred Seventeenth Illinois*, 1–2.

20. Ibid., 5–6.

21. Ibid., 145, 155, 185, 200.

22. Ibid., 15.

23. Ibid., 93.

24. Stone, "Repelling Hood's Invasion," 453.

25. Sylvia Burbank Morris, *Jerome: To My Beloved Absent Companion: Letters of a Civil War Surgeon to His Wife at Home, Caring for Their Family* (Cullman, AL: Author, 1996), 9–13.

26. Ambrose, *Wisconsin Boy*, xi–xiv; emphasis in original.

27. Ibid., xiii.

28. Byron R. Abernethy, ed., *Private Elisha Stockwell, Jr., Sees the Civil War* (Norman: University of Oklahoma Press, 1958), ix, 206.

29. Ibid., 160.

30. Boatner, *Civil War Dictionary*, 328.

31. Andrews, *Campaign of Mobile*, 53; Daryl A. Bailey, "The 8th Iowa," *America's Civil War* (May 1996), 8; Kathy Fisher, *In the Beginning There Was Land: A History of Washington County, Iowa* (Washington, IA: Washington County Historical Society, 1978), 292.

32. Bailey, "8th Iowa," 62–63.

33. Britton, *Snedeker Diary*.

34. Hearn, *Mobile Campaign*, 148; Abernethy, *Stockwell*, 152.

35. Hearn, *Mobile Campaign*, 148–149; Britton, *Snedeker Diary*.

36. Ambrose, *Wisconsin Boy*, 143–145.

37. Abernethy, *Stockwell*, 156–157.

38. Andrew Thompson, Diary, 1864–1865, Auburn University Archives, RG 446, 46. (hereafter cited as Thompson Diary).

39. Britton, *Snedeker Diary*; Anders, *Twenty-First Missouri*, 224.

40. Abernethy, *Stockwell*, 157.

41. Bryner, *Bugle Echoes*, 151; Zeitlin, *Old Abe*, 73; Abernethy, *Stockwell*, 158, 205; Morris, *Jerome*, 216.

42. Abernethy, *Stockwell*, 160; Morris, *Jerome*, 214.

43. Edward Q. Nye, Diary, in "We Will Be Apt to Have a Hard Fight," *Baldwin Today*, April 10–April 11, 1991, C1 (hereafter cited as Nye Diary).

44. Ibid.

45. Britton, *Snedeker Diary*; Thompson Diary, 47.

46. Nye Diary, C1, C5; Britton, *Snedeker Diary*; Morris, *Jerome*, 217; Nye Diary, 5C.

47. Nye Diary, C5.

48. Hearn, *Mobile Campaign*, 162–164.

49. Andrews, *Campaign of Mobile*, 53, 58; Abernethy, *Stockwell*, 160; Britton, *Snedeker Diary*.

50. Morris, *Jerome*, 218–219.

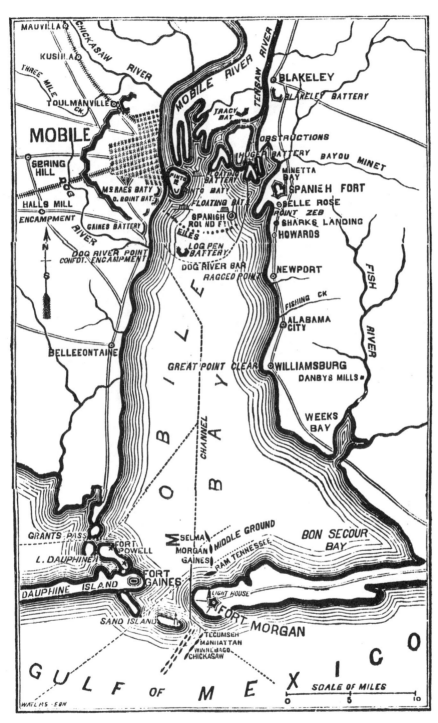

Mobile and Defenses, 1865. (Alabama Department of Archives and History, Montgomery, Alabama)

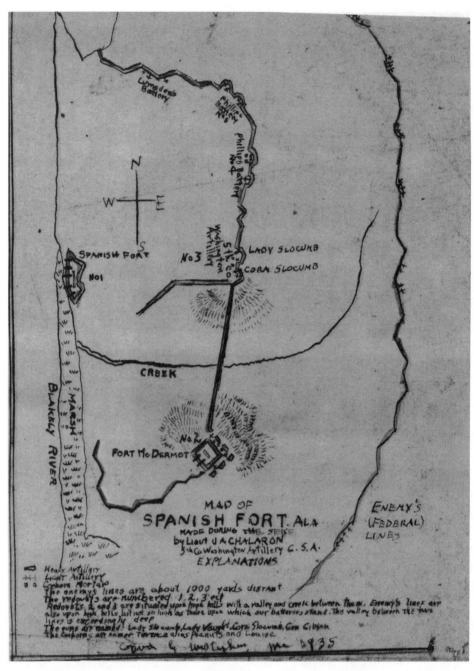

Confederate Defenses at Spanish Fort, from a sketch by Lieutenant J. A. Chalaron. (Alabama Department of Archives and History, Montgomery, Alabama)

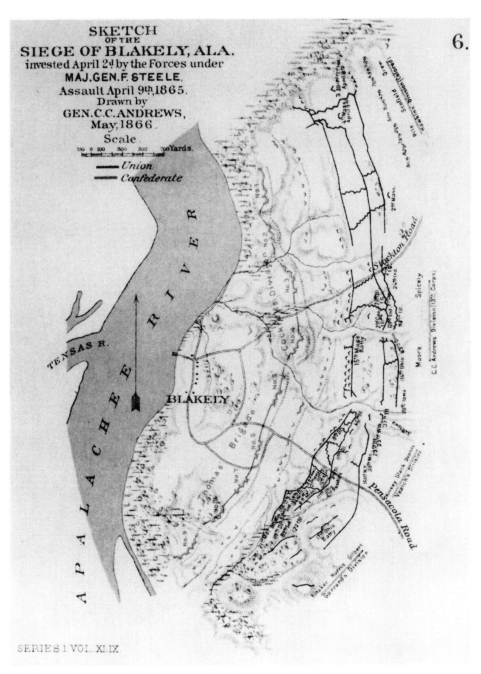

Siege of Fort Blakely, from a sketch by Brigadier General C. C. Andrews. (William Stanley Hoole Special Collections Library, The University of Alabama)

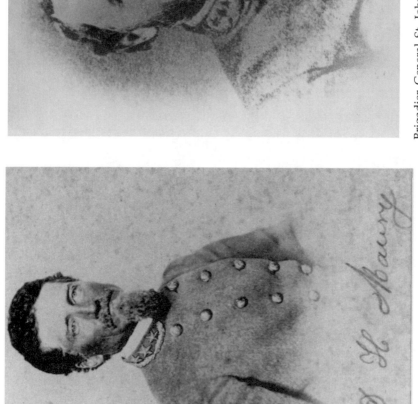

Brigadier General St. John R. Liddell commanded Fort Blakely, last major Confederate stronghold to fall to a Federal assault. (Reproduced from the Collections of the LIBRARY OF CONGRESS)

Major General Dabney H. Maury supervised the Confederate defense of Mobile. (Alabama Department of Archives and History, Montgomery, Alabama)

Brigadier General Francis M. Cockrell, commander of the Missouri brigade, rendered able assistance in the defense of Fort Blakely. (Alabama Department of Archives and History, Montgomery, Alabama)

Brigadier General Randall L. Gibson conducted a brilliant defense of Spanish Fort. (Alabama Department of Archives and History, Montgomery, Alabama)

Brigadier General Bryan M. Thomas. His teenage Alabama soldiers fought well at Fort Blakely. (Alabama Department of Archives and History, Montgomery, Alabama)

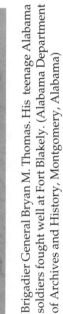

Colonel William S. Barry commanded the Mississippi brigade defending Fort Blakely. (Courtesy of Mississippi Department of Archives and History)

Lieutenant General Richard Taylor surrendered the last Confederate forces east of the Mississippi. (Alabama Department of Archives and History, Montgomery, Alabama)

Brigadier General James T. Holtzclaw commanded the Alabama brigade at Spanish Fort. (Alabama Department of Archives and History, Montgomery, Alabama)

Major General Gordon Granger commanded the Federal XIII corps. (Reproduced from the Collections of the LIBRARY OF CONGRESS)

Major General E.R.S. Canby directed the Federal campaign to capture Mobile. He was under pressure to take the Gulf City. (Reproduced from the Collections of the LIBRARY OF CONGRESS)

Major General Frederick Steele commanded the Federal column from Pensacola that invested Fort Blakely. (Seward R. Osborne, Jr. Collection, U.S. Army Military History Institute)

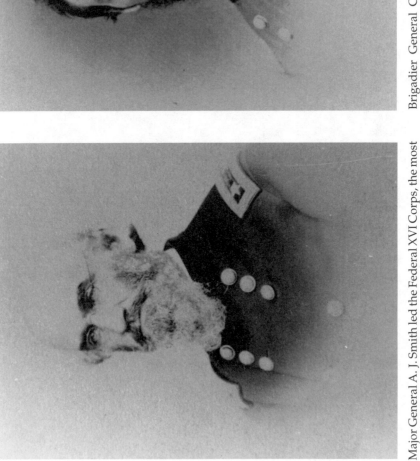

Major General A. J. Smith led the Federal XVI Corps, the most combat-hardened troops in Canby's army. (Randy Beck Collection, U.S. Army Military History Institute)

Brigadier General C. C. Andrews. His division saw the toughest fighting in the storming of Fort Blakely. (Albion Historical Society Collection, U.S. Army Military History Institute)

Captain Charles Lumsden. His Alabama artillerists made things hot for Federals at Spanish Fort. (William Stanley Hoole Special Collections Library, The University of Alabama)

Colonel David Coleman. His North Carolina troops in Ector's brigade made the last stand at Spanish Fort. (Courtesy of the North Carolina Division of Archives and History, Raleigh)

Die-Hard Rebels. Brothers William H., Benjamin H., and Francis M. Cathey served in the 39th North Carolina Infantry, one of the regiments defending Spanish Fort. (Courtesy of the North Carolina Division of Archives and History, Raleigh)

King of the Battlefield. Big guns, like these Columbiads manned by Rebel troops at Pensacola in 1861, were used in siege operations at Spanish Fort and Blakely. (Real War Photos)

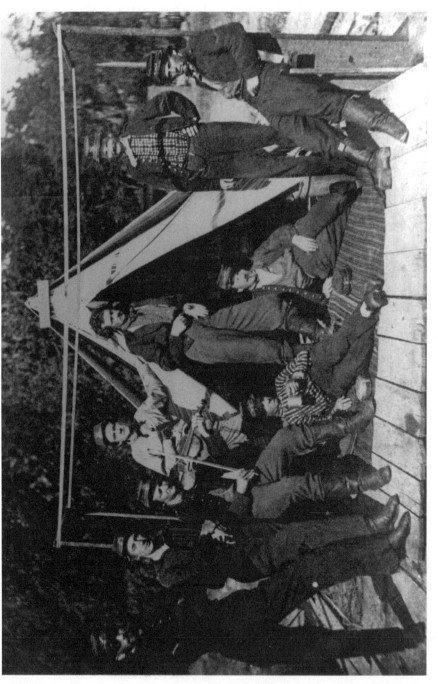

Defiant Rebel Gunners. Members of the 5th Company, Washington Artillery of New Orleans, in a photo taken early in the war. (U.S. Army Military History Institute)

Yankee Firepower. Captain Clayton Cox's battery, 1st Indiana Heavy Artillery in a photo taken in 1863. (National Archives)

Captain Lysander K. Weeks, 8th Iowa Infantry, was commended for bravery in his regiment's assault on Spanish Fort. (Roger Davis Collection, U.S. Army Military History Institute)

Captain Thomas N. Stevens, 28th Wisconsin Infantry, served in the siege of Spanish Fort. He believed that the war would not be over until the last Rebel stronghold was conquered. (U.S. Army Military History Institute)

Federal Monitor. The U.S.S. *Osage* in 1864. A Rebel naval mine sank the vessel on March 29, 1865, with the loss of four sailors. (Real War Photos)

Terror from under the Sea. Rebel submarines used in the Mobile campaign were patterned after the *David*, seen here in Charleston in 1865. (Real War Photos)

The Last Grand Assault. In this sketch from *Harper's Weekly*, May 27, 1865, the 83rd Ohio Infantry attacks Redoubt 4, the strongest part of the Confederate lines at Fort Blakely, while members of the 15th Massachusetts Light Artillery lend their support.

The 69th Indiana Infantry advances in the assault on Redoubt 4, held by Cockrell's Missouri Brigade, April 9, 1865. (Originally published in *Harper's Weekly*, May 27, 1865)

Terrain in front of Redoubt 4 at Fort Blakely. This modern photo shows a portion of the difficult terrain that Federal attackers had to overcome. (Author's photo)

Colonel Thomas Kinney, 119th Illinois Infantry, led the attack on Confederate Redoubt 9 at Fort Blakely. (Roger Hunt Collection, U.S. Army Military History Institute)

Members of the 117th Illinois Infantry. More than a quarter of Canby's troops in the Mobile campaign hailed from the Prairie State. (U.S. Army Military History Institute)

Corps D'Afrique. Black troops, shown at Port Hudson in 1863, made up ten percent of the Federal forces in the Mobile campaign and at least a quarter of those besieging Fort Blakely. (National Archives)

A Proud Union Veteran. 1st Sergeant William R. Eddington, 97th Illinois Infantry, in a photo taken many years after the war, with his grandson. The 97th Illinois sustained the highest casualties of any Federal regiment in the April 9 assault on Fort Blakely. (William F. Steudt Collection, U.S. Army Military History Institute)

Chapter 10

"Digging All Night and Fighting All Day"

By 1865 Rebel and Union armies conducted siege operations routinely. Field earthworks, formerly used only in formal sieges, became common as the firepower of infantry rifle muskets became increasingly deadly, and veteran soldiers expected to dig in as soon as they came under fire. The fourth year of the long conflict found experienced infantrymen as familiar with the entrenching tool as they were with the musket.

The war had witnessed many sieges. Veterans at Spanish Fort and Blakely remembered the two-month siege of Vicksburg in the summer of 1863. Federal forces shelled the city night and day, and civilians took refuge in caves dug into the bluffs as food and supplies gradually gave out. As the troops at Spanish Fort and Blakely began skirmishing and digging trenches, Lee's army in Petersburg, Virginia—enclosed by 37 miles of earthworks—neared the end of a punishing ten-month siege begun in June 1864.

Gibson described the siege of Spanish Fort as "digging all night and fighting all day." Siege warfare was a tiresome duty for soldiers, and crowded living conditions in trenches and bombproof shelters made life even more unpleasant. Plus there was always an unseen danger from enemy artillery, snipers, land mines, and booby traps.[1]

Still most soldiers found siege duty preferable to the suicidal frontal assaults favored by commanders earlier in the war. Fighting in the open was one thing, Wisconsin soldier James K. Newton wrote home, "but charging on fortifications with an almost impregnable abattis in front besides a ditch from 8 to 12 feet deep & as many wide is altogether a different matter." A Federal artillery officer recalled Vicksburg: "There it was charge! charge!

charge! Here a little more good sense is shown, and a regard had for human life; and the end approaches much more rapidly."[2]

Siege operations had changed little since being perfected by European armies in the eighteenth century, the objective being to get as close to a forti-fied enemy position as possible while minimizing casualties. It was meticu-lous, time-consuming work, calling for patient, steady labor. Soldiers dug a series of saps, or approach trenches, in the direction of the enemy lines. The saps ran in a zigzag pattern, rather than directly toward the enemy, so as to prevent enfilade fire delivered straight down the trench that could bring heavy casualties. These ditches also allowed the soldiers to remove their wounded and dead from the advance rifle pits. When the saps reached out to a certain point, soldiers would burrow out of the far ends to connect them, creating a parallel trench, bringing their whole line closer to the enemy with-out costly frontal charges to capture ground. Then the whole pattern would repeat itself, with forward saps going out and another parallel being dug, yet closer to the enemy. It was common for a besieging army to dig two or three parallels. By then, if they hadn't starved the enemy into surrendering, they were usually close enough to risk a frontal assault and take the fort by storm. Federal troops at Spanish Fort had finished two parallels and part of a third before the fort fell. At Blakely, they had dug three parallels.[3]

"It looked rather funny," the 117th Illinois' Adolph Wolf wrote on March 31, "to see several hundred men scattered through the woods making bas-kets while a war is being fought." The "baskets" or gabions that Wolf and other soldiers were put to work on were simply large open-ended wicker-work frames, filled with earth, and these protected soldiers while they were digging trenches. Gabions served as a retaining wall or bracing to hold the sides of trenches in place and to keep breastworks from caving in.[4]

The Yankees also tried filling large barrels with dirt and rolling them in front of skirmishers who used them for cover as they advanced closer to the enemy works. Rebel gunfire from the "Lady Slocomb" and other big guns blew the barrels apart, and the bluecoats were forced to abandon the idea.[5]

The Federals were relentless. "I never saw such digging as the enemy does," Gibson wrote Maury, "he is like a mole." And each day of digging brought the Federals closer. "The enemy's skirmish line of yesterday is a line of battle today," Liddell wrote. "I have never seen men work as we did there," wrote a soldier in the 19th Iowa. "Men were posted to give warning when they fired and every man dropped to the ground until the shell passed over and then up and at it we went again." Captain Thomas N. Stevens of the 28th Wisconsin wrote, "the men dig, dig, dig, day & night, with accou-trements on, & their trusty rifles by their sides in the trenches. The rebels dig too, and we have to be cautious not to expose ourselves too far, or *whiz* goes a bullet, much too close to one's head to be pleasant for a timid man." Half of every Federal regiment was on duty each day, part of them standing guard on the skirmish line and part burrowing away in the trenches; and E. A. Carr reported that at one time officers and N.C.O.s in one of his brigades manned the trenches while privates took a welcome sleep break.[6]

The Federals besieging Spanish Fort had rough work entrenching. Topped in some places with heavy logs, the rocky ground seemed filled with tree roots and stumps. The work was also difficult for the bluecoats at Blakely, where C. C. Andrews wrote, "there were numerous stumps, and the surface was strewn with fallen pines." Adding to the difficulty, Rebel snipers watched diligently for any chance to pick off a Yankee soldier who became careless while doing the exhausting work of digging rifle pits, earthworks, and trenches.[7]

Digging at night provided little safety. The sound of a spade striking a root or the flash of light reflected from a shovel in the moonlight would bring a swift volley from the Rebel works. "Then we would hug the ground," Elisha Stockwell wrote, "or if in the ditch would hug the bottom of that." Stockwell noted that soldiers did not mind the shoveling, it kept them from getting cold. Two men were assigned to a shovel; one dug while the other rested.[8]

The Federals attacked the task before them with grim professionalism, showing steady determination, with the war's end clearly in sight. "This work of taking Mobile is a job of more magnitude than I at first imagined," an Iowa soldier, one of "Smith's Guerrillas," confessed, "but it must come at last." And a newspaperman for the *Chicago Tribune* confidently reported from Spanish Fort, "Inch by inch we are moving on the Gibraltar that protects Mobile."[9]

The Yankees came up with some novel ways to annoy the Rebels. Iowa soldiers found that by cutting a 3-foot-long section out of a gum tree trunk, hollowing it out, and banding it with iron, they could convert it into a wooden mortar. By placing just a small charge of powder in the "barrel," they could lob a shell into the Rebel lines, and they could do it from their own advanced rifle pits. Primitive but deadly, a number of these "wooden mortars" were used with good effect. Charles Henry Snedeker in the 124th Illinois recorded in his diary on April 3 that a couple of them were placed in front of Geddes' brigade.[10]

While the bluecoats busied themselves like moles, the Confederates were far from passive. "The defence was active, bold and defiant," Maury wrote; and Gibson reported, "Enemy is busy, and so are we." The Rebels had spent considerable time in strengthening the forts on the eastern shore. At Fort Blakely, Missouri officer O. F. Guthrie called Redoubt 4 "the best works we ever fought behind with nice head logs and a battery on each flank."[11]

Slowing the Federal approach was a prime objective of the graycoats, and they used all the standard methods of defensive siege warfare. They capitalized on their woodland surroundings of yellow pines to construct a formidable abatis, an obstacle course of felled trees with their limbs sharpened. Alabama soldier Edgar Jones remembered that the sharpened ends stood 6 feet high, pointing outward toward the Federals. Twenty-five feet long or more, the trees were lashed together to make it harder for the bluecoats to remove the obstructions. In some parts of the line there were two or more rows of them. The Rebels had been thorough.[12]

Thirty yards in front of their main works, the Rebels had dug a line of rifle pits large enough to hold three or four soldiers apiece. Edgar Jones described a rifle pit as "a hole in the ground much the size and shape of a common grave, with some large logs piled up on the side next to the enemy." The soldiers covered the logs with dirt from digging out the pit. While in the pits, they kept a watch out for enemy soldiers trying to remove the obstructions. They also kept their eyes peeled for enemy snipers. Alerted by the smoke from their guns, a Rebel infantryman recalled spotting three Federal sharpshooters posted in a sweet gum tree some two hundred yards in front of his rifle pit. "We fired on them," he wrote, "and two fell out like squirrels; the other came down and ran as I never saw a man run before."[13]

Fearful of exposing themselves during daylight, Rebel sharpshooters went into the rifle pits at 8:00 P.M. and stayed there until 8:00 P.M. the next night. They had to bring enough to live on for twenty-four hours. Jones recalled being stuck without water with two very young recruits who had also failed to bring enough to drink. All Jones had was some uncooked bacon and corn bread. But he wrote that he was too busy ducking enemy bullets to get too thirsty.[14]

Jones' position was about 20 yards in front of the Red Fort, and he recalled one particularly rough night during a jarring artillery duel between the "Lady Slocomb" and a Federal battery—"something like I imagine would be if a dozen earthquakes were turned loose. . . . I was bouncing like a rubber ball." Every concussion filled the rifle pit with dirt and debris, and the boy recruits became more terrified, crying and praying. When the firing finally let up, Jones admitted, "I was almost as deaf as a stump."[15]

Inside the forts, Rebel engineers had built defensive screens—half-inch-thick steel plates 2-by-3 feet square—over the cannon embrasures. The plates, or mantlets, shielded the Rebel gunners from enemy snipers. The artillerymen would raise the mantlets when ready to roll the gun into battery, then would lower them quickly after the gun recoiled.

To protect their own sharpshooters, the Confederates used "Beauregard screens," wooden embrasures covered with sandbags. General P.G.T. Beauregard had perfected the screens at Charleston. Gibson requisitioned 400 of them to shield his snipers at Spanish Fort.[16]

Soldiers of both armies built bombproof shelters, sometimes called "gopher holes," to protect them from shot and shell. These structures were small log houses covered with three layers of pine logs and 6 feet of earth. They generally held three to eight men. Charles Henry Snedeker wrote on March 31, "As soon as we got breakfast we set to work on our Bomb proof, and by the middle of the afternoon we had it done." In Slocomb's battery, Phil Stephenson recalled working on one bombproof about 16 by 20 feet and 10 to 12 feet deep.[17]

Bombproofs were not always equal to the task of protection. Rebel naval officer George S. Waterman, visiting friends in Slocomb's battery, wrote, "We were counting up the missing, and became absorbed, when a crash at the door brought an end to roll call and lo! a fuse shell had come to see us, and was about two feet within the door of our 'gopher.' Not a syllable was uttered, but . . . there were more artillerists in the flesh and spirit stowed into one corner than Armour, Swift, or Morris could pack in an hour. Here we huddled—minutes? no, seconds. . . . Orderly Serg. John Bartley seized the unwelcome tongue-tied visitor and threw it out."[18]

At Fort Blakely, soldiers seem not to have built the network of bombproofs common at Spanish Fort. Mississippi artillery officer J. L. Bradford wrote his mother that the Blakely defenders lived in caves and holes and were under constant fire from enemy sharpshooters. He asked her to send a servant with rags for the soldiers. "We fire constantly," he explained, "& the men have literally nothing to wipe out their rifles with."[19]

Everyone feared the unseen sniper. Edgar Jones wrote, "If a man only lifted his hand above the breastworks a Yankee would take a crack at it." At Fort Blakely, Liddell wrote that Federal sharpshooters could pick off his soldiers as far away as the wharf. J. L. Bradford was struck near the heart by an enemy bullet, but fortunately two letters folded in his pocket kept the wound from killing him.[20] Others were not so lucky. Captain Samuel Barnes, who had already lost more than half of his company of the 22nd Louisiana at Fort McDermott, was observing the effect of mortar fire on April 5. A Federal musket ball struck him in the face, went in to one side of his nose and came out on the opposite side of his skull. And in Lumsden's battery, a Yankee sniper's bullet struck just under a head-log and ricocheted downward, hitting Lieutenant A. C. Hargrove in the head just in front of his ear. A transport carried Hargrove—accompanied by Sergeant Jim Maxwell, who had finally received orders to go to Tuscaloosa to bring back clothing—across the Bay to Mobile that night. After carefully probing the wound, surgeons were unable to remove the bullet, and Hargrove carried it in his head for the rest of his life.[21]

Rebel sharpshooters proved deadly too. Through their small portholes—just big enough for a musket barrel to poke through—they presented as small a target as possible while they pecked away at the enemy. Any moving target was fair game. Elisha Stockwell recalled a careless young soldier from the 48th Missouri reloading while standing in front of his porthole. Stockwell, digging a trench nearby, cautioned him against it. "I told him he ought to stand to one side," he wrote, "as the Rebs were good at shooting." The young Missourian laughed and took no heed. To demonstrate his bravery, the lad leapt atop the works and fired a shot at the Rebel rifle pits. "This was what we called foolhardy," Stockwell wrote, wasting no time with further warnings. Later that same day, a bullet came through the porthole and killed the boy.[22]

Sometimes the tedium of life in the trenches could tempt a restless soldier to do something foolish. In Slocomb's battery, a gunner named Ferand, "a big, handsome Frenchman, with dancing, fun-lit, black eyes," crouched too close to the metal screens over one of the cannon's embrasures. As lead from enemy sharpshooters peppered the outside of the shield, Ferand clowned and grinned for his pals as he wagged his red cap up and down on the end of a ram rod. A few minutes of this horseplay, and a Federal bullet finally penetrated the crack between the screen and the embrasure and struck Ferand in the hip. He was out of action and had earned a painful furlough home.[23]

The Rebel garrisons were badly undermanned. Whereas the Federals could afford to let half their troops rest while the other half dug trenches and served on the skirmish line, the graycoats had to do double duty to keep the works manned. Edgar Jones wrote, "There was no time announced to eat or sleep. You just did these things as you could." When they were not at the guns, artillerymen doubled as riflemen. Lumsden's gunners were issued rifles, and James Maxwell wrote, "our shoulders got sore with the continued kick of the firing." It was also important to conserve ammunition. Maury and Gibson urged their soldiers to gather spent bullets and shells to send back to Mobile to be melted down and used again.[24]

Confederate mortars proved a menace to the Federals. One of the best shots in the 14th Wisconsin, Frederick B. Mattice, laughed at his comrades who cringed against the breastworks when the mortar shells burst overhead. A popular soldier, Mattice had never been injured since enlisting in October 1861, but a mortar shell exploded and a piece struck him in the head. He never regained consciousness and died three days later. Stockwell wrote that his death saddened his company. Mattice, whose wife had died shortly after his enlistment, left four orphaned children in Wisconsin.[25]

Rebel troops at Blakely used their coehorn mortars to send up fireballs in front of their works at night, lighting up the sky and exposing Federal work parties to fire, or scattering troops from their shelters into the mud and drizzle. "Sleep had to be snatched at any moment," the 83rd Ohio's Frank McGregor wrote, because no one knew when an enemy shell might strike.[26]

Fire from the Federal mortars plagued the Johnnies too. They could see the glow of an incoming round at night and would try to gauge its path and move out of the way. With this happening every fifteen minutes or so, the soldiers learned to dart into their bombproofs, sometimes diving in headfirst like a rabbit into his burrow. Slower men could expect some ribbing. The 18th Alabama's surgeon, Dr. L. W. Shepherd, out of breath and cringing in the pit, caught Edgar Jones laughing at him. "Jones," he said, shaking his finger, "I don't see anything funny about this business, and I want you to hush it."[27]

Jones remembered a soldier literally being blown to bits by an enemy shell. The man had taken shelter in a niche in the earthworks, giving him protection on three sides, but somehow the shell came down directly above him landing on his head as it detonated. Jones and his comrades searched for his body, "but little of it was found."[28]

Called torpedoes by the Federals and sub-terra shells by the Confederates, land mines were one of the biggest concerns of the bluecoats. A New York artilleryman wrote that a fellow soldier lost an arm and a leg when someone carelessly tossed a torpedo down in front of him. "That is what boys get," he wrote, "by fooling with these things. So goes soldiering."[29]

Rebel Brigadier General Gabriel Rains, credited with introducing land mines at Yorktown in May 1862, proposed using them in the Mobile defenses as early as August 1863. Maury at first was opposed, but by March 1865 he was all in favor of them. The typical land mine was an 8- or 10-inch Columbiad shell buried in the ground. A friction primer in a wooden plug was pushed into the shell, and a tin cup placed over the plug. When soldiers buried the shell, they carefully left just an inch or so of dirt covering the bottom of the cup. When an enemy soldier stepped on it, the primer would ignite the shell. Soldiers also would bury mines inside the wheel ruts in a road. The explosion would disable enemy wagons or caissons. Another favorite technique was to arrange two or three mines in a row, with a wooden plank over them. If an enemy soldier stepped on one of the tin cups, he would detonate all the shells.[30]

The wounds produced by an exploding land mine were appalling and added to the terror these weapons inspired. The 2nd Connecticut Light Artillery lost only one man in the siege of Fort Blakely. The victim was actually killed after the battle on April 9, when he stepped on a torpedo. The explosion blew his left leg off, tore two holes in his other leg, and wounded him in the genitals, typical injuries for a land mine casualty. He lived only three hours.[31]

Riding south from Blakely with a communications team making for Spanish Fort, Lieutenant Colonel Jonathan Merriam narrowly escaped death on April 2, when the horse behind him stepped on a land mine. A sudden and powerful blast shook the column, as sand and smoke temporarily blinded them, and they reeled in their saddles. Merriam marveled that they were not all killed. The two horses behind Merriam fell dead. The shaken officer simply sat on his horse for a few moments and reflected on his good fortune at being alive.[32]

Federal soldiers found and disarmed fifty land mines along the bank of D'Olive's Creek, where the Confederates had expected an initial attack. At Spanish Fort, several skirmishers of the 8th Wisconsin surprised three Rebel pickets one night and took them prisoner. The Yanks asked their captives if they had placed any torpedoes in the ground behind the pits. One of the Rebels, an Irishman from his accent, replied, "I trod light when I came out."[33]

As the more desperate of the two belligerents, Confederates regarded the use of land mines as a regrettable but justifiable method of war, but the Federals condemned it as uncivilized. "In regard to this system of warfare," C. C. Andrews wrote, "I cannot omit here to observe that it seems inhuman on this account, that after a battle is over it may be out of the enemy's power to prevent the disaster which they are calculated to produce, as in this instance, non-combatants searching for the wounded and the dead were liable to destruction." "It is horribly barbarous," wrote Captain Thomas L. Evans of the 96th Ohio, "and I can think of nothing which would be so as severe to use in retaliating. Up to this time, I have felt like dealing honorably with Rebels, but the last spark of such feeling is gone." Isaac Jackson of the 83rd Ohio wrote, "This is a very mean way of fighting." Long after the war, civilians walking in the woods around Blakely and Spanish Fort stood the risk of being maimed or killed by an undiscovered land mine.[34]

But the true king of the killing field remained the heavy artillery. The contest for Spanish Fort hinged on artillery supremacy. From the beginning of the siege, Federal troops sought to neutralize the big guns of Batteries Huger and Tracy that supported Spanish Fort. At first, Fort Huger vexed the Federal troops on the right in Carr's division. Private Elisha Stockwell remembered shells from Huger dropping unpredictably in the lines. "We could see it coming," he wrote, "but couldn't tell where the darned thing was going to light." Some shells fell short, others overshot the Yankee trenches. "But it always looked like it was coming right where you were," Stockwell observed, making it necessary for soldiers to do some fast moving. Edward Nye recorded the curious sight of a shell, fired from a Rebel gunboat toward the Federal camp, slowly "rolling end over end way up in the air." "It looked like a bird," he added.[35]

The Federals countered Rebel gunners with heavy artillery of their own. Brigadier General James Totten, a Regular Army man and a veteran of the Mexican War and the fighting in Missouri, arrived with the Federal siege train. With him was the 1st Indiana Heavy Artillery, originally an infantry outfit converted to heavy artillery in February 1863. The regiment had served in the Red River campaign and in the bombardment of Forts Morgan and Gaines. By March 31, eight 30-pounder Parrotts of Captain William P. Wimmer's Battery H and Captain Clayton Cox's Battery K were in position on the northern shore of Bay Minette. The heavy guns focused their fire on Batteries Huger and Tracy and on Rebel transports in the river. Yankee shelling of the little forts prevented them from aiding Spanish Fort.[36]

Soon a strategically placed Yankee battery was able to provide relief to Carr's hard-pressed troops on the far right of the Union line. After working all night in a heavy downpour on March 28, Captain W. H. Blankenship with Battery B of the 1st Indiana Heavy Artillery set up eight 8-inch mortars on a hilltop to the rear of Geddes' brigade. Meanwhile, the 8-inch howitzers of Battery C and six 20-pounder Parrotts of Captain Albert Mack's 18th New York Light Artillery (known as the Black Horse Battery) pounded away at Fort McDermott on the Confederate right and forced Rebel gunners to seek shelter in their bombproofs. Captain Isaac Hendricks' 1st Indiana Battery L placed their 30-pounder Parrotts in the rear between Carr's and McArthur's divisions.[37]

But the Rebels had an April 1 surprise for the Yanks. Captain John B. Grayson brought up two 10-pounder rifles from Fort Blakely and placed them in the woods on the north bank of Bay Minette. At daybreak, he opened fire on the troublesome Captain Wimmer's battery. Already in the midst of a duel with the guns of Fort Huger and the Rebel gunboat *Morgan*, the Indiana boys hastily threw up earthworks to protect their right flank and especially their magazine, which Wimmer feared would be blown up. Although Cox's and Wimmer's batteries lost only three men wounded, their position was compromised. But Steele's Federal troops were arriving to invest Fort Blakely, and by day's end Grayson was forced to withdrew his guns into the Rebel works.[38]

The Yankees particularly targeted the Red Fort, where the "Lady Slocomb" posed such a formidable menace. "Artillery duels became of daily occurrence," Phil Stephenson wrote, "our 'head logs' were constantly knocked down upon us, bruising and crippling us; squads of sharpshooters devoted their especial attention to our port holes or embrasures and poured a steady stream of bullets through them from early morn till dewy eve."[39]

A major duel commenced on April 2, a clear Sunday morning. Brass bands played in the Federal camps, and the breeze carried snatches of their music over the Rebel lines. Mack's 18th New York Battery began the action, hammering away at Fort McDermott. Barnes' artillery from the fort responded and showered the New Yorkers with solid shot and shells, and Slocomb's battery joined in around 11:00 A.M. Blankenship's Battery B of the 1st Indiana hurled a hundred mortar shells at the Red Fort. Meanwhile, the 30-pounders of Wimmer's and Cox's batteries at Bay Minette were keeping Forts Huger and Tracy occupied. Mack succeeded in disabling Slocomb's 24-pounder howitzer. Rebel firing ceased but began again at 4:00 P.M., and the duel between Slocomb's and Mack's batteries continued until dark. Mack estimated the Rebel gunners had hit his works thirty-eight times during the day, but remarkably none of the New Yorkers was injured. Fort McDermott, though, had received considerable damage. Mack's gunners were busy during the night making repairs to their works.[40]

Firing continued throughout the next day and on through the night. George S. Waterman, with the Washington Artillery, wrote, "Mortar shells were thrown into our garrison throughout the night with perfect periodicity." When the firing finally eased, Holtzclaw's Alabama infantrymen crept into the Red Fort to sit around a dim campfire with the Louisiana gunners puffing on their pipes and talking about the day's action and what the next day would bring. A few, weighted down with canteens, slipped down to a small spring behind the works to get water and risk the occasional shot from the watchful Yankee snipers.[41]

A lovely morning greeted the combatants on April 4. The glow of the eastern sky preceded the bright rising sun itself, lending a blood-red hue to the low-lying smoke in the dark ravines and along the fields. It was unusually quiet, and then a few scattered shots broke the stillness as snipers from both sides tried to bring down a marsh bird that had flown between the lines. As the lone bird fell from the sky, angry voices of graycoats and Yankees were heard arguing over whose shot had brought him down. A soldier from the 9th Minnesota jumped from his rifle pit and ran forward shouting, "He belongs to the side that gets him!" The graycoats held their fire, as the bold Yankee scooped up his trophy and with a wave of his cap bounded back into his pit.[42]

Other than the periodic thudding of the mortars, firing was light during the day. Then with seventy-five cannon—thirty-eight siege guns and thirty-seven field guns—in place by the evening of April 4, the Federals opened a two-hour bombardment of Spanish Fort at 5:00 P.M. Each Yankee gun was firing every three minutes—like "rolling thunder," a Connecticut artilleryman recalled—and Rebel gunners could do little but reply sporadically. A Rebel soldier wrote, "the entire length of their works was one blaze of artillery." "A well-sustained and grand bombardment," Andrews wrote. "Clouds of dust rose from their parapets." Mack's New York battery fired 360 rounds at Fort McDermott; one of the New Yorkers was killed when a gun exploded prematurely.[43]

At the Red Fort, Lady Slocomb, snug behind three embrasures, was relatively safe. Lady Slocomb could be pivoted so as to be run out three different embrasures, front, right, or left. The Louisiana gunners did not fire it often, because ammunition was low and the Rebels had to bring it up from the magazine at Old Spanish Fort to the Red Fort by a road open to Federal artillery fire. The bluecoats watched the Red Fort carefully, and whenever the Lady Slocomb's muzzle appeared, they would loose a bombardment.[44]

But when the Louisiana gunners noticed a new Federal battery—anxious to join in the bombardment—coming into the open in order to get off a shot, they scrambled to throw screens and sandbags to one side and shove the Lady Slocomb into firing position. The Lady Slocomb spoke, a direct hit that left the Yankee battery in ruins. But before the graycoats could replace the sandbags and screen, Captain Isaac Hendricks' 1st Indiana battery sent a shell from a 30-pounder Parrott sailing directly into Redoubt Blair, and then another. The explosion killed three New Orleans gunners and shattered the right trunnion of the Lady Slocomb.[45]

As the pounding continued all along the line at Spanish Fort, civilians in Mobile could hear the cannon and feel the ground rumble. All the way to Fort Blakely, Federal besiegers could hear the thunderous shelling, prompting Yankee skirmishers to begin cheering. Bluecoats back in the trenches quickly took up the cheer, and Rebel soldiers in the advance rifle pits fell back fearing an assault on their lines. The Federal skirmishers moved ahead and occupied more ground without a fight. As the cannons fell silent in front of Spanish Fort, officers issued a ration of whiskey to the Yankee gunners, and their brass bands broke into rousing music.[46]

Morning revealed the extent of the Federal bombardment. The Rebel parapets were nearly flattened. "We could see the marks of our shot and shell," Snedeker wrote, "on the trees inside of the fort." Weary foot soldiers were relieved that the shelling was over for now. In the rifle pits of the 94th Illinois, William Macy wrote, "dont feel very well on account of being up so much The cooks brought out some hot coffee which is rellished very much."[47]

In the Red Fort, the Lady Slocomb lay disabled. Maury put in an appearance in the Rebel works and spoke with Slocomb. He proposed to bring up a fresh battery from Mobile to relieve Slocomb's gunners. "We respectfully decline to be relieved," Slocomb replied after a short conference with his men.[48]

Batteries Huger and Tracy also had taken a pounding. At the start of the siege, the little forts had only about 200 rounds of ammunition per gun. Maury ordered them to hold their fire. Under murderous bombardment from the Federal heavy batteries at Bay Minette, they could not return fire. The shelling was annoying but so far had done little damage. The garrison troops kept busy carrying sandbags and repairing the works. Being at the big guns was about the safest place to be, because they were less exposed to enemy fire. "About the only leisure time we have is when the enemy are firing on us," 24-year-old Louisiana soldier Mark Lyons wrote his wife from Fort Huger. The men's spirits were good. The graycoats brought sandbags downriver by flatboats on the night of April 4 and strengthened the parapets between the gun embrasures.[49]

The Federal artillery was running short of ammunition, so there was little shelling on April 5, 6, and 7. Mortar shells accounted for many of the casualties in the Rebel forts. A 10-inch mortar shell weighed about ninety pounds. On April 5, such a shell fired by the 6th Michigan Heavy Artillery scored a direct hit on a bombproof in Battery 5, occupied by Phillips' Tennessee battery. It penetrated 6 feet of earth and three layers of logs and buried twenty-six men, injuring five and killing one instantly. George Waterman marveled "that while this man was hurled twenty feet in air and every bone was broken when he fell he sustained no mangling whatever." Phillips' battery lost more than fifty men during the siege and had to be relieved by Garrity's Alabama battery.[50]

Most of the Federal heavy artillery was at Spanish Fort, but only a few light field pieces opposed the Rebels at Blakely. The Federals had a ten-pounder rifle of the 2nd Connecticut battery in place near the Stockton road on the night of April 4. On April 5, near the rear of Moore's brigade, they began work on a battery for the 15th Massachusetts with four 12-pounder Napoleons. The 17th Ohio light battery was in front of Garrard's division, and the 2nd Massachusetts had two guns in front of Hawkins' division. The Federals wished they had a few heavy guns to reply to the Rebel pieces. A member of the 117th Illinois recalled Rebel soldiers taunting them with offers to let them borrow some of their artillery. The bluecoats replied that they would be hearing Federal guns soon enough.[51]

The Rebels at Blakely would soon feel the sting of heavy guns. By noon on April 8, Wimmer's Battery H, 1st Indiana, had been moved from their position on Bay Minette to the right of Hawkins' division, which had been shelled daily by the Rebel gunboats. Wimmer's four 30-pounder Parrott guns would now give some relief to Hawkins' hard-pressed troops.[52]

Although most of what soldiers did at Spanish Fort and Blakely amounted to boring, tedious, hard work, duty during the siege had its share of close calls and tense moments. "Every day was full of incident," Phil Stephenson reported, "and it soon got so that we had no rest day or night."[53]

Federal skirmishers had a close call on the night of March 29. Captain L. K. Myers of the 29th Iowa was in charge of a small party of soldiers sent to dig rifle pits. Shortly before daybreak, the bluecoats had completed a line of pits just 50 yards from the advance line of Gibson's Louisiana brigade. While leading eight unarmed soldiers carrying ammunition boxes, Myers made his way back to what he assumed were the Federal lines. "Boys," Myers called out into the darkness, "I am coming back again." The answer came back, "Come on." Myers and his men stumbled into the trench and found themselves suddenly face to face with a Rebel officer and a dozen armed enemy soldiers.[54]

The graycoat officer eyed Myers suspiciously. "Do you know where you are?" he asked, "Do you belong to us?" Myers thought quickly. "Of course we belong to you," he replied, "ain't you confederate soldiers?" "Yes," the man replied. Myers told him they were carrying ammunition to one of the Rebel posts further down the line, but the Southern officer was cautious. "I knew the reb. knew what we were," Myers reported later, "and was afraid to order us to surrender; perhaps wanted to first double his force at the next post." Finally one of the Rebel soldiers blurted out, "Hold on, these are not our men!" Guns began to fire, as both the Rebels and the unarmed Yankee party scattered.[55]

The bluecoats scrambled away in the direction of what they hoped were their own lines, a shower of Rebel lead following. Myers stumbled into an enemy picket, squatting in the bushes ahead, and the Rebel fired his musket, striking Myers in the hip. The Yankee officer returned fire with his revolver and killed the graycoat. Eventually he managed to crawl back to his own lines. In the following days of the siege, Reb pickets would call out to their counterparts asking, "How is Captain Myers?" and the Yanks would reply, "He is not dangerous. How about your officer who ran from unarmed men?"[56]

Confederates often became disoriented too. Soldiers of McArthur's division on duty in the Federal rifle pits one night spotted a party of Rebel sharpshooters sliding over the walls of the fort to relieve the skirmishers in their own rifle pits. The bluecoats loosed a volley that scattered the Rebs and sent most of them scrambling back to their works. One graycoat became confused and stumbled toward the Yankee rifle pits. He ran up to one, stooped down, whispered, "Is this No. 3?" "Yes," a voice replied, "jump down quick!" The Reb jumped down into the pit and found himself a prisoner of Federal soldiers.[57]

On March 31 just after noon a Union sharpshooter in the rifle pits about 150 yards in front of the Rebel works fired a shot that instantly killed Colonel William E. Burnett, Gibson's chief of artillery. Burnett apparently had decided to take a potshot at enemy soldiers across the lines and had just picked up a rifle and taken aim from behind the breastworks when the Yankee bullet struck him in the head. The shot narrowly missed Gibson.[58]

The Rebel gunners replied by shelling the enemy position, occupied by twenty-one soldiers of the 7th Vermont Infantry under Captain Riley B. Stearns. In fact the Rebel gunners and the Yankee skirmishers had been shooting at each other for most of the day. But Stearns, described by the 7th Vermont's Colonel William C. Holbrook as "one of the most efficient officers in my regiment," stubbornly refused to withdraw.[59]

Perhaps the Vermont boys felt that they had something to prove. They had been censured by Major General Benjamin Butler in an action at Baton Rouge on August 5, 1862, in which Butler charged them with cowardice under fire. The 7th Vermont's colonel, quarry manager George T. Roberts, was killed in the engagement, and Butler alleged, "He was worthy of a better disciplined regiment and a better fate." The Vermonters, whose numbers had fallen to 250 men because of rampant malaria, argued that Butler had it in for the 7th Vermont because of an earlier run-in in which he had accused them of insubordination. Although a court of inquiry cleared the Vermonters of Butler's charge that they had abandoned their colors, the regiment was forbidden to inscribe them with the name "Baton Rouge." Their bad reputation had followed them to Spanish Fort where they marched in the same brigade with the 29th Iowa. Thomas Stevens of the 28th Wisconsin called the 7th Vermont "the White Reg't" and "a pack of cowards."[60]

Unable to dislodge the Vermont detachment by shelling, the Rebels set fire to the brush and fallen tree limbs to the right of Stearns' skirmishers, and soon the Yankees were enveloped in smoke. Fearing they were about to be burned out, Stearns ordered his men to fall back to the Federal lines one at a time, but the first one who tried was stopped by a hail of gunfire. Stearns was unable to pull back and was pinned down in his position by Rebel fire. He had already sent word back that he expected to be attacked before nightfall, and now he ordered his men to fix bayonets and prepare to receive an assault.[61]

At sunset a detachment from the Louisiana brigade—about thirty soldiers led by Captain Clement Watson, an officer on Gibson's staff, and Lieutenant A. C. Newton—jumped over the works of the garrison and charged the Vermonters. The smoke from the burning brush was so thick that Stearns could no longer see his own lines behind him much less the Rebels in front. Suddenly the graycoats were upon them, and the Yankees were overwhelmed before many of them could even discharge their weapons. "The charge was so sudden and vigorous," Stearns reported, "that we could offer but little resistance. . . . I found two muskets and a revolver pointing at me, with a request to come out of the pit."[62]

The Rebels quickly hustled their captives into the fort. Stearns was led to Gibson's tent, nestled protectively inside a triangular shaped ravine behind the Rebel earthworks. With Watson and Newton also present, Gibson extended Stearns an invitation to share supper with them, and the Federal officer accepted. The men then sat down to partake of a rather Spartan meal of cold chicken and water. Gibson complimented Stearns on the bravery of his men. When the meal was ended, Stearns was escorted from the tent. The Yankee officer from the Green Mountain State was bound for a Rebel prison camp at Meridian, Mississippi, but before he was taken away, he spoke with some Rebel enlisted men. The ragged graycoats admitted to him that they had lost hope in the Confederacy's chances of victory.[63]

After the sortie against the Vermont boys, Gibson wrote, "the enemy guarded carefully against sudden dashes, and though frequent combats at particular points took place, and a few more sorties were contemplated, none could be undertaken with a reasonable prospect of success."[64]

There were not nearly enough Rebel soldiers to man the rifle pits. They had to make the best use of the troops they had, relying on the most veteran soldiers like the Missourians at Fort Blakely to do more than their share of duty. On April 1, Liddell ordered Cockrell to "fill the whole line of skirmish pits with the men of your own brigade, as they are the only ones here that can be relied upon thoroughly, and in all probability the enemy will endeavor to take these works by storm, and therefore it is necessary to have the best men in those pits."[65]

Maury had promised Liddell to bring Ector's brigade back up from Spanish Fort, a decision that set off a flurry of messages late into the night of April 1 as Gibson apparently went into a panic at the thought of losing the Texans. "Can't you let me keep Ector's brigade a day or two longer?" he wired Maury. "The withdrawal of it just now renders this position hazardous in the extreme. Answer." Apparently annoyed with Gibson's insistence, Maury at first was unyielding. "I decided this matter when at Blakely," he telegraphed Liddell. "Ector's brigade must come up to Blakely." But finally Maury thought better of his decision and allowed the Texans to remain at Spanish Fort. Gibson breathed a sigh of relief. Also Liddell reconsidered his order to Cockrell to spread the Missourians out along the entire skirmish line at Blakely. The Missouri brigade instead would man the rifle pits along the left of the Rebel line, and the Alabama reserves would man the skirmish line in front of their lines.[66]

Although hard-pressed and incredibly shorthanded as the siege wore on, the stubborn defenders displayed steady bravado. C. C. Andrews recorded that the Rebels made sorties against his lines at Blakely for three nights in a row.

At 3:00 A.M. on April 6, the nighttime stillness was shattered as a mass of screaming graycoats swarmed over the parapets near Redoubt 4 and very nearly overwhelmed the surprised Federals in their rifle pits. The Rebs seemed to have targeted a work party for the 15th Massachusetts battery in front of Andrews' division. For about half an hour there was heavy firing, and Andrews had some tense moments, but the bluecoats held their ground. The Rebel sortie then moved to their right down the Federal line and finally came within a few feet of the rifle pits in front of Garrard's division. Quick-thinking Federal Lieutenant Angus McDonald of the 11th Wisconsin bellowed out for the Rebs to hear, "First and Second brigade supports, forward!" The Rebels withdrew, although they could not know that the Wisconsin boys only had about four rounds of ammunition each and that there were no supports in the rear.[67]

The Rebels launched another sortie against troops on the Federal left just before daylight the following morning, again advancing up to the Yankee rifle pits, firing several volleys and cheering. Cannon from the fort leant supporting fire, answered by Federal artillery. The bluecoats drove the Rebel attackers back again. The attack was costly for the Rebels; Lieutenant Colonel Junius Law's 63rd Alabama Regiment withdrew with fifteen men killed and twenty-two wounded. The fighting left one Yankee dead and two wounded.[68]

And at 1:00 A.M. on April 8, the Rebels made yet another sortie. This time a blue signal light preceded the attack. With artillery in support, the graycoats sent out skirmishers in front of Veatch's division and the right of Andrews' division. There was heavy firing for about an hour, especially in front of Hawkins' division, but once again the Rebs made no progress. The Federals had learned to take such incidents in their stride. "I am becoming so accustomed to it," an Illinois officer wrote, "that it doesn't disturb me much. In fact, I begin to feel fidgety when there is a lull in the discharge of artillery & musketry."[69]

Nearly four years of combat had taught Johnny Reb and Billy Yank to have a healthy respect for one another, and when fighting appeared pointless to the common soldier, he left the foe alone. Elisha Stockwell recalled going out on picket duty one night accompanied by another soldier. After taking their position behind a small log, the two Federals spotted two Rebel pickets behind a log no more than 15 yards away. When his companion raised his rifle, Stockwell dissuaded him. "No," he admonished, "they are there to watch us and as long as they keep quiet we are to do the same." All night long the pickets watched each other, and Stockwell could hear the graycoats whispering but could not make out what they said. With daybreak, the Rebs crawled back to their works, and Stockwell and his pal followed suit. "I had lost my pocket knife and my bayonet," Stockwell added, "but I didn't want them bad enough to go after them."[70]

By April 4, the Federal advance parallel was within a hundred yards of the Spanish Fort garrison, and sharpshooters of both sides "were within talking distance." Occasional lulls in the fighting led to good-natured banter between pickets. "Hello, Johnny," a bluecoat near Fort McDermott called out to his counterpart one day. When he received no reply, the Federal hailed the enemy picket again. After several minutes of calling and getting no answer, the bluecoat finally asked why the Rebel was keeping silent. A voice came back, "Because you all insult us so when we talk with you." Soldiers would frequently exchange jests with one another during momentary calms in the storm. Confederate humor grimly reflected their grave plight. "Jeff Davis," one graycoat was heard to say, "will have to rent a piece of land to fight the war out on."[71]

At Blakely, along the skirmish line between Garrard's division and Thomas' Alabama reserves, there were unofficial truces, sometimes lasting more than an hour, in which skirmishers met to exchange the latest news and swap coffee and sugar for tobacco. They would call out when back in position or warn the enemy when about to fire. Liddell attempted to put a stop to this. On April 7, he instructed Thomas that because "the enemy in your front is very bold," he should exchange a company of his men with one of Cockrell's and scatter the veteran soldiers in the rifle pits to discourage further contact with the enemy.[72]

Apparently the fraternizing continued. The 21st Missouri was posted at the extreme left of the Federal line, a few hundred yards from the Blakely River. Colonel Charles Hills of the 10th Kansas recalled that at times the Federal Missourians found themselves separated by only 80 yards from Cockrell's Missourians in the Rebel rifle pits. Occasionally they would strike up a conversation with the Rebels. "This led to quiet little truces," the colonel remembered, "when the muskets would be left in the trenches, and the blue and grey meet each other socially, half-way, to swap lies for the ten minutes, and at other times to trade coffee for a Mobile paper and a plug of tobacco."[73]

There was no friendly banter between the African American pickets and the Mississippians at Fort Blakely, but even here soldiers could find some humor in their situation. First Sergeant Cassius M. Clay Alexander of the 50th U.S.C.T. recalled a running exchange with a Confederate soldier during the siege:

> We were only ten days on the siege, and had nothing to eat but Parched Corn. But as luck would have it, I crept out of my hole at night and scared one of the Jonnys so bad that he left his rifle pit, gun and accouterments, also one corn dodger and about one pint of buttermilk, all of which I devoured with a will, and returned to my hole safe and sound. After sleeping the remainder of the night . . . I forgot myself and poked my head out of my hole, and came very near getting one of Jonny's cough pills. We had to keep our heads down all the time or else run the risk of getting shot. So me and my friend of whom I was speaking had it all that day, shooting at each other. Finally, he got hungry and cried out to me, "Say, Blacky, let's stop and eat some Dinner." I told him, "All right." By the time I thought he was done eating, I cried, "Hello, Reb." He answered, "What do you want?" I said, "Are you ready?" "No, not yet," he said. Then I waited for a while. I finally got tired and cried for a chew of tobacco. He then shot at me and said, "Chew that!" I thanked him kindly and commenced exchanging shots with him.[74]

Morale at Blakely remained fairly high. "If we only had plenty of ammunition," J. L. Bradford wrote, "we would hold the dogs at bay forever, but we are stinted, & they will gain on us little by little I fear." At Spanish Fort, Gibson did what he could to raise the men's morale. He made himself visible in the trenches often, and he encouraged his officers to cheer their soldiers and bolster their faith. "It is morale that defeats a charge," he wrote, "it increases as the great Napoleon said—a resisting power tenfold." He also tried to provide incentives to the men to keep up the fight. Because ammunition was scarce, he offered an immediate twenty-four-hour leave of absence to any man who could gather up twenty-five pounds of lead, and soon eager graycoats could be seen scouring the ground for spent bullets.[75]

Thanks to generous food donations of Mobile's civilians, the Rebel soldiers ate fairly well, when they found the time to eat. The cooks were busy in the rear of Spanish Fort near the water's edge. The soldiers still complained of not having enough, and when they did find time to eat, a Yankee bullet might interrupt their meal. The Yankees had to make do with hardtack, bacon, and coffee. "I guess that if I Stay in the army much longer,"

Elisha Stockwell wrote his mother, "I will haf to get a new set of teeth." He went on to complain of how it was to eat hardtack, but added, " I can make out to eat all I draw."[76]

The Union morale continued to be high. News of the fall of Richmond and of Selma reached the Federal troops at Spanish Fort on April 5. These reports encouraged the Yankees but brought despair to the graycoats, who had hoped that Forrest would create some diversion to take the pressure off them.[77]

Even the most naive Rebel could see the handwriting on the wall now. Sergeant Maxwell of Lumsden's Battery wrote:

Closer and closer, came the parallels, each morning finding the Federal trenches closer than the day before, until any exposure of any part of the body, or either Yank or Confederate, would draw several bullets, men standing with rifles at shoulder beneath the head logs and finger on trigger, ready to fire at the least motion shown on opposite entrenchment.[78]

The Rebel lines were getting thinner and thinner. Gibson wired Maury on April 5, "My men are wider apart than they ever were under Generals Johnston and Hood." He sent a gloomy message to his commander on the morning of April 7: "I can't get along without subterra shells, hand-grenades, more negroes, a company of sappers and miners, a cutter or launch from the navy, two howitzers. The enemy made great progress yesterday and last night in his approaches. He will soon dig up to my main line at the rate he is advancing. Must do something to meet his night approaches."[79]

Gibson was increasingly worried about the vulnerability of his left flank, a marsh about 200 yards wide extending to the river. The Confederates had never fortified this section of the line and felt it highly unlikely the Yankees would get through it. But this almost proved to be a fatal error.

Although they hoped against hope that they could hold Spanish Fort, the Confederates knew that its capture was a strong probability. As early as March 30, Gibson began constructing a means of flight. The escape route was a narrow footpath or treadway—just 18 inches wide and about 1,200 yards long—built on pilings and running from a peninsula on the Confederate left across the swamp and a shallow part of the river to a point opposite Fort Huger. High grass screened the Rebel work parties from the eyes of the enemy, and each day the laborers spread moss over the trail to keep it hidden. Although random Federal shells occasionally scattered the workers, construction went on each day, and each day the treadway extended.[80]

Maury also had a backup plan, in case the garrison had to evacuate directly to Blakely. Engineer officers and several soldiers from the 9th Texas Infantry formed a special detail to scout and stake out an alternate route through the swamp above Spanish Fort overland to Fort Blakely.[81]

The escape route was ready none too soon. "I found by the 8th of April," Gibson wrote, "that all my artillery was about silenced; that the enemy had largely increased his; that his working parties, greatly re-enforced at every point and carefully protected against sorties, were pushing forward at a rate that would bring them up to our main works . . . that unless extraordinary re-enforcements could be had, the moment had at length arrived when I could no longer hold the position without imminent risk of losing the garrison."[82]

Meanwhile, Canby had pressures of his own to deal with, in particular a restless brigadier general, 34-year-old Cyrus Comstock, sent by Grant to observe the progress of the Mobile campaign while serving as senior engineer. Comstock viewed Canby's careful maneuvering with impatience, felt he had missed several chances to crush the Rebels. Canby should get on with the operation against Mobile—so that he could free up at least 8,000 of his troops to send to Wilson in central Alabama—and should launch an immediate assault against the Rebel works at Spanish Fort. "Think we might & should do it, at once," he wrote in his diary on April 5.[83]

In the siege of Spanish Fort, Colonel Lucius F. Hubbard reported that his brigade in McArthur's division excavated 7,000 cubic yards of earth and fired 169,000 rounds of ammunition. His losses—five men killed and ninety-four wounded—were relatively light considering the hazards of combat involved. Historian Chester Hearn writes, "the light casualty list reflects a new concern for the lives of men. At this stage in the war, commanders had learned how to attack strong fortifications without excessive bloodshed. Spades and axes had replaced glorious charges. Four years of fighting had taught the men how to protect themselves, and they no longer took unnecessary risks with their lives." Soldiers of both armies endured the dangers and hardships of siege and trench warfare with bravery and resolve. Their experiences would be repeated by a later generation of young Americans in the trenches of France during World War I.[84]

NOTES

1. Christopher C. Andrews, *History of the Campaign of Mobile* (New York, 1867), 136.

2. Stephen E. Ambrose, ed., *A Wisconsin Boy in Dixie: The Selected Letters of James K. Newton* (Madison: University of Wisconsin Press, 1961), 148–149; Andrews, *Campaign of Mobile*, 147.

3. Andrews, *Campaign of Mobile*, 149, 190.

4. Edwin G. Gerling, *The One Hundred Seventeenth Illinois Infantry Volunteers (The McKendree Regiment), 1862–1865* (Highland, IL: Author, 1992), 101.

5. Vincent Cortright, "Last-Ditch Defenders at Mobile," *America's Civil War* (January 1977), 61.

6. Andrews, *Campaign of Mobile*,136; *War of the Rebellion: A Compilation of the Official Records of the Union and Confederate Armies* (Washington, DC: Government Printing Office, 1880–1901) (hereafter cited as *OR*), Series I, Vol. 49, Part I, 268; Part II, 1173; Donald C. Elder III, ed., *A Damned Iowa Greyhound: The Civil War Letters of William Henry Harrison Clayton* (Iowa City: University of Iowa Press, 1998), 160; George M. Blackburn, ed., *"Dear Carrie . . .": The Civil War Letters of Thomas N. Stevens* (Mount Pleasant, MI: Clarke Historical Library, Central Michigan University, 1984), 307.

7. Andrews, *Campaign of Mobile*, 171.

8. Byron R. Abernethy, ed., *Private Elisha Stockwell, Jr., Sees the Civil War* (Norman: University of Oklahoma Press, 1958), 163–164.

9. Noah Andre Trudeau, *Out of the Storm: The End of the Civil War, April–June 1965* (Boston: Little, Brown & Co., 1994), 154, 159, 168.

10. John E. Peck, Letter, Alabama Department of Archives and History, SG11132, Folder #16, "Spanish Fort and Blakely, Battles," 2; Chester G. Hearn, *Mobile Bay and the Mobile Campaign: The Last Great Battles of the Civil War* (Jefferson, NC: McFarland and Company, Inc., Publishers, 1993), 175; Mildred Britton, ed., *The Civil War Diary of Charles Henry Snedeker*, 1966, Auburn University Archives, RG 844 (hereafter cited as *Snedeker Diary*).

11. Dabney H. Maury, "Defence of Mobile," *Southern Historical Society Papers* 3 (1877), 7; *OR*, Series I, Vol. 49, Part II, 1195; Phil Gottschalk, *In Deadly Earnest: The History of the First Missouri Brigade, C.S.A.* (Columbia: Missouri River Press, 1991), 521.

12. Edgar Wiley Jones, *History of the 18th Alabama Infantry Regiment*, compiled by C. David A. Pulcrano (Birmingham, AL: C.D.A. Pulcrano, 1994), 218.

13. Ibid., 222; Eli Davis, "That Hard Siege of Spanish Fort," *Confederate Veteran* 12 (1904), 591.

14. Jones, *18th Alabama*, 221–222.

15. Ibid., 222–223.

16. Arthur W. Bergeron, Jr., *Confederate Mobile* (Jackson: University Press of Mississippi, 1991), 176–177.

17. Britton, *Snedeker Diary*; Philip D. Stephenson, "Defence of Spanish Fort," *Southern Historical Society Papers* 39 (1914), 121.

18. George S. Waterman, "Afloat—Afield—Afloat, Notable Events of the Civil War," *Confederate Veteran* 8 (1900), 24.

19. Bergeron, *Confederate Mobile*, 185.

20. Jones, *18th Alabama*, 221; Bergeron, *Confederate Mobile*, 185.

21. Arthur W. Bergeron, Jr., "The Twenty-Second Louisiana Consolidated Infantry in the Defense of Mobile, 1864–1865," *Alabama Historical Quarterly* 38 (1976), 211; James Robert Maxwell, *Autobiography of James Robert Maxwell* (New York: Greenburg, Publisher, 1926), 281.

22. Abernethy, *Stockwell*, 166–167.

23. Nathaniel C. Hughes, Jr., ed., *The Civil War Memoirs of Philip Daingerfield Stephenson, D. D.* (Conway, AR: UCA Press, 1995), 362.

24. Jones, *18th Alabama*, 221; George Little and James R. Maxwell, *A History of Lumsden's Battery C.S.A.* (Tuscaloosa: United Daughters of the Confederacy, 1905), 66; Bergeron, *Confederate Mobile*, 178.

25. Abernethy, *Stockwell*, 165.

26. Bergeron, *Confederate Mobile*, 184; Carl E. Hatch, ed., *Dearest Susie: A Civil War Infantryman's Letters to His Sweetheart* (Jericho, NY: Exposition Press, Inc., 1971), 110–111.

27. Jones, *18th Alabama*, 218–219.

28. Ibid., 219.

29. Trudeau, *Out of the Storm*, 7.

30. Mark Mayo Boatner III, *The Civil War Dictionary* (New York: David McKay Co., Inc., 1959), 470; Cortright, "Last-Ditch Defenders," 62.

31. Letter of H. W. Hart, April 10, 1865, Mobile Public Library, Local History and Genealogy Division.

32. Trudeau, *Out of the Storm*, 159.

33. Cortright, "Last-Ditch Defenders," 62; Andrews, *Campaign of Mobile*, 237.

34. *OR*, Series I, Vol. 49, Part I, 202; Sidney Adair Smith and C. Carter Smith, Jr., eds., *Mobile: 1861–1865 Notes and a Bibliography* (Chicago: Wyvern Press, 1994), 40; Joseph Orville Jackson, ed., *"Some of the Boys . . .": The Civil War Letters of Isaac Jackson, 1862–1865* (Carbondale: Southern Illinois University Press, 1960), 246; Hearn, *Mobile Campaign*, 200.

35. Abernethy, *Stockwell*, 161–162; Edward Q. Nye, Diary, in "We Will Be Apt to Have a Hard Fight," *Baldwin Today*, April 10–April 11, 1991, C5.

36. Phillip E. Faller, "Battery H, 1st Indiana Heavy Artillery, Took Part in Civil War's Last Siege," *The Artilleryman* (Summer 1991), 14; Bergeron, *Confederate Mobile*, 177, 187.

37. Andrews, *Campaign of Mobile*, 81–82; 92; Hearn, *Mobile Campaign*, 176.

38. Andrews, *Campaign of Mobile*, 91–92.

39. Stephenson, "Defence of Spanish Fort," 122–123.

40. Andrews, *Campaign of Mobile*, 130–131.

41. Waterman, "Afloat—Afield—Afloat," 54; Letter of George Grant, Alabama Department of Archives and History, SG11124, Folder #3, "Cannons and Artillery: 'Lady Slocomb,'" 14; Stephenson, "Defence of Spanish Fort," 122.

42. Letter of George Grant, 16; Cortright, "Last-Ditch Defenders," 62.

43. Trudeau, *Out of the Storm*, 169; Letter of George Grant, 18; Andrews, *Campaign of Mobile*, 139–140.

44. Letter of George Grant, 13–14.

45. Cortright, "Last-Ditch Defenders," 62; Letter of George Grant, 18–19; *OR*, Series I, Vol. 49, Part II, 1199; Andrews, *Campaign of Mobile*, 140.

46. Bergeron, *Confederate Mobile*, 178–179; Andrews, *Campaign of Mobile*, 139–140, 171–172.

47. Britton, *Snedeker Diary*; William M. Macy, "Civil War Diary of William M. Macy," *Indiana Magazine of History* 30 (1934), 194.

48. Dabney H. Maury, "Defence of Spanish Fort," *Southern Historical Society Papers* 39 (1914), 132.

49. Mark Lyons, Letters, Alabama Department of Archives and History, SPR 194, 492–493; Bergeron, "Twenty-Second Louisiana," 210.

50. Cortright, "Last-Ditch Defenders," 62; Andrews, *Campaign of Mobile*, 141; Waterman, "Afloat—Afield—Afloat," 54; John A. Thomas, "Mebane's Battery," *Confederate Veteran* 5 (1897), 167.

51. Bergeron, *Confederate Mobile*, 184–185; Hatch, *Dearest Susie*, 108; Gerling, *One Hundred Seventeenth Illinois*, 102; Andrews, *Campaign of Mobile*, 185–186.

52. Faller, "Battery H," 18.

53. Stephenson, "Defence of Spanish Fort," 122.

54. Andrews, *Campaign of Mobile*, 73–75.

55. Ibid., 75.

56. Ibid., 76–77.

57. Ibid., 237.

58. Ibid., 84; Hearn, *Mobile Campaign*, 173.

59. Andrews, *Campaign of Mobile*, 84–85; *OR*, Series I, Vol. 49, Part I, 225.

60. Howard Coffin, *Full Duty: Vermonters in the Civil War* (Woodstock, VT: Countryman Press, Inc., 1993), 151–153; Blackburn, *"Dear Carrie . . . ,"* 306.

61. Andrews, *Campaign of Mobile*, 85–87; *OR*, Series I, Vol. 49, Part I, 225–226.

62. Ibid.

63. Ibid.

64. *OR*, Series I, Vol. 49, Part I, 316.

65. Ibid., Part II, 1188.

66. Ibid., 1185–1186; Gottschalk, *In Deadly Earnest*, 515.

67. Andrews, *Campaign of Mobile*, 178; *OR*, Series I, Vol. 49, Part I, 204; Hearn, *Mobile Campaign*, 185.

68. Andrews, *Campaign of Mobile*, 180–181.

69. Ibid., 184–185; Trudeau, *Out of the Storm*, 171.

70. Abernethy, *Stockwell*, 166.

71. Andrews, *Campaign of Mobile*, 137, 237–238.

72. Ibid., 184.

73. Leslie Anders, *The Twenty-First Missouri: From Home Guard to Union Regiment* (Westport, CT: Greenwood Press, 1975), 227.

74. Edwin S. Redkey, *A Grand Army of Black Men: Letters from African-American Soldiers in the Union Army, 1861–1865* (Cambridge, MA: Cambridge University Press, 1992), 157.

75. Bergeron, *Confederate Mobile*, 178, 185–186; Andrews, *Campaign of Mobile*, 90.

76. Bergeron, *Confederate Mobile*, 178; Jones, *18th Alabama*, 221; Abernethy, *Stockwell*, 205.

77. Trudeau, *Out of the Storm*, 153–154, 169; Andrews, *Campaign of Mobile*, 142.

78. Little and Maxwell, *History of Lumsden's Battery*, 66.

79. *OR*, Series I, Vol. 49, Part II, 1204, 1215.

80. Hearn, *Mobile Campaign*, 174.

81. Maury, "Defence of Spanish Fort," 131.

82. *OR*, Series I, Vol. 49, Part I, 316.

83. Trudeau, *Out of the Storm*, 174.

84. Hearn, *Mobile Campaign*, 200.

CHAPTER 11

"Not One Is Even *American*"

On the night of January 27, 1865, just two months before the start of the siege at Spanish Fort, a large cigar-shaped metallic object slid into the waters of upper Mobile Bay and headed out to do battle with a Union naval vessel. The occasion marked the first combat appearance of the Rebel torpedo boat *St. Patrick*. Patterned after the *David*, a steam-powered torpedo boat built in Charleston, the *St. Patrick* had not been ready for use in the naval battle of Mobile Bay. John P. Halligan, the designer, had the boat built at Selma and brought it to Mobile in September 1864. The *St. Patrick* was a steam-powered vessel about 50 feet long, 6 feet wide, and 10 feet deep, pointed at each end like a trout, with a copper torpedo affixed to a 12-foot pole at the bow. The craft carried a steam engine for propulsion on the surface of the water, but it also could be submerged and then driven by cranks operated by a six-man crew.[1]

The Rebels had experimented with primitive submarines earlier in the war at Mobile. Maury, seizing on the significance of such a weapon, provided a work site to New Orleans entrepreneur Horace L. Hunley and his partner, former steamboat skipper James R. McClintock. He assigned two young engineers from the 21st Alabama Infantry, Lieutenants George E. Dixon and William A. Alexander, to help with the design and construction of the vessel. The *H. L. Hunley*, built in the spring of 1863, carried a crew of nine and was powered by a hand-driven crank, which operated the propeller. Eight men turned the crank, while one (the commander) steered and directed. The iron 30-foot-long craft was shipped by rail to Charleston—where the Federal siege was growing particularly intense—in August 1863.

Everyone knew that the *Hunley* was an experimental craft, and on August 29 tragedy struck when five Confederate sailors drowned during testing of the vessel at the Charleston wharf. Undaunted, the submariners raised the boat and pushed ahead with the project. Dixon commanded the craft during several successful test dives, sometimes submerging for as long as thirty minutes at a time. But on October 15, Hunley himself and seven members of his crew were killed when the submarine filled with water and sank on a test run. The *Hunley* with the bodies of the unfortunate victims was recovered three weeks later.

Still determined to give the submarine a chance, Dixon boldly took the *Hunley* out to attack the U.S.S. *Housatonic* in Charleston harbor on the night of February 17, 1864. Dixon's torpedo blew a hole in the wooden hull of the *Housatonic*, and the Yankee ship went down within five minutes. Five sailors died, the rest managed to get off the ship. The successful Rebel attack ushered in a revolution in naval warfare. But the *Hunley* failed to return to port that night. Although it is not clear exactly what happened, the submarine apparently was disabled during the attack and sank to the bottom of Charleston harbor. Dixon and his eight crew members perished with the vessel.

All through the fall of 1864, Maury pressured John Halligan, now a commissioned Confederate naval lieutenant, to take the *St. Patrick* out into Mobile Bay and try her out against Union vessels. But Halligan continued to drag his feet. Exasperated, Maury appealed to the Secretary of War to put someone else in command of the boat. Commodore Ebenezer Farrand, commander of the Mobile naval squadron, declined to cooperate, so Maury appealed straight to President Jefferson Davis, who directed that the vessel be turned over to Maury.[2]

Maury assigned the *St. Patrick* to a Rebel naval officer, Lieutenant John T. Walker, who prepared to take the boat into action. An inspection of the craft revealed that Halligan had removed part of the vessel's machinery, and the *St. Patrick* lay idle until Walker managed to retrieve the lost parts. At last, on the night of January 27, 1865, the *St. Patrick* got underway, steaming out into the Bay for its first encounter with the enemy. The target was the U.S.S. *Octorara*, a paddle-wheel gunboat built in Brooklyn in 1862, nearly four times as long as the Rebel torpedo boat and equipped with an impressive array of guns. The *St. Patrick* opened fire on the enemy vessel at 1:00 A.M., but the torpedo struck the gunboat slightly behind its wheelhouse and failed to detonate. The *Octorara* returned fire, blasting the Rebel boat with musket fire and artillery fire. The two vessels were so close that one of the Yankee sailors even managed to grab hold of the *St. Patrick*'s smokestack;

he let go when one of the Rebels fired at him. The *St. Patrick* hobbled back to Mobile with some of her machinery damaged.[3]

The *St. Patrick*'s later history is shadowy. After the unsuccessful attack on the *Octorara*, the Rebels developed—and then abandoned—a plan to use the torpedo boat to stage a diversion that would allow the blockade runner *Red Gauntlet* to slip out of the Bay. Later the Confederates used the *St. Patrick* and the *S. D. Lee*, a new torpedo boat launched in February, to carry supplies to Spanish Fort. It is believed that the vessels were scuttled by the Rebels when Mobile was evacuated.[4]

The fates of the *Hunley* and the *St. Patrick* underscore the problems that the nonindustrial Confederacy faced in creating a viable navy. Ironically, the South could have channeled more money and effort into building submarines, which required only a fraction of the cost of building ironclads. Mobile witnessed more testing of submarines than any other Southern port. Unfortunately, Confederate naval officials failed to see the clear potential of these revolutionary new weapons and failed to put their development under a central control. Instead, Confederate naval planners concentrated on building ironclads. Five of these monsters were built in Mobile.[5]

Commodore Ebenezer Farrand, former chief of the Confederate naval station at Selma, had replaced "Old Buck" Buchanan as commander of Mobile's small naval squadron after the battle of Mobile Bay. Starting with their disagreements over use of the *St. Patrick*, Maury and Farrand—who was inclined to be bullheaded and slow to act—had engaged in an ongoing spat over control of the handful of Rebel naval vessels at Mobile. Maury had taken the matter to his superior, Richard Taylor, who soon addressed the problem. "The navy at Mobile is a farce," the no-nonsense Taylor bluntly wrote Jeff Davis. "Its vessels are continually tied up at the wharf; never in co-operation with the army." Farrand's expenses were "a waste of money." By March 1865, Farrand had been persuaded to cooperate with Maury: "He says he will place his vessels in any position I desire," Maury wrote, "and do all in his power to aid me."[6]

The Confederate Mobile squadron consisted of two gunboats, the *Nashville* and the *Morgan*, and two "floating batteries," the *Tuscaloosa* and the *Huntsville*, originally designed to be ironclads of the *Tennessee* class but never completely armed or armored. The Confederates had just decommissioned the *Baltic*, a converted riverboat described by her skipper as "rotten as punk, and . . . about as fit to go into action as a mud scow." The *Nashville*, *Morgan*, and *Huntsville* operated in the river between Blakely and Spanish Fort. Apparently, the *Tuscaloosa* was not in good enough working order to take an active role in these operations. Gunfire from the Rebel vessels was effective, especially against the Federal right flank at Blakely.[7]

The *Nashville* was a large side-wheeler patterned after the ironclad ram *Tennessee* but not completed in time for the naval battle of Mobile Bay. The shortage of iron had led the Rebels to armor the *Nashville* with plate removed from the older *Baltic*. The big vessel, 271 feet long, had a 24-pounder gun and three 7-inch muzzle loading rifles. Lieutenant John W. Bennett commanded the *Nashville*. In the Battle of Mobile Bay, Bennett had commanded the Rebel side-wheel gunboat *Gaines*, which was disabled by fire from the U.S.S. *Hartford*, Farragut's flagship, then beached and burned by her crew.

The *Morgan*, a wooden gunboat, was the only Rebel vessel to survive the defeat at Mobile Bay. The side-wheel steamer was 202 feet long and carried a 6-inch Brooke gun, a 7-inch Brooke gun, and two 32-pounder guns. The *Morgan*'s skipper was Lieutenant Joseph Fry. In 1873 Fry would be executed by the Spanish for running guns to the insurgents in Cuba.

Filling crews for the Rebel ships was an ongoing dilemma for the Confederate navy. Few recruits had ever been to sea. Desertion was a persistent problem. By 1864 most of the crews were formed from conscripts or transfers from the army. A large percentage of them were foreigners, recruited from recent immigrants in the South's coastal cities. A considerable number were African Americans who served as cooks, servants, and seamen.[8]

Old Buchanan had complained of the quality of the crews in 1863, calling the sailors "some of the greatest vagabonds you will ever read of." "One or two such hung during this time," he went on, "would have a wonderful effect." An officer on the *Morgan* wrote, "To call the *Morgan*'s crew sailors would be disgracing the name. Out of a hundred and fifty not one is even *American*, much less a Southerner . . . a desperate set of cut throats. But worst of all their loyalty is doubtful." William Lochiel Cameron, an officer aboard the flagship *Nashville*, wrote that "the men before the mast, or sailors, in the Confederate navy were, as a rule, not Americans at all, but Scotch, Irish, English, Italian, German, etc.—all soldiers of fortune. There did not seem to be an excess of 'fortune' in our service, as a day's liberty ashore easily consumed a month's pay—Confederate money." But he added that they "never were backward when a fight was on hand." Lieutenant Bennett, commander of the *Nashville*, seemed to echo these sentiments. "Frequently under fire," he reported, "their bearing was always admirable."[9]

Serving on a Confederate ironclad was difficult duty, particularly because poor ventilation made the vessel a virtual sweatbox. The few portholes along the sides of the ship and gratings on top of the shield provided the only fresh air, and heat was unbearable during the summer and during a naval action. The interior of the ship was dark and damp. An officer on the *Huntsville* called the vessel "terribly disagreeable for men to live on"; an officer on the Rebel ironclad *Atlanta* wrote, "I would defy anyone in the world to tell when it is day or night if he is confined below without any way of marking time." Such conditions led to sickness, poor morale, and desertion. Naval commanders tried to alleviate the problem by quartering the seamen outside the ships when possible. The crews of the *Huntsville* and *Tuscaloosa* spent much of their off-duty time sleeping in cotton warehouses in Mobile.[10]

Engines and boilers were constantly breaking down, and repairs were difficult because there were few qualified machinists. The danger of a boiler explosion was a real concern. Such a fate befell the Rebel gunboat *Chattahoochee*, a 130-foot vessel operating on the Apalachicola River. On May 27, 1863, the *Chattahoochee*'s boilers exploded, sending scalded crewmen screaming with pain onto the deck. Confusion and panic reigned, as the ship's skipper ordered the powder magazine, which was only a few feet from the boilers, flooded to prevent a worse explosion. Eighteen sailors died, and many more were seriously burned.[11]

Still, life for Rebel crewmen was not all that bad. They ate well compared to the Rebel soldiers, and captains still issued a ration of grog or a half-pint of wine to seamen each day. Off-duty sailors could enjoy the distractions of Mobile; and the Gulf City, with its cosmopolitan atmosphere, was especially genial for the young officers. One such officer, William Lochiel Cameron, was still a teenager when transferred to Mobile in the fall of 1863. He had enlisted at age 16 as a Confederate army private in his older brother's company in Memphis in June 1861. Later he found himself in charge of war materials at the Confederate arsenal at Selma, and soon he received an appointment as an officer in the Confederate States Navy. Now Cameron was serving aboard the *Nashville*, where he described himself as "a very small, young, and not especially significant officer."[12]

From their positions in the river, the *Nashville*, *Morgan*, and *Huntsville* lobbed shells at Federal positions during the day. At night, the officers manned boats carrying fresh troops bound for Spanish Fort and bringing wounded soldiers back. Still, a frustrated Gibson felt that the Rebel gunboats were not doing all they could do. When they did shell the Federal troops, they seemed to have a good effect, especially in breaking up work parties. On one occasion, a shell from one of the gunboats killed two soldiers in the 8th Iowa, and eighteen men in the 32nd Wisconsin were wounded in another attack. One witness gave a grisly description of a soldier in the 124th Illinois cut in half by a shell fragment: "cut off both his hands, and cut him so nearly in two that . . . a part of him fell one side up, and a part the other."[13]

Rebel gunboats also pounded Hawkins' division, on the right of the Federal line at Blakely. The black soldiers took the worst of the Rebel cannon fire, and the gunboats added to their misery with the effect of, to some degree, an enfilading fire. On March 28, to combat Rebel fire from Battery Huger and from the gunboats, the Federals placed two guns—a Whitworth and a steel rifle—on a high bluff along Bay Minette's eastern shore. Within two days, their other heavy guns were in place on Bay Minette, and from then on, they were able to protect the right flank of Carr's division and keep the Rebel gunboats out of range.[14]

The Rebels also pressed a number of old blockade-runners—including veteran craft like the *Red Gauntlet*, *Virgin*, *Mary*, and *Heroine*—into service as transports carrying men and supplies between Mobile, Blakely, and Spanish Fort. The Confederates used whatever they could get. George Waterman, who had served on the gunboat *Gaines*, accompanied a flotilla of small boats loaded with ammunition and supplies bound from Blakely for Spanish Fort, on the night of March 31. Not too seaworthy, with inexperienced soldiers at the oars, the skiffs made their way downstream. One got caught on obstructions in the river, but Waterman's vessel behind bumped into it and freed it. In the night, they passed the *Nashville*—damaged during an artillery duel earlier that day and on the way to Mobile for repairs—and at daybreak, they spotted Spanish Fort off to the left, across the marsh—in the wrong river. The little convoy had taken the wrong fork below Fort Huger and was heading down the Apalachee River into a mine field. Waterman's party had to row back upstream to Fort Huger, where, breakfasting with officers there, they learned that Federal heavy batteries and sharpshooters awaited them on the other side of the Blakely River. While sailing to Spanish Fort that afternoon, they heard the explosion of the Federal vessel *Rodolph*, which had struck a Rebel naval mine.[15]

The trip back upriver to Blakely could also be hazardous. Waterman described his return from Spanish Fort on the blockade runner *Heroine*, transporting dead and wounded soldiers from the garrison on the night of April 5. The little vessel got underway at 10:00 P.M. with all lights on board extinguished. Even the engine room hatchways were covered with tarpaulins to keep any glimmer of light from being spotted by the watchful eyes of Yankee pickets on Bay Minette. With only the sound of the engine and the paddles beating on the dark water, the *Heroine* made her way slowly past the Federal batteries. Then, ready to make a run for it, the skipper ordered full speed ahead, and the *Heroine*, which had a reputation for speed, surged ahead. Soon the Federal guns began to boom, and shells began to streak overhead, many of them plunging into the water with a hiss. But the captain and the pilot, both old veterans of blockade-running days, seemed amused by the whole situation. The *Heroine* avoided the Yankee shells and steamed on safely to the Blakely landing.[16]

Rebel transports and gunboats had more to fear from the Federal shore batteries than from the Yankee fleet. Canby had hoped for a quick end to the siege of Spanish Fort if the Federal navy could invest the Rebel garrison by its water side, as the army was doing by land. He had not reckoned on the extent of Rebel naval mines in the shallow river. Maury credited the network of torpedoes with drastically slowing down the Federal advance by preventing the Yankee ships from getting close to the rear of Spanish Fort. "Our torpedoes were of rude construction," he wrote. "The best were beer casks charged with gunpowder and anchored two to three feet below the surface of the water by an iron chain to a mushroom anchor. Many fuses with sensitive primers were set around the kegs, and as they rolled under a passing ship one or another primers would be discharged. They usually blew out a section of the bottom eight feet by ten. The ships sunk immediately. As the water was shoal, few of the people were killed on these ships." He added that the mere danger was enough to keep the Federal ships away.[17]

"We dreaded torpedoes more than anything else," a Federal seaman acknowledged, and Rear Admiral Henry K. Thatcher termed the naval mines as "the only enemies that we regard." The Confederates had made free use of these new weapons—feared as much by sailors as by the soldiers on land—and hundreds of them dotted the river approaches to Spanish Fort. Their presence virtually held the superior Federal fleet at bay.[18]

From his flagship, the *Stockdale*, Thatcher commanded the Federal fleet of fifteen monitors and gunboats, and on board these vessels men much the same as those in the Rebel navy went about their duties faithfully, coping with the transition of naval warfare from wooden sailing craft to steam-powered armorclads.

As much as half the Federal navy's manpower came from immigrants; twenty-five different nationalities were represented on the *Hartford*. Irishmen, Englishmen, Germans, and Scandinavians constituted the largest numbers of foreign-born. African Americans served in large numbers on Federal ships, enduring the same racial prejudice from their white shipmates as found in the army. Most performed well. As in the Rebel navy, most Federal seamen had no previous experience on ships. The captain of the U.S.S. *Fernandina* in October 1864 called a draft of new recruits "about the greenest specimens of humanity who ever went on board a ship."[19]

Life for the blue jackets was similar to that of their counterparts on Confederate ships. Duty was monotonous, punctuated only by occasional chases of blockade runners and even rarer combat with enemy vessels. In the Gulf, sailors coped with a repetitious diet supplemented only rarely by fresh meat and vegetables. Pork and beans seemed to be the steady diet for the *Hartford*'s crew during the spring of 1864. Oppressive heat and sickness contributed to the discomforts of seamen whose most treasured moments came with intermittent shore leaves and the chance for a night of drinking and merriment.[20]

As in the Rebel navy, the Yankee tars found duty on the ironclads especially difficult. Although they received slightly higher pay than sailors on the wooden ships, seamen serving on the monitors were subject to intolerable heat and sickness because of the poor ventilation. Temperatures often exceeded 100 degrees below deck. The captain of the *Chickasaw* wrote his mother after the action at Mobile Bay, "these iron-clads are pretty rough on a fellow, they are not and have no comforts." And an officer on the *Manhattan*, another vessel in that battle, wrote, "a man who would stay in an ironclad from choice is a candidate for the insane asylum."[21]

On March 28, as the bluecoats strengthened their own earthworks and Gibson braced for an attack on Spanish Fort, Federal monitors and supporting gunboats probed the Rebel defenses by water, steaming menacingly into the mouth of the Blakely River. The guns of the Yankee ships and Spanish Fort, supported by Batteries Huger and Tracy, hammered away at each other but did little damage. Barely a mile and a half from the fort, the *Milwaukee* and the *Winnebago*, two double-turreted ironclad monitors with four 11-inch guns, opened fire on a Rebel steamer conveying supplies to the garrison.

Suddenly, a resounding blast struck the *Milwaukee*, and the big monitor started going down. The skipper, Lieutenant Commander James H. Gillis, reported that he "felt a shock and saw at once that a torpedo had exploded on the port side of the vessel." In barely three minutes, the rear of the *Milwaukee* had sunk, but the bow remained above water for almost an hour giving the crew time to escape. The survivors were rescued and taken aboard the monitor *Kickapoo*. The sinking of the *Milwaukee* astonished the Federals because they had conducted mine-sweeping operations in the same area the previous night and felt the waters had been cleared.[22]

A less serious accident befell the *Octorara*, a veteran of the battle at Mobile Bay and survivor of the *St. Patrick*'s abortive attack two months earlier. The side-wheel steam gunboat—equipped with two 9-inch guns, two 32-pounders, four 24-pounder howitzers, a 100-pounder Parrott rifle, and a 9-inch smooth-bore rifle—was conducting supporting operations on March 28 when she ran aground in 8 feet of water while attempting to cross the Blakely bar. Then a tube in her starboard boiler burst, putting the *Octorara* out of action. Repairs to her boiler would delay the vessel's crossing the bar for another twenty-four hours.[23]

But the next day Yankee sailors were not so lucky. After a strong east wind blew the *Winnebago* from where she was anchored and nearly caused her to collide with the *Osage,* a single-turret monitor, Lieutenant Commander William M. Gamble ordered the latter vessel to raise anchor and move forward. Suddenly the *Osage* struck a torpedo and sank in 12 feet of water. This time the Rebel mine claimed casualties, four men killed and eight wounded.[24]

That same day, Thatcher himself barely escaped injury. Sailors had recovered one of the Rebel naval mines and taken it aboard one of the gunboats. It was supposed to have been disabled and emptied out, then taken to the *Stockdale* for Thatcher to look at. While two sailors were dismantling the mine, it exploded. The two blue jackets were wounded, but Thatcher, sitting just five yards away from the torpedo, was unhurt.[25]

Another setback occurred on April 1. At 2:40 in the afternoon, the steamer *Rodolph* struck a torpedo while engaged in an attempt to raise the *Milwaukee.* The explosion tore a 10-foot-diameter hole in her starboard bow, and the *Rodolph* quickly sank in 12 feet of water. Four sailors died.[26]

Thatcher was loath to expose his ships to further danger. He had already lost three vessels and felt that the torpedoes posed too great a risk. The Rebels, he believed, were laying them at night. For the time being, the fear of torpedoes had the Union fleet stymied. Canby was disappointed in the lack of support from the navy, much as Gibson was with the Confederate gunboats.[27]

The Federals undertook the tedious and time-consuming chore of mine-sweeping to remove the dangerous torpedoes and cut a passage through for the squadron. The *Metacomet,* with Commander Pierce Crosby at the helm, was active in this work. The swift *Metacomet*—a paddle wheel, "double-ender," gunboat, armed the same as the *Octorara*—had pursued and captured the Rebel gunboat *Selma* in the Battle of Mobile Bay. Crosby supervised mine-sweeping operations involving twenty rowboats moving up and down the Blakely River with large nets dangling between them. The sailors dragged the channel to bring up torpedoes, then disarmed them by carrying them onto the marsh and puncturing them with an auger or a musket ball.[28]

Meanwhile, some of the Yankee sailors got their first chance to see some real action. Lieutenant Commander Gillis, captain of the ill-fated *Milwaukee,* landed with a party of blue jackets on the banks of the Blakely River and set up a naval battery of three thirty-pounder Parrott rifles. The seamen were to assist in the bombardment of Spanish Fort, and Canby reported that they "behaved admirably." The *Octorara,* back in action with her boiler repaired, began hurling 100-pound shells at the Rebel fort. And after one of her shells struck the steamer *Jeff Davis* on April 2 and drove the little vessel back upriver, Confederate transports suspended trips to the fort during the daytime.[29]

Although the Yankee ships couldn't reach them, the *Nashville, Morgan,* and *Huntsville* soon felt the impact of the Federal heavy guns. As the morning mist cleared on March 31, the Confederate seamen spotted the enemy's 30-pounder Parrotts just placed on the northern shore of Bay Minette and made ready to fire, but too late. Lieutenant Cameron noted that the attack took the officers of the *Nashville* by surprise as they were finishing breakfast: "[S]uddenly a solid shot struck the wheel house, then another, and splinters began to fly."[30] The big Yankee guns "opened a rapid and accurate fire" on the Rebel gunboats. "We responded with a few shots," Lieutenant Bennett reported, "but finding our elevation inefficient to reach, we steamed a little above Tracy and anchored beyond range. The ship was struck eight times, but without serious injury." The *Nashville* moved off to Mobile for repairs.[31]

The *Nashville* was back in service on April 3, and Liddell sent a staff officer aboard to point out enemy positions he wanted the gunboat to shell. Bennett set up a signal post below the bluff at Blakely to report on the effectiveness of the fire. At 1:00 P.M. the *Nashville* opened fire on the Federal right at Blakely and did not let up for four hours. Cheering from the Rebel lines and reports from the signal post told Bennett that his shots were punishing the black division. The *Nashville* fired sporadically at the enemy for the next three days until nearly out of ammunition.[32]

The big Federal guns kept the Rebel gunboats at bay, but the Rebel naval mines kept the Federal ships at bay throughout the siege. By April 12, the Federal mine-sweepers had recovered 150 torpedoes from the waters of upper Mobile Bay. Thatcher commended his men for their "coolness, judgement and perseverance." In spite of these efforts, the tug *Ida* struck a Rebel torpedo on April 13 and sank after the explosion burst her boilers. A Federal seaman described the scene: "I think, her smoke stack must have gone fifty feet into the air." The next day two more ships, the gunboat *Sciota* and a launch from the *Cincinnati*, went down. Five sailors died and six were wounded on the *Sciota*, and three died on the launch. Even as late as May 12, an army transport, the *R. B. Hamilton*, struck a mine and sank with thirteen men killed or injured.[33]

Confederate torpedoes sank nine Federal warships and one launch in the operations in upper Mobile Bay and killed or wounded some 200 sailors. Of all the weapons available to the Rebels in the Mobile campaign, Maury rated the naval mines as "the most striking and effective." Torpedoes sank more Federal ships than all Confederate ironclads combined. If the

Confederates had done more to develop torpedoes earlier in the war, they might have thwarted Farragut's entrance into Mobile Bay in August 1864. They could have seriously hampered or slowed Canby's advance. The Confederacy also could have taken submarine technology more seriously. The damage that a whole fleet of *St. Patrick*s might have done to Thatcher's naval squadron could have been substantial.[34]

NOTES

1. Arthur W. Bergeron, Jr., *Confederate Mobile* (Jackson: University Press of Mississippi, 1991), 169; Louis S. Schafer, *Confederate Underwater Warfare* (Jefferson, NC: McFarland and Co., Inc., Publishers, 1996), 155–156.
2. Bergeron, *Confederate Mobile*, 169.
3. Ibid., 170.
4. Ibid., 170; Sidney H. Schell, "Submarine Weapons Tested at Mobile during the Civil War," *Alabama Review* 45 (1992), 181–182.
5. Schell, "Submarine Weapons," 163.
6. Chester G. Hearn, *Mobile Bay and the Mobile Campaign: The Last Great Battles of the Civil War* (Jefferson, NC: McFarland and Company, Inc., Publishers, 1993), 138, 145; Bergeron, *Confederate Mobile*, 170–171.
7. William N. Still, Jr., *Iron Afloat: The Story of the Confederate Armorclads* (Columbia: University of South Carolina Press, 1971), 204, 224.
8. William N. Still, Jr., John M. Taylor, and Norman C. Delaney, *Raiders and Blockaders: The American Civil War Afloat* (London: Brassey's, 1998), 86–87.
9. Still, *Iron Afloat*, 197–198; William Lochiel Cameron, "The Battles Opposite Mobile," *Confederate Veteran* 23 (1915), 306; *War of the Rebellion: A Compilation of the Official Records of the Union and Confederate Armies* (Washington, DC: Government Printing Office, 1880–1901) (hereafter cited as *OR*), Series I, Vol. 49, Part I, 322.
10. Still, *Iron Afloat*, 100–101.
11. Ibid.; Maxine Turner, *Navy Gray: A Story of the Confederate Navy on the Chattahoochee and Apalachicola Rivers* (University: University of Alabama Press, 1988), 99.
12. Still, Taylor, and Delaney, *Raiders and Blockaders*, 92–93; Still, *Iron Afloat*, 199; Cameron, "The Battles Opposite Mobile," 305.
13. Cameron, "Battles Opposite Mobile," 305; Hearn, *Mobile Campaign*, 173.
14. Christopher C. Andrews, *History of the Campaign of Mobile* (New York, 1867), 62, 168.
15. George S. Waterman, "Afloat—Afield—Afloat," *Confederate Veteran* 8 (1900), 21–22.
16. Ibid., 24–25.
17. Andrews, *Campaign of Mobile*, 66; Dabney H. Maury, "Defence of Spanish Fort," *Southern Historical Society Papers* 39 (1914), 134.
18. Milton F. Perry, *Infernal Machines: The Story of Confederate Submarine and Mine Warfare* (Baton Rouge: Louisiana State University Press, 1965), 188.
19. Still, Taylor, and Delaney, *Raiders and Blockaders*, 56–57.
20. Ibid., 74–76.
21. Ibid., 77–78.

22. Perry, *Infernal Machines*, 185; U.S. Naval History Division, *Civil War Naval Chronology, 1861–1865*, vol. 5, *1865* (Washington, DC: U.S. Government Printing Office, 1965), 69.

23. Andrews, *Campaign of Mobile*, 79.

24. Hearn, *Mobile Campaign*, 169–170; Perry, *Infernal Machines*, 185–186; Vincent Cortright, "Last-Ditch Defenders at Mobile," *America's Civil War* (January 1997), 61.

25. Perry, *Infernal Machines*, 186.

26. Andrews, *Campaign of Mobile*, 94.

27. Hearn, *Mobile Campaign*, 170.

28. Perry, *Infernal Machines*, 187; Andrews, *Campaign of Mobile*, 132–133.

29. U. S. Naval History Division, *Naval Chronology*, vol. 5, 79–80; Andrews, *Campaign of Mobile*, 132, 139.

30. Cameron, "Battles Opposite Mobile," 305.

31. *OR*, Series I, Vol. 49, Part I, 320.

32. Ibid., 320–321.

33. Perry, *Infernal Machines*, 187, 188.

34. Ibid.; Dabney H. Maury, "Defence of Mobile," *Southern Historical Society Papers* 3 (1877), 11; Hearn, *Mobile Campaign*, 205.

CHAPTER 12

"A Splendid Defense and They Knew It"

By April 8, Federal work parties were burrowing close to the Rebel garrison at Spanish Fort, and Yankee artillery fire had become so intense that the graycoats could do little about it except dig in and take it. Bertram's brigade was now within 100 yards of Fort McDermott. In Carr's division, Jonathan Moore's brigade was within 100 yards of Redoubt 6. In McArthur's division, Lucius Hubbard's brigade had dug a sap to within 60 yards of the Red Fort. Inside the Rebel lines, men in Lumsden's and Garrity's Alabama batteries and Ector's Texas brigade may have wondered if a rematch with some of the same troops they had fought at Nashville was in the making.[1]

Although morale was still good, the garrison's situation was poor. The Rebels had endured several days of heavy bombardment, and Lieutenant Cameron on board the *Nashville* wrote, "a view of the fort in the morning showed plainly what a wreck had been made of it." Gibson brought up slaves from the fort's cooking yard to help repair the earthworks and asked Maury for more laborers. The Rebels were so short of ammunition that Gibson ordered his men to hold their fire, except for sharpshooters in the advanced rifle pits.[2]

After a heavy rain on April 7, the night turned chilly and clear. Federal pickets could hear heavy firing of artillery and small arms off in the direction of Blakely around midnight. During the night, Alabama artillery officer James Garrity and one of his men stealthily crept close to one of McArthur's work parties busily shoveling away. Although a bright moon illuminated the landscape, the Federals were so intent on their digging that they never realized Garrity was there, so close that a spadeful of dirt cascaded down on him, and he clearly heard one of the bluecoats declare, "We'll give the rebels hell tomorrow."[3]

Heavy artillery fire greeted Gibson on Saturday morning, April 8, and he feared that the enemy would assault his works that day. He ordered his skirmishers to harass the Federal work parties as much as they could and cautioned his men to watch for a sudden attack. "Every precaution must be taken to prevent a surprise," he warned.[4]

Meanwhile, Maury paid a visit on Saturday, along with chief engineer Samuel Lockett. The garrison's situation looked precarious. Although evacuating the fort seemed unavoidable, Maury felt that Gibson's defenders would be safe for a few more days and set April 11 as the day for the garrison to withdraw. Gibson was not so confident. He conferred with Holtzclaw that morning, and the two men agreed that they should evacuate Spanish Fort that day. But Lieutenant Colonel Williams persuaded them to hold off a little longer. Williams wanted to place four twelve-pounders on the left of the Rebel line. He felt that he could finish the battery by nightfall and slow down the Yankees' work details by enfilade fire. Gibson agreed to wait. It was almost a fatal decision.[5]

Federal artillery at Blakely also opened a heavy bombardment of the Rebel garrison there. Although Liddell had ordered his own gunners to shell the Yankees at 8:00 A.M., heavy fire from the bluecoat batteries quickly suppressed the Rebel guns.[6]

The afternoon proved climactic for the Rebel gunboats. At 2:00 P.M., three thirty-pounder Parrotts of Wimmer's 1st Indiana Battery H—just relocated from Bay Minette to the rear of Hawkins' battered division— opened fire on the three vessels in the Tensas River about a mile away. The first shot hit the *Morgan*, completely unaware that heavy artillery was that near. Rebel seamen were unable to see the Yankee guns, hidden among the trees. After a few minutes' pause, the *Morgan* and *Nashville* returned fire, gauging the enemy position by smoke from the Yankee guns and wounding two of the cannoneers. Lieutenant Bennett complained that many of the *Nashville*'s shells were defective or partly damaged, especially the fuses, causing fragments to fall like canister far short of their targets. The duel continued until the *Morgan* and *Nashville*, disabled and low on ammunition, moved back out of range. The *Morgan* apparently suffered the worst of the encounter, having been struck near the waterline. The Indiana gunners then focused their fire on the *Huntsville*, which also steamed off as soon as darkness fell.[7]

Gibson had been especially concerned about enemy movement on his unprotected left flank. He had even considered launching an attack there but hesitated to commit troops without the support of the Rebel gunboats.

Gibson finally gave up the idea, but he placed a heavier concentration of his own troops on his left in case of an enemy attack.[8]

Gibson instructed his gunners in Fort McDermott to shell Yankee work parties to their front. The Rebel cannoneers obeyed and were answered by a fire so intense that they could no longer man their guns. Enemy fire destroyed an ammunition chest and disabled one gun. Gibson was now even more convinced that the Federals had something big in the works. He determined to probe the enemy's intentions and ordered his artillery to begin a general shelling of the Yankee lines at sundown.[9]

But no sooner had the Rebel batteries opened fire at 5:30 P.M. than the Yanks replied with a staggering barrage of their own. The fire was devastating, as Federal mortars rained down destruction on the Spanish Fort garrison, and bombproofs no longer afforded protection. Yankee shells pierced the toughest "gopher hole" and sent graycoat riflemen scrambling for cover of any kind. Phil Stephenson wrote, "There was no shelter from these bombs—no defense from that fire. We had to stand and take it." Federal shells blasted through their stout bombproof "as though it was paper." Reeling from the concussions, Rebel soldiers staggered about, blood rushing from ears, mouths, and eyes.[10]

Canby was ready to deal the death blow to Spanish Fort; and Grant's watchdog, Brigadier General Comstock, finally seemed pleased. "At last," he wrote in his diary, "the general decided to assault in about 36 hours. A little bombardment [scheduled] in pm. beginning at 5 1/2 pm." The Federals had ninety-six guns in place now—fifty-three siege guns and thirty-seven field guns, plus four thirty-pounders and two hundred-pounder rifles on Bay Minette—and A. J. Smith ordered his gunners to open fire at 5:30 "with every piece that could throw iron into the fort, and continue until dark." The "little bombardment" lasted until 7:30 P.M. Canby planned a general assault for the following morning.[11]

It was the most devastating pounding the Rebels had taken yet. Phil Stephenson described what it was like:

> Think of seventy-five or a hundred guns massed in a semi-circle thick around us. . . . The din was so great it distracted our senses. We could hardly hear each other speak and could hardly tell what we were doing. The crackling of musketry, the unbroken roaring of artillery, the yelling and shrieking of the shells, the bellowing boom of the mortars, the dense shroud of sulphurous smoke thickening around us—it was thought the mouth of the pit had yawned and the uproar of the damned was about us.[12]

"I never heard the like of it before," wrote a soldier in the 19th Iowa. "I have often heard of terrific cannonading but this was the first time that I could realize what it was like." The Federal artillery fire was so intense, C. C. Andrews wrote, "There is scarcely anything in the phenomena of nature to which it could be compared." And another Iowa soldier wrote, "This firing . . . made it seem impossible for any in the fort to survive."[13]

And yet survive they did. Stephenson and many of the gunners in Slocomb's battery soon gave up trying to hide in the redoubt and actually came out to cringe in the open area behind. There they could at least see the mortar shells as they curved toward them. Stephenson became particularly adept at observing the path of the shell and gauging where it would hit. "Sing out, Stephenson," the officers would yell, "and tell us which way to run!"[14]

Hoping to exploit the confusion created by the heavy bombardment, Carr conferred with Colonel James L. Geddes and instructed him to "press with skirmishers on his right against the rebel left, feel their strength, ascertain the nature of the ground, and take as much as he could hold." The ailing Geddes—"shaking with a chill," Carr noted—took in the division chief's orders, nodded, then sprinted back to his brigade to select the troops to carry out the operation. The objective was a pine-covered hilltop in the marsh on the Rebel left. If the Federals took it, they could place a battery there and enfilade the Rebel lines.[15]

At about 6:00 P.M., Geddes gave the assignment to Colonel William B. Bell in his old command, the 8th Iowa. Two companies were to advance, take the crest, and begin digging in for the night. Geddes asked Bell how soon he could be ready, and Bell replied, "Fifteen minutes." Bell quickly collected Captain Henry Muhs' Company A and Lieutenant Henry Vineyard's Company G. The soldiers pushed off from behind the gabion wall on the extreme right flank and into the swamp opposite the Rebel left. The rest of the Iowans let out a loud cheer, hoping the Rebs would think a general assault was in progress.[16]

The path to the hilltop objective was far from inviting. Bell's troops must cross a hundred yards of "an almost impassable swamp, thickly strewn with fallen trees and brush, and in which the water and mud were very deep." One soldier recalled felled trees slashed waist high "and left hanging to the stumps and lying criss-cross in all shapes." No wonder the graycoats had failed to fortify this swampy area. The Iowans struggled forward, sloshing their way through the water and mud, and immediately they drew fire from the Rebel works.[17]

Ector's Texans continued to peck away at the Federals, and soon the Iowans were bogged down in the marsh, taking cover as best they could and returning fire from behind the naked trunks and branches of the felled trees. In the rapidly falling dusk, Yankee heavy guns continued to boom all along the line as the bombardment of the Rebel fort continued. Bell made his way back to the trenches and ordered another company forward to support his men in the marsh.

Almost immediately the colonel had second thoughts. If the Rebs counterattacked, his three small companies would be thrown back and annihilated in the swamp. Bell hastily dispatched a courier to Geddes. Could he send in *all* his companies? No reply came back. Fearing to delay any longer, he ordered the entire 8th Iowa to advance.[18]

It was one of those rare impulsive actions on which the outcome of a battle frequently hinged. Bell himself took the lead, as his men—already anxious to join their comrades in the swamp—rushed out of their trenches. Meanwhile, the leading companies had already gained the hilltop, and Lieutenant Vineyard, hit in the left arm, fell near the crest as another enemy bullet struck him in the left thigh. As his men hesitated, he waved them on. "Pay no attention to me, boys," he urged, "Move on." Vineyard's wounds would prove fatal.[19]

The Iowans held the hilltop, but what now? No one had ordered a general advance, and the 8th Iowa was unsupported. If the Rebels launched a counterattack, everything gained could be lost. "Come on! Come on!" some of the Iowans turned and shouted to the troops in the rear. Bell made another split-second decision and ordered his command forward. Under heavy fire, the Iowans plunged ahead. In one bold surge, they overwhelmed the Rebel rifle pits manned by Ector's Texans. Bell quickly observed that the enemy's rifle pits were the *only* works on the Confederate left and that they were not connected with each other or with the main works. "This enabled us to attack them in detail," he later wrote, "and we had carried a considerable portion of their works before their main force was aware that we had turned their left."[20]

Momentum carried the Iowans on into the enemy's main works. Federal mortar shells were still falling as the Iowans planted their flag on the ramparts, and Bell, waving his hat, signaled the friendly gunners to cease fire.[21]

Ector's troops weren't about to give up without a fight. Captain James A. Howze rallied thirty men in his "Star Company." With a Rebel yell, the Texans threw themselves against the 8th Iowa in a desperate counterattack in the moonlight, but they were quickly thrown back. Federal gunfire cut down their young color bearer, and the Rebs fell back in confusion. "This checked us," a Texas soldier recalled. "Some one gathered up the colors and we retreated. This was the last gun we fired."[22]

Rebel determination persisted as a final desperate gray-clad column—about 200 of David Coleman's mountain boys from North Carolina and 100 of Lieutenant Alfred G. Clark's provost guard—launched another counter-attack. Again the graycoats hurled themselves against the Iowans, but Yankee gunfire cut Clark down, and the Rebel lunge faltered, then fizzled out. But the Federal advance had been temporarily halted as well.[23]

The 8th Iowa encountered isolated pockets of Rebels still resisting in their trenches. The Federals rooted them out ditch by ditch. Many of the Texans fought to the bitter end. "We here witnessed," Bell reported, "the spectacle of dying in the last ditch, as quite a number of the rebels refused to surrender." He also noted that a number of the Rebels fired a final defiant shot before throwing up their hands and surrendering. The Iowans captured about 300 yards of the Rebel works and took 350 prisoners. They had lost five men killed and twenty wounded in the assault.[24]

The other regiments in Geddes' brigade moved in to support the 8th Iowa, but not immediately. It was well after dark before they arrived. The bluecoats had a foothold now and had no intention of giving it up. They did not realize how close to victory they were. Had they pushed forward, they could have taken the Rebel fort. At the very least, they could have cut off Gibson's troops from their only escape route. They were just a few hundred yards in the rear of the Red Fort, and Stephenson wrote, "we could see them moving about in the moonlight. Why they did not come right on and take us, too, we could never understand." But with night coming on, the bluecoats were satisfied just to secure their position. In the darkness, the Yankees began throwing up earthworks, digging until nearly midnight.[25]

In Benton's division, pickets of the 96th Ohio had made their way close to the Red Fort, so close that they could hear the graycoats on the other side. "Johnnie," one of the Yanks shouted, "listen a minute. Lee's surrendered to Grant; you're gone up. Don't I often told you so!" There was only stillness in the darkness ahead. "Yank," a voice finally replied, "if that's so, we don't need this old fort; come and take it!"[26]

Nightfall proved a blessing for Gibson. There was no way now to hold the fort, but he still had one chance to get his men out. In the darkness, his troops might be able to slip away via the prepared escape route. Gibson telegraphed Maury—just returned to Mobile—about 10:00 P.M. and broke the news that his left had been turned and that his escape route was also in jeopardy. Maury ordered him to evacuate. Gibson's Louisiana brigade fell back from their position behind Fort McDermott and—as they had done at Nashville—prepared to cover the Rebel retreat.[27]

Whispered orders made the rounds to puzzled men, unaware that Gibson had planned for this for some time. Captain Garrity sent an officer with a request for ammunition. When the officer returned with only a handful of spikes, the Alabama cannoneers knew what they must do. They spiked their guns and moved toward the treadway. In Slocomb's battery, Sergeant John Bartley slipped the company's guidon off its pole and wrapped it inside his jacket, carried it with him as they evacuated the Red Fort. The Louisianans also spiked their guns and left them behind, including their favorite, the disabled Lady Slocomb.[28]

The scene on the beach was an eerie one, as soldiers, gunners, sick and wounded, slaves—the whole garrison—made their way carefully and silently down a steep ravine and gathered for the march across the treadway in the dark. The graycoats slipped off their shoes, slung their rifles on their left shoulders—away from the enemy so that the glint of metal would not give them away.[29]

Although the shattering Federal bombardment had long since ceased, occasional shells still burst over the Rebel works. As Phil Stephenson and Tony Barrow hurried toward the beach in the dark, a large artillery shell exploded in the air, showering Barrow with fragments. Barrow fell with a cry, and as the rest of Slocomb's gunners pushed on, Stephenson bent to help his fallen pal. "Where are you hit, Tony?" "Oh, Phil," Barrow moaned, "I'm killed. Tell my mother I died for my country!" Stephenson frantically looked for a wound, but there was none. Barrow's blanket roll had absorbed the shock of the shell fragment and knocked him to the ground, but he was all right. The two men sprang to their feet and ran to catch up with their comrades.[30]

The whole gray column seemed to have dissolved into the darkness ahead, as if it had melted into the earth. In fact, the troops had only gone out of Stephenson's line of sight as they disappeared over the edge of the bluff. "Down we followed," Stephenson wrote, "pell mell, right down the almost perpendicular sides of the gorge, clinging to vines, saplings, the sides of rocks; any way to keep our hold, until we reached the bottom, fifty feet or so below. And there, to our amazement, we found the beginning of a treadway."[31]

The graycoats followed Gibson's extraordinary escape route along the beach behind Spanish Fort, then along the shore to the north. The Rebels passed so close to the swamp just taken by Bell's Iowans that they could actually hear the voices of the Federal pickets in the darkness. The narrow treadway turned into the bay. "The water was shallow," Stephenson wrote, "and we walked just above the water's surface." A Federal shore battery fired a shot, causing quite a scare in the Rebel ranks; but the Yankees had not spotted them, it was only a routine shot to discourage Rebel vessels in the Bay.[32]

To Stephenson's surprise, the treadway ended on one of those same marshy offshore islands that he himself had mused about as an escape route. As they jumped from the end of the treadway to the island, they could make out the dark shapes of several Rebel gunboats in the water beyond. "When I jumped from the treadway," Stephenson wrote, "I sank to my waist in mud." A bad time to be discovered, he thought, hearing shouting and small arms fire from the shore. But still there was no sign of detection from the Yankees.[33]

Meanwhile, Edgar Jones and his mates in the 18th Alabama were scrambling out of the marsh too. Once again surgeon Shepherd cut a comical figure as he swashed along carrying a jug of whiskey. Not a good jumper, he quickly became bogged down and yelled for help, promising to share his whiskey when he got on board the ship.[34]

"Looking out on the water," Stephenson remembered, "we saw a yawl pulled cautiously to the shore. . . . In we plunged, rushing up to our necks in water, and throwing our guns in first, pitched into the boat, head over heels, laughing, spluttering, struggling." In minutes the boat was packed "full to sinking" with gray-clad soldiers. Federal cannon fire ripped through the Rebel ship's rigging. Curled up on deck, the wringing wet Stephenson thought "what a shame to be sunk in this boat after what we have gone through this day."[35]

The evacuees had reached a site on the Blakely River across from Fort Huger. Transports carried the Spanish Fort troops up the bay to Blakely, and part of the garrison—a couple hundred soldiers under Colonel Bush Jones—made their way north across the swamp to Fort Blakely. The exhausted Rebels disembarked and spent about an hour at the landing where they built some fires and waited to hear news of their fate. Would they stay here or move on to Mobile? In the early predawn darkness, they could hear sporadic firing from the direction of the Confederate works, and an occasional musket ball struck a nearby tree. Finally the word came. They were pulling out. The soldiers climbed aboard the transports, which sailed away in the darkness.[36]

By midnight, most of the Spanish Fort garrison had slipped away, but part of the Rebel picket line did not receive the orders to evacuate. Edgar Jones estimated that about one third of the 18th Alabama fell captive when the Federals overran the fort—sacrificed so that the bulk of Gibson's force could get away in the dark. Realizing that they were alone, many of the graycoats simply gave up. "Don't shoot, Yanks," one of them called, "we are coming in."[37]

As the abandoned earthworks of Spanish Fort lay quiet, the Federals gingerly sent out patrols to probe the Rebel defenses. Now the moon was high, and light gleamed from Yankee bayonets as troops entered the redoubts all along the line. By midnight, Carr's troops milled about on the

Rebel left, and McArthur's veterans cautiously entered the Red Fort. On the right, Bertram sent out a reconnaissance party into Fort McDermott and was astonished to find no Rebel resistance. Bertram's brigade moved in and occupied the redoubt and Old Spanish Fort as well.[38]

The graycoats had evacuated Spanish Fort so skillfully that many Federal troops still in their own lines mistook their Yankee comrades in the deserted earthworks for the enemy and opened fire. The *Octorara*, unaware of the circumstances, also lobbed several shells into the fort. Signal officers waved torches as a sign to the Federal gunboats and to the troops on land that they now had possession of Spanish Fort. "For God's sake," screamed one officer, "cease firing. We have the fort!"[39]

Thomas Stevens of the 28th Wisconsin led his troops over the parapet, and was surprised to find groups of Federals already there. He took in the extent of damage the Federal guns had already done. "It was a sight," he wrote. Bluecoats began raising their flags over the fort. "You ought to have heard the cheers," Stevens wrote, "when the stars & stripes were flung to the breeze."[40]

Soldiers could hear the cheers of Union troops at Spanish Fort all the way to Fort Blakely. For the Federals, the sounds were assuring, but they brought no good cheer to the Rebels. Mississippi soldier Henry Lacy, on picket duty, reported seeing the flash of gunfire to the south. Shortly afterward he heard a soldier of Hawkins' division call out, "Dat rackit down de crick means you is guine slide into de reunion tomorrow."[41]

At Spanish Fort, blue-coated victors wandered over the Rebel earthworks, looking like snow drifts in the moonlight, and swarmed over abandoned clothing and articles the Rebs could not take with them. Captain Charles J. Allen, acting chief engineer for the 16th Corps, was mulling over the fate of the Confederate dead strewn about the fort, when a voice sounded out, "Who goes there?" "An officer of the Union Army," he responded. He looked down to see a wounded Confederate officer. It was Lieutenant Alfred Clark, who had led the failed counterattack by the Rebel provost guard. Clark asked for water, and Allen found three Yankee soldiers to carry him to the field hospital. Watching him go, Allen hoped he would make it, but the bold Rebel officer died later.[42]

The Federals' spirits were lifted. "We feel first-rate," Edward Nye's journal entry on April 8 records, "Weather fine. Not much sleep tonight. Too busy collecting spoils and picking up Johnnie around in the bushes."[43]

With daylight, the extent of damage was evident at Spanish Fort. "The whole interior is in a perfect smash," newspaperman Benjamin C. Truman of the *New York Times* wrote. "All the debris of a battlefield met our gaze." Dead Rebel soldiers littered the fort.[44]

Gibson estimated that he lost 20 men killed and 45 wounded on the evening of the evacuation, bringing his total casualties during the siege to 93 killed and 395 wounded. He counted 250 captured, although Federal estimates ran much higher; the true figure probably is close to 325. Holtzclaw's brigade alone lost 110 soldiers killed, wounded, and captured. The price exacted from the Federals during the operation was 52 killed, 575 wounded, and 30 missing.[45]

The Confederates had held Spanish Fort for thirteen days against remarkably heavy odds of eight to one. Maury wrote, "It is not too much to say that no position was ever held by Confederate troops with greater hardihood and tenacity, nor evacuated more skillfully after hope of further defense was gone." He went on to compliment the garrison. "They were the very flower of our Western army," he wrote. "They had made a splendid defense and they knew it." Gibson praised his men for their "steady valor and cheerful endurance"; and Richard Taylor wrote, "Gibson's stubborn defense and skillful retreat make this one of the best achievements of the war."[46]

Ironically, Canby reported that he was aware that Gibson had been constructing a treadway between Spanish Fort and Battery Tracy. He had planned to launch a foray by boat in order to cut the treadway but was unable to do so because of lack of boats. Had the Federals implemented this plan, they would have effectively isolated the Rebel garrison in Spanish Fort and cut off their only means of flight.[47]

Now time was running out for the defenders at Blakely. The Federals were enjoying a renewed drive now, as Canby was already moving his divisions toward the last Rebel stronghold. Writing to his parents on April 9, James Newton of the 14th Wisconsin was very upbeat at reports from Rebel prisoners that Petersburg and Richmond had fallen and that the Mobilians themselves were even hoping for a Union victory now. The graycoats seemed thoroughly sick of the war. "Really," Newton wrote, "dont you begin to see the 'beginning of the end'? I do."[48]

NOTES

1. Chester G. Hearn, *Mobile Bay and the Mobile Campaign: The Last Great Battles of the Civil War* (Jefferson, NC: McFarland and Company, Inc., Publishers, 1993), 187–188.

2. William Lochiel Cameron, "The Battles Opposite Mobile," *Confederate Veteran* 23 (1915), 305; Arthur W. Bergeron, Jr., *Confederate Mobile* (Jackson: University Press of Mississippi, 1991), 179–180.

3. Christopher C. Andrews, *History of the Campaign of Mobile* (New York, 1867), 236–237.

4. Bergeron, *Confederate Mobile*, 180.

5. Dabney H. Maury, "Defence of Spanish Fort," *Southern Historical Society Papers* 39 (1914), 131–132; Andrews, *Campaign of Mobile*, 148.

6. Bergeron, *Confederate Mobile*, 186.

7. Ibid.; Andrews, *Campaign of Mobile*, 187–188; *War of the Rebellion: A Compilation of the Official Records of the Union and Confederate Armies* (Washington, DC: Government Printing Office, 1880–1901) (hereafter cited as *OR*), Series I, Vol. 49, Part I, 321.

8. Bergeron, *Confederate Mobile*, 179.

9. Ibid., 180; Noah Andre Trudeau, *Out of the Storm: The End of the Civil War, April–June 1865* (Boston: Little, Brown & Co., 1994), 174.

10. Philip D. Stephenson, "Defence of Spanish Fort," *Southern Historical Society Papers* 39 (1914), 123–124.

11. Trudeau, *Out of the Storm*, 174; Andrews, *Campaign of Mobile*, 149; *OR*, Series I, Vol. 49, Part I, 229.

12. Stephenson, "Defence of Spanish Fort," 124.

13. Donald C. Elder III, ed., *A Damned Iowa Greyhound: Civil War Letters of William Henry Harrison Clayton* (Iowa City: University of Iowa Press, 1998), 161; Andrews, *Campaign of Mobile*, 151; Trudeau, *Out of the Storm*, 176.

14. Nathaniel C. Hughes, Jr., ed., *The Civil War Memoirs of Philip Daingerfield Stephenson D.D.* (Conway, AR: UCA Press, 1995), 364.

15. Andrews, *Campaign of Mobile*, 151; *OR*, Series I, Vol. 49, Part I, 267.

16. Andrews, *Campaign of Mobile*, 152.

17. *OR*, Series I, Vol. 49, Part I, 277; Trudeau, *Out of the Storm*, 176.

18. Andrews, *Campaign of Mobile*, 153.

19. Ibid., 154.

20. Ibid., 153–154; Trudeau, *Out of the Storm*, 176; *OR*, Series I, Vol. 49, Part I, 278.

21. Andrews, *Campaign of Mobile*, 153.

22. Bergeron, *Confederate Mobile*, 181; W. Bailey, "The Star Company of Ector's Texas Brigade," *Confederate Veteran* 22 (1914), 405.

23. Bergeron, *Confederate Mobile*, 181; Andrews, *Campaign of Mobile*, 156–157.

24. *OR*, Series I, Vol. 49, Part I, 278; Andrews, *Campaign of Mobile*, 155.

25. Andrews, *Campaign of Mobile*, 155; Stephenson, "Defence of Spanish Fort," 126; Mildred Britton, ed., *The Civil War Diary of Charles Henry Snedeker*, 1966, Auburn University Archives, RG 844.

26. Hearn, *Mobile Campaign*, 189.

27. Maury, "Defence of Spanish Fort," 132; Bergeron, *Confederate Mobile*, 181; Andrews, *Campaign of Mobile*, 157–158.

28. Andrews, *Campaign of Mobile*, 158; Powell A. Casey, *An Outline of the Civil War Campaigns and Engagements of the Washington Artillery of New Orleans* (Baton Rouge: Claitor's Publishing Division, 1986), 90.

29. Bergeron, *Confederate Mobile*, 181.

30. Hughes, *Stephenson*, 365.

31. Stephenson, "Defence of Spanish Fort," 126.

32. Ibid., 127.

33. Ibid., 127–128.

34. Edgar Wiley Jones, *History of the 18th Alabama Infantry Regiment*, compiled by C. David A. Pulcrano (Birmingham, AL: C.D.A. Pulcrano, 1994), 224.

35. Stephenson, "Defence of Spanish Fort," 128.

36. Bergeron, *Confederate Mobile*, 181; Andrews, *Campaign of Mobile*, vi, 162; Stephenson, "Defence of Spanish Fort," 128.

37. Trudeau, *Out of the Storm*, 178; J. W. DuBose, Historic sketch, Clayton's-Holtzclaw's Brigade File (Montgomery: Alabama Department of Archives and History), 64; Jones, *18th Alabama*, 224–225; Andrews, *Campaign of Mobile*, 159.

38. *OR*, Series I, Vol. 49, Part I, 207.

39. Trudeau, *Out of the Storm*, 178.

40. George M. Blackburn, ed., *"Dear Carrie . . .": The Civil War Letters of Thomas N. Stevens* (Mount Pleasant, MI: Clarke Historical Library, Central Michigan University, 1984), 309.

41. John E. Peck, Letter, Alabama Department of Archives and History, SG 11132, Folder #16, "Spanish Fort and Blakely, Battles," 2; Mamie Yeary, compil., *Reminiscences of the Boys in Gray, 1861–1865* (Dayton, OH: Morningside House, 1986), 414.

42. Trudeau, *Out of the Storm*, 179.

43. Edward Q. Nye, Diary, in "We Will Be Apt to Have a Hard Fight," *Baldwin Today*, April 10–April 11, 1991, C5.

44. Trudeau, *Out of the Storm*, 180.

45. *OR*, Series I, Vol. 49, Part I, 318; Joseph Wheeler, "Alabama," in Clement Evans, ed., *Confederate Military History*, vol. 7 (Atlanta, 1899), 381; Bergeron, *Confederate Mobile*, 182; Milton E. Henderson, *History of Edmond Waller Henderson: His Civil War Service: The Thirty-Sixth Alabama Infantry Regiment in Holtzclaw's Brigade* (N.p., n.d.), in 36th Alabama Infantry Regiment File, Alabama Department of Archives and History, 28.

46. Maury, "Defence of Spanish Fort," 130, 132; *OR*, Series I, Vol. 49, Part I, 317; Bergeron, *Confederate Mobile*, 182.

47. *OR*, Series I, Vol. 49, Part I, 96.

48. Stephen E. Ambrose, ed., *A Wisconsin Boy in Dixie: the Selected Letters of James K. Newton* (Madison: University of Wisconsin Press, 1961), 151.

CHAPTER 13

"The Spirit of Killin'"

Palm Sunday, April 9, dawned warmer than previous days, but it brought only greater apprehension to the Fort Blakely garrison. As uneasy troops looked on, the last of the exhausted, mud-encrusted survivors of Spanish Fort arrived only to be bustled aboard transports bound for Mobile. Before they shoved off, some of them relayed grim rumors of Ector's Texans being massacred at Spanish Fort. They left a sense of foreboding as they sailed away, and one Missouri soldier reflected, "we knew we were 'gone up' unless the enemy deferred the attack on our position until the transports could return for us."[1]

But the transports would not return. Canby was up from Spanish Fort, and he planned to launch a general assault on the Blakely garrison that very day. A. J. Smith gave the news to Garrard that morning. Canby's orders were to storm the Rebel fort. Already Old Baldy had McArthur's and Carr's divisions on the march from Spanish Fort, and Garrard could expect their support as well. Garrard met with his brigade commanders at 2:00 P.M., with Veatch sitting in. Garrard explained the plan of attack: Half of their troops to go into the rifle pits as a strong skirmish line, the other half in reserve as an even stronger line of battle. At 5:30 P.M., half of the skirmishers to advance; as soon as they could be seen gaining ground, then the other half to follow. When the first line reached the enemy works, the whole reserve line would go in. The Federals fervently hoped the skirmishers would be able to get through the obstructions in time to keep the Rebs occupied while the line of battle advanced. In this way, the attackers could drive off the Rebel skirmishers before exposing too many men to enemy fire. The plan was one of the best conceived and best executed in the war, "well and quickly done," Liddell later conceded.[2]

Victory now seemed so close that the Federals could almost taste it. Rumors began to spread that the graycoats were evacuating Fort Blakely. Indeed, firing along the lines seemed to have slackened during the morning hours. (The Rebels, anticipating an assault, actually were trying to save their ammunition.) Besides, Federal lookouts in the tall trees could see the transports heading downriver carrying Rebel troops from the river landing. What they did not know was that these were survivors of the Spanish Fort evacuation, that the Fort Blakely garrison was preparing to make a stand.[3]

Liddell had already received a message that morning from Colonel Patton at Battery Tracy: "Wagon trains and heavy columns of infantry have been crossing Bay Minette bridge all the morning." Liddell anticipated that the blow would come on his right, where a quarter of a mile from Thomas' brigade through the swamp to the river was unoccupied, like Gibson's left at Spanish Fort. He moved his headquarters there and prepared to receive the Federal attack.[4]

As soon as Spanish Fort was taken, Canby had begun shifting troops north to Blakely and beefing up his heavy artillery there. Captain Mack pulled out of Spanish Fort at 4:00 A.M. and had his New York battery in place on Garrard's right by 5:00 P.M. Captain Wimmer's battery of 30-pounder Parrotts was already in place on the far right, supporting Hawkins' division, and had driven off the Rebel gunboats the previous afternoon. Garrard placed two more heavy batteries just up from Spanish Fort—Cox's and Hendricks', whose 30-pounder Parrotts had silenced the Lady Slocomb—on his extreme left to check any attempt of the Rebel gunboats to menace his flank. The arrival of lighter pieces—four 10-pounder Parrotts of Captain John W. Lowell's 2nd Illinois, three Napoleons of Captain Rice's 17th Ohio, and late in the afternoon, four 10-pounder Parrotts of Captain Thomas J. Ginn's 3rd Indiana Light—augmented the Federal firepower in this sector.[5]

On the Federal right, Hawkins' black troops wondered if the Rebels were indeed withdrawing, robbing them of the chance to avenge Fort Pillow. The 73rd U.S.C.T.'s Lieutenant Colonel Henry C. Merriam had heard of the Rebel garrison's withdrawal from Spanish Fort and was concerned that the graycoats in Fort Blakely would also elude them. "The effect upon us was very depressing," he wrote. "To me it appeared that the escape of the garrison in our front also would be simply disgraceful." And brigade commander Colonel Hiram Scofield echoed these feelings "that the prize was slipping through our fingers."[6]

The 73rd's Captain Henry C. Nichols volunteered to lead a small reconnaissance of the Rebel position. Nichols' patrol silently stole out to verify whether the fort had been vacated, and a blistering volley from Redoubts 1 and 2 let the Federals know that Blakely was still held.

But how strongly held? Merriam asked his brigade commander, William A. Pile, to let him attempt a surprise assault on the Rebels' advanced line of rifle pits in front of Redoubt 2. Pile agreed. A little after 3:00 P.M., two parties of thirty men each—one from the 73rd U.S.C.T. led by Captain John C. Brown and one from the 86th led by Captain Jenkins—moved out to "feel the enemy" in front of Piles' brigade. A scorching fire from the Rebel sharpshooters and gunners greeted them immediately. The black soldiers moved more carefully, seeking protection behind logs and stumps, working their way through 300 yards of difficult terrain. Captain Brown fell mortally wounded, many others hit as well.[7]

The Rebs saw that the black soldiers meant business, and more graycoats slipped over the parapets to stiffen the skirmish line. Firing intensified, but the bluecoats came ahead. Pile sent in five more companies to reinforce them, and gradually the attackers gained ground. Captain Lewis A. Snaer, the single black officer on the field, went down with a shell fragment in his left foot, but he refused to be borne to the rear and continued brandishing his sword and waving his men onward. It took about an hour of hard fighting, but the black troops captured the Rebel rifle pits, and the graycoats scrambled back to the redoubt. The 73rd's Henry Crydenwise, in command of one of the attacking companies, left this account of the action:

> Cautioning my men to follow me in one rank & keep close to me, I sprang over our rifle pit & away we went on a hard run for the rebel pits. The Rebs saw us coming & swept the ground with shot, shell & tried to stop our advance, but to no purpose. Onward, still onward we went, down a slope, across a ravine filled with logs, brush, stumps & trees but these we hardly noticed. Then up a little rise & were soon in possession of the desired line.[8]

There was also some rough fighting in the other two African American brigades, Scofield's and Drew's. Starting at about 4:00 P.M., a skirmish line moved out in front of Drew's brigade, on the far right. Colonel J. Blackburn Jones of the 68th U.S.C.T. led four companies each from his regiment and the 76th. The men slipped off their coats so as to move more freely and advanced in their shirt sleeves through the thick brush and logs. Cheering and moving forward, they braved heavy gunfire from Barry's Mississippians in Redoubt 1. Jones was wounded in the hand, and several of his men fell. Af-

ter gaining 100 yards, Jones could see Rebel sharpshooters pulling back
from their advance rifle pits.

Back in the Federal trenches, Colonel Charles Drew, carried away by the
moment, waved his hat and shouted, "Forward on the enemy's works."
The rest of the 68th and 76th Regiments surged forward but soon became
bogged down by heavy fire. Private Andrew Turner of the 68th U.S.C.T. recalled the "charge was made under a terrible fire from the enemy, the men
dashing forward with all their might." One lieutenant was killed instantly
by grapeshot, and a captain fell mortally wounded. Colonel Jones felt something tugging at his pants leg, looked down, and there lay a soldier,
wounded in the first advance and in desperate pain. He clutched his unused
cartridges in his hands and pressed them into Jones' to take "to the boys."
Moments later Jones fell, stunned by the concussion of an exploding shell.[9]

The Rebels kept up a stubborn fire, and casualties among the black
troops mounted. An officer in the 68th asked for volunteers to push forward and clean out a group of Rebel snipers. A dozen eager men raised
their hands, including a young Missourian, Private Pless Adams, already
wounded. The black soldiers charged forward and were raked by enemy
fire. Young Adams fell a second time. He died later, "as good and worthy a
soldier," the white officer declared, "as ever drew a bead on a rebel."[10]

Drew decided to try a different approach. He ordered his men to shift to
their right and advance up the bluff side of the Rebel fort where he hoped
they would find more cover nearer to the river. The soldiers had to work
their way up the steep bluff, and exhaustion and enemy bullets claimed
many. Only a small number made it to within 100 paces of Redoubt 1. The
men kept firing and cheering, as if about to charge, looking to their rear for
more support.

But Colonel William Barry's Mississippians inside Redoubt 1 were preparing a countercharge. Leaving Lieutenant Colonel Densmore in command, Drew clambered back to the trenches to order in his reserves (the
48th U.S.C.T.). The Rebel assault party came out of the fort, but was soon
turned back by fire from Densmore's troops. Suddenly three gunboats appeared in the river. Thinking at first they were Federal, the black soldiers
began cheering but fell silent when Densmore made out a Confederate flag
on one of them. Still menacing, the Rebel vessels *Nashville*, *Morgan*, and
Huntsville lobbed a few shells in their direction.

Densmore was frantic now. Where were the reserves? He sent back an officer for word from Drew; and when no answer came back, he sent a second
officer. Meanwhile, all the men could do was hug the ground and wait for
help. Densmore was ready to send yet a third man back to the trenches
when he noticed an officer in the brush behind them madly waving them

back. It seemed a shame to give up their hard-won ground, but reluctantly Densmore and his troops began moving back, withdrawing the same way they had come. When they finally reached the Federal trenches, the reserves arrived.[11]

One small detachment remained isolated from the rest of the party. This group of soldiers, under Captains Holcomb and Norwood, had reached within 100 yards of the fort before they were cut off from the rest of their comrades. Fearful of being overrun by a Rebel countercharge and captured or killed, the black soldiers gritted their teeth, fixed bayonets, charged the enemy sharpshooters, and actually overran the Rebel riflemen at the interior line of abatis. They held their position there and waited.[12]

The Mississippians had their hands full. Soldiers in the second line of rifle pits—just 40 yards away from the black troops of the 68th U.S.C.T.—were told to hold their positions to the end. Welcome aid from Cockrell's Missouri boys quickly came in as troops from Redoubt 4 hustled to their left to reinforce the beleaguered works. But this left the Missouri brigade spread dangerously thin. Lieutenant George Warren wrote, "it was necessary to stretch the line out until the men were deployed ten paces apart."[13]

Near Redoubts 3 and 4, Cockrell's skirmishers under 40-year-old Captain Davis Lanter anticipated the worst as they huddled inside their rifle pits and listened to the din of musketry over to their left. Gates had issued grim orders: If the enemy advances in force, stand your ground and fight. It was necessary to delay the Federals as long as possible before they could reach the rest of the Missouri brigade behind their breastworks. Corporal William Kavanaugh sullenly mused, "skirmishers with such orders seldom live to run in."[14]

Lanter, a respected veteran officer, was determined to stay with his men to the end. The 20-year-old Kavanaugh, captured at Franklin and since exchanged, vowed to fight to the end rather than surrender. "Just the thought of going back to prison," he wrote, "made me desperate." Another Missourian who vowed not to be taken alive was Captain Joseph Neal, commanding Redoubt 4 and dressed in his new uniform coat bought in Mobile. Neal made a pledge with another officer that if the fort were overrun—and that looked pretty likely—that they would take to the river and hide out in the swamps.[15]

The black troops had made impressive gains at great cost, but so far they only held the advance rifle pits of the Mississippi brigade. Merriam asked to be allowed to attack the main works as well. "We have already fought the battle," he argued, turning to Pile, "but unless we go over the main works we will not get the credit." Pile finally agreed. "You are right, Colonel," he replied. "When you see Andrews' Division start to advance, charge the main works with your regiment and I will follow you with the rest of the brigade."[16]

But now it was 5:00 P.M., and the black assault on the Confederate left seemed to have stalled. As nightfall approached, weary Rebel defenders hoped for a badly needed break. It seemed they had survived to fight another day. But about that time, Federal batteries—stiffened by the addition of the heavy guns from Spanish Fort—opened up and began pounding the Rebel lines. Hawkins' black troops greeted the sound of heavy artillery fire with shouts of "Another through train to Mobile."[17]

While the African American soldiers—with no support from the white divisions—fought and bled keeping the Rebel left occupied, the Yankee troops all along the line were getting into position for the storming of Fort Blakely. The assault was to be delivered in echelon, from left to right, starting with Garrard's division in front of Redoubt 9.

Frank McGregor was in the middle of writing a letter to Susie when the command came to fall in, and he observed, "all could see that there was something unusual up. Our rifle pits were soon filling up as far as could be seen." As they moved into their forward rifle pits, the soldiers of the 83rd Ohio prepared themselves for what lay ahead. "We knew what was coming next, of course," Isaac Jackson recalled. He added, "I never saw the Boys in better spirits nor seem cooler."[18]

"The waiting and suspense was a severe test of courage," an Iowa infantryman recalled. Soldiers, jostling and clowning with one another, masked their apprehension with false bravado. But although a mere 40 yards separated the bluecoats crouching in their advanced rifle pits from those of the enemy, another 500 yards of obstructions, abatis, and land mines lay beyond and in front of the Rebel fort. "I will own," confessed an Illinois soldier, "that I never wanted to go home so badly in all my life."[19]

At 5:30 P.M., the waiting ended, as the whole Federal front erupted in a massive assault by 16,000 troops, in a line 3 miles long. On the Federal left, Garrard's division of "Smith's Guerrillas" overflowed their advanced trenches and swelled like a torrent toward Redoubts 6 through 9.

Although the 21st Missouri held the extreme left of the Federal line, the 119th Illinois, manning the rifle pits in front, stepped off first. Lieutenant Colonel Thomas J. Kinney had formed the Illinois regiment in a single line and had the men count off. Odd numbers would lead the advance; even numbers would remain in the rifle pits and give fire support.[20]

A bugle blared, and Kinney reported, "As a cloud, we raised from the rifle-pits and with a shout and cheer onward we went." As the first line plunged ahead through the swampy terrain—over felled trees, snarled vines, and brush—Rebel artillery in the redoubts let loose with grape and canister.

Three hundred yards to go. The supporting line—the 21st Missouri, 122nd Illinois, and 89th Indiana—made ready to follow at a second bugle signal.[21]

The rising blue tide was a sign to Rebel sharpshooters in the opposing rifle pits to abandon their works and fall back to Redoubts 8 and 9. C. C. Andrews wrote, "it seemed to be a race between them and the assaulting troops as to which should reach them first." Twenty-four-year-old Missouri soldier Aron Wilburn, stationed in one of the rifle pits with several young Alabama teenagers, ordered the boys to run for the breastworks. One of them finally scrambled away after Wilburn yelled at him a second time to flee. Wilburn managed to get off one shot, then turned and made for the fort at top speed. Forty yards from the redoubt, Wilburn stumbled over the body of the Alabama boy, the top of his head shot away. "I have no doubt," he wrote later, "that his parents never heard from him again or ever saw his corpse." Wilburn barely made it to the fort himself, just managing to scale the works as a pursuing Federal soldier struck him between the shoulder blades with the butt of his rifle.[22]

The bluecoats plowed ahead, and now the second wave of attacking troops poured out of the Yankee works. As they reached the ditch that protected the redoubts, they discovered to their glee that the Rebels had failed to remove two footbridges; so they charged forward and soon were inside the works. Most of the Rebel infantry—the Alabama reserves—fell back toward the river. But at Redoubt 9, the South Carolina gunners, armed with rifles, stood their ground, and their commander, 25-year-old Lieutenant J. L. Moses, was struck down. First to burst into the fort was Colonel Kinney. The 21st Missouri quickly planted their colors on the Rebel fort, claiming to be the first to do so—a feat disputed by the 178th New York in Harris' brigade. Hundreds of Rebel prisoners fell into Federal hands, including Brigadier Generals Thomas and Liddell. Surrounded by Yankee troops, the grizzled Rebel commander reluctantly handed his sword to a young Federal captain. The ground behind Colonel John Rinaker's victorious brigade was littered with forty-six bluecoats wounded and fourteen dead. It had taken less than ten minutes to carry the enemy works.[23]

Seeing the blue-clad soldiers pouring into the works, some of the 62nd Alabama's boy soldiers formed a second line between Redoubts 8 and 9 in a futile effort to quell the Union tide. The graycoats could not hold for long, and quickly both the impromptu "traverse line" and the skirmish line broke and fell back.[24]

An Indiana bluecoat credited the Alabama teenagers with putting up a spirited defense. "Young as they were," he wrote, "they fought like devils." Swinging his sword and yelling "Surrender!" Lieutenant Angus R. McDonald of the 11th Wisconsin took on several of these young defenders as he leapt into the Rebel works at Redoubt 7. A cluster of graycoats quickly threw up their hands, but to their right a Confederate officer, with a dozen armed soldiers, yelled, "No quarter to the damned Yankees!" The Rebels opened fire, and Sergeant Daniel B. Moore went down with a musket ball in the thigh and two bayonet wounds in the shoulder, but not before he had laid low several young Rebels. One of the graycoats fell on top of McDonald, who used him as a shield. Although wounded himself, Moore grabbed a Rebel musket and fired, killing McDonald's attacker. Moore's quick actions won him the Medal of Honor.[25]

Surging down the Pensacola road, James I. Gilbert's brigade braved intense fire from Redoubt 6. In the lead, the 10th Kansas—"a little band of heroes," Gilbert called them—raced over 1,000 yards of ground "covered with timber felled in every possible direction, torpedoes planted in front of the works, wire stretched from stump to stump, a double line of abatis, and in rear of all a very strong line of fortifications." The Kansans, led by Lieutenant Colonel Charles Hills, struggled through the abatis and the ditch, breached the embrasures, and attacked the 63rd Alabama's works. A Rebel captain with a well-aimed pistol shot brought down a Yankee flag bearer, but the blue lines plowed over the Alabamians and overwhelmed them. Inside the fort, the Kansans wheeled to their right and charged down the Rebel line, scooping up hundreds of prisoners.[26]

So sudden and swift was the collapse of the Rebel right flank that the colors of Garrard's leading regiments were already fluttering above the captured parapets as the other Federal divisions got under way. Elias Dennis' brigade of Veatch's division charged toward Redoubt 5, defended by the last of the teenage Alabama reserves. The assault here was spearheaded by the 8th Illinois Infantry, and Veatch wrote, "No regiment could have done better." The Illinoisans clambered over three lines of abatis, sometimes stopping to pull the sharpened branches of the felled trees to one side while dodging trip wires and standing heavy fire from shell and canister, served up by Captain William C. Winston's Tennessee gunners. At the second line of abatis they overran the Rebels' rifle pits, either killed or captured the sharpshooters there, and in minutes were pouring into the Rebel works. First in were Sergeant John M. Switzer and Lieutenant Colonel Lloyd Wheaton, at the embrasure for a 30-pounder Parrott. After securing the fort, the Yankees formed ranks and moved toward the river landing.[27]

But it would be at Redoubts 3 and 4, where the veteran Missouri brigade stoically waited, that the combat at Fort Blakely would be the fiercest. In C. C. Andrews' division, the two advancing regiments—the 83rd Ohio in Moore's brigade and the 97th Illinois in Spicely's—received the command to move forward and assault Redoubt 4, the strongest fort in the Rebel line.

Just as the 97th Illinois prepared to charge, the noise of a land mine caused heads to jerk as the explosion tore the leg off a Federal captain and killed several other soldiers. Many of the bluecoats cringed with dread. But Lieutenant Colonel Victor Vifquain raised his sword high and bellowed, "Forward, Ninety-Seventh!" With a vigorous cheer, the Illinois troops plunged ahead.[28]

The Missourians poured on the fire, and before the 97th had covered 20 yards, bluecoats began to drop. At 80 yards, the Illinoisans opened fire, as the Rebel sharpshooters began to fall back. Vifquain quickly interrogated a Rebel prisoner snatched up from an advance rifle pit: What was the enemy strength? The Reb replied that the fort had not been evacuated; the whole garrison was still there. Even as they spoke, Vifquain could see swarms of Rebel sharpshooters falling back from the rifle pits, and hordes of graycoat defenders looming up behind their breastworks. Vifquain hurried back to his men. It would be much harder going than he had hoped.[29]

Led by Lieutenant Colonel William H. Baldwin, the 83rd Ohio rushed forward at the double quick, 600 yards from the Rebel lines. The ground here was more uneven, with a number of ravines, and the going was slower than in front of Garrard's division. The Buckeyes clawed their way over three lines of abatis, tangled pine limbs, and a long strand of telegraph wire strung knee high along the ground. Isaac Jackson recalled, "The wire tripped nearly every man. I did not see it. I must have jumpd in running." A third of the way through the obstructions, the men had to stop to catch their breath before pushing on. Frank McGregor recalled "scrambling in the brush, jumping over logs, now stumbling over sharpened stakes, at another time tripping up with the telegraph wires that were laced through here and there." McGregor added, "they were all prepared for us, and such a storm of grape shells, cannister, etc.—I never wish to see again."[30]

The surging blue tide quickly overwhelmed the Rebel rifle pits. William Kavanaugh wrote, "they advanced in our immediate front in solid columns. An imposing sight indeed was this, but one never to be forgotten. Our little thin line of skirmishers loaded and fired as rapidly as possible, but on they came as though no one could harm them."[31]

Bluecoats swarmed over the rifle pits, clubbing and bayoneting many Rebels who stood their ground to the very end, as Gates had ordered. Only when annihilation seemed certain did Captain Davis Lanter and the Missourians begin to fall back to the Rebel earthworks 200 yards in their rear. Corporal Kavanaugh bolted from his rifle pit and raced for Redoubt 4 with Yankee soldiers just paces behind him.

Under a rain of bullets, Kavanaugh and two of his comrades ran for their lives. He later recalled, "it appeared to me that all hell had turned loose and that every man in the U. S. was practicing on us with repeating rifles." The smack of bullets into bodies told him that the two Missourians running behind him had been shot down. Kavanaugh somehow managed to reach the ditch in front of Redoubt 4, but he fell too exhausted to climb to the top of the parapet.[32]

Suddenly, determined arms were pulling Kavanaugh up the embankment. Eighteen-year-old Private Philip Hamilton Devinnie, braving a storm of lead, had jumped from behind the parapet to pull Kavanaugh to safety. Risking his own life, Devinnie—who had been badly wounded in the face at Vicksburg—dragged the corporal inside the fort. The troops inside held their fire as their comrades scrambled over the parapet—unwittingly giving the Yanks more time to advance.

Fifty yards from the fort, the 83rd Ohio had emerged from the closest ravine and spent several minutes pulling sections of the last abatis apart. The rest of Moore's brigade poured through the gaps. In front of the Rebels works the ground was filled with torpedoes. Incredibly, the bluecoats managed to get through the mine field without injury.[33]

The going was slow, and when the Buckeyes at last reached Redoubt 4, a blistering musket volley greeted them as the Missourians determined to make their last stand. Astonished at the Rebels' resistance—much stiffer than the bluecoats had expected—C. C. Andrews recorded, "These troops stood up in a bold manner behind their breastworks, firing on their assailants as if they hoped to repulse them. There seemed to be a constant blaze of musketry along the breastworks." Captain George F. Abbay's Mississippi gunners continued to serve the Rebel guns with fury.[34]

Captain John D. Gary and Private William M. Rooke of the 83rd Ohio were the first on the parapet. Meanwhile, the 97th Illinois, which had led the attack and sustained the heaviest casualties—sixty-one men killed and wounded—was also breaching the Rebel defenses. As the 83rd Ohio's bullet-ridden colors went up, Sergeant Edwin D. Lowe placed the torn colors of the 97th Illinois on the works just south of the Stockton road, and immediately a Rebel defender shot him down, only to be himself shot down by another Union soldier. Captain Neal's Missouri troops and Abbay's Mississippi gunners continued putting up a stiff resistance even as more blue-clad soldiers swarmed into the Rebel fort. The Federal assault, Vifquain declared, was "brilliant and a complete success"; and Andrews praised his troops for showing "cool and splendid soldiership in every respect."[35]

Close behind the 97th Illinois and 83rd Ohio, Lieutenant Colonel Oran Perry's 69th Indiana and Colonel Samuel T. Busey's 76th Illinois were on the move. The Hoosiers charged down the left of the Stockton road and poured into Redoubt 4 just behind the 97th Illinois; Perry fell badly wounded. The 76th Illinois made directly for Redoubt 3 just 50 yards above the Stockton road, and Captain Charles Edmondson's Missourians peppered them with musket fire. Hit in the leg, Lieutenant William F. Kenaga managed to keep going; then a Rebel bullet struck him in the ankle of his other leg. Kenaga fell, but on his knees kept cheering his men onward. Twenty feet to go. When the color-sergeant fell, Corporal Charles Goldwood scooped up the colors. Onto the parapet. Goldwood was about to plant the colors when three Rebel soldiers shot him down point blank, and he fell, colors in his arms, his clothes in flames.[36]

Now Busey was on the parapet, shooting down a Rebel gunner preparing a double charge of grape and canister, and he continued firing his revolver at close range at other cannoneers. Busey quickly divided his men and charged the Rebel works from front and right flank. Bayonet-wielding bluecoats soon scrambled into the fort, and fierce fighting continued there, as at Redoubt 4. Andrews said of the 76th Illinois, "No regiment on the field that day suffered so heavily, none exhibited more intrepid bravery."[37]

On the Federal right, Hawkins' black troops, who had been under heavy fire most of the day, heard the cheering of the white regiments to their left. Not fully certain whether a general assault was under way or whether the white divisions were merely attempting to capture the advanced Rebel rifle pits, as the black soldiers had done earlier in the afternoon, Pile sent a staff officer to investigate. Anxious eyes watched as the U.S. flag went up above the Rebel works to their left, and when the news came back that Andrews' division was indeed moving on the redoubts, Pile ordered his own brigade ahead. Hawkins' other brigades quickly followed suit.[38]

In the action that earned him the Medal of Honor, Henry C. Merriam led the men of the 73rd U.S.C.T. surging toward Redoubt 2. The 73rd swept forward with a shout and scrambled through the killing field, shells bursting overhead and torpedoes exploding. A wounded soldier in the 97th Illinois recalled seeing the black troops "now dropping forward out of sight as a volley of canister passed over them, then up and onward with thinned ranks, always keeping an eye on the guns for smoke—again to fall as the charge passed over them. As the storming column passed over the works, I could distinctly hear their yell 'Fort Pillow, Fort Pillow.'" Merriam and Color Sergeant Edward Simon were the first into the fort, the 73rd's colors the first to wave over the works. Merriam called it "the last assault of our great and bloody Civil War." Pile reported, "All my officers and men behaved splendidly."[39]

A similar scene was repeated on the far right, as Scofield's and Drew's black brigades headed for Redoubt 1. The men were eager to go. Colonel Scofield wrote, "Men actually wept that they were placed in reserve and could not go with their comrades into the thickest of the fight." "I cannot speak in terms of too much praise of the officers and men of my command," Drew reported. "Each and every one did willingly all that was asked." Struggling through the same bloody ground that had claimed so many of their comrades earlier in the afternoon, the black troops quickly overran the last of the Rebel rifle pits. Defiant soldiers of the Mississippi brigade coolly remained outside of Redoubt 1, brandishing their muskets and refusing to surrender; but the rising black tide from Drew's brigade quickly overcame them. To their left, a single exploding land mine sent a whole group of soldiers in the 51st U.S.C.T. sprawling, leaving half a dozen killed or wounded. But in moments, the 50th U.S.C.T. was inside the fort, and their commander, Colonel Charles A. Gilchrist wrote, "The enthusiasm of the men was unbounded."[40]

The entire Federal front had moved forward now, and boisterous cheering from center, then left, then right along the line of redoubts told the Yankees that Fort Blakely had been taken. Anxiously watching the blue tide swell over the Rebel works, General Steele became ecstatic, turning to his staff officers. "I knew they would do it," he cried, "I told you they would go over those works." "It was the greatest sight I ever saw," a Connecticut artilleryman recalled.[41]

But the battle still raged hotly at Redoubts 3 and 4. Musket fire from the Rebel strongholds was so intense that many Federal soldiers were forced back to temporary shelter in ravines in front of the forts. But within minutes, the Union attackers' sheer weight of numbers breached the Rebel lines. Defenders in both forts discovered they were outflanked and turned to find bluecoats entering the works behind them. At Redoubt 3, 1st Sergeant John Corkery recalled, "we were so busy beating back the lines in our front that they surrounded us before we knew it, and we surrendered." As Colonel Busey's 76th Illinois, closely followed by the 24th Indiana, swarmed into Redoubt 3 from front and right, Captain Charles Edmondson's Missouri troops were overwhelmed. "Is it fight or surrender?" a young Federal lieutenant demanded. "Talk Damn quick!" Realizing the hopelessness of further resistance, Edmondson conceded defeat. "Surrender," he uttered, throwing down his sword.[42]

In Redoubt 4, where Captain Joseph H. Neal's Missouri troops fought to the bitter end, some of the most vicious hand-to-hand combat of the war played itself out. Federal troops crying, "Torpedoes! Torpedoes!" poured into the redoubt. Here the Rebels feared Yankee retribution for the losses inflicted by land mines, and in the smoke, shouting, and confusion, they doubted their foe would grant them quarter. Neal defiantly bellowed to his troops, "No quarter to the damn Yankees." In the struggle at close range, a

Federal soldier shot him point-blank in the face. Neal fell, his head nearly blown off, to the horror of fellow officers and men nearby.[43]

Raw instinct and pumping adrenaline took control, as the bluecoats scrambled over the works, and savage fighting raged. "We . . . jumped down in the (trench) right on top of them," 1st Sergeant W. R. Eddington of the 97th Illinois Infantry wrote, "too close to shoot them; too close to stick them with bayonets, but we could use the butts of our guns." In the melee, Frank McGregor remembered, "it was no time to think." And Private T. J. Stow, 37th Illinois, observed, "You would have thought if you have been there that all the fiends in human shape had broken loose from the lower regions and like an angel of light from Hell were on the point of visiting death and destruction to the southern chivalry in the last ditch."[44]

The die-hard Rebs grasped at every last wisp of hope. Lieutenant Orlando F. Guthrie noticed a white flag fluttering from Redoubt 5—being overrun by the 8th Illinois—thought maybe the Federals were surrendering. But it was the 63rd Alabama and Winston's Tennessee gunners running up the white flag, not the Yanks. "I knew better in a minute," Guthrie wrote, "as they came pouring in around us." Just then he felt something hit him, looked down in horror to see the front of his coat splashed with the brains of a nearby soldier.[45]

Lieutenant Colonel Baldwin, at the head of his troops, leapt down into the Rebel works crying, "Surrender!" "To whom do we surrender?" a Confederate officer shot back. "To the Eighty-third Ohio," Baldwin replied. "I believe we did that once before," the Missouri officer said, remembering Vicksburg.[46]

Yankee troops quickly zeroed in on Cockrell, boldly waving a battle flag, and Gates, still trying to rally his men. The Federals surrounded and captured both defiant officers. Captain Patrick H. Pentzer of the 97th Illinois reported that men were so enraged over the casualties caused by the land mines and by the savagery of the Rebel resistance in the redoubt that they were ready to kill the Confederate commander on sight. Cockrell surrendered the headquarters flag of his division to Pentzer. Just as Private Nathaniel Bull pointed his musket at the general and prepared to pull the trigger, Pentzer jerked it away. Later Pentzer was awarded the Medal of Honor.[47]

Gates was obstinate to the end. As he reluctantly surrendered his sword, Federals demanded that he show them where the land mines were buried. "I don't know where they are," the scrappy Missourian snapped, "and by the lord Harry if I did I would not tell you." Fed up with Rebel insolence and angry over the deaths and maiming of their comrades, the bluecoats were at the end of their patience. They would take Gates along with them by force, they told him, and make him show where the torpedoes were. "All right," he replied. "I have the satisfaction of knowing you will be blown up with me!"[48]

Resistance continued because in the confusion and smoke of battle in the falling dusk few soldiers heard their commanders' cries to cease fire. But within minutes the last major battle of the Civil War came to an end as the remaining Confederates conceded defeat. Outnumbered graycoats surrendered by the score. Many cowered in fear; but when a Yankee officer insolently demanded Colonel Stephen Cooper's sword, the one-armed officer presented it to him point first. "Reverse it!" the soldier demanded. Cooper hurled it away as far as he could throw it. "Go and get it," he growled, "I hand nothing to a federal soldier!"[49]

Major Thomas Carter, covered with grime and powder, agonizingly ordered his men to cease fire, then burst into tears and "cried like a child." The graycoats gave up hesitantly, some cursing, some silently. Corporal Kavanaugh—feeling that "to be killed outright in battle was far preferable to being murdered by inches in a loathsome dirty northern prison"—in rage shot the nearest Federal soldier before bluecoats overpowered him and took him prisoner.[50]

One last Rebel unit remained fairly intact. Lieutenant Colonel James C. McCown's 3rd and 5th Missouri Infantry, returning once again from aiding the hard-pressed Mississippians in Redoubt 2, reached Redoubt 3 just as the fort was taken by the Federals. The Missourians could see the Rebel lines to their right crumbling, as swarms of bluecoats poured into the redoubts to the south. Lieutenant Warren wrote, "We saw in a moment 'the jig was up.'" McCown massed his troops in the cover of a brushy area 50 yards behind the captured Redoubt 3. The Missourians fired one final defiant volley at the bluecoats on the ramparts—wounding several Federals, including Colonel Busey—then dropped their weapons and made a mad dash for the Tensas landing in hopes of escaping across the river.[51]

At Redoubt 1, Scofield's and Drew's brigades were overwhelming the Mississippians. As the black mass hurtled down on them, a Rebel officer shouted to his men, "Lay low and mow the ground—the damned niggers are coming!" As the Federals poured over the parapet, fighting became frantic.[52]

Clearly out for blood now, black soldiers poured into Redoubt 1 in droves. "[T]he very devil could not hold them," Lieutenant Walter Chapman of the 51st U.S.C.T. wrote. "Their eyes glittered like serpents and with yells & howls like hungry wolves they rushed for the rebel works." Numbers of them reportedly had tied pieces of red cloth around their muskets as a reminder to give no quarter. Screaming, "Remember Fort Pillow!" one soldier received a bullet that entered his open mouth and passed out through his cheek; unfazed, he charged straight ahead until into the fort.[53]

Sergeant John J. Gray of Tarrant's Alabama Battery whirled his twelve-pounder James rifle about and fired a final round of canister into the bluecoats. This was probably the last shot fired by the Rebels that day and angered the blacks even more. Fearful of being taken prisoner by the black soldiers, many of the Mississippians—apparently including Colonel Barry—clambered over the works toward Redoubt 3, hoping to surrender to white troops. Those captured in the earthworks huddled together in groups, fearing for their lives while black troops poured over the earthworks, screaming, "Remember Fort Pillow!"[54]

Losing control, some of the black troops began bayoneting and shooting Rebel soldiers who had already surrendered. Private Ben H. Bounds of the 4th Mississippi, with forty or fifty of his comrades, raised their hands only to be fired on. Bounds, who saved himself by keeping a white Federal officer between him and the black soldiers, maintained that more Rebel soldiers were killed after surrendering at Redoubt 1 than during the fighting. "It looked as though we were to be butchered in cold blood," Lieutenant Ed Tarrant wrote, "so I passed word along our line that if another man was shot I would seize a musket, as would every man of us, and would die fighting to the last." The 51st U.S.C.T.'s Lieutenant Chapman declared, "the niggers did not take a prisoner, they killed all they took to a man."[55]

Trying to intervene to stop a massacre, two white officers in the 68th U.S.C.T. were fired on by their own men. Captain Fred W. Norwood, who earlier in the day had led a detachment of black troops pinned down in the no man's land in front of Redoubt 1, fell with a bullet in his knee. Also shot while attempting to save the prisoners was Lieutenant Clark Gleason, who died two days later. It seems likely that other white officers stepped in and restored order.[56] Apparently not all the black soldiers took out their wrath on the Rebels. One man in the 50th U.S.C.T. even discovered his former master among the prisoners. Andrews wrote, "They appeared happy to meet, and drank from the same canteen."[57]

In spite of Lieutenant Chapman's assertions, most Federal officers strongly denied that anything like a massacre occurred at Redoubt 1. Captain J. L. Coppec of the 47th U.S.C.T. wrote, "every officer of the colored troops will testify that not a rebel soldier was shot by the darkies after they had surrendered," although he added that they surely had ample provocation. Chaplain Thomas Calahan of the 48th U.S.C.T. insisted that no atrocities were committed. And Lieutenant Colonel Samuel M. Quincy of the 73rd U.S.C.T. maintained that although many of the Rebel soldiers "fell on their knees expecting Fort Pillow treatment," the black troops showed remarkable discipline and restraint.[58]

Probably black soldiers did kill some Rebel prisoners after they had surrendered, but nothing on the scale of a massacre took place. Circumstantial evidence for the offenses points to soldiers in the 68th U.S.C.T., although if any of the black units could be blamed for losing control, it would probably be the 76th U.S.C.T., with its history of abuse by white officers. The same type of conduct undoubtedly occurred in the aftermath of the savage fighting at Redoubts 3 and 4, and one Federal soldier admitted that some of his white comrades also became possessed by the "spirit of killin.'"[59]

The fierce combat for Fort Blakely had taken just twenty minutes, and Federal victory seemed complete. Steele sent a triumphant dispatch to Canby: "We have stormed the entire line of works, and our troops are now in full possession." "God bless you," Canby replied, "and God bless your brave command." Canby later commended the Federal troops for "a gallantry to which there were no exceptions."[60]

Just six hours earlier, General Robert E. Lee had surrendered the Confederate Army of Northern Virginia to General Ulysses Grant at Appomattox.

A pitiful spectacle unfolded at the landing, as Rebel defenders who had not been killed or taken prisoner fled to the banks of the river. With blue-coated pursuers closing in on them, Rebel soldiers commandeered boats and tore wooden planks from the wharf to use as makeshift floats in a desperate attempt to carry them to safety. Some even tried to swim the muddy Tensas.

Lieutenant George Warren, Captain Young (Cockrell's aide-de-camp), and about forty other men quickly boarded a flatboat loaded down with cargo. Anxious to get underway, they yelled to anyone on the riverbank to cut the rope securing the vessel to the wharf. No one would help. Warren plunged into the water and sawed the hawser in two with his knife. As the current began to move the vessel off, the soldiers pulled the soaked Warren into the boat. "The boat is loaded with powder!" someone from the bank shouted. Whipping off the tarpaulin that covered cases of artillery gunpowder, the horrified men began frantically to toss them overboard. Several terrified men decided to take their chances in the water.[61]

Others tried similar means of escape. Several officers seized a small skiff, but a few yards from shore the boat sank and left them struggling in the water. Captain William Conway Zimmerman of the 63rd Alabama—one of a handful from his regiment to escape—pried a wooden plank from the landing wharf and floated a mile and a half downstream until he reached a swamp on the opposite side of the river and safety. More soldiers tried floating out to the sandbars in the river, where they hid in the tall cane.[62]

Warren and his comrades began to move rapidly downstream, and they could see at the landing Colonel McCown and the remnant of his command with no where else to go. As pursuing Federals overtook them, McCown and the last of the Missouri brigade brought the proud record of a command that had never surrendered to a painful end as the colonel agonizingly hoisted a white handkerchief on the end of a ramrod. Warren's craft escaped in a hail of Federal bullets that splashed in the water or thudded into the thick oak gunwale of the boat, while the men on board lay low on the bottom. The current carried the boat downriver and out of range.[63]

As his friends rushed toward the river, Mississippi artillery officer Alden McLellan was holding down the leg of a wounded soldier at the field hospital while the surgeon prepared to amputate it. The two men waited anxiously while the chloroform took effect. As soon as the operation was finished, McLellan and the hospital steward made a break for the river landing, where they found other soldiers scrambling to find anything to get them to safety across the river.

McLellan and the hospital steward tossed several loose planks into the water, but by now it was too late. Swarms of bluecoats suddenly appeared on the bluffs above them and began firing at the men in the river. "I concluded not to take a plank ride just then," McLellan wrote, "and was busy fastening a twenty-dollar gold piece in the lining of my cap and dropping my watch into my bootleg when a Federal called out: 'say, you fellow with a green shirt on, come up or you will get hulled [shot] next time.' " McLellan did as he was told and sadly joined other groups of Rebels bound for captivity.[64]

Hovering nearby in the river, the *Nashville* hoped to provide cover and rescue for the Rebel withdrawal but could not fire, because soldiers of both armies were mixed together on the bank. "It was evident to even the youngest of us," Lieutenant Cameron wrote, "that the end was near." Cameron lamented the fate of the Rebels:

Our men jumped into the water. Many could not swim, and those who could were an easy mark for the negro soldiers, who fired at them from the bank and at us in the boats. We picked up all we could and quickly retired to our respective vessels, where we landed them and returned for more. I do not know how many were rescued; but many were drowned, some killed in the water and some on the shore, and the rest surrendered. . . . We had to sit calmly under direct fire from the shore, to which, in our eagerness to rescue our poor fellows, we had approached pretty close.[65]

As the fateful Sunday drew to a close, the last Rebel hopes vanished with the setting red sun in the west. Cameron recalled, "That night was a sorry one for all of us."[66]

The assault cost the bluecoats 127 men killed and 527 wounded. The heaviest losses were in Andrews' division with 41 killed and 192 wounded. "The 9th day of April will ever be a memorable day," Colonel Spicely noted in his brigade, where the 97th Illinois lost 61 men killed or wounded. The 83rd Ohio lost 7 killed and 21 wounded. Thirteen men died and 64 were wounded in Veatch's division; Garrard reported 41 killed and 124 wounded. In Rinaker's brigade, half the casualties were Missourians of the 21st Regiment, including three color-bearers. But it was in Hawkins' black division—where 32 died and 147 were wounded in the assault—that the highest number of casualties were reported for the entire siege (48 killed, 323 wounded). Lieutenant Colonel Merriam attributed this to the damage done by the Rebel gunboats. The 68th U.S.C.T. reported 12 killed and 88 wounded, the highest of any single regiment. Total Federal losses in the siege were 116 killed, 655 wounded, 4 missing.[67]

Confederate losses are harder to assess, because no official report was made. Probably 100 graycoats died in the assault, not counting those who were shot or drowned trying to swim the river. The bulk of the 2,700-man garrison fell into Union hands, while between 150 and 200 lucky survivors managed to escape to the Rebel gunboats. George A. Callaway, a boy soldier in the 62nd Alabama, recalled that he was the only one out of six messmates who was not killed or wounded. "My hat and clothes were riddled," he wrote, "and my canteen was shot away, but I was not scratched."[68]

Some of the Rebel prisoners, especially the Alabama boys, were astounded at the staggering number of the Union troops. "Where did you Yanks all come from?" one of them asked. They had no idea of the odds they had faced. And Thomas N. Stevens with the 28th Wisconsin remarked that gray-clad prisoners he talked with later—mostly Alabama and Mississippi soldiers—predicted that Mobile would be evacuated. "They say they don't see how 'our fellers' can dig & advance our rifle pits so fast under their fire," he wrote. "It puzzles them." The prisoners appeared to be "intelligent, well fed, & pretty well clothed. Many of them did not seem to feel very bad at falling into our hands."[69]

Casualties continued to mount even after the fighting was over. As he was escorting Rebel prisoners to the rear, Private Josias Lewis of the 47th U.S.C.T. lost a leg when he stepped on a land mine. All through the night, the Federals could hear the explosions of torpedoes accidentally trod on by soldiers searching for the dead and wounded. Rebel prisoners would be put to work the following day digging up the land mines.[70]

The battle over, soldiers reflected on the day's events and on the high cost of victory. "Now is the time when sorrow is mixed with joy," Isaac Jackson wrote. "We began now to learn who of our comrades had fallen." And the next day Frank McGregor wrote, "Ten steps from where I am writing this morning, they are placing six of my comrades in rough boxes to be buried."[71]

McGregor had survived the fighting without injury. But he had lost his pictures again and his memorandum book, which had fallen out of the breast pocket of his coat as he jumped over the Rebel rifle pits. The next morning he was up at daybreak and spent two hours combing the battlefield looking for the lost articles, but to his dismay he found only fragments of the broken photos. Someone had removed the money from his memorandum book.[72]

Twenty-Seventh Iowa soldier John E. Peck marveled, "The next day as I took a look at the ground we passed over in that charge I could hardly believe that we ever went over the ground, although when we made the assault I did not experience much difficulty in getting along." And in the 6th Minnesota, which had moved its camp into Fort Blakely, fellow "Smith's Guerrilla" Andrew Thompson wrote that the former Rebel stronghold "seems like a very strange place."[73]

As Elisha Stockwell watched the Rebel prisoners being marched back from Blakely, one of his comrades suddenly brightened with recognition. "Oh," he cried out, stepping into the road, "there comes Jimmy." "Hello, Jimmy," he greeted, approaching one bedraggled Confederate. There was no reply from the sullen graycoat, who only looked down at the ground. The Federal tugged on the man's sleeve. "To hell with you," the Reb finally snarled. The exchange made both the Union soldiers and some of the Rebel prisoners laugh. The two men had known each other before the war and had worked together on river steamboats in St. Louis.[74]

The world looked much brighter for the Federals. Edward Nye, arriving with his regiment from Spanish Fort, wrote on April 10, "Moved out and camped near Blakely. Seen the prisoners pass. They are mostly boys and look down in the mouth. Tonight, we hear that Grant has taken Richmond and Petersburg. Think the war will soon be over."[75]

NOTES

1. Phillip Thomas Tucker, "The First Missouri Confederate Brigade's Last Stand at Fort Blakely on Mobile Bay," *Alabama Review* 42 (October 1989), 277.

2. *War of the Rebellion: A Compilation of the Official Records of the Union and Confederate Armies* (Washington, DC: Government Printing Office, 1880–1901) (hereaf-

ter cited as *OR*), Series I, Vol. 49, Part I, 248–249; Nathaniel C. Hughes, ed., *Liddell's Record* (Dayton, OH: Morningside House, Inc., 1985), 196.

3. Christopher C. Andrews, *History of the Campaign of Mobile* (New York, 1867), 191–192.

4. *OR*, Series I, Vol. 49, Part II, 1222.

5. Andrews, *Campaign of Mobile*, 189–190; *OR*, Series I, Vol. 49, Part I, 248.

6. Henry C. Merriam, "The Capture of Mobile," in *War Papers (Read before the Commandery of the State of Maine. Military Order of the Loyal Legion of the United States)*, vol. 3 (Wilmington, NC: Broadfoot Publishing Co., 1992), 244; *OR*, Series I, Vol. 49, Part I, 291.

7. Andrews, *Campaign of Mobile*, 194–195.

8. Ibid., 195; Merriam, "Capture of Mobile," 245–246; Noah Andre Trudeau, *Like Men of War: Black Troops in the Civil War, 1862–1865* (Boston: Little, Brown & Co., 1998), 403–404.

9. Trudeau, *Like Men of War*, 404; Andrews, *Campaign of Mobile*, 196–197.

10. Trudeau, *Like Men of War*, 404.

11. Andrews, *Campaign of Mobile*, 197–199.

12. Ibid., 199.

13. Roger B. Hanson and Norman A. Nicolson, *The Siege of Blakeley and the Campaign of Mobile* (N.p.: Historic Blakeley Press, 1995), 42; Robert S. Bevier, *History of the Confederate First and Second Missouri Brigades, 1861–1865* (St. Louis, 1879), 265.

14. Tucker, "Last Stand," 278–279.

15. Ibid.

16. Merriam, "Capture of Mobile," 246.

17. Andrews, *Campaign of Mobile*, 189.

18. Carl E. Hatch, ed., *Dearest Susie: A Civil War Infantryman's Letters to His Sweetheart* (Jericho, NY: Exposition Press, Inc., 1971), 113; Joseph Orville Jackson, ed., *"Some of the Boys . . .": The Civil War Letters of Isaac Jackson, 1862–1865* (Carbondale: Southern Illinois University Press, 1960), 244.

19. Noah Andre Trudeau, *Out of the Storm: The End of the Civil War, April–June 1865* (Boston: Little, Brown & Co., 1994), 181–182.

20. Leslie Anders, *The Twenty-First Missouri: From Home Guard to Union Regiment* (Westport, CT: Greenwood Press, 1975), 228–229.

21. *OR*, Series I, Vol. 49, Part I, 252–253; Andrews, *Campaign of Mobile*, 218–219.

22. Andrews, *Campaign of Mobile*, 218–219; Mamie Yeary, compil. *Reminiscences of the Boys in Gray, 1861–1865* (Dayton, OH: Morningside House, 1986), 794.

23. Andrews, *Campaign of Mobile*, 218–219; *OR*, Series I, Vol. 49, Part I, 252–253; Anders, *Twenty-first Missouri*, 229–230; Hughes, *Liddell's Record*, 196.

24. David Marshall Scott, letter to Thomas M. Owen, September 24, 1910, Alabama Department of Archives and History (hereafter cited as ADAH), 62nd Alabama Infantry Regiment File, 3–4.

25. Trudeau, *Out of the Storm*, 183; Andrews, *Campaign of Mobile*, 215.

26. *OR*, Series I, Vol. 49, Part I, 255; Letter of Zach T. Smith to T. M. Owen, October 15, 1910, ADAH, 63rd Alabama Infantry File; Phil Gottschalk, *In Deadly Earnest: The History of the First Missouri Brigade, C.S.A.* (Columbia: Missouri River Press, 1991), 519–520.

27. *OR*, Series I, Vol. 49, Part I, 157, 176, 230.

28. Andrews, *Campaign of Mobile*, 202–203.

29. Ibid.

30. Jackson, *"Some of the Boys . . . ,"* 244–246; Hatch, *Dearest Susie*, 113.

31. Tucker, "Last Stand," 279.

32. Ibid., 280.

33. Jackson, *"Some of the Boys . . . ,"* 246.

34. Andrews, *Campaign of Mobile*, 208.

35. *OR*, Series I, Vol. 49, Part I, 201–202, 214; Andrews, *Campaign of Mobile*, 206–207; Chester G. Hearn, *Mobile Bay and the Mobile Campaign: The Last Great Battles of the Civil War* (Jefferson, NC: McFarland and Company, Inc., Publishers, 1993), 196–197.

36. Andrews, *Campaign of Mobile*, 204.

37. Ibid., 204–205.

38. Ibid., 200.

39. Merriam, "Capture of Mobile," 247; Carlos W. Colby, "Memoirs of Military Service," Joseph G. Bilby, ed., *Military Images* 3: 2 (September–October 1981), 29; *OR*, Series I, Vol. 49, Part I, 289–290.

40. *OR*, Series I, Vol. 49, Part I, 291, 294–296.

41. Andrews, *Campaign of Mobile*, 221; Trudeau, *Out of the Storm*, 182–183.

42. Tucker, "Last Stand," 283.

43. Ibid., 284.

44. Hatch, *Dearest Susie*, 113–114; Hanson and Nicolson, *Siege of Blakeley*, 25, 27.

45. Gottschalk, *In Deadly Earnest*, 521; Tucker, "Last Stand," 284.

46. Andrews, *Campaign of Mobile*, 209.

47. Gottschalk, *In Deadly Earnest*, 521.

48. Ibid., 521–522.

49. Tucker, "Last Stand," 287; Hatch, *Dearest Susie*, 114.

50. Gottschalk, *In Deadly Earnest*, 522; Tucker, "Last Stand," 287.

51. Bevier, *First and Second Missouri Brigades*, 265; Tucker, "Last Stand," 288; Andrews, *Campaign of Mobile*, 205.

52. Andrews, *Campaign of Mobile*, 200–201.

53. Trudeau, *Like Men of War*, 406; Hanson and Nicolson, *Siege of Blakeley*, 21, 41, 42.

54. E. W. Tarrant, "After the Fall of Fort Blakely," *Confederate Veteran* 25 (1917), 152; Tucker, "Last Stand," 287; *OR*, Series I, Vol. 49, Part I, 210.

55. Andrews, *Campaign of Mobile*, 201; Trudeau, *Like Men of War*, 406; E. W. Tarrant, "Siege and Capture of Fort Blakely," *Confederate Veteran* 23 (1915), 457.

56. Trudeau, *Like Men of War*, 406.

57. Andrews, *Campaign of Mobile*, 201.

58. Trudeau, *Like Men of War*, 407.

59. Trudeau, *Like Men of War*, 407; Hanson and Nicolson, *Siege of Blakeley*, 42; James Huffstadt, "The Last Great Assault: Campaigning for Mobile," *Civil War Times Illustrated* (March 1982), 17.

60. Andrews, *Campaign of Mobile*, 221; *OR*, Series I, Vol. 49, Part I, 98.

61. Bevier, *First and Second Missouri Brigades*, 266.

62. Ibid.; Tucker, "Last Stand," 290.

63. Bevier, *First and Second Missouri Brigades*, 267.

64. Alden McLellan, "Vivid Reminiscences of War Times," *Confederate Veteran* 14 (1906), 264.

65. William Lochiel Cameron, "The Battles Opposite Mobile," *Confederate Veteran* 23 (1915), 305–306.

66. Ibid., 306.

67. Andrews, *Campaign of Mobile*, 201, 209–210, 213, 220; *OR*, Series I, Vol. 49, Part I, 110–115, 210, 214; Anders, *Twenty-First Missouri*, 231–232; Trudeau, *Like Men of War*, 408; Merriam, "Capture of Mobile," 243; Arthur W. Bergeron, Jr., *Confederate Mobile* (Jackson: University Press of Mississippi, 1991), 186.

68. Hanson and Nicolson, *Siege of Blakeley*, 36; Bergeron, *Confederate Mobile*, 186; Yeary, *Reminiscences*, 113.

69. Hearn, *Mobile Campaign*, 199; George M. Blackburn, ed., *"Dear Carrie . . .":The Civil War Letters of Thomas N. Stevens* (Mount Pleasant, MI: Clarke Historical Library, Central Michigan University, 1984), 310.

70. Trudeau, *Like Men of War*, 407; Jackson, *"Some of the Boys . . . ,"* 246; *OR*, Series I, Vol. 49, Part I, 202.

71. Jackson, *"Some of the Boys . . . ,"* 245; Hatch, *Dearest Susie*, 115.

72. Hatch, *Dearest Susie*, 115.

73. John E. Peck, Letter, Alabama Department of Archives and History, SG 11132, Folder #16, "Spanish Fort and Blakely, Battles," 3; Andrew Thompson, Diary, 1864–1865 (Auburn University Archives, RG 446), 50.

74. Byron R. Abernethy, ed., *Private Elisha Stockwell, Jr., Sees the Civil War* (Norman: University of Oklahoma Press, 1958), 167.

75. Edward Q. Nye, Diary, in "We Will Be Apt to Have a Hard Fight," *Baldwin Today*, April 10–April 11, 1991, C5.

CHAPTER 14

"A Good Run Instead of a Bad Stand"

The day after the storming of Fort Blakely, Federal guards escorted Liddell to Canby's headquarters. The meeting between the two commanders was a cordial one. Perhaps they spoke of their days at West Point, because they had attended the academy at the same time. Soon the discussion turned to the outcome of the war. "I suppose now slavery is gone," Liddell lamented, "and with it goes the cotton interest in our country." Canby was more optimistic. "No, not so," he corrected him, "for more cotton under free labor will be made in three years than ever before." Liddell was not convinced, but was confident in his own ability to bounce back. He was a ruined man now, but he expected that in three years he would be back on top again and asked Canby if he would care to make a wager on it. "He declined," Liddell later wrote, "likely from principle." He added, "I felt surer of winning such a bet than of holding Blakely with one-half of the men that the works required against fifty thousand men."[1]

For Canby, there still remained Batteries Huger and Tracy to deal with. On April 9, Colonel Isaac Patton—with four companies of the 22nd Louisiana evacuated from Spanish Fort—took command of the two forts, determined to hold them until Maury evacuated Mobile. With eleven guns, including two 10-inch Columbiads, and a 25-foot-high bombproof, Huger was still a formidable obstacle and was prepared to hold out a while longer. Battery Tracy had five 7-inch rifle guns. The forts were still safe from the Federal navy, as ten rows of pilings across the Apalachee River and seven across the Blakely separated them from the enemy fleet. And they had plenty of ammunition, because Maury had instructed them to hold their fire so far. Now Maury directed Patton, "Open all your guns upon the enemy, keep up an active fire, and hold your position until you receive orders to retire." The two forts probably threw 250 shells at the Yankees during the next two days.[2]

The Yanks had been preparing for this moment too. On April 9, Federal gunners in Captain Joseph Foust's 1st Missouri light battery unspiked two 100-pounder Brooke rifles in the captured Old Spanish Fort and turned the big guns toward the two little Rebel forts. Also firing were two 100-pounder Parrotts of the 1st Indiana on the southern shore of Bay Minette and two more 100-pounder rifles and four 30-pounder rifles on the northern shore.[3]

The *Octorara* soon added its guns to the bombardment. The blue jackets had been working steadily to take up Rebel naval mines and had already removed about 150. By the afternoon of April 9, the gunboat was 1,000 yards below Old Spanish Fort. After sailors hacked a way through the thick growth of tall reeds on the marsh islands, the crew of the *Octorara* was able to sight its guns on Fort Huger. The tars sent several shots from their hundred-pounder Parrott—expertly handled by veteran gunner Chief Boatswain's Mate James Welsch—hurtling toward the Rebel fort. The garrison, including some of the evacuees from Spanish Fort waiting to be transported to Mobile, cheered heartily when the first few shots fell short. But the next shot dropped into the water 300 yards above the fort and the following was a direct hit on the fort itself. The *Octorara* began to pummel the little fort, and one soldier was killed.[4]

Downcast after the fall of Fort Blakely, Louisiana soldier Mark Lyons wrote his wife from Battery Huger that he expected the fort to be cut off and the garrison taken prisoner, but he reassured her that he would be all right: "I suppose they know as soon as Mobile falls they have us without trouble. Rest easy about me as I hope to come out safe and will never get caught in another affair of this kind."[5]

On April 10, Huger and Tracy unleashed all their firepower and "made it deathly hot around Old Spanish fort," according to C. C. Andrews. But the Federal guns responded. The *Octorara* got into action again when the Confederate gunners began to target the Federals' minesweeping boats. Foust's battery at Old Spanish Fort kept firing all night, and gunners of the 6th Michigan worked through the night to get a 100-pounder Brooke rifle mounted and serviceable in Fort McDermott.[6]

April 11, Andrews wrote, "was the last day for great guns in Mobile bay—the last for the war." The guns of the Rebel forts blazed away, and Federal guns continued to hammer back. The four big guns on the northern shore of Bay Minette pounded Fort Tracy. The 1st Indiana's two 100-

pounders and eight 30-pounders on the south side of Bay Minette and the Missouri battery in Old Spanish Fort, as well as the *Octorara*, continued shelling Huger. The Yankees had about twenty big guns in action and were building another battery on the north shore of Bay Minette for two more 100-pounders and four more 30-pounders.[7]

The Federals had every intention of assaulting the two Rebel forts that night. A. J. Smith and his staff officers waited on the shore of Bay Minette, a detachment of his "Guerrillas" ready to move out by boats and attack the forts. At 10:00 P.M., the Federal officers turned their field glasses on Huger and saw signal lights flashing. The Rebels were evacuating the fort. Meanwhile a cutter from the *Octorara* intercepted a small skiff with several Rebel deserters who confirmed the suspicion. Sailors from the Federal mine-sweepers landed at the two forts and occupied them that same night.[8]

Three days after Gibson's troops evacuated Spanish Fort over a make-shift treadway across the marsh, the defenders of Batteries Tracy and Huger had escaped these now-vulnerable outposts in a similar fashion. As at Spanish Fort, Confederate engineers had constructed a 2-mile-long bridge stretching from behind Tracy through the bayou. The graycoats stole si-lently out on this foot bridge, boarded a steamer at about 2:00 A.M., and headed for Mobile.[9] The next day the Federals continued sweeping the channel for torpedoes, and the *Octorara* and the *Glasgow* approached the obstructions below Fort Huger. All was done but continued cleanup on this side of the Bay, and the prize of Mobile was now ready for the taking.

Maury simply did not have enough men to hold Mobile, and the grim news of Forrest's defeat at Selma meant that there would be no reinforce-ments coming. In fact, there was nothing but grim news coming in from all around. Maury wired Taylor that if Canby attacked the city, he would not be able to hold out even for one day. The Rebel commander later acknowl-edged that he hadn't enough troops to hold Mobile two weeks earlier had Canby chose to attack it from the western side of the Bay instead of moving against the eastern defenses. In Mobile, alarm bells announcing the evacua-tion of the city clanged throughout a gloomy overcast April 10 morning. Eighteen steamers carried most of the soldiers away that day, but a small rear guard of infantry and cavalry remained. There was a somber mood in the city, as townspeople sadly watched the graycoats—including the wearied, muddy evacuees of Spanish Fort—pull out. "Never have I experi-enced such feelings," one resident noted, "perfectly miserable, as may be imagined."[10]

At sunrise on the morning of April 12, Maury and his rear guard—about 300 of the Louisiana brigade under Colonel Robert Lindsay—abandoned Mobile. Maury's army of 4,500 weary troops followed the Mobile and Ohio

Railroad north. Before he too finally pulled out, Gibson and Colonel Philip Spence's 16th Confederate Cavalry performed one last chore—burning the 3,500 bales of confiscated cotton piled up north of the city. By noon the last of the Confederate army was gone. Even as these graycoats rode away, some residents ran to save as much of the cotton as they could, and nearly half was extracted from the flames. Meanwhile the specter of anarchy loomed. Although Maury had left food supplies to be distributed to the poor, unruly mobs scrambled to get what was left.[11]

The Confederate navy evacuated the city at the same time the army did. Commodore Farrand ordered his remaining gunboats—the *Nashville* and the *Morgan*, joined at Mobile by the decrepit *Baltic*—up the Mobile River. Because they had no towboats for the floating batteries *Huntsville* and *Tuscaloosa*, the sailors scuttled them and left them in the river. The steamers *Black Diamond* and *Southern Republic* and former blockade runners *Heroine*, *Red Gauntlet*, *Mary*, and *Virgin*, accompanied the Rebel fleet that sailed up the Tombigbee River toward Demopolis, about 140 miles north of Mobile. The Rebel sailors also planted torpedoes at the junction of the Alabama and Tombigbee to impede enemy pursuit.[12]

"Although the river was deep," Lieutenant William L. Cameron wrote, "it was narrow and crooked. Our vessels were long and wide, and every once in a while we were into the bank, first on one side and then on the other." The weather was warm with spring foliage in bloom, and it almost seemed to the young officers like a "pleasure journey." Formal discipline practically disappeared. Farrand stayed in his quarters most of the time brooding about the morrow. There was plenty of food—coffee, sugar, molasses, navy beans, rice, salt pork, grog three times a day—because the sailors had cleaned out the navy storehouse in Mobile before leaving.[13]

Everyone knew in their hearts that the war was practically over, and the ships' captains were afraid to stay too close to the river bank for fear that the sailors might jump ship. One night when the *Nashville* was tied up at the bank, the officers posted ten marines as a shore guard. In the morning the marine guard and many of the sailors were gone.

The little Rebel fleet reached Demopolis, where, Cameron recalled, "the ladies were especially kind to the men who were inclined to accept their hospitality." The squadron spent several days there and enjoyed one last fling before facing the inevitable end of their naval careers. Cameron and his pals enjoyed dinner with the ladies where they had "strawberries and cream out of real china plates with silver spoons," drank "cool lemonade from cut glass tumblers offered by lovely maidens who had beautiful eyes, rosy lips, and altogether engaging manners!"[14]

Canby already was putting in motion the final phase of the Mobile campaign. On the day after the capture of Fort Blakely, Major General Gordon Granger had ordered Veatch's and Benton's divisions to prepare to move again, and in the wee hours of the morning of April 12—"after a hard march, which nearly played out a good many of us," the 28th Wisconsin's Captain Thomas Stevens wrote—the Union column reached Starke's Landing below Spanish Fort. The bluecoats loaded themselves and their equipment aboard transports and—accompanied by Federal gunboats—steamed across the Bay for a landing 5 miles below Mobile and a march directly on the Rebel stronghold. At the same time, A. J. Smith's 16th Corps would march north from Blakely toward Montgomery and Selma for a linkup with Wilson's cavalry.[15]

The Union flotilla was prepared for the final battle. As the Mobile shoreline approached, a lone Federal gunboat ploughed ahead and fired a shot at the shore. There was no response. From his flagship, Rear Admiral Thatcher signaled Granger on board the *General Banks*, "I propose to shell the shore." Scrutinizing the tranquil shoreline with his field glass, the general smiled as he saw only white flags. "By ____," he signaled Thatcher, "you'll shell a flag of truce if you do."[16]

The Federal army landed at Catfish Point, just below the city, and waited for the Mobile townspeople to make the next move. Mayor R. H. Slough, accompanied by two other civilian representatives, drove his carriage—carrying a large white sheet as a flag of truce—down the Shell Road to meet with Granger. Slough told Granger that the Rebel soldiers were gone and that the city was undefended. At noon he formally surrendered Mobile to the Federal army. The 8th Illinois Infantry entered the city, and soon the U.S. flag waved over the customhouse for the first time in four years.[17]

One eager soldier from the 8th Illinois asked if he could ride in advance of the column and be the first to plant the national colors on the Battle House Hotel. Receiving an affirmative, the young bluecoat galloped into the city to find the streets choked with curious and anxious civilians. "They treated me kindly," he reported, even furnished him with a hammer and nails, and directed him to the top of the five-story hotel, "where I nailed Old Glory."[18]

All there remained to do was to occupy the Gulf City, the object of so much Federal activity for so long. To the strains of blaring bands, the Federal troops marched into Mobile. The crowds watched with interest, some with apprehension, others with relief. Captain Thomas L. Evans of the 96th Ohio recalled, "We saw many ragged women and children." African Americans seemed delighted and relieved that their deliverance had come at last. A few of the townspeople cautiously approached the Yanks and slowly initiated dialogue. Some were clearly relieved to find that the bluecoats were not the monsters that many had feared. One man gingerly walked up to a young soldier. "I don't see any horns on your head," he remarked. "No," the lad cheerfully shot back, "I got mine knocked off at Blakely."[19]

But many Mobilians eyed the bluecoats with distrust. "I have a sad tale to tell you," teenager Willie Fulton wrote his sister. "Mobile has fallen and we are now under Yankee dominion." The youngster witnessed with sour contempt the arrival of the first groups of Federal soldiers and the raising of the "flag of the dis-United States" over the Battle House Hotel. "In a little while," he wrote, "the officers were riding all over the city. One group passed me and I gave three hearty *groans*."[20]

As the euphoria of victory began to abate, Federal soldiers began to take in the sights of Mobile. After getting a closer look at the strong lines of fortifications surrounding the city, Captain Thomas Stevens reflected that the Confederates must have been badly pressed for manpower, or else they could have put up a severe fight. He cynically observed that many of the Mobile townspeople now claimed they were " 'good Union men,' *of course.*" On April 16, Stevens was delighted to receive fresh potatoes and beans, sugar and coffee, "some *eatables* once more—something beside 'hardtack' & hog meat." The same day, he learned that Lee's surrender had been confirmed. "Didn't we cheer?" he noted.[21]

The occupation of Mobile and the news of Lee's surrender and Federal victories on all fronts did not mean that fighting was over for Canby's army in Alabama. Since April 5, Brigadier General Thomas Lucas' cavalry had been trotting northward from Blakely, heading for the town of Claiborne about 40 miles up the Alabama River, a town said to be held by Rebel troops. Canby intended for Lucas to block the Alabama to navigation in case Maury's army tried to escape by that route. By April 11, part of the blue-coated 1st Louisiana Cavalry galloped into Mount Pleasant just south of Claiborne and found that Rebel militia had abandoned their camp there. But the Federals ran into trouble three miles north, drawing heavy fire from Rebel troops drawn up in a stubborn battle line partly concealed in the swamp ahead.

The Rebel force was 450 men of the 15th Confederate Cavalry led by Lieutenant Colonel Thomas J. Myers. Formed at Mobile in the spring of 1864, the 15th Confederate Cavalry had patrolled approaches to the city. The Rebel attack momentarily stunned the Federals, who fell back in confusion. But Lucas, nearby, sent up Lieutenant Colonel Algernon Badger with the rest of the 1st Louisiana Cavalry while he followed with the balance of the column. Badger's men gamely charged the Rebels, and the skirmish was over in a few minutes. The Rebels broke and retreated leaving five dead and six wounded. The 1st Louisiana Cavalry lost two men killed and five wounded. Lucas captured sixty of the graycoats and three of their officers. The Confederate horsemen withdrew and rumbled through Claiborne, abandoning it to the Yankees. Lucas was unable to cross the Alabama because the river was too high.[22]

On the morning of April 13, Colonel Henry M. Day's brigade took out after Maury's retreating Rebel army. Following the Mobile and Ohio Railroad a few miles north of Mobile, an advance detachment from the 91st Illinois ran upon Colonel Philip Spence's 16th Confederate Cavalry, a Mississippi command, in the process of burning a railroad bridge at Whistler. Spence—described by Maury as "one of the most efficient and comfortable out-post commanders I ever had to deal with," who "always took what was given to him and made the most of it"—was doing what he did best, impeding the pursuing Yankee army and making (as a young Rebel cavalryman said earlier in the campaign) a "good run instead of a bad stand." Day quickly deployed the 91st Illinois and 29th Iowa, while the 7th Vermont moved up in support, and heavy gunfire spattered for several minutes. The Rebels already had fires lit on the bridge, but Captain Augustus P. Stover and twenty Illinoisans charged and dislodged the graycoats, who retreated, leaving one bluecoat killed and two wounded plus four of their own dead and two wounded. Day complimented the much-maligned 7th Vermont for its promptness in the action. The volleys fired at Whistler proved to be the last shots of the Mobile campaign.[23]

While Benton's and Veatch's divisions occupied Mobile and nipped at the heels of Maury's retreating graycoats, a lumbering Yankee war machine was gobbling up the rest of southern Alabama. A. J. Smith's corps was marching north toward Montgomery where they expected to link up with Wilson's cavalry. To the east of Smith's corps, Major General Benjamin H. Grierson's cavalry column up from Pensacola—joined by Lucas' horsemen after their capture of Claiborne—rode toward Eufaula on the Chattahoochee River. And to the west of Smith, plodding north up the Alabama River, came Steele with Hawkins' black division and the two brigades of C. C. Andrews' division.

Smith's Guerrillas left Blakely on April 13 in a heavy rainstorm. As his division moved into the road headed north, John McArthur rode out to meet them, and they cheered. "Boys," he said, waving his Scottish cap, "we'll soon be in out of the wet." The bluecoats were eager for the campaign to end and anxious to finish the Rebels off, although how the graycoats could go on fighting after the fall of Mobile was a mystery to them. "I can't imagine," wrote Edward Nye, "where they intend to make a stand."[24]

The Federals made their way overland toward Greenville. "Country very lonely indeed," Nye wrote in his diary. "Trees green, woods full of beautiful flowers." The weather turned hot, and sunstroke claimed several victims as the Federal column plodded through the pine forests and swamps of southern Alabama. More than once, drenching spring rains soaked them. Easter Sunday passed, a beautiful day, just a week since the storming of Fort Blakely. There was no sign of the Rebels. "In the 55 miles that we have marched," Nye observed, "I have not seen but nine houses. Miserable huts at that. They are generally inhabited by from 10 to 12 white-headed children each." As if aware of the Yankees' approach, many houses displayed white flags, and a sign on one of them proclaimed, "The Union forever."[25]

The white inhabitants may have seemed aloof, but the reaction of the African Americans the Federals encountered was quite different. "It would be a novelty to you," Surgeon Jerome Burbank wrote his wife, "to see the negroes that follow us. They are of all ages from a few weeks old up to 60 years of age and both sexes. Ask them where they are agoing. Their reply is universally the same—that they are going with you'all or Im goin with you all." Now that the war was over, blacks were deserting the plantations. "A great many Negro families are following the Army," Charles Henry Snedeker wrote. "Some are carrying their children on their heads and picking up beef bones left by the soldiers, to live on."[26]

The official news of Lee's surrender reached Smith's Guerrillas as they marched through the little town of Greenville on April 22. A staff officer came galloping along the column waving a dispatch and proclaiming, "Lee has surrendered, Lee has surrendered!" At first there was stunned silence, then wild cheers as the soldiers fired their guns into the air. "For the first time," a private in the 47th Illinois wrote, "the roar of the guns of the 16th corps proclaimed the glad tidings of peace—upon that afternoon—amid the pines of Alabama." Elisha Stockwell recalled that the exultant bluecoats "lay there all day and celebrated."[27]

Although soldiers in the advance cautiously threw up breastworks regularly as they moved through enemy country, Smith's troops encountered no opposition on the march north. The monotonous stretches of pine timber gradually gave way to oaks and gumtrees, and on April 24, Smith's corps reached Montgomery, only to learn that Wilson had already occupied the city without firing a shot on April 12, then had moved on to Columbus, Georgia. Smith sent word to Canby, "I am out of rations but can get along until the 27th."[28]

Smith's Guerrillas marched into Montgomery with flags flying and bands blaring. Lieutenant Hieronymus in the 117th Illinois noted that it

was "the grandest parade many of us ever witnessed," and the Federal officers were decked out in their best uniforms. The former Confederate capital was "quite a pleasant place," Jerome Burbank wrote, and Snedeker
called it "a pretty little city." There was evidence of recent evacuation by
Rebel troops who had set fire to cotton bales in part of the town. An Iowa
soldier remembered that the streets were "full of negroes and a few citizens." And as freedmen crowded along the river bank cheering and waving, Hawkins' black division arrived by boat on April 30. Snedeker
observed that they "are doing a big business recruiting here."[29]

Hieronymus commented with some bitterness that Montgomery was
the place where "the first Rebel Congress met, planned and caused these
past four years of bloody war." As a jest, members of Edward Nye's regiment, the 33rd Illinois, occupied the state capitol, "elected" its own senate
and passed laws, among others, to have Jeff Davis hanged for treason, to
raise each soldier's pay to $100 a month, and to replace army rations of
hardtack with turkey, cranberries, and roast beef.[30]

While the Federal army was overrunning southern Alabama unop-
posed, Maury's army—now consisting of Gibson's, Holtzclaw's, and Ector's
brigades and the artillery commands from Spanish Fort and Mobile—had
been retreating northward from Mobile along the Tombigbee River. The
graycoats finally congregated near Meridian, Mississippi, where Taylor
had his headquarters. The 22nd Louisiana evacuees from Batteries Huger
and Tracy caught up with the main column on April 18. On April 19, Sergeant Pitt Chambers—having hid out in the swamps after the rout of the
46th Mississippi in the Federal cavalry attack of April 1 and after a remarkable seventeen-day odyssey through southern Alabama—finally reached
the Rebel army's camp and rejoined what was left of Sears' brigade—about
a dozen officers and fifty-five enlisted men who had managed to escape
from Blakely—now attached to Ector's brigade.[31]

"We had plenty to eat," Edgar Jones recalled, "and there seemed no disposition to drill or do anything of the kind." There were plenty of rations for
a change and plenty of rumors about Lee's surrender. In spite of it all,
Maury reported, the army "remained steadfastly together, and in perfect
order and discipline." With their world crumbling around them, the soldiers still kept up their spirits with dark humor. "Boys," one graycoat began seriously as he approached a group of his comrades, "the Confederacy
has run the blockade with forty thousand bales of cotton and laid it all out
in tin." When a naive soldier asked him what they intended doing with so
much tin, the man replied with a sardonic grin, "To make spouts for the
Confederacy to go up in."[32]

On April 21, Maury moved his command to Cuba Station, on the Mississippi-Alabama line, in preparation for a possible movement by rail to North Carolina to join General Joseph E. Johnston's army, still fighting against Sherman. Anticipating the coming collapse, a number of soldiers slipped away during the march, and the Mississippi brigade was down to thirty-five men by the time they reached Cuba Station on April 24. It was at this little railroad junction that Maury's army received official confirmation of the surrender of Lee's army and of the capture of Jefferson Davis by Federal cavalry in Georgia.[33]

In Holtzclaw's Alabama brigade, the soldiers were told to assemble that evening at brigade headquarters. Colonel Bush Jones, under obvious strain, stepped up on a box and quieted the troops, told them that the rumors were true. Lee had surrendered in Virginia. Johnston had surrendered. The Confederacy was gone. "Strong men bowed their heads in sorrow," Edgar Jones wrote, "and tears trickled down the cheeks of many. . . . I drew apart from the throng, and seated on a log I wept as I had not done for many a day."[34]

Reaction was similar in the other Rebel units. "Hard as it is to say it," Pitt Chambers wrote in his diary, "*we have failed.*" From the Rebel army's camp Robert Tarleton wrote his young bride Sallie on April 27, "The surrender of Lee is not doubted here and our cause is looked upon as gone. This is the bluest place I have seen and I shall be glad to get away from it today."[35]

Now there seemed nothing left to do but to wait for the appearance of Yankee gunboats coming up the Tombigbee River. There was nowhere else to go.

Sad intelligence of a different sort reached the Federal Army on April 26. The news of President Abraham Lincoln's assassination filled the Yankee soldiers with shock and anger. Many of the men were predictably outraged and vengeful toward the South. "[L]et the army destroy everything from the face of the land they claim," Captain Thomas Stevens wrote. "[L]et them reap the whirlwind of destruction & shame, desolation & sorrow." Charles Musser in the 29th Iowa wrote, "the whole Army is enraged." There was an overriding sense of loss in the Federal Army. In Montgomery, Smith's Guerrillas took the news of the assassination hard. Flags were lowered to half mast, and guns fired every half hour. "At the north I doubt not his death is felt to be a great national calamity," James Newton of the 14th Wisconsin wrote, "but nowhere is such sincere sorrow felt as here in the army. . . . We mourn him not only as a President but as a man." For the African American troops the news was especially shocking, for the "Great Emancipator" had created the black commands in the Union army, and his death was a special loss to them.[36]

Confederate soldiers also were shocked at news of Lincoln's murder, which they regarded as a cowardly and stupid act. Fear of Yankee retribution was also a prime concern. "I am fearful the war will be prosecuted more barbarously than ever," Pitt Chambers wrote. Charles Musser wrote that the Rebel civilians and prisoners he had talked to expressed great regret at the president's death, "are very tired of the war here and all are willing to submit to the U. S. authorities."[37]

But beyond all of the tragedy of Lincoln's death, most Union soldiers looked forward to the end of the war. For them, all that remained was to wait for the inevitable Rebel surrender. On duty with his regiment guarding a captured Rebel arsenal at Mount Vernon, Alabama, Musser was having the most enjoyable time since joining the army, and he rejoiced on May 1: "*there is no more fighting for us during this war*, and how thankful I am for it."[38]

Richard Taylor's command—including the Mobile troops under Maury and Forrest's cavalry defeated at Selma—was now the last organized Confederate army east of the Mississippi. Taylor came from a distinguished family; his father was military hero and U.S. President Zachary Taylor. He also had close ties with his former brother-in-law Jefferson Davis, whose first wife was the old general's daughter. A Harvard and Yale graduate as well as a planter and legislator in Louisiana, Taylor had become colonel of the 9th Louisiana Infantry in July 1861. He had skillfully directed Confederate forces in the 1864 Red River campaign and had defeated Major General Nathaniel Banks at Mansfield.[39]

The Confederate commander faced a sad decision. He had actually seen the inevitable back in September 1864 when he told Jeff Davis that "the best we could hope for was to protract the struggle until spring." Now there seemed no way that he could avoid going the way of Lee and Johnston. Taylor and Canby had exchanged notes on April 14 and April 19 concerning a prisoner swap, and the Confederate commander had picked up from the "tone" of Canby's message that a meeting between the two men might be useful. Taylor suggested a parley and asked Canby to pick the place.[40]

The meeting between the two commanders took place at noon on April 29 at Magee's Farm, a site along the railroad line 12 miles north of Mobile. On hand for the occasion were a Federal brass band and a full brigade of spiffy blue-coated troops as a guard of honor. If Canby anticipated the arrival of a similar retinue with his Rebel counterpart, he was in for a letdown. The commander of the Confederate Department of Alabama, Mississippi, and East Louisiana arrived at Magee's Farm riding in a railroad handcar, with one aide and with two black men operating the handle. In contrast to Canby and his large staff all decked out in their best dress, both Taylor and his aide, Colonel William M. Levy, looked pretty scruffy.[41]

Taylor recognized Canby, whom he knew from before the war, as well as several of the Federal officers. The men chatted for a few minutes, then Taylor and Canby withdrew to a separate room in the farmhouse and got down to business. They agreed not to a surrender but to a truce between the two armies, same as the one just agreed to by Sherman and Johnston, with forty-eight hours' notice if either side decided to end it. The two generals then rejoined the staff officers. Although obviously relieved that the fighting seemed to be over, the men made no more mention of this. Instead, the conversation turned to more pleasant past experiences.

"A bountiful luncheon was soon spread," Taylor wrote, "and I was invited to partake of patis, champagne-frappe, and other 'delights,' which, to me, had long been as lost arts." Outside, Canby's military band broke into a rousing "Hail Columbia." Canby excused himself, left the table, and moved to the door. A few moments later, the music stopped, then the band struck up "Dixie." Moved by this gesture of consideration, Taylor thanked Canby and requested that the band switch back to "Hail Columbia." Taylor "proposed we should unite in the hope that our Columbia would soon be, once more, a happy land." Champagne flowed, and Taylor quipped that the popping of the corks were "the first agreeable explosive sounds I had heard for years."[42]

The Rebel commander returned to his camp. "Circumstances," Taylor wrote sadly, "had appointed me to watch the dying agonies of a cause that had fixed the attention of the world." Almost immediately a dispatch came to him with news from Canby. The Federal government had rejected the peace agreement between Johnston and Sherman, so the truce was off. As an alternative, Canby proposed that the Confederate commander surrender his army to him on the same terms that Grant had offered to Lee.[43]

Should he make a last stand? "There was no room for hesitancy," Taylor later wrote. "Folly and madness combined would not have justified an attempt to prolong a hopeless contest." The alternative to fighting a last bloody battle was disbandment and guerrilla warfare. Taylor gave serious thought to the idea but decided against it. He was adamant on this point. If any of his troops chose this course of action, he cautioned, "they will be hunted down like beasts of prey." Taylor also advised several Confederate congressmen, who had recently arrived in his camp, to accept the inevitable, to go home, and respect the peace. On the evening of May 2, Taylor accepted Canby's offer.[44]

Taylor and Canby held their second meeting—this time for the purpose of negotiating a surrender—at Citronelle, Alabama, on the rail line about 40 miles north of Mobile, on May 4. Taylor formally surrendered his entire command—on paper 25,000 men, of whom far less were actually present.

Commodore Farrand surrendered his gunboats as well. Taylor noted that Canby "was ready with suggestions to soothe our military pride" and to make the details of the surrender as painless for the Rebels as possible. The Confederate officers would be allowed to retain their side-arms, the troops would turn in their weapons and equipment, and transportation home would be provided for the men.[45]

News of the surrender spread like wildfire through the Federal camps. As soon as Taylor had accepted his proposal, Canby had telegraphed A. J. Smith in Montgomery to "desist from all aggressive operations." Old Baldy was to maintain the "strictest discipline" among his troops and to respect the civilian population, "the people at all times treated with leniency." Smith's Guerrillas were overjoyed. Lieutenant Morrey of the 21st Missouri, camped north of Montgomery, wrote, "Oh what a glorious termination of things."[46]

Soldiers of Benton's division were throwing up earthworks at a bluff on the Tombigbee. As soon as the news of the Confederate surrender reached him, Benton mounted his horse, and galloped out to the works. "Boys," he yelled, "the war is over, throw down your spades and let the Fort go to Hell. We dont want it." The troops broke into cheering, and shots from the *Octorara*—coming up the river in pursuit of the Rebel gunboats after winding through the Alabama delta—boomed in celebration.[47]

Thomas Stevens heard the welcome news of the Rebel surrender on his birthday, May 6. He and the Wisconsin boys of his company spent the day partying, many of them drinking toasts and too excited to do much of anything else. Charles Musser and his Iowa comrades still camped near Mount Vernon had already begun to relax, spending their time fishing on the river or sailing in small boats. There was little else to do, and the local people seemed to be warming up to them now. Even the returning Rebel soldiers seemed inclined to be amiable now that the war was truly over.[48]

Maury's little army—now the size of a regular brigade—had just one final duty to perform—to lay down its arms. Gibson's Louisiana brigade, Holtzclaw's Alabama brigade, Ector's Texans, the artillerymen, and the few remaining members of Sears' Mississippians, Cockrell's Missourians, Alabama reserves, all made their way toward Meridian. Many of the soldiers saw no sense in carrying their weapons any longer, piled them into the ordnance wagons or simply left them propped up by trees on the side of the road. The troops bundled aboard freight cars and rode the rails one last time, some of them reaching Meridian on the night of May 7, others early the next morning. Maury's concluding message to his troops was to "let us tomorrow, with the dignity of the veterans who are the last to surrender, perform the duty which has been assigned to us."[49]

And now the time had come. On the morning of May 8, the troops fell in one last time. Commanding officers choked back tears as they thanked their men for their loyalty and respect. In the 18th Alabama, Lieutenant Colonel Peter F. Hunley reminded his soldiers of the fine record they left behind them, told them they could walk away from all this with heads held high. "You will now march with me into the town," Hunley directed them, "where you will turn over your guns and receive your parole." The troops marched into Meridian, filed into an old wooden warehouse, where each man deposited his weapons and equipment onto a growing pile of guns. They then moved through a small office, where a Federal officer filled in their names on individual forms and handed them their paroles.[50]

In Slocomb's battery, Phil Stephenson left this account of the surrender:

> The agony of the formalities took several days. We were surrendered on parole, each officer and private receiving a separate paper. Everything was perfectly businesslike and humdrum, no excitement, no disorder. The Federal troops were kept well in hand, were not allowed to insult us, and they showed no disposition to do so. There was no marching out, lining us up opposite the Federal forces, and our general surrendering his sword to the victor, no pomp and parade of triumph. We saw very little of the Federal troops.[51]

Pitt Chambers took the responsibility of gathering up the Mississippi brigade's remaining guns—all three of them—and he and two other soldiers carried them to a Federal officer in his tent where he "politely informed him that that was Sears' brigade, and asked *where* he would have it stack its arms." The Yankee officer simply smiled and pointed to a spot nearby.[52]

Gibson delivered his farewell address to the Louisiana brigade. "There is nothing in your career to look back upon with regret," he told them. "As soldiers, you have been among the bravest and most steadfast, and as citizens, be law abiding, peaceable, and industrious. You have not surrendered and will never surrender your self-respect and love of country. You separate not as friends, but brethren whom common hopes, mutual trials, and equal disasters have made kinsmen."[53]

Surprisingly a large number of Confederate deserters turned up in Meridian, having heard of the surrender and eager now to receive their paroles. The arrival of these men filtering in slowed down the paroling process. At first no one really tried to interfere, but Taylor finally recommended that no more paroles be given them. The Rebel commander had reported some 8,000 men to be surrendered, but 20,000 showed up to claim their paroles! A number of the veterans let it be known that they resented the deserters, and several scuffles broke out. Some men finally lost patience with the whole process and left without their paroles, heading for home. Throughout all this, the Federal troops kept their composure and seemed happy to provide rations to the former Rebel soldiers, as well as transportation home.[54]

And soon it was all over. "I am a soldier no longer," Pitt Chambers recorded in his diary on May 9; and Phil Stephenson wrote, "There was nothing else left to keep us together." While waiting to board freight cars to carry them home—and anxious to let off some steam—the Rebs organized a boxing match—"the most terrific fist fight I ever witnessed," Edgar Jones recalled—between one of their own and a big Irish Yankee. The Rebel won. Finally a train arrived to carry the 18th Alabama to Demopolis. With the bridge out over the Cahaba River, the men had to walk the rest of the way to Selma, where they dispersed to their homes.[55]

For the senior officers, the breakup of the little Rebel army was a bitter pill to swallow, but they had made a good run. At Meridian, Maury and the men he had worked so closely with during the war spent a melancholy night on May 13, as the small brass band of Gibson's Louisiana brigade played nostalgic music. Then the officers paid their final respects to Maury and bid him good-bye. There was nothing else to do but go home.

The end had finally come for the little Confederate navy bottled up at Demopolis with nowhere else to go. Rear Admiral Thatcher—who had dispatched the *Octorara* and several monitors up the Tombigbee after the fall of Mobile—was satisfied that the Rebel gunboats "must soon fall into our hands or destroy themselves." Word of the capitulation of Lee and Johnston had already reached the Rebel sailors, and Farrand had signed the surrender agreement between Taylor and Canby as well. So on May 8, the same day that the graycoats were laying down their arms at Meridian, the tiny Rebel fleet steamed downriver toward Nanna Hubba Bluff on the Tombigbee and arrived there the next day. The Federal gunboats were waiting for them there.[56]

On May 10, Lieutenant Commander Julian Myers, representing Farrand, boarded the Federal ironclad *Cincinnati* and met with Fleet Captain Edward Simpson, representing Thatcher. The Rebel naval officer formally surrendered the vessels of the Confederate squadron. Once the formalities were done with, members of the former enemy fleets relaxed and began to mix with one another. Lieutenant Cameron wrote, "I found myself in the quarters of the young officers on board the *Cincinnati* drinking iced wine and smoking Havana cigars, having eaten a 'square' meal with them as an honored guest." For senior officers, this was a chance to get reacquainted with former classmates from Annapolis and friends from the old navy.[57]

Paroles were given to the officers, seamen, and marines aboard the Rebel ships. On the *Nashville*, the crew played out the final scene of the surrender, assembling on deck for the lowering of the Confederate colors, which they saluted by raising their caps as many of them burst into tears. After turning over their vessels to the Federals, the former officers and men of the Rebel navy boarded the old transport *Southern Republic*, nicknamed the "Three-Story House Afloat," and steamed down the Tombigbee toward Mobile. A Rebel seaman stepped up to the keyboard of an old calliope and broke into the popular tune, 'O, ain't I glad to get out of the wilderness!' "[58]

The surrender of Taylor's army left Canby with one final matter to take care of—accepting the surrender of the last organized Confederate army, Edmund Kirby Smith's command west of the Mississippi. Feelers from Kirby Smith indicated that he was agreeable to a meeting, and Canby returned to New Orleans for the parlay. On the morning of May 25, the conference was held at the St. Charles Hotel in the Crescent City. Canby, Steele, and Major General F. J. Herron met their Rebel counterparts Generals Simon B. Buckner, Sterling Price, and J. L. Brent. Because he was anxious to prevent needless further bloodshed, Taylor also was on hand. By the end of the day, the Rebel generals agreed to lay down their arms, and the war was over.[59]

The burning question for the Union troops now was when they would be mustered out. "Since the war is over," Surgeon Jerome Burbank wrote, "it appears to me as though we all ought to be at home." Still in Montgomery, Burbank noticed that the Rebel soldiers were coming home now. "Nearly all of them say that the war is played," he observed, "that they are tired of it and are glad of an opportunity to return home."[60]

Charles Musser's regiment returned to Mobile. "I am tired of marching and fighting," the young Iowan wrote, "and want to get where I will no longer hear the Drum and fife or Bugle or the Booming of canons or the rattle of Musketry." But this was not to be. Rumors already had the bluecoats being sent to Texas, where a confrontation between U.S. troops and the French in Mexico seemed likely. France's military intervention in Mexico—a problem Washington had put on the back burner until the Confederacy could be defeated—now appeared to be possibly a cause for a new war; and Musser, seeing Mobile crowded with paroled Rebel soldiers waiting for transportation home, even speculated that Rebel and Federal veterans might join up with Benito Juarez' army fighting the French in Mexico. Now that North and South were at peace, Musser marveled at how well the former enemies got along: "you will see 'Graybacks' and 'Blue Coats' in crowds on the streets most any time in the day, talking about the war and jokeing as if they had not been trying to kill each other only a short time before."[61]

NOTES

1. Nathaniel C. Hughes, ed., *Liddell's Record* (Dayton, OH: Morningside House, Inc., 1985), 197.

2. Dabney H. Maury, "Defence of Mobile," *Southern Historical Society Papers* 3 (1877), 10; George S. Waterman, "Afloat—Afield—Afloat, Notable Events of the Civil War" *Confederate Veteran* 8 (1900), 55.

3. Christopher C. Andrews, *History of the Campaign of Mobile* (New York, 1867), 227.

4. Ibid., 227–228.

5. Mark Lyons Letters, Alabama Department of Archives and History, SPR 194, 501.

6. Andrews, *Campaign of Mobile*, 229.

7. Ibid., 230.

8. Ibid., 230–231.

9. Maury, "Defence of Mobile," 10; Dabney H. Maury, "Defence of Spanish Fort," *Southern Historical Society Papers* 39 (1914), 131.

10. Arthur W. Bergeron, Jr., *Confederate Mobile* (Jackson: University Press of Mississippi, 1991), 188–189.

11. Ibid., 190–191.

12. Ibid., 190.

13. William Lochiel Cameron, "The Battles Opposite Mobile," *Confederate Veteran* 23 (1915), 306–308.

14. Ibid., 308.

15. *War of the Rebellion: A Compilation of the Official Records of the Union and Confederate Armies* (Washington, DC: Government Printing Office, 1880–1901) (hereafter cited as *OR*), Series I, Vol. 49, Part I, 143; George M. Blackburn, ed., *"Dear Carrie . . .": The Civil War Letters of Thomas N. Stevens* (Mount Pleasant, MI: Clarke Historical Library, Central Michigan University, 1984), 310.

16. Chester G. Hearn, *Mobile Bay and the Mobile Campaign: The Last Great Battles of the Civil War* (Jefferson, NC: McFarland and Company, Inc., Publishers, 1993), 201.

17. Ibid.; *OR*, Series I, Vol. 49, Part I, 143, 175.

18. Noah Andre Trudeau, *Out of the Storm: The End of the Civil War, April–June 1865* (Boston: Little, Brown & Co., 1994), 185.

19. Sidney Adair Smith and C. Carter Smith, Jr., eds., *Mobile: 1861–1865 Notes and a Bibliography* (Chicago: Wyvern Press, 1994), 41; Trudeau, *Out of the Storm*, 185.

20. Smith and Smith, *Mobile: 1861–1865*, 42–43.

21. Blackburn, *"Dear Carrie . . . ,"* 311–313.

22. Andrews, *Campaign of Mobile*, 239–240; Joseph Wheeler, "Alabama," in Clement Evans, ed., *Confederate Military History*, vol. 7 (Atlanta, 1899), 298; *OR*, Series I, Vol. 49, Part I, 303–305.

23. *OR*, Series I, Vol. 49, Part I, 223; Maury, "Defence of Mobile," 3.

24. Byron Cloyd Bryner, *Bugle Echoes: The Story of Illinois 47th Infantry* (Springfield, IL, 1905), 154; Edward Q. Nye, Diary, in "We Will Be Apt to Have a Hard Fight," *Baldwin Today*, April 10–April 11, 1991 (hereafter cited as Nye Diary), C5.

25. Nye Diary, C5; Edwin G. Gerling, *The One Hundred Seventeenth Illinois Infantry Volunteers (The McKendree Regiment), 1862–1865* (Highland, IL: Author, 1992), 103; Mildred Britton, *The Civil War Diary of Charles Henry Snedeker*, 1966, Auburn University Archives, RG 844 (hereafter cited as *Snedeker Diary*).

26. Sylvia Burbank Morris, *Jerome: To My Beloved Absent Companion: Letters of a Civil War Surgeon to His Wife at Home, Caring for Their Family* (Cullman, AL: Author, 1966), 224; Britton, *Snedeker Diary*.

27. Bryner, *Bugle Echoes*, 155; Byron R. Abernethy, ed., *Private Elisha Stockwell, Jr., Sees the Civil War* (Norman: University of Oklahoma Press, 1958), 168.

28. Leslie Anders, *The Twenty-First Missouri: From Home Guard to Union Regiment* (Westport, CT: Greenwood Press, 1975), 233; Morris, *Jerome*, 225; Abernethy, *Stockwell*, 168.

29. Gerling, *One Hundred Seventeenth Illinois*, 104; John E. Peck, Letter, Alabama Department of Archives and History, SG 11132, Folder #16, "Spanish Fort and Blakely, Battles," 4; Morris, *Jerome*, 225; Joseph T. Glatthaar, *Forged in Battle: The Civil War Alliance of Black Soldiers and White Officers* (New York: Macmillan, Inc., 1990), 208; Britton, *Snedeker Diary*; Trudeau, *Out of the Storm*, 259.

30. Gerling, *One Hundred Seventeenth Illinois*, 104; Victor Hicken, *Illinois in the Civil War* (Urbana: University of Illinois Press, 1966), 344.

31. Arthur W. Bergeron, Jr., "Twenty-Second Louisiana Consolidated Infantry in the Defense of Mobile, 1864–1865," *Alabama Historical Quarterly* 38 (1976), 212; William Pitt Chambers, *Blood and Sacrifice: The Civil War Journal of a Confederate Soldier*, ed. Richard A. Baumgartner (Huntington, WV: Blue Acorn Press, 1994), 220.

32. Edgar Wiley Jones, *History of the 18th Alabama Infantry Regiment*, compiled by C. David A. Pulcrano (Birmingham, AL: C.D.A. Pulcrano, 1994), 226; Bergeron, "Twenty-Second Louisiana," 213.

33. Chambers, *Blood and Sacrifice*, 221; Bergeron, "Twenty-Second Louisiana," 213.

34. Jones, *18th Alabama*, 222.

35. Chambers, *Blood and Sacrifice*, 222; William N. Still, Jr., ed., "The Civil War Letters of Robert Tarleton," *Alabama Historical Quarterly* 32 (1970), 80.

36. Blackburn, *"Dear Carrie . . . ,"* 314–315; Barry Popchock, ed., *Soldier Boy: The Civil War Letters of Charles O. Musser* (Iowa City: University of Iowa Press, 1995), 203; Stephen E. Ambrose, ed., *A Wisconsin Boy in Dixie: The Selected Letters of James K. Newton* (Madison: University of Wisconsin Press, 1961), 152; Glatthaar, *Forged in Battle*, 209.

37. Hearn, *Mobile Campaign*, 207; Chambers, *Blood and Sacrifice*, 220; Popchock, *Soldier Boy*, 203.

38. Popchock, *Soldier Boy*, 202–203

39. Hearn, *Mobile Campaign*, 144.

40. Shelby Foote, *The Civil War, a Narrative: Red River to Appomattox* (New York: Random House, 1974), 998; Max L. Heyman, Jr., *Prudent Soldier: A Biography of Major General E.R.S. Canby, 1817–1873* (Glendale, CA: Arthur H. Clarke Co., 1959), 232.

41. Heyman, *Prudent Soldier*, 232.

42. Ibid., 233; Richard Taylor, "The Last Confederate Surrender," *Annals of the War Written by Leading Participants, North and South* (Philadelphia, 1879), 69.

43. Taylor, "Last Confederate Surrender," 69.

44. Ibid., 69–70; Trudeau, *Out of the Storm*, 260; Heyman, *Prudent Soldier*, 234.

45. Taylor, "Last Confederate Surrender," 70; Heyman, *Prudent Soldier*, 234.

46. Anders, *Twenty-First Missouri*, 233–234.

47. Popchock, *Soldier Boy*, 204–205.

48. Ibid.; Blackburn, *"Dear Carrie . . . ,"* 316.

49. Jones, *18th Alabama*, 229; Chambers, *Blood and Sacrifice*, 223; Maury, "Defence of Mobile," 13.

50. Jones, *18th Alabama*, 229, 241.

51. Nathaniel C. Hughes, Jr., ed., *The Civil War Memoirs of Philip Daingerfield Stephenson, D.D.* (Conway, AR: UCA Press, 1995), 371.

52. Chambers, *Blood and Sacrifice*, 224.

53. *OR*, Series I, Vol. 49, Part I, 319.

54. Chambers, *Blood and Sacrifice*, 224; Hughes, *Stephenson*, 371–372.

55. Hughes, *Stephenson*, 372; Chambers, *Blood and Sacrifice*, 224; Jones, *18th Alabama*, 241.

56. U.S. Naval History Division, *Civil War Naval Chronology, 1861–1865*, vol. 5, *1865* (Washington, DC: U.S. Government Printing Office, 1965), 95; Cameron, "Battles Opposite Mobile," 308.

57. Cameron, "Battles Opposite Mobile," 308; Waterman, "Afield—Afloat—Afield," vol. 9 (1901), 26–27.

58. Ibid.

59. Heyman, *Prudent Soldier*, 234–235.

60. Morris, *Jerome*, 227.

61. Popchock, *Soldier Boy*, 205–206.

CHAPTER 15

No Longer an Army

After the fall of Fort Blakely, the captured Rebel commanders—Liddell, Cockrell, Thomas—and their staff officers were taken to Dauphin Island and spent six weeks there before being paroled on May 16. Liddell wrote that the Federals treated him courteously and—with the exception of the dark days following Lincoln's assassination, when the Rebel officers were confined to quarters—allowed him free rein of the island. While at Dauphin Island, the three generals visited a Mississippi officer sick in the hospital there, and the patient jokingly asked them what their plans were now that the war was lost. Thomas had in mind making for Mexico and starting a coffee plantation there. Cockrell planned on returning to Missouri where he was confident that with hard work he could rebuild his fortune, adding, "If they don't hang me, and I don't believe they will." These thoughts were echoed by Liddell, who soon found himself paroled and back in New Orleans, "a sadder if not a wiser man, than I started out four years since."[1]

The Rebel enlisted men and officers captured at Fort Blakely and Spanish Fort found themselves confined in the prison camp on Ship Island, in the Gulf of Mexico south of Biloxi, Mississippi. As transports carried the prisoners across Mobile Bay, defiant Colonel Elijah Gates hatched a plot to take over one of the ships. Gates had noted the rather loose discipline on the steamer where he and about 300 other Rebel officers were allowed to mix with the forty or so Yankee guards on board. Gates enlisted others in a plan to seize the vessel. At a given signal, the prisoners would overpower the guards and turn the ship toward Havana, Cuba. The plot was a bold one, but an alert Federal lieutenant got wind of the conspiracy, and the guards then kept a wary eye on the Rebels until they were delivered safely at Ship Island.[2]

Federal soldier Isaac Jackson had called Ship Island "nothing but a heap of sand surrounded by water" when the transport carrying his regiment to Pensacola stopped there briefly in January. For Missouri soldier Ephraim Anderson it was "nothing but a bleak sand-bar, without any shade or shelter upon it of any kind." The eastern end of the island was wooded, but the rest was barren indeed, with a fort, a wharf, and a little village on the western end. The prison camp was next to the village.[3]

The bitterness of defeat and capture became even more galling to the prisoners at Ship Island when they found their guards to be black soldiers of the 74th U.S.C.T., a regiment that had not taken part in the Mobile campaign. Alabama artillery officer Ed Tarrant wrote that the prisoners were "under guard of mean sugar plantation negroes, commanded by even meaner white officers." "They cursed us and called us by all vulgar names they could think of," Alabama infantryman Asa Piper wrote, "and we had to take it or be shot." The guards, making sure the Rebels understood that the "bottom rail on top dis time sure," made life miserable for the prisoners. Treatment became much worse when the news of Lincoln's assassination reached the island. "This was an unfortunate thing for the Southern country," Alden McLellan wrote, "and we felt the effects of it at once, the guards treating us very badly. . . . One night a man stood up to shake the sand from his blanket and was shot."[4]

Prisoners on the barren sandy island endured searing hot sun in the day time, followed by chilly wind at night. "The limit, or 'dead line,' of our camp," McLellan wrote, "was a low ridge made by scraping up the sand. The men had no protection from the sun or rain; the officers had small A tents. The rations were bad and the water bad, as we got only the seepage from barrels sunk in the sand three-fourths of their length. The wood we had to bring two and a half miles from the east end of the island."[5]

Fed up with the abuse, the heat, and the rations ("A fourth of a pound of old salt horse, a half pint of yellow mush"), Asa Piper and some of his chums let their anger out by composing a song:

> Ship Island is an awful place, I'd have you understand,
> They starve a rebel most to death, the guards are contraband,
> They dress in Yankee uniforms, their faces black as tar,
> And when they take us after wood, they make us "Close up dar!"[6]

The confinement on Ship Island lasted two to three weeks, depending upon the Rebel units, which were gradually shipped out as the war ground to a close. The Missouri brigade was transported to New Orleans, marched to a cotton press in the city where they were confined again, then were taken by boat to Vicksburg and by train to Jackson where they received their final paroles—in conjunction with the surrender of Taylor's army—on May 13. Then the veterans parted. Corporal William Kavanaugh recalled it as "one of the saddest days I ever experienced." Even including all the sick and missing at the time of paroling, the Missouri brigade numbered less than 500 out of 8,000 who had originally crossed the Mississippi.[7]

Now the Rebel soldiers made their way back to their homes to face a grim and unsure future. They faced it with a mixture of pride and sadness. They had done their duty, and they would always have that. "In the sanctioned memory of the war," historian Reid Mitchell writes, "the Confederate soldier achieved an odd kind of victory. Defeat itself became glorious." Reflecting on his service with Slocomb's battery, among the last to surrender, Phil Stephenson wrote, "Of that I am proud, have a right to be proud, and shall never cease to be proud." For Pitt Chambers, the outcome of the war and their failure to stave off the South's defeat marked the downfall of American democracy itself. "As Americans," he wrote, "it seems to me, we have demonstrated that we are incapable of governing ourselves."[8]

The graycoats arrived home with a sense of melancholy mixed with grief. Many veterans, like R. P. Womack of the 46th Mississippi "found everything gone, and started life anew." "It seemed that it was impossible," Edgar Jones wrote of the South's surrender, "that it could not be, and how were we ever to endure Yankee domination." The physical destruction the war had brought to home communities in the South was only compounded by the horrendous losses incurred during the conflict and the deaths of family members. "I had three brothers in the same company"; J. A. Dozier of the 18th Alabama remembered, "but when the surrender came, I was the only one."[9]

Some men postponed the return home, unwilling to face what they might find there. Phil Stephenson, a Missourian, did not return to St. Louis until June 1865, because bitter feelings were still so intense there. Instead, he went to the Canebrake country east of Demopolis, where he awaited the arrival of five of his friends in the Rebel army. The six pals, now scattered in different parts of the defeated South, had promised to meet in the Canebrake if they survived the war and then go home together. The last to arrive traveled from North Carolina, much of the way on foot, to be at the friends' reunion. Before going home, there were things they intended to do—relaxing, playing jokes on each other, and gathering intelligence on the situation in Missouri. Still clowning even in defeat, Stephenson wrote, "it was simply frolicking and playing pranks. . . . We simply *had* to have vent."[10]

But sooner or later former Rebel soldiers had to grapple with weightier problems. Lieutenant Colonel James M. Williams had sent his wife Lizzy and their son to stay with friends near Prattville, Alabama, in August 1864. Now that the war was lost, his main concern was how to support his family. "I have arrived in Mobile," he wrote Lizzy on May 16, "—am well—paroled— I will try to find something to do but I fear it will be very hard to make even a living. . . . [As] soon as I can make some arrangements for employment I will try to get leave to visit you." Williams did find work in Mobile with John King, a fellow officer in the 21st Alabama. He still remained a loyal Southerner in spite of the war's outcome and stayed in Mobile for the rest of his life, but like most Confederate veterans he resolved to get on with his life and accept the South's defeat.[11]

For the Federals, the Confederate surrender did not mean they would be going home, at least not immediately like their former antagonists. A. J. Smith's corps performed occupation duty in Alabama. McArthur's division went to Selma, Garrard's to Mobile. The 21st Missouri boys, itching to get out of the service, were still on duty in the fall of 1865. The 8th Iowa was stationed in Montgomery—where some of the men had been held as prisoners of war after Shiloh—then in Tuscaloosa, and finally in Selma, where the regiment became the last Iowa command to be mustered out on April 20, 1866. But most of Smith's Guerrillas gradually left the service during the summer and fall of 1865. Old Baldy bid farewell to them on August 8, disbanding the 16th Corps, and expressing his appreciation for their courage and loyalty. "You have never experienced defeat nor repulse," Smith told them. "Let the memory of what you have endured endear to you every foot of American soil."[12]

After assembling at Mobile, Granger's 13th Corps was moving west to Texas as part of a show of force aimed at the French in Mexico. Much to the frustration of Frank McGregor, the 83rd Ohio left on ships bound for Galveston, where the men arrived seasick, angry, and ready to vent their rage on the local townsfolk. A number of fist fights between the Yankees and ex-Rebel soldiers broke out, provoking Frank to write, "Texas never was a law abiding community." The 7th Vermont received orders to head for the Rio Grande and was stationed there until March 1866. Not until April did they return to Vermont. In July 1866 the War Department finally authorized the 7th Vermont to carry the name Baton Rouge on their colors. The last two actions inscribed there were Spanish Fort and Whistler, the last skirmish of the Mobile campaign.[13]

The 97th Illinois—battle-scarred from the bloody assault on Redoubt 4 at Blakely—mustered out at the end of July 1865 and returned to Springfield to be discharged on August 18. "That night we had a great jollification meeting," one soldier wrote, "over the fact that we could now return to our homes and loved ones as citizens; but there was sadness mixed with joy when the original roll was called, to see how many answered to their names of those who so proudly marched to the front three years before."[14]

The war had changed all of them in many ways. When his fiancée wrote asking him to describe how he looked after three years in the army, Frank McGregor took pen in hand. He suggested that Susie picture a Frank "stouter than you used to see," bearded, with grayer hair, and sunburned skin. But he was looking forward to their life together. And finally Frank, like thousands of other young ex-soldiers, went back home. The veterans returned to their farms and businesses; and some sought better opportunities in the west. Most lived out their days as respected members of their communities, many taking an active role in civic and political life.[15]

Veterans of Hawkins' black division faced a more uncertain future. The African American troops also did police duty in the occupied South after the war, and then they were mustered out. They had served with distinction in the last major assault of the war in a battle hardly anyone in the civilian world would remember, a needless battle that came when the war was really over. Blakely was final indisputable proof of the fighting quality and loyalty of black soldiers, but the general public would never know or care.

The 73rd U.S.C.T.'s postwar odyssey took it from Montgomery to Selma, then to Mobile, to Vicksburg, and to Jackson, where the regiment was stationed in June 1865. The 73rd returned to New Orleans in July and was discharged on September 23, observing the occasion with a grand parade down Conti Street. Marching to the beat of fife and drum, proud black veterans—some 250 strong—filed by the office of the New Orleans *Tribune*, the first African American daily newspaper in the United States, and was saluted with three rousing cheers from the crowd of black citizens that turned out to watch. The *Tribune*'s editor, in his next issue, vowed, "we'll battle with pen in hand, for the same noble cause for which they all suffered, fought, and bled."[16]

With the ratification of the 15th Amendment to the U.S. Constitution, blacks now began to vote for the first time. In Louisiana, African Americans took an active part in the state's constitutional convention. Six delegates were veterans of the old Louisiana Native Guards, including 27-year-old Louis Francois, a former sergeant in the 73rd U.S.C.T. Pinckney B. S. Pinchback, also a veteran of the Native Guards, later became lieutenant governor of Louisiana. The new Louisiana constitution contained provisions guaranteeing African Americans equal rights with whites in the business place and on common carriers, a provision struck down by the U.S. Supreme

Court in 1878. Veterans of the old Louisiana Native Guards also served in the state legislature, five in the House and four in the Senate.[17]

Most black veterans received no reception like that of the Native Guards, no parades, and no recognition. Some of them chose to remain in the service, and several new African American regiments in the Regular Army attracted blacks with wartime experience. With the old battles for equal pay over, the army provided security and a sense of pride.[18]

Black veterans faced the hostility of white Southerners toward African Americans after the war, hostility that could manifest itself in terrible ways. Even as the war was ending, Charles Henry Snedeker of the 124th Illinois recorded in his diary on May 14 that three blacks, a man and two women, turned up at the guard house with their ears cut off and that one of the women had part of her face and the right side of her head skinned, a hideous mutilation. Black veterans faced intimidation of other sorts. When the mother of Private Pless Adams, killed in the attack of Drew's brigade on Fort Blakely, applied for a pension for her son, she provoked the wrath of white neighbors who declared they would "never assist any damned nigger in getting a pension, so long as pensions are denied to the widows of southern soldiers."[19]

For Mobile, the end of the fighting came as a welcome relief. The Federal occupation there was remarkably peaceful. "The city is full of Yanks black and white," James M. Williams wrote on May 17, 1865, "so far they have behaved well." The restrained conduct of the soldiers surprised many Mobilians who had expected the worst of the Yankees.[20]

But just as the Gulf City seemed to be bouncing back from defeat, a tragic explosion shattered the early afternoon calm of May 25, 1865. A detachment of black soldiers of the 51st U.S.C.T. unloading captured Rebel munitions from the railroad to a warehouse—and carelessly handling the boxes of shells—accidentally set off a horrendous blast. General C. C. Andrews, working on reports in the military headquarters on Government Street, was thrown against a wall by the explosion. Brigadier General James Slack, taking a nap in a nearby boardinghouse, woke up with a start as the window above his bed shattered. He got out fast, to find the streets filled with men, women, and children screaming and running for their lives. The downtown business district of Mobile was a raging inferno. The fires destroyed eight city blocks and left a 10-foot-deep, 57-by-254-foot-wide hole where the warehouse once had stood. The explosion created a mushroom cloud over Mobile that could be seen by soldiers three miles away and a blast wave that could be felt by civilians on the eastern side of Mobile Bay. Two steamers in the harbor were destroyed.

Slack described the scene: "Shells were constantly exploding, men crying most piteously for help, the fire approaching them and no helping hand could save them." Major General Gordon Granger was at the scene quickly and took charge of the containment operation. Firefighters worked through the night to quell the blaze, many of them—terrified by continuing explosions—with armed soldiers at their backs. A detachment of sailors arrived to help, and two of the blue jackets died in the operation. Cleanup and rescue operations went on for several more days, as work crews continued to uncover the dead buried in the debris. Somewhere between two and three hundred people, military and civilian, perished. The disaster retarded Mobile's economic recovery for years.[21]

Several days after the explosion, a Northern newspaper reporter described a scene of fearful destruction, blocks and blocks of Mobile a "waste of broken brick and mortar, still smoldering and smoking," buildings "flattened as a whirlwind might flatten a house of card-boards." Kate Cummings, returning from Montgomery, wrote, "As we neared Mobile my heart sank within me at the desolate appearance of every thing." The "best fortified place in the Confederacy," the last great Rebel stronghold that withstood an overwhelming Federal army until the very end of the war, was in the end leveled with terrific loss of life because a careless soldier dropped a box of explosives.[22]

The military operation against Mobile—with its costly siege at Spanish Fort and bloody storming of Fort Blakely—was a needless one. The campaign cost the Federals 1,678 senseless casualties (including 232 men killed), while Confederate losses were probably about 500. In an attempt to distance himself from criticism, Grant commented, "I had tried for more than two years to have an expedition sent against Mobile when its possession by us would have been of great advantage. It finally cost lives to take it when its possession was of no importance, and when, if left alone, it would within a few days have fallen into our hands without any bloodshed whatever."[23]

A Federal occupation of Mobile earlier in the war could most certainly have affected the war's outcome and brought about the Confederacy's fall much sooner. Mobile was the "soft underbelly" of the Confederate heartland, and the capture of the Gulf City could have allowed the Yankees to slash the rail link into this heartland. Federal troops could have used the rail line and the Alabama and Tombigbee River systems to move against Montgomery and against Atlanta, forcing the Confederacy to divert significant numbers of troops away from other critical areas. They might even have prevented Confederate offensives into the North in 1862 and 1863. Because Union forces were drawn away to other areas of the conflict in 1863 and 1864, and because Northern military strategists overestimated the strength of Mobile's defenses, Federal movement against Mobile was de-layed to the end of the war.[24]

When the Federals finally moved decisively against Mobile, its occupa-tion made virtually no difference anymore. Lee's surrender on April 9, plus Wilson's capture of Selma on April 2 and subsequent occupation of Mont-gomery on April 12, rendered Canby's occupation of Mobile and the bloody sieges of Blakely and Spanish Fort completely unnecessary. Sherman's march through Georgia in late 1864 had already dealt such an effective blow to the South's economy and will to fight that both Wilson's and Canby's offensives were needless. But the Mobile operation was an integral part of Grant's grand strategy, his policy of "total war" implemented in 1864 to bring the South to her knees; and the Federal war machine, once set in motion, was hard to revoke.[25]

If Canby had marched on Mobile after the Battle of Mobile Bay, while Sherman was taking Atlanta, the two commanders could have linked up, severing the eastern Confederacy from the central heartland and rendering Sherman's "march to the sea" through Georgia unnecessary (or perhaps transposing it to central Alabama). Grant had originally planned to have Sherman, after taking Atlanta, set out overland through Alabama to Mo-bile, linking up with Canby's forces and thus severing the Confederacy. The lateness of the Federal movement against Confederate defenses in Mobile Bay caused the generals to revise their plan.[26]

Even in moving against Mobile in the spring of 1865—long after the city's importance had been neutralized by Federal control of Mobile Bay—if Canby had sidestepped Spanish Fort and Fort Blakely, concentrated his heavy guns along the shore of Bay Minette, and focused his artillery fire on Batteries Huger and Tracy, he would have forced their surrender (and the evacuation of Mobile) in two weeks. Canby could also have bypassed the eastern shore garrisons altogether and moved north to the junction of the Alabama and Tombigbee Rivers. There he could have severed Mobile from reinforcements and supplies and eventually starved the city out. Canby's reply to this argument was that Spanish Fort and Blakely could have been used by the Rebels to disrupt Federal communications and that it was too risky to allow a large enemy force to remain behind the advanc-ing Yankee army.[27]

Even though Canby seemed to be operating under pressure from Grant—pressure to "take Mobile and hold it," although Grant later contended Mobile was not the major objective—he knew it was not strategically neces-sary to capture the city. By bypassing the western defenses and moving to the eastern shore, he would be able to open up the Alabama River as a sup-ply route for the Federal army on its offensive into central Alabama. He also would siphon off Maury's troops from Mobile and force him to defend the eastern forts against possible attack. Canby considered Selma and Montgomery his primary objectives.[28]

Some Confederate strategists questioned the wisdom of defending Spanish Fort and Fort Blakely at all. General P.G.T. Beauregard contended that they would have been better off in simply strengthening Batteries Huger and Tracy and withdrawing the bulk of troops to Mobile. Garrisoning Spanish Fort made no sense, if its purpose was to protect Huger, because the Federals put batteries on Bay Minette that neutralized Huger and, according to C. C. Andrews, "in two weeks time would have crushed Huger and Tracy."[29]

Tactical errors by the Confederate commanders included their oversight in not effectively fortifying their flanks in the swamps at Spanish Fort and Blakely. Although they felt an attack was highly unlikely at these points, it was precisely there that the Federals made their breakthroughs. Maury probably could have saved the Fort Blakely garrison had he gone ahead and evacuated the post at the same time that Gibson's troops pulled out of Spanish Fort. He actually planned to evacuate Blakely on the night of April 9, but he delayed one day too long. Liddell, on the other hand, contended he could have held Blakely had Maury allowed him to retain the Spanish Fort troops, an unlikely boast in the face of the vast Federal numerical strength. In any event, the capture of these posts was only a matter of time.[30]

Although forgotten by the American public and largely ignored by historians, the Mobile campaign of 1865 actually marked the zenith of America's war-making science of the Civil War. Brigadier General James R. Slack, who commanded a brigade in Veatch's division, wrote on April 29, 1865, "Thus terminated a very severe and highly successful campaign of twenty-six days, in which time perhaps more was accomplished than in any one campaign that preceded it of no greater length during a four years' war." And Major General Dabney Maury commented, "The defense of Spanish Fort was the last death grapple of the veterans of the Confederate and Federal armies. They brought to it the experience of four years of incessant conflict, and in the attack and defense of that place demonstrated every offensive and defensive art then known to war."[31]

The casualties at Spanish Fort and Fort Blakely could have been much higher, but, Chester Hearn writes, "after four years of war, men had learned how to protect themselves, and officers no longer insisted on frontal attacks against heavily fortified and strongly held earthworks." Ironically, Liddell said that his lack of manpower caused him to disperse his troops so widely that the Federals need not have feared any serious concentration of fire, and the final assault on Fort Blakely demonstrated how easy it was to take the Rebel fort by storm.[32]

The Mobile campaign had no effect on the outcome of the war. But the strategies, tactics, and technologies used underscored just how far these had evolved since the start of the war—a war that had begun like most nineteenth century conflicts, with tactics basically unchanged since the time of Napoleon—and provided a lesson that European military observers were quick to study. Innovations included trench warfare, rifled artillery, land mines, hand grenades, army-and-navy combined amphibious operations, submarines, naval mines, and minesweeping operations. Germany, France, Great Britain, and Japan quickly took the lead in building modern navies—phasing out their old wooden warships with armored ones. The European military professionals improved on and completed the development of these new technologies by 1914, and all of these would play a major role in World War I. The Mobile campaign illustrated their potential.[33]

The men who had fought at Spanish Fort and Fort Blakely remembered the struggles and sacrifices of these last days of the war. The "Lady Slocomb" remained at rest exactly where her gunners had abandoned her, in the overgrown earthworks at Spanish Fort. In March 1891 a Union and Confederate veterans' group in Mobile secured title to the cannon and moved the five-ton, 10-foot-long behemoth to Mobile. It was intended to be placed on a "peace monument" in the city, but the monument was never finished. The veterans finally moved the cannon to New Orleans, and to-day it sits outside the Confederate Museum on Camp Street.

The pride and mutual respect of the veterans endured. Writing from his home in Columbus, Ohio, in 1912, P. B. Darling, a Federal army veteran who had served at Blakely, penned an affectionate tribute to a recently de-ceased former Confederate lieutenant, William Curtis Mayes, who had es-caped after the fall of Fort Blakely, and—after turning 18 on April 13—was said to be the senior officer among the survivors of Thomas' brigade who surrendered at Meridian. Darling and Mayes had never met but had be-come acquainted through correspondence, and gradually they formed a mutual friendship. Over the years, they had planned on meeting at some veterans' reunion but had never done so. Darling wrote, "We fought each other at Spanish Fort and Blakely, Ala., in March and April, 1865, for thir-teen days, and much of the time we were not more than two hundred yards apart." He concluded, "Mr. Mayes and I believed that after those two great men, Lee and Grant, signed those papers at the McLean House, Appomat-tox, all of us were American citizens. . . . We knew that the war was over."[34]

NOTES

1. Phil Gottschalk, *In Deadly Earnest: The History of the First Missouri Brigade, C.S.A.* (Columbia: Missouri River Press, 1991), 526–527; Nathaniel C. Hughes, ed., *Liddell's Record* (Dayton, OH: Morningside House, Inc., 1985), 198.

2. E. W. Tarrant, "After the Fall of Fort Blakely," *Confederate Veteran* 25 (1917), 152.

3. Joseph Orville Jackson, ed., *"Some of the Boys . . .": The Civil War Letters of Isaac Jackson, 1862–1865* (Carbondale: Southern Illinois University Press, 1960), 232; Ephraim M. Anderson, *Memoirs: Historical and Personal; Including the Campaigns of the First Missouri Confederate Brigade* (Dayton, OH: Press of the Morningside Bookshop, 1972), 400; "The Siege of Blakeley and Imprisonment of Confederates on Ship Island," *Montgomery Advertiser*, July 18, 1886.

4. Tarrant, "After the Fall of Fort Blakely," 152; Asa M. Piper, "Some Recollections of an Old Soldier," 62nd Alabama Infantry Regiment File, Alabama Department of Archives and History, 2; Anderson, *Memoirs*, 400–401; Alden McLellan, "Vivid Reminiscences of War Times," *Confederate Veteran* 14 (1906), 265.

5. McLellan, "Vivid Reminiscences," 265.

6. Piper, "Some Recollections," 3.

7. Gottschalk, *In Deadly Earnest*, 528.

8. Reid Mitchell, *Civil War Soldiers: Their Expectations and Their Experiences* (New York: Simon and Schuster, 1988), 179; Nathaniel C. Hughes, Jr., ed., *The Civil War Memoirs of Philip Daingerfield Stephenson, D.D.* (Conway, AR: UCA Press, 1995), 368; William Pitt Chambers, *Blood and Sacrifice: The Civil War Journal of a Confederate Soldier*, ed. Richard A. Baumgartner (Huntington, WV: Blue Acorn Press, 1994), 225.

9. Edgar Wiley Jones, *History of the 18th Infantry Regiment*, compiled by C. David A. Pulcrano (Birmingham, AL: C.D.A. Pulcrano, 1994), 226; Mamie Yeary, compil., *Reminiscences of the Boys in Gray, 1861–1865* (Dayton, OH: Morningside House, 1986), 814; J. A. Dozier, "Concerning Hood's Tennessee Campaign," *Confederate Veteran* 16 (1908), 192.

10. Hughes, *Stephenson*, 372–373.

11. John Kent Folmar, "Post Civil War Mobile: The Letters of James M. Williams, May–September, 1865," *Alabama Historical Quarterly* 32 (1970), 187.

12. Leslie Anders, *The Twenty-First Missouri: From Home Guard to Union Regiment* (Westport, CT: Greenwood Press, 1975), 234–237; Daryl A. Bailey, "The 8th Iowa," *America's Civil War* (May 1996), 64; Byron Cloyd Bryner, *Bugle Echoes: The Story of Illinois 47th Infantry* (Springfield, IL, 1905), 158–159.

13. Carl E. Hatch, ed., *Dearest Susie: A Civil War Infantryman's Letters to His Sweetheart* (Jericho, NY: Exposition Press, Inc., 1971), 123; Howard Coffin, *Full Duty: Vermonters in the Civil War* (Woodstock VT: Countryman Press, Inc., 1993), 353.

14. Carlos W. Colby, "Memoirs of Military Service," Joseph G. Bilby, ed., *Military Images* 3, 2 (September–October 1981), 29.

15. Hatch, *Dearest Susie*, 117.

16. James G. Hollandsworth, Jr., *The Louisiana Native Guards: The Black Military Experience during the Civil War* (Baton Rouge: Louisiana State University Press, 1995), 102–103.

17. Ibid., 108–109.

18. Joseph T. Glatthaar, *Forged in Battle: The Civil War Alliance of Black Soldiers and White Officers* (New York: Macmillan, Inc., 1990), 234–235.

19. Milton Britton, ed., *The Civil War Diary of Charles Henry Snedeker*, 1966, Auburn University Archives, RG 844; Noah Andre Trudeau, *Like Men of War: Black Troops in the Civil War, 1862–1865* (Boston: Little, Brown & Co., 1998), 404.

20. Folmar, "Post Civil War Mobile," 188.

21. Trudeau, *Out of the Storm: The End of the Civil War, April–June 1865* (Boston: Little, Brown & Co., 1994), 324–334.

22. Ibid., 334; Richard Barksdale Harwell, ed., *Kate: The Journal of a Confederate Nurse* (Baton Rouge: Louisiana State University Press, 1959), 305.

23. *War of the Rebellion: A Compilation of the Official Records of the Union and Confederate Armies* (Washington, DC: Government Printing Office, 1880–1901) (hereafter cited at *OR*), Series I, Vol. 49, Part I, 115; Chester G. Hearn, *Mobile Bay and the Mobile Campaign: The Last Great Battles of the Civil War* (Jefferson, NC: McFarland and Company, Inc., Publishers, 1993), 206; E. B. Long, ed., *Personal Memoirs of Ulysses S. Grant* (New York: Da Capo, 1982), 571–572.

24. Arthur W. Bergeron, Jr., *Confederate Mobile* (Jackson: University Press of Mississippi, 1991), 195–197.

25. Ibid., 193; Herman Hattaway and Archer Jones, *How the North Won: A Military History of the Civil War* (Urbana: University of Illinois Press, 1982), 669.

26. Hattaway and Jones, *How the North Won*, 633.

27. Christopher C. Andrews, *History of the Campaign of Mobile* (New York, 1867), 163–164; Hearn, *Mobile Campaign*, 202.

28. Hearn, *Mobile Campaign*, 206.

29. Andrews, *Campaign of Mobile*, 163.

30. Hearn, *Mobile Campaign*, 203–204; Hughes, *Liddell's Record*, 196; Bergeron, *Confederate Mobile*, 186–187.

31. *OR*, Series I, Vol. 49, Part I, 162; Dabney H. Maury, "Defence of Spanish Fort," *Southern Historical Society Papers* 39 (1914), 130.

32. Hearn, *Mobile Campaign*, 206.

33. Ibid., 211.

34. P. B. Darling, "Tribute to W. C. Mayes from the Other Side," *Confederate Veteran* 20 (1912), 18; W. C. Mayes obituary, *Confederate Veteran* 19 (1911), 489.

APPENDIX

"We Knew That the War Was Over"

The young men who closed the last major chapter of the Civil War remained loyal to their families, their communities, and their fellow veterans. Many were leaders in their home towns in civic, political, and religious roles. Most were very active in veterans' affairs, participating in organizations like the United Confederate Veterans and the Grand Army of the Republic, the powerful Union veterans' organization. The bond that the war had created among them held steady. The war had shaped their lives and would ever be a part of it.

THE CONFEDERATES

WILLIAM S. BARRY, Colonel, 35th Mississippi Infantry Regiment, fought a losing struggle to adjust to life in a defeated South. "My thinking in the past has not been profitable," he wrote, "my hopes for my county have all been blasted, and as far as I can, I will quit thinking and for a while lead a negative existence." Depressed and ailing from his wartime shoulder injury, Barry became a recluse. He died at his sister's home in 1868, at the age of 47.[1]

JIM BOBBETT, Lumsden's Alabama Battery, returned home and found his wife still living in their cabin on the Maxwell plantation. At the prompting of the Maxwells, Jim took up a new trade as a barber and clothes cleaner, and the thrifty freedman soon set aside enough money to go into business for himself.[2]

JOSEPH BOYCE, Captain, 1st/4th Missouri Infantry Regiment, became a prosperous tobacco wholesaler and realtor. Historian of the Missouri brigade and a founder of the Missouri Historical Society, Boyce was president of the St. Louis city council and helped promote the World's Fair of 1904.[3]

WILLIAM LOCHIEL CAMERON, Lieutenant, Confederate States Navy, moved to Galveston, Texas, where he became an engineer and a waterworks management constructor. He died in 1918.[4]

JOSEPH ADOLPH CHALARON, Lieutenant, Slocomb's Louisiana Battery, was a planter and an insurance executive. He played a very active role in the Confederate veterans' organization and died in New Orleans in July 1909 at the age of 73. The bugler of the old Slocomb's battery played taps at his funeral.[5]

WILLIAM PITT CHAMBERS, Sergeant, 46th Mississippi Infantry Regiment, made his way back home, married Sarah Ann Robertson in 1866, and the couple moved to Alabama. Chambers returned to teaching and eventually began copying his wartime diary as a record of his experiences. After his wife died in 1900, Chambers lived with his two daughters in Hattiesburg, Mississippi. He kept in touch with his old comrades and wrote short stories, poetry, and essays. He died after falling victim to influenza in 1916 at 76 years of age.[6]

JAMES HOLT CLANTON, Brigadier General, returned to his law practice and was active in Democratic party politics in Alabama. On September 26, 1871, Clanton was shot and killed by a former Federal army officer in an altercation stemming from an argument in court in Knoxville, Tennessee. Clanton was 44.[7]

FRANCIS MARION COCKRELL, Brigadier General, resumed his law practice in Missouri, but it was in the political arena that he left his greatest mark. He was elected to the U.S. Senate to succeed Carl Schurz in 1874 and retained his seat there for the next thirty years. In 1905, President Theodore Roosevelt appointed him to serve on the Interstate Commerce Commission. Cockrell died in Washington in 1915 at the age of 81.[8]

DAVID COLEMAN, Colonel, 39th North Carolina Infantry, practiced law in Asheville and was a delegate to the state constitutional convention in 1875. The colonel became a town eccentric, insisting on wearing only gray clothing manufactured in local mills. Local people often observed Coleman spending hours on solitary walks through the countryside with his hands crossed behind him or with his hat in his hands. He died at Asheville in 1883, at age 59.[9]

MATTHEW DUNCAN ECTOR, Brigadier General, returned to Marshall, Texas, and his law practice. He was elected judge of the Seventh Judicial District in 1874 and was presiding judge of the Texas Court of Appeals 1876–1879. He died in 1879, at the age of 57.[10]

ELIJAH GATES, Colonel, 1st/3rd Missouri Cavalry, was active in Democratic party politics and held several positions, including sheriff of Buchanan County, state treasurer of Missouri, and U. S. marshal. For a number of years the one-armed veteran was in the transfer and bus business in St. Joseph. Gates died in 1915 at the age of 88.[11]

RANDALL LEE GIBSON, Brigadier General, was a successful attorney in New Orleans. Elected to the U. S. Congress in 1872, Gibson was denied admission by the Radical Republican majority, but he later served in the U.S. House of Representatives from 1875 to 1882 and in the U.S. Senate from 1883 to 1892. Gibson was one of the founders of Tulane University and was president of its board of administrators from 1882 until his death in 1892 at the age of 60.[12]

ANDREW COLEMAN HARGROVE, Lieutenant, Lumsden's Alabama Battery, was an attorney, professor at the University of Alabama, and state senator. During all these years he still carried the bullet in his head from his wound at Spanish Fort on March 30, 1865. Constant pain from headaches plagued him until he finally committed suicide in 1895 at the age of 58.[13]

JAMES THADEUS HOLTZCLAW, Brigadier General, returned to Montgomery and his law practice. He was active in Democratic party politics and served on the Alabama state railway commission. He died in 1893 at the age of 59.[14]

BUSH JONES, Colonel, 58th Alabama Infantry, was an attorney in Perry County, Alabama. Jones died in 1872 at the age of 36.[15]

EDGAR WILEY JONES, Private, 18th Alabama Infantry Regiment, entered the ministry. He edited the *Jones Valley Times* in his community near Birmingham and in 1904 to 1905 wrote a series of articles telling of his experiences in the war.

WILLIAM H. KAVANAUGH, Corporal, 2nd/6th Missouri Infantry Regiment, returned to his farm in central Missouri.

DANVILLE LEADBETTER, Brigadier General, reportedly fled to Mexico and finally surfaced in Canada where he died in 1866 at the age of 55.[16]

ST. JOHN RICHARDSON LIDDELL, Brigadier General, was unable to adjust to the myriad of economic and social changes in postwar Louisiana—falling cotton prices, difficulty in getting laborers, deepening debts, poor crops aggravated by floods and drought. Liddell seriously considered emigrating to Brazil. "Everything seems to work against me," he wrote, "and ruin stares me full in the face." His wife Mary died in 1869, and the bank foreclosed on his plantation. His ongoing quarrel with neighboring planter Charles Jones took a fatal turn on a Black River steamer on February 14, 1870, when a confrontation with Jones and his two sons ended in tragedy. Liddell was eating dinner in the cabin when Jones and his sons entered. Liddell started to rise, reaching for his gun. Two shots to the chest brought him down, but before he fell he got off one shot at Jones, which missed. As other passengers scrambled for cover, Jones' other sons fired five more bullets into Liddell. The former Rebel commander was 54. A pro-Liddell mob later killed Jones and one of his sons.[17]

ROBERT HUME LINDSAY, Lieutenant Colonel, 1st/16th/20th Louisiana Infantry, went home to Shreveport, where he became a familiar figure in the town's business and political life. He married Margaret Blake of Nashville in 1875, and the couple had two daughters. He died in 1910 at the age of 77.[18]

CHARLES L. LUMSDEN, Captain, Lumsden's Alabama Battery, went into the lumber business and was killed in a sawmill accident in 1867 at the age of 33.[19]

ALDEN McLELLAN, Lieutenant, quartermaster section, Cockrell's Missouri brigade, went to work with his father's contracting business in New Orleans and later became president of the company.[20]

DABNEY HERNDON MAURY, Major General, returned to his home in Fredericksburg, Virginia, to found a boys' academy where he served as an instructor. He relocated to New Orleans where he was an express agent and naval stores manufacturer. In 1868 he formed the Southern Historical Society and was active as its executive chairman until 1886. Maury was U.S. minister to Colombia from 1885 to 1889. He then lived with his son in Peoria, Illinois, where he died at the age of 77 in 1900.[21]

JAMES ROBERT MAXWELL, Sergeant, Lumsden's Alabama Battery, had just arrived at his father's plantation south of Tuscaloosa when word came to him that the army had surrendered. He married Kittie Tutwiler in 1867, and the couple moved to a cabin on Maxwell's father's land where they farmed and raised two children. Maxwell later served on the county commission.[22]

DAVID MARSHALL SCOTT, Sergeant, 62nd Alabama Infantry Regiment, became a merchant and postmaster in Selma, Alabama. He married in 1872 and had three children. Scott was an active member of the Alabama National Guard and served as its quartermaster general for sixteen years.[23]

CLAUDIUS SEARS, Brigadier General, was released from prison in June 1865. The Mississippi brigade's former commander returned to education and was chairman of the mathematics department at the University of Mississippi in Oxford. He died in 1891 at the age of 72.[24]

CUTHBERT H. SLOCOMB, Captain, Slocomb's Louisiana Battery, became a successful hardware merchant in New Orleans, where he died in 1874.[25]

PHILIP DAINGERFIELD STEPHENSON, Slocomb's Louisiana Battery, floundered searching for direction in his life. After working as a clerk and a bookkeeper, he finally decided on the ministry. At seminary in Virginia, he met socially prominent Jane Minge Fried of Petersburg and married her in 1875. Stephenson became a Presbyterian minister and died in Richmond, Virginia, in 1916.[26]

ROBERT TARLETON, Lieutenant, 1st Alabama Artillery Battalion, farmed in Louisiana, but returned to Mobile two and a half years later. He and Sallie had three children. Tragically he died at age 30 in 1868 following a short illness.[27]

EDWARD WILLIAM TARRANT, Lieutenant, Tarrant's Alabama Battery, became a Methodist preacher and an educator, always active in Confederate veterans affairs. The old artilleryman died at the home of his youngest daughter in Bryan, Texas, in 1921, at the age of 79.[28]

RICHARD TAYLOR, Major General, became a peacemaker after the war, trying to influence President Andrew Johnson to steer the country toward a more lenient Southern Reconstruction policy and a more sympathetic treatment of former Confederate president Jefferson Davis. Taylor played an important role in the Compromise of 1877 that settled the controversial Hays-Tilden election for president and brought Reconstruction to an end in the South. A victim of rheumatoid arthritis, he died in New York City in 1879 at the age of 53.[29]

BRYAN MOREL THOMAS, Brigadier General, returned to Georgia where he was a farmer, a deputy U.S. marshal, and superintendent of schools in Dalton, Georgia. He died in 1905 at the age of 69.[30]

GEORGE W. WARREN, Captain, 3rd/5th Missouri Infantry Regiment, was a successful realtor and stockbroker in Richmond, Virginia. He married the daughter of a socially prominent Virginia family, had three sons, and served as a member of the Richmond city council. Warren died in 1890 at age 53.[31]

JAMES MADISON WILLIAMS, Lieutenant Colonel, 21st Alabama Infantry, struggled for a decade to make ends meet—in a steam laundry business that failed, as a bookkeeper, in an unsuccessful venture with a life insurance company, as clerk for the Mobile and Ohio Railroad Company. Finally he landed a position as clerk with the Mobile County probate court. Williams remained an eager participant in state military affairs. When the Alabama state militia was revived in 1872, Williams became a major in the 1st Infantry Battalion in Mobile and was an energetic member of the Alabama State Troops for twenty years. He formed the first chapter of the United Confederate Veterans in Alabama and was active in other civic organizations. James and Lizzy had three daughters and two more sons. Williams died in 1903 at age 65.[32]

THE FEDERALS

CHRISTOPHER COLUMBUS ANDREWS, Brigadier General, enjoyed a colorful and dynamic career after the war. Minnesota state politics first beckoned, then the former general served as U.S. minister to Sweden and Norway from 1869 to 1877. Andrews was a newspaper editor, consul general to Brazil, chief warden and forest commissioner of Minnesota, and wrote extensively on law, history, travel, and military tactics. He died in 1922 at age 92.[33]

WILLIAM B. BELL, Lieutenant Colonel, 8th Iowa Infantry Regiment, was a prominent fixture in the civic life of the town of Washington, Iowa, where the old veteran served as county marshal and postmaster.[34]

WILLIAM P. BENTON, Brigadier General, resumed his law practice in Indiana and died of yellow fever in New Orleans in 1867. He was 38 years old.[35]

DR. JEROME BURBANK, Surgeon, 33rd Wisconsin Infantry Regiment, left the army in August 1865. Still suffering from effects of dysentery and overwork, he relocated with his family to Waverly, Iowa, and opened a drug store in nearby Allison with his son (who also became a doctor) in 1882. Jerome died in 1897 at age 70, and his wife Jerusha remained lively until her death at age 83.[36]

EDWARD RICHARD SPRIGG CANBY, Major General, continued to follow an army career. The man who received the surrender of two Confederate armies was murdered on April 11, 1873—almost eight years to the day after the fall of Mobile—while attempting to negotiate a peace agreement with Modoc Indians in northern California. The murderers—two Indians who opposed the peace treaty—shot him through the head and stabbed him. He was 55 years old. [37]

EUGENE A. CARR, Brigadier General, served on the western frontier after the war and retired from the army in 1893. He died in 1910 at the age of 80.[38]

MICHAEL CASHMAN, Private, 21st Missouri Infantry Regiment, was a plumber and produce dealer in Quincy, Illinois. He lived to see the outbreak of World War II, outlasting his old comrades, and died in 1941 at the age of 95.[39]

KENNER GARRARD, Brigadier General, resigned from the army in November 1866. He was active in business and civic affairs in Cincinnati, Ohio, and died in 1879 at 51 years of age.[40]

JAMES L. GEDDES, Brevet Brigadier General, devoted much of his postwar life to the development of Iowa State College. He died in 1887.

JAMES I. GILBERT, Brigadier General, left the army in August 1865. He went back into the lumber business with his two brothers in Burlington, Iowa, and in 1877 got involved in a mining deal in Colorado that "proved disastrous." He died of a heart attack in Topeka, Kansas, in 1884 at 60 years of age.[41]

GORDON GRANGER, Major General, remained in the army. He commanded the District of Memphis from 1867 to 1869 and the District of New Mexico from 1871 to 1876. Granger died in Santa Fe in 1876. He was 53 years old.[42]

JOHN P. HAWKINS, Brigadier General, also made the army a life career, holding commissary posts and heading the Subsistence Department. He retired in 1894, lived in Indianapolis, and died there in 1914 at the age of 83.[43]

BENJAMIN R. HIERONYMUS, Lieutenant, 117th Illinois Infantry Regiment, was active in banking and in veterans affairs and lived in Springfield, Illinois. He died in 1926 at age 84.[44]

ISAAC JACKSON, Private, 83rd Ohio Infantry Regiment, returned to Ohio. The shy Jackson eventually married late to a woman twenty-six years younger. Isaac was active in the G.A.R. and died in 1903 at the age of 61.[45]

THOMAS J. LUCAS, Brigadier General, returned to civilian life in Lawrenceburg, Indiana. The former cavalry officer worked in the U.S. Revenue Service, then was postmaster in Lawrenceburg. He made an unsuccessful bid for Congress in 1886. Lucas died in 1908 at age 82.[46]

JOHN McARTHUR, Brigadier General, faced failures after the war. He was unable to revive his ironworks. While he was commissioner of public works, the great Chicago fire of 1871 took place. He was embarrassed by a bank failure and was held personally liable by the courts. McArthur was active in Scottish organizations and in veterans' affairs. He died in Chicago in 1906 at age 79.[47]

FRANK McGREGOR, Corporal, 83rd Ohio Infantry Regiment, finally returned home to Ohio in August 1865. He married Susie Brown in 1866, and the couple raised seven children. Frank and his brother ran a florist business in Springfield, Ohio. He died in 1920 at age 82, Susie in 1931.[48]

HENRY C. MERRIAM, Lieutenant Colonel, 73rd U.S.C.T., made the army his career and retired as a major general in 1901. He died in 1912 at age 75.[49]

JONATHAN MERRIAM, Lieutenant Colonel, 117th Illinois Infantry, returned to McKendree College and received his degree in 1869. He and his new wife Lucy raised six children. Merriam was active in Illinois state politics, served in the state legislature and in state constitutional conventions. He was a collector for the Internal Revenue Service, was U.S. pension commissioner in Chicago, and a McKendree trustee. He died in 1919 when he was struck by a train.[50]

RISDON M. MOORE, Colonel, 117th Illinois Infantry Regiment, turned down an offer of a brigadier general's commission and left the army in 1865. He returned to McKendree College but a year later he was back in Selma, Alabama, where he "lost thousands of dollars" in an unsuccessful venture in the coal business. He took a job with the U.S. Treasury Department in San Antonio, Texas, in 1877. Moore died in 1909 in San Antonio.[51]

CHARLES O. MUSSER, Sergeant, 29th Iowa Infantry Regiment, returned to his parents' farm in Iowa. He married Emily Jane Triplett in 1867, and the young farm couple raised ten children. In 1884 the Mussers moved west, homesteading in Nebraska. Emily died in 1933. Plagued for many years by severe rheumatism and heart and kidney disease, Musser died at age 95 in 1938, possibly the last surviving veteran of the 29th Iowa.[52]

JAMES K. NEWTON, Sergeant, 14th Wisconsin Infantry Regiment, received a lieutenant's commission in July 1865. His duties mainly consisted of administering the amnesty oath in Alabama. The young officer was mustered out in October 1865 and returned to Wisconsin. He embarked on a career in education and by 1873 was an instructor in German and French at Oberlin College in Ohio. James married Frances Woodrow, a widow and Oberlin alumna, in 1870. Newton retired in 1880, and he and Frances moved to California, where he died in 1892 at age 49.[53]

WILLIAM A. PILE, Brigadier General, embraced Radical Republican politics after the war and was elected to Congress, calling for "death to all supporters of the South, past and present." He was defeated for reelection in 1868. Pile was appointed territorial governor of New Mexico and was minister to Venezuela in 1871. He moved to California and died near Los Angeles in 1889 at age 60.[54]

JAMES R. SLACK, Brigadier General, went back to his law practice in Indiana. He became a judge and made an unsuccessful try for Congress in 1880. Slack died of a heart attack in 1881 at age 62.[55]

ANDREW JACKSON SMITH, Major General, stayed on in the army and in 1866 commanded the 7th U.S. Cavalry, famous later as George A. Custer's regiment. Smith left the service and became postmaster of St. Louis in 1869. He died in 1897 at age 81.[56]

LOUIS A. SNAER, Captain, 73rd U.S.C.T., moved to California. He died there at the age of 75 in 1917.[57]

NEHEMIAH D. STARR, Lieutenant, 21st Missouri Infantry Regiment, won election as county clerk in Lewis County, Missouri, in 1866, and was active as a Republican in state politics.[58]

FREDERICK STEELE, Major General, remained in the army and was stationed in Texas in command of the 20th U.S. Infantry. Just two days short of his 49th birthday in 1868, he was on leave in San Mateo, California, when he was killed in an accidental fall from the buggy he was driving.[59]

THOMAS N. STEVENS, Captain, 28th Wisconsin Infantry Regiment, moved his family to Greenville, Michigan, early in 1866. He and his wife had five children. Stevens was in the abstract business and later was mayor of Greenville. He was tireless in his involvement with politics and veterans affairs and was a delegate to the Republican Party national convention in Chicago in 1880. Stevens died on New Years Day in 1908 at age 72.[60]

ELISHA STOCKWELL, JR., Corporal, 14th Wisconsin Infantry Regiment, returned to his young bride, and the couple farmed near Alma, Wisconsin. They tried their hand at homesteading for four years in Minnesota and in 1876 moved back to Wisconsin, where they lived for thirty years. The

Stockwells moved west again in 1906, when Elisha was 60 years old, this time settling for good in North Dakota. Elisha's wife Katherine died in 1927, and shortly afterward family members cajoled the old veteran into writing the story of his wartime experiences. Although in his 80s and hand-icapped by cataracts, he wrote his story from memory, relying on the vivid impressions still stamped upon his mind so many years later. Elisha died in 1935 at age 89, one of only two surviving veterans of the 14th Wisconsin.[61]

JAMES CLIFFORD VEATCH, Brigadier General, was adjutant general of Indiana and a U.S. collector of internal revenue. He died in 1895 at 76.[62]

ADOLPHUS PHILLIP WOLF, Corporal, 117th Illinois Infantry Regiment, returned to Illinois and married 20-year-old Albina Jane Kinder, his com-pany commander's niece. Wolf was in the hardware business, in the coal business with two of his brothers (including Otto, the drummer boy), and banking. He was the last surviving Civil War veteran in Madison County, and the license plate on his automobile read "Illinois 117." Wolf died in 1935 at age 94.[63]

NOTES

1. Lee T. Wyatt III, "William S. Barry, Advocate of Secession, 1821–1868," *Journal of Mississippi History* 39 (1977), 354–355.

2. James Robert Maxwell, *Autobiography of James Robert Maxwell* (New York: Greenburg, Publisher, 1926), 293.

3. Phil Gottschalk, *In Deadly Earnest: The History of the First Missouri Brigade, C.S.A.* (Columbia: Missouri River Press, Inc., 1991), 77.

4. "Our Veteran Helpers," *Confederate Veteran* 24 (1916), 236; Cameron obitu-ary, *Confederate Veteran* 26 (1918), 534.

5. Joseph Adolph Chalaron Obituary, *Confederate Veteran* 18 (1910), 384.

6. William Pitt Chambers, *Blood and Sacrifice: The Civil War Journal of a Confed-erate Soldier*, ed. Richard A. Baumgartner (Huntington, WV: Blue Acorn Press, 1994), 5.

7. Arthur W. Bergeron, Jr., "James Holt Clanton," in William C. Davis, ed., *The Confederate General*, vol. 1 (Harrisburg, PA: National Historical Society, 1991), 191.

8. Anne Bailey, "Francis Marion Cockrell," in William C. Davis, ed., *The Con-federate General*, vol. 1 (Harrisburg, PA: National Historical Society, 1991), 7.

9. F. A. Sondley, *A History of Buncombe County, North Carolina* (Spartanburg: Reprint Co., 1977), 768–769.

10. Lawrence L. Hewitt, "Matthew Duncan Ector," in William C. Davis, ed., *The Confederate General*, vol. 1 (Harrisburg, PA: National Historical Society, 1991), 95.

11. E. L. McDonald and W. J. King, compilers, *History of Buchanan County and St. Joseph, Missouri* (St. Joseph, 1915), 282–283.

12. Arthur W. Bergeron, Jr., "Randall Lee Gibson," in William C. Davis, ed., *The Confederate General*, vol. 1 (Harrisburg, PA: National Historical Society, 1991), 188.

13. Roger B. Hansen and Norman A. Nicolson, *The Siege of Blakeley and the Cam-paign of Mobile* (N.p.: Historic Blakely Press, 1995), 21.

14. Joseph Wheeler, "Alabama," in Clement Evans, ed., *Confederate Military History*, vol. 7 (Atlanta, 1899), 419.

15. Thomas M. Owen, *History of Alabama and Dictionary of Alabama Biography*, vol. 3 (Spartanburg, SC: Reprint Co., 1978), 925–926.

16. Ezra J. Warner, *Generals in Gray: Lives of the Confederate Commanders* (Baton Rouge: Louisiana State University Press, 1959), 176–177.

17. Nathaniel C. Hughes, ed., *Liddell's Record* (Dayton, OH: Morningside House, Inc., 1985), 199–206.

18. Lindsay Obituary, *Confederate Veteran* 18 (1910), 581.

19. Owen, *History of Alabama*, vol. 4, 1076.

20. Alden McLellan, "Vivid Reminiscences of War Times, *Confederate Veteran* 14 (1906)," 266.

21. Arthur W. Bergeron, Jr., "Dabney Herndon Maury," in William C. Davis, ed., *The Confederate General*, vol. 4 (Harrisburg, PA: National Historical Society, 1991), 168.

22. Maxwell, *Autobiography*, 307–315.

23. Owen, *History of Alabama* vol. 4, 1510.

24. Warner, *Generals in Gray*, 271–272.

25. Powell A. Casey, *An Outline of the Civil War Campaigns and Engagements of the Washington Artillery of New Orleans* (Baton Rouge: Claitor's Publishing Division, 1986), 90.

26. Nathaniel C. Hughes, Jr., *The Civil War Memoirs of Philip Daingerfield Stephenson, D.C.* (Conway, AR: UCA Press, 1995), x, 390–391.

27. William N. Still, Jr., ed., "The Civil War Letters of Robert Tarleton," *Alabama Historical Quarterly* 32 (1970), 51.

28. Tarrant Obituary, *Confederate Veteran* 30 (1922),108.

29. Warner, *Generals in Gray*, 299–300; Noah Andre Trudeau, *Out of the Storm: The End of the Civil War, April–June 1865*, (Boston: Little, Brown & Co., 1994), 394.

30. Benjamin E. Snellgrove, "Bryan Morel Thomas," in William C. Davis, ed., *The Confederate General*, vol. 6 (Harrisburg, PA: National Historical Society, 1991), 43.

31. Gottschalk, *In Deadly Earnest*, 536.

32. John Kent Folmar, ed., *From That Terrible Field: Civil War Letters of James M. Williams, Twenty-First Alabama Infantry Volunteers* (University: University of Alabama Press, 1981), xv–xvi.

33. Ezra J. Warner, *Generals in Blue: Lives of the Union Commanders* (Baton Rouge: Louisiana State University Press, 1964), 8–9.

34. Kathy Fisher, *In the Beginning there Was Land: A History of Washington County, Iowa* (Washington, IA: Washington County Historical Society, 1978), 97, 109, 352.

35. Warner, *Generals in Blue*, 30–31.

36. Sylvia Burbank Morris, *Jerome: To My Beloved Absent Companion: Letters of a Civil War Surgeon to His Wife at Home, Caring for Their Family* (Cullman, AL: Author, 1996), 13.

37. Warner, *Generals in Blue*, 67–68.

38. Ibid., 70–71.

39. Leslie Anders, *The Twenty-First Missouri: From Home Guard to Union Regiment* (Westport, CT: Greenwood Press, 1975), 273–274.

40. Warner, *Generals in Blue*, 167–168.

41. Ibid., 174–175.

42. Ibid., 181.

43. Ibid., 218–219.

44. Edwin G. Gerling, *The One Hundred Seventeenth Illinois Infantry Volunteers (The McKendree Regiment), 1862–1865* (Highland, IL: Author, 1992), 155.

45. Joseph Orville Jackson, ed., *"Some of the Boys . . .": The Civil War Letters of Isaac Jackson, 1862–1865* (Carbondale: Southern Illinois University Press, 1960), xvii.

46. Warner, *Generals in Blue*, 285–286.

47. Ibid., 288–289.

48. Carl E. Hatch, ed., *Dearest Susie: A Civil War Infantryman's Letters to His Sweetheart* (Jericho, NY: Exposition Press, Inc., 1971), "Epilogue."

49. Joseph T. Glatthaar, *Forged in Battle: The Civil War Alliance of Black Soldiers and White Officers* (New York: Macmillan, Inc., 1990), 235.

50. Gerling, *One Hundred Seventeenth Illinois*, 6–7.

51. Ibid., 3.

52. Barry Popchock, ed., *Soldier Boy: The Civil War Letters of Charles O. Musser* (Iowa City: University of Iowa Press, 1995), 4–6.

53. Stephen E. Ambrose, ed., *A Wisconsin Boy in Dixie: The Selected Letters of James K. Newton* (Madison: University of Wisconsin Press, 1961), xv.

54. Warner, *Generals in Blue*, 371–372.

55. Ibid., 449–450.

56. Ibid., 454.

57. Camille Corte, "History of 73rd U.S.C.T.," online, Historic Blakeley State Park, www.siteone.com/tourist/blakeley/73rdUSCT.htm, 29 March 1999.

58. Anders, *Twenty-First Missouri*, 260, 266.

59. Warner, *Generals in Blue*, 474–475.

60. George M. Blackburn, ed., *"Dear Carrie . . .": The Civil War Letters of Thomas N. Stevens* (Mount Pleasant, MI: Clarke Historical Library, Central Michigan University, 1984), xiii–xiv.

61. Byron R. Abernethy, ed., *Private Elisha Stockwell, Jr., Sees the Civil War* (Norman: University of Oklahoma Press, 1958), ix–x.

62. Warner, *Generals in Blue*, 525–526.

63. Gerling, *One Hundred Seventeenth Illinois*, 200.

Bibliography

Abernethy, Byron R., ed. *Private Elisha Stockwell, Jr., Sees the Civil War*. Norman: University of Oklahoma Press, 1958.

Allmon, William B. "The 21st Missouri." *America's Civil War* (September 1996): 10+.

Ambrose, Stephen E., ed. *A Wisconsin Boy in Dixie: The Selected Letters of James K. Newton*. Madison: University of Wisconsin Press, 1961.

Anders, Leslie. *The Twenty-First Missouri: From Home Guard to Union Regiment*. Westport, CT: Greenwood Press, 1975.

Anderson, Ephraim M. *Memoirs: Historical and Personal; Including the Campaigns of the First Missouri Confederate Brigade*. Dayton, OH: Press of the Morningside Bookshop, 1972.

Andrews, Christopher C. *History of the Campaign of Mobile*. New York, 1867.

Bailey, Anne. "Francis Marion Cockrell." In William C. Davis, ed., *The Confederate General*, vol. 1. Harrisburg, PA: National Historical Society, 1991.

Bailey, Daryl A. "The 8th Iowa." *America's Civil War* (May 1996): 8+.

Bailey, W. "The Star Company of Ector's Texas Brigade." *Confederate Veteran* 22 (1914): 404–405.

Barnard, Harry Vollie. *Tattered Volunteers: The 27th Alabama Infantry Regiment, C.S.A.* Northport, AL: Hermitage Press, 1965.

Bergeron, Arthur W., Jr. *Confederate Mobile*. Jackson: University Press of Mississippi, 1991.

———. "Dabney Herndon Maury." In William C. Davis, ed., *The Confederate General*, vol. 4, pp. 165–168. Harrisburg, PA: National Historical Society, 1991.

———. "James Holt Clanton." In William C. Davis, ed., *Confederate General*. Vol. 1, pp. 189–191.

———. "Randall Lee Gibson." In William C. Davis, ed., *Confederate General*. Vol. 1, 185–188.

------. "The Twenty-Second Louisiana Consolidated Infantry in the Defense of Mobile, 1864–1865." *Alabama Historical Quarterly* 38 (1976): 204–213.

Berry, Mary F. "Negro Troops in Blue and Gray: The Louisiana Native Guards, 1861–1863." In Donald G. Nieman, ed., *The Day of the Jubilee: The Civil War Experience of Black Southerners*. New York: Garland Publishing, Inc., 1994.

Bevier, Robert S. *History of the Confederate First and Second Missouri Brigades, 1861–1865*. St. Louis, 1879.

Biographical and Historical Memoirs of Louisiana, Vol. 1. Baton Rouge: Claitor's Publishing Div., 1975.

Blackburn, George M., ed. *"Dear Carrie . . .": The Civil War Letters of Thomas N. Stevens*. Mount Pleasant, MI: Clarke Historical Library, Central Michigan University, 1984.

Boatner, Mark Mayo, III. *The Civil War Dictionary*. New York: David McKay Co., Inc., 1959.

Bradley, James. *Confederate Mail Carrier*. Mexico, MO, 1894.

Brewer, Willis. *Alabama: Her History, Resources, War Record, and Public Men from 1540 to 1872*. Montgomery, 1872.

Britton, Mildred, ed. *The Civil War Diary of Charles Henry Snedeker*. 1966. RG 844. Auburn University Archives, Auburn, AL.

Bryner, Byron Cloyd. *Bugle Echoes: The Story of Illinois 47th Infantry*. Springfield, IL, 1905.

Cameron, William Lochiel. "The Battles Opposite Mobile." *Confederate Veteran* 23 (1915): 305–308.

Cameron Obituary. *Confederate Veteran* 26 (1918): 236.

Casey, Powell A. *An Outline of the Civil War Campaigns and Engagements of the Washington Artillery of New Orleans*. Baton Rouge: Claitor's Publishing Division, 1986.

Catton, Bruce. *The Centennial History of the Civil War*. Vol. 3, *Never Call Retreat*. Garden City, NY: Doubleday & Co., 1965.

Chalaron, J. A. "Hood's Campaign at Murfreesboro." *Confederate Veteran* 11 (1903).

------. "Slocomb's Battery in Tennessee Army." New Orleans *Times-Democrat*, November 22, 1903.

------. "The Slocomb's History." *Mobile Register*, January 3, 1896.

Chalaron Obituary. *Confederate Veteran* 18 (1910): 384.

Chambers, William Pitt. *Blood and Sacrifice: The Civil War Journal of a Confederate Soldier*. Ed. Richard A. Baumgartner. Huntington, WV: Blue Acorn Press, 1994.

Civil War Centennial Commission. *Tennesseans in the Civil War: A Military History of Confederate and Union Units with Available Rosters of Personnel*. Nashville, 1964.

Coffin, Howard. *Full Duty: Vermonters in the Civil War*. Woodstock, VT: Countryman Press, Inc., 1993.

Colby, Carlos W. "Memoirs of Military Service." ed. Joseph G. Bilby. *Military Images* 3, 2 (September–October 1981): 24–29.

Cornish, Dudley Taylor. *The Sable Arm: Negro Troops in the Union Army, 1861–1865*. New York: Longmans, Green, and Co., 1956.

Corte, Camille. "History of 73rd U.S.C.T." Online. Historic Blakeley State Park. www.siteone.com/tourist/blakeley/73rdUSCT.htm. 29 March 1999.

Cortright, Vincent. "Last-Ditch Defenders at Mobile." *America's Civil War* (January 1997): 58–64.

Crenshaw, Edward. "Diary of Captain Edward Crenshaw of the Confederate States Army." *Alabama Historical Quarterly* 1 (1930): 438–452.

Crute, Joseph H., Jr. *Units of the Confederate States Army.* Midlothian, VA: Derwent Books, 1987.

Dabney, T. G. "On Hood's Campaign into Tennessee." *Confederate Veteran* 30 (1922): 408–409.

Daniel, Larry J. *Cannoneers in Gray: The Field Artillery of the Army of Tennessee, 1861–1865.* University: University of Alabama Press, 1984.

Darling, P. B. "Tribute to W. C. Mayes from the Other Side." *Confederate Veteran* 20 (1912): 18.

Davis, Eli. "That Hard Siege of Spanish Fort." *Confederate Veteran* 12 (1904): 591.

Davis, William C., ed. *The Confederate General.* 6 vols. Harrisburg, PA: National Historical Society, 1991.

Dent, Stouten Hubert. Papers. RG #86, Confederate Letters. Auburn University Archives, Auburn, AL.

Dimitry, John. "Louisiana." In Clement Evans, ed., *Confederate Military History*, Vol. 10, Atlanta, 1899.

Dowdey, Clifford, ed. *The Wartime Papers of Robert E. Lee.* New York: Da Capo, 1987.

Dozier, J. A. "Concerning Hood's Tennessee Campaign." *Confederate Veteran* 16 (1908): 192.

DuBose, J. W. Historic Sketch. Clayton's-Holtzclaw's Brigade File. Montgomery, AL: Alabama Department of Archives and History.

Elder, Donald C. III, ed. *A Damned Iowa Greyhound: Civil War Letters of William Henry Harrison Clayton.* Iowa City: University of Iowa Press, 1998.

Evans, Clement, ed. *Confederate Military History.* 13 vols. Atlanta, 1899.

Faller, Phillip E. "Battery H, 1st Indiana Heavy Artillery, Took Part in Civil War's Last Siege." *The Artilleryman* (Summer 1991): 14–20.

Fisher, Kathy. *In the Beginning There Was Land: A History of Washington County, Iowa.* Washington, IA: Washington County Historical Society, 1978.

Folmar, John Kent, ed. *From That Terrible Field: Civil War Letters of James M. Williams, Twenty-First Alabama Infantry Volunteers.* University: University of Alabama Press, 1981.

———. "Post Civil War Mobile: The Letters of James M. Williams, May–September, 1865." *Alabama Historical Quarterly* 32 (1970): 186–198.

Foote, Shelby. *The Civil War, a Narrative: Red River to Appomattox.* New York: Random House, 1974.

Fullerton, J. S. "Reenforcing Thomas at Chickamauga." In Robert Underwood Johnson and Clarence Clough Buel, eds., *Battles and Leaders of the Civil War.* Vol. 3. New York: Castle Books, 1956.

Gerling, Edwin G. *The One Hundred Seventeenth Illinois Infantry Volunteers (The McKendree Regiment) 1862–1865.* Highland, IL: Author, 1992.

Gilmore, Jasper. Diary. Mobile Public Library, Living History and Genealogy Division, Mobile, AL.

Glatthaar, Joseph T. *Forged in Battle: The Civil War Alliance of Black Soldiers and White Officers*. New York: Macmillan, Inc., 1990.

Gottschalk, Phil. *In Deadly Earnest: The History of the First Missouri Brigade, C.S.A.* Columbia, MO: Missouri River Press, Inc., 1991.

Grant, George. Letter. "Cannons and Artillery: 'Lady Slocomb.'" SG11124, Alabama Department of Archives and History.

Hansen, Roger B., and Norman A. Nicolson. *The Siege of Blakeley and the Campaign of Mobile*. N.p.: Historic Blakeley Press, 1995.

Harrington, Fred Harvey. "The Fort Jackson Mutiny." In Donald G. Nieman, ed., *The Day of the Jubilee: The Civil War Experience of Black Southerners*. New York: Garland Publishing, Inc., 1994.

Harris, Richard N. "Historic Sketch of Selden's-Lovelace's Battery" (c. 1907)." Selden's-Lovelace Battery File. Montgomery: Alabama Department of Archives and History.

Harris, W. Stuart. *Perry County Heritage*, Vol. 2. N.p.: 1991.

Hart, H. W. Letter, April 10, 1865. Mobile Public Library, Local History and Genealogy Division, Mobile, AL.

Harwell, Richard Barksdale, ed. *Kate: The Journal of a Confederate Nurse*. Baton Rouge: Louisiana State University Press, 1959.

Hatch, Carl E., ed. *Dearest Susie: A Civil War Infantryman's Letters to His Sweetheart*. Jericho, NY: Exposition Press, Inc., 1971.

Hattaway, Herman, and Archer Jones. *How the North Won: A Military History of the Civil War*. Urbana: University of Illinois Press, 1982.

Hearn, Chester G. *Mobile Bay and the Mobile Campaign: The Last Great Battles of the Civil War*. Jefferson, NC: McFarland and Company, Inc., Publishers, 1993.

Henderson, Milton E. *History of Edmond Waller Henderson: His Civil War Service: The Thirty-Sixth Alabama Regiment in Holtzclaw's Brigade*. N.p., n.d. 36th Alabama Infantry Regiment File. Montgomery: Alabama Department of Archives and History.

Herndon, Thomas H. Obituary. *Confederate Veteran* 8 (1900): 542.

Hewitt, Lawrence L. "Matthew Duncan Ector." In William C. Davis, *The Confederate General*. Vol. 1, 94–91. Harrisburg, PA: National Historical Society, 1991.

Heyman, Max L., Jr. *Prudent Soldier: A Biography of Major General E.R.S. Canby, 1817–1873*. Glendale, CA: Arthur H. Clarke Co., 1959.

Hicken, Victor. *Illinois in the Civil War*. Urbana: University of Illinois Press, 1966.

Hollandsworth, James G., Jr. *The Louisiana Native Guards: The Black Military Experience during the Civil War*. Baton Rouge: Louisiana State University Press, 1995.

Hood, John B. "The Invasion of Tennessee." In Robert Underwood Johnson and Clarence Clough Buel, eds., *Battles and Leaders of the Civil War*, Vol. 4. New York: Castle Books, 1956.

Hooker, Charles E. "Mississippi." In Clement Evans, ed., *Confederate Military History*. Vol. 12. Atlanta, 1899.

Horn, Stanley F. *The Army of Tennessee*. Norman: University of Oklahoma Press, 1941.

Hubbell, John T., and James W. Geary, eds. *Biographical Dictionary of the Union: Northern Leaders of the Civil War*. Westport, CT: Greenwood Press, 1995.

Hubbs, G. Ward. *Tuscaloosa: Portrait of an Alabama County*. Northridge, CA: Windsor Publications, Inc., 1987.

Huffstadt, James. "The Last Great Assault: Campaigning for Mobile." *Civil War Times Illustrated* (March 1982): 9–17.

Hughes, Nathaniel C., ed. *The Civil War Memoirs of Philip Daingerfield Stephenson, D.D.* Conway, AR: UCA Press, 1995.

———. *Liddell's Record*. Dayton, OH: Morningside House, Inc., 1985.

Jackson, Joseph Orville, ed. *"Some of the Boys . . .": The Civil War Letters of Isaac Jackson, 1862–1865*. Carbondale: Southern Illinois University Press, 1960.

Jefferson County National Guard Association. *The History of the Alabama National Guard of Jefferson County*. Birmingham, 1909.

John, Samuel Will. "Alabama Corps of Cadets, 1860–1865." *Confederate Veteran* 25 (1917): 12–14.

Johnson, Robert Underwood, and Clarence Clough Buel, eds. *Battles and Leaders of the Civil War*. 4 vols. New York: Castle Books, 1956.

Jones, Charles T. "Five Confederates: The Sons of Bolling Hall in the Civil War." *Alabama Historical Quarterly* 24 (1962).

Jones, Edgar Wiley. *History of the 18th Alabama Infantry Regiment*. Compiled by C. David A. Pulcrano. Birmingham, AL: C.D.A. Pulcrano, 1994.

Jones, Terry L. "St. John Richardson Liddell." In William C. Davis, ed., *The Confederate General*, vol. 4, 74–75. Harrisburg, PA: National Historical Society, 1991.

Klinger, Michael J. "Gallant Charge Repulsed." *America's Civil War* (January 1989): 26–33.

Lindsay, R. H. "Trick to Learn Position of the Enemy." *Confederate Veteran* 8 (1900): 75.

Lindsay, Obituary. *Confederate Veteran* 18 (1910): 581.

Little, George. *Memoirs of George Little*. Tuscaloosa, AL: Tuscaloosa Chamber of Commerce, 1929.

Little, George, and James R. Maxwell. *A History of Lumsden's Battery, C.S.A.* Tuscaloosa: United Daughters of the Confederacy, 1905.

Long, E. B., ed. *Personal Memoirs of Ulysses S. Grant*. New York: Da Capo, 1982.

Lyons, Mark. Letters. SPR 194. Alabama Department of Archives and History.

McCaslin, Richard B. *Portraits of Conflict: A Photographic History of North Carolina in the Civil War*. Fayetteville: University of Arkansas Press, 1997.

McDonald, E. L., and W. J. King, compil. *History of Buchanan County and St. Joseph, Missouri*. St. Joseph, 1915.

McDonough, James Lee, and Thomas L. Connelly. *Five Tragic Hours: The Battle of Franklin*. Knoxville: University of Tennessee Press, 1983.

McLellan, Alden. "Vivid Reminiscences of War Times." *Confederate Veteran* 14 (1906): 264–266.

McNeilly, James H. "The Retreat from Nashville." *Confederate Veteran* 26 (1918): 305–306.

McPherson, James M. *For Cause and Comrades: Why Men Fought in the Civil War*. New York: Oxford University Press, 1997.

Macy, William M. "Civil War Diary of William M. Macy." *Indiana Magazine of History* 30 (1934): 181–197.

Maury, Dabney H. "Defence of Mobile." *Southern Historical Society Papers* 3 (1877): 1–13.

———. "Defence of Spanish Fort." *Southern Historical Society Papers* 39 (1914): 130–136.

Maxwell, James Robert. *Autobiography of James Robert Maxwell.* New York: Greenburg, Publisher, 1926.

———. "Lumsden's Battery in the Battle of Nashville." Lumsden's Battery File. Montgomery: Alabama Department of Archives and History.

Mayes, W. C. Obituary. *Confederate Veteran* 19 (1911): 489.

Merriam, Henry C. "The Capture of Mobile." In *War Papers (Read before the Commandery of the State of Maine. Military Order of the Loyal Legion of the United States)* Vol. 3. Wilmington, NC: Broadfoot Publishing Co., 1992.

Mitchell, Reid. *Civil War Soldiers: Their Expectations and Their Experiences.* New York: Simon and Schuster, 1988.

Mobley, Joe A. "The Siege of Mobile, August, 1864–April, 1865." *Alabama Historical Quarterly* 38 (1976): 250–270.

Moneyhon, Carl, and Bobby Roberts. *Portraits of Conflict: A Photographic History of Louisiana in the Civil War.* Fayetteville: University of Arkansas Press, 1990.

———. *Portraits of Conflict: A Photographic History of Mississippi in the Civil War.* Fayetteville: University of Arkansas Press, 1993.

———. *Portraits of Conflict: A Photographic History of Texas in the Civil War.* Fayetteville: University of Arkansas Press, 1998.

Morris, Sylvia Burbank. *Jerome: To My Beloved Absent Companion: Letters of a Civil War Surgeon to his Wife at Home, Caring for Their Family.* Cullman, AL: Author, 1996.

Nichols, James L. "Confederate Engineers and the Defense of Mobile," *Alabama Review* 12 (1959): 181–194.

Nieman, Donald G., ed. *The Day of the Jubilee: The Civil War Experience of Black Southerners.* New York: Garland Publishing, Inc., 1994.

Nye, Edward Q. Diary, in "We Will Be Apt to Have a Hard Fight." *Baldwin Today,* April 10–April 11, 1991.

O'Bannon, W. H. Letter to T. M. Owen, June 1910. 8th Alabama Cavalry Regiment File. Alabama Department of Archives and History.

Oliver, C. C. Letter to Thomas M. Owen, February 22, 1911. 63rd Alabama Infantry Regiment File. Alabama Department of Archives and History.

"Our Veteran Helpers." *Confederate Veteran* 24 (1916): 236.

Owen, Thomas M. *History of Alabama and Dictionary of Alabama Biography.* Vols. 3 and 4. Spartanburg, SC: Reprint Co., 1978.

Peck, John E. Letter. "Spanish Fort and Blakely, Battles." SG11132, Folder #16. Alabama Department of Archives and History.

Perry, Milton F. *Infernal Machines: The Story of Confederate Submarine and Mine Warfare.* Baton Rouge: Louisiana State University Press, 1965.

Piper, Asa M. "Some Recollections of an Old Soldier." 62nd Alabama Infantry Regiment File. Alabama Department of Archives and History.

Pitcher, Charlie Holcombe. "Spencer-Holcombe Letters Written in the 1860s." *Louisiana Genealogical Register* (March 1972): 44–47.

Popchock, Barry, ed. *Soldier Boy: The Civil War Letters of Charles O. Musser*. Iowa City: University of Iowa Press, 1995.

Rea, R. N. "Gen. C. W. Sears: A Pathetic Incident." *Confederate Veteran* 11 (1903): 327.

———. "A Mississippi Soldier of the Confederacy." *Confederate Veteran* 30 (1922): 262–289.

Redkey, Edwin S. *A Grand Army of Black Men: Letters from African-American Soldiers in the Union Army, 1861–1865*. Cambridge, MA: Cambridge University Press, 1992.

Rich, Doris. *Fort Morgan and the Battle of Mobile Bay*. Foley, AL: Underwood Printing Co., 1986.

Rietti, J. C., compil. *Military Annals of Mississippi*. Spartanburg: Reprint Co., 1976.

Robertson, Felix I. "Service of Dr. James Thomas Searcy." *Confederate Veteran* 28 (1920): 250–252.

Robertson, James I., Jr. "Negro Soldiers in the Civil War." *The Negro in the Civil War*. Eastern Acorn Press, 1988.

Rollins, Richard. *Black Southerners in Gray*. Murfreesboro: Southern Heritage Press, 1994.

Rosser, Levin Vinson. "Tarrant Family—Columbia Institute," *Alabama Historical Society Collections* vol. 2 (1897–1898), Tarrant's Battery File. Alabama Department of Archives and History.

Rowland, Dunbar. *Military History of Mississippi, 1803–1898*. Spartanburg, SC: Reprint Co., 1978.

Schafer, Louis S. *Confederate Underwater Warfare*. Jefferson, NC: McFarland and Co., Inc., Publishers, 1996.

Schell, Sidney H. "Submarine Weapons Tested at Mobile during the Civil War." *Alabama Review* 45 (1992): 163–183.

Scott, David Marshall. "The Evolution of the Alabama National Guard." Jefferson County National Guard Association. *The History of the Alabama National Guard of Jefferson County*. Birmingham, 1909.

———. Letter to Thomas M. Owen, July 1, 1910, September 24, 1910. 62nd Alabama Infantry Regiment File. Alabama Department of Archives and History.

"The Siege of Blakeley and Imprisonment of Confederates on Ship Island." *Montgomery Advertiser*, July 18, 1886.

"The Situation at Mobile." Mobile *Daily Advertiser*, August 11, 1864.

Smartt, Eugenia Persons. *History of Eufaula, Alabama, 1930*. Eufaula: Author, 1933.

Smith, Sidney Adair, and C. Carter Smith, Jr., eds. *Mobile: 1861–1865 Notes and a Bibliography*. Chicago: Wyvern Press, 1994.

Smith, Zach T. Letter to T. M. Owen, October 15–November 3, 1910. 63rd Alabama Infantry File. Alabama Department of Archives and History.

Snead, Thomas L. "The Conquest of Arkansas." In Robert Underwood Johnson and Clarence Clough Buel, *Battles and Leaders of the Civil War*. Vol. 3. New York: Castle Books, 1956.

Snellgrove, Benjamin E. "Bryan Morel Thomas." In William C. Davis, ed., *The Confederate General*, vol. 6, 42–43. Harrisburg, PA: National Historical Society, 1991.

Sondley, F. A. *A History of Buncombe County, North Carolina.* Spartanburg: Reprint Co., 1977.

Starr, Stephen Z. *The Union Cavalry in the Civil War.* Vol. 3, *The War in the West, 1861–1865* . Baton Rouge: Louisiana State University Press, 1985.

Stephenson, Philip D. "Defence of Spanish Fort." *Southern Historical Society Papers* 39 (1914): 118–129.

Still, William N., Jr. *Iron Afloat: The Story of the Confederate Armorclads.* Columbia: University of South Carolina Press, 1971.

Still, William N., Jr., ed. "The Civil War Letters of Robert Tarleton." *Alabama Historical Quarterly* 32 (1970): 51–80.

Still, William N., Jr., John M. Taylor, and Norman C. Delaney. *Raiders and Blockaders: The American Civil War Afloat.* London: Brassey's, 1998.

Stone, Henry. "Repelling Hood's Invasion of Tennessee." In Robert Underwood Johnson and Clarence Clough Buel, eds., *Battles and Leaders of the Civil War.* Vol. 4. New York: Castle Books, 1956.

Sword, Wiley. *Embrace An Angry Wind: the Confederacy's Last Hurrah: Spring Hill, Franklin, and Nashville.* New York: HarperCollins, 1992.

Tancig, W. J. *Confederate Military Land Units, 1861–1865.* New York: Thomas Yoseloff, 1967.

Tarrant, Edward William. "After the Fall of Fort Blakely." *Confederate Veteran* 27 (1917): 152.

———. "Siege and Capture of Fort Blakely." *Confederate Veteran* 23 (1915): 457–458.

Tarrant Obituary. *Confederate Veteran* 30 (1922): 108.

Taylor, Richard. "The Last Confederate Surrender." *Annals of the War Written by Leading Participants, North and South.* Philadelphia, 1879.

Terry, James G., compil. "Record of the Alabama State Artillery." *Alabama Historical Quarterly* 20 (1958).

Thomas, John A. "Mebane's Battery." *Confederate Veteran* 5 (1897): 167.

Thompson, Andrew. Diary, 1864–1865. RG 446. Auburn University Archives, Auburn, AL.

Thompson, Mattie Thomas. *History of Barbour County, Alabama.* Eufaula: N.p., 1939.

Todd, Frederick P. *American Military Equipage, 1851–1872. Vol. 2, State Forces.* New York: Chatham Square Press, Inc., 1983.

Todhunter, R. "Ector's Texas Brigade." *Confederate Veteran* 7 (1899): 312.

Trudeau, Noah Andre. *Like Men of War: Black Troops in the Civil War, 1862–1865.* Boston: Little, Brown and Co., 1998.

———. *Out of the Storm: The End of the Civil War, April–June 1865.* Boston: Little, Brown and Co., 1994.

Tucker, Phillip Thomas. "The First Missouri Confederate Brigade's Last Stand at Fort Blakeley on Mobile Bay." *Alabama Review* 42 (October 1989): 270–291.

———. *The South's Finest: The First Missouri Confederate Brigade from Pea Ridge to Vicksburg.* Shippensburg, PA: White Mane, 1993.

Tunnell, J. T. "Ector's Brigade in Battle of Nashville." *Confederate Veteran* 12 (July 1904): 348–349.

Turner, Maxine. *Navy Gray: A Story of the Confederate Navy on the Chattahoochee and Apalachicola Rivers.* University: University of Alabama Press, 1988.

U.S. Naval History Division. *Civil War Naval Chronology, 1861–1865*. Vol. 5: *1865*. Washington, DC: U.S. Government Printing Office, 1965.

War of the Rebellion: A Compilation of the Official Records of the Union and Confederate Armies. Washington, DC: Government Printing Office, 1880–1901.

Warner, Ezra J. *Generals in Blue: Lives of the Union Commanders*. Baton Rouge: Louisiana State University Press, 1964.

———. *Generals in Gray: Lives of the Confederate Commanders*. Baton Rouge: Louisiana State University Press, 1959.

Waterman, George S. "Afloat—Afield—Afloat, Notable Events of the Civil War." *Confederate Veteran* 7, 8, 9 (1899–1901).

Wheeler, Joseph. "Alabama." In Clement Evans, ed., *Confederate Military History*, Vol. 7. Atlanta, 1899.

Whitman, William E. S., and Charles H. True. *Maine in the War for the Union: A History of the Part Borne by Maine Troops in the Suppression of the American Rebellion*. Lewiston, ME, 1865.

Wiley, Bell I. *The Life of Billy Yank*. Baton Rouge: Louisiana State University Press, 1978.

———. *The Life of Johnny Reb*. New York: Bobbs-Merrill, 1962.

Wyatt, Lee T., III. "William S. Barry, Advocate of Secession, 1821–1868." *Journal of Mississippi History* 39 (1977): 339–355.

Yeary, Mamie, compil. *Reminiscences of the Boys in Gray, 1861–1865*. Dayton, OH: Morningside House, 1986.

Zeitlin, Richard H. *Old Abe the War Eagle*. Madison: State Historical Society of Wisconsin, 1986.

Index

About the Author

SEAN MICHAEL O'BRIEN is the author of *Mountain Partisans: Guerrilla Warfare in the Southern Appalachians, 1861–1865* (Praeger, 1999) and of numerous articles on Southern military history. Trained in the U.S. military, he has also taught at the college level.